Journal of the British Archaeological Association

by British Archaeological Association

Journal of the British Archaeological Association

British Archaeological Association

THE JOURNAL

OF THE

𝕭ritish
𝕬rchaeological 𝕬ssociatioɴ

ESTABLISHED 1843,

FOR THE

ENCOURAGEMENT AND PROSECUTION OF RESEARCHES
INTO THE ARTS AND MONUMENTS OF THE
EARLY AND MIDDLE AGES.

VOL. XVI.

London :

LONGMAN, GREEN, LONGMAN, & ROBERTS.

MDCCCLX.

CONTENTS.

CONTENTS.

THE JOURNAL

OF THE

𝕭𝖗𝖎𝖙𝖎𝖘𝖍 𝕬𝖗𝖈𝖍𝖆𝖊𝖔𝖑𝖔𝖌𝖎𝖈𝖆𝖑 𝕬𝖘𝖘𝖔𝖈𝖎𝖆𝖙𝖎𝖔𝖓.

MARCH 1860.

THE ARCHÆOLOGY OF BERKSHIRE.

INAUGURAL ADDRESS DELIVERED AT THE OPENING OF THE CONGRESS AT NEWBURY.

BY THE EARL OF CARNARVON, PRESIDENT.[1]

IN opening the proceedings of the Congress, and in discharging the duties which this chair has devolved upon me, I shall at once proceed to draw the attention of the meeting, first to the reasons which have brought us together ; next, to the particular sphere of labour which is before us; and lastly, to the general character and objects of such a study as that of archæology. In the first place, allow me to say, that nowhere in the south of England could this meeting have been called together with greater advantage. In Newbury we occupy a central position ; we are placed on the borders of two counties, rich in the associations of the past, but to which as yet scant justice has been done either by the historian or the archæologist. From the dawn of English history down to a period comparatively recent, great events and names are of no infrequent occurrence ; but not only can neither Hampshire nor Berkshire claim any work which rises to the dignity and importance of a county history, but as regards Berkshire there is a dearth of written record or information, almost incredible except to those who, like

[1] This paper presents the substance of the address; other portions, not strictly archæological, will be found *in extenso*, published by the president. (Murray, 1859.)

myself, have been compelled to look with some care and particularity into this subject. These deficiencies we must, to the best of our power, remedy, and, by the researches we make and the interest we excite, pave the way towards the future accomplishment of a county history; though it is fair to add, that on ground as yet so unbroken, we shall probably, during the proceedings of this week, encounter a difficulty, not so much in finding frequent objects of interest or an ample field of inquiry, as in limiting that field to a reasonable extent.

It is then our duty to undertake the task : but it is not a matter of indifference when that task is undertaken. Day by day as it is deferred, the difficulty becomes greater and more formidable. Those local traditions and legends, sometimes too little considered by county-historians, but which are the most precious heirlooms of archæology, because in an especial degree they breathe the life and the habits, the thoughts and the faith of our ancestors, are year by year perishing from amongst us.

Antiquities resolve themselves into two classes : 1st, the local traditions and legends to which I have alluded ; 2nd, the visible and material monuments of the past, and especially the ruins in stone and mortar. It has curiously so happened that the same age is not favourable in its tendencies to the preservation of both. It was reserved for the advanced and sceptical period of the Roman Empire to appoint public officers for the preservation of antiquities, and to dote upon each fragment of the past with a fondness that provoked the bitter sarcasm of Juvenal : but the generation which cherished, because it believed in, the wildest and most fantastic legends, was the same which converted the Coliseum into a stone quarry for modern palaces, and which, in spite of the reproaches of Petrarch, trafficked away the statuary that had graced the world's capital to feed the taste and to enrich the halls of indolent Naples. Legends are of so delicate, so evanescent, a character, that they may perhaps best be compared to those beautiful insects of the eastern seas, of which travellers tell—gorgeous and dazzling in their ten thousand colours, when seen under the soft splendour of a tropical moonlight ; but touch them, handle them, and they break and scatter into countless and colourless fragments ; bid them even stay till daybreak, and they vanish, for they cannot look on the face of the sun and live. The old story, that fairies fly from the spot where they have once been seen by men, is true of these legends. They are trampled under the march of an indiscriminating education ; they will scarcely bear the more delicate touch of philosophy or criticism ; they can only really thrive in an atmosphere of tenderness, and respect, and faith.

This belongs not to our spirit nor our age. But, if under these circumstances old legends are rapidly perishing, there never was a time when the actual ruins of stone and mortar were more respected, cared for, or even honoured. And this is the result of several causes. Each fresh meeting, such as the present, both creates and confirms this feeling of respect ; but there lies a still deeper cause in the fact, that whilst formerly all knowledge of antiquities was confined to some few individuals, now, however vague and imperfect it may be, it is diffused through the body of the community, and is yearly widening its circle. The wider indeed that circle grows, the stronger will become the feeling ; for with Englishmen there is that unmistakeable instinct of conservation, which consecrates, and recognises a value in every such association of the great past of this country ; which, fragmentary and uncertain as it may be—meaningless, perhaps, except to the eye of faith and imagination—is yet as inseparably married to history as the ivy to the mouldering wall on which it hangs.

I now proceed to invite your attention to the particular field of labour which presents itself to us as archæologists assembled on the borders of Hampshire and Berkshire.

The first in order is the Roman period, but I will not linger long over it, nor will I wander back into it to establish archæological claims which cannot be fairly substantiated. I will not even delay you by attempting to trace the campaigns of Vespasian in Hampshire and Berkshire ; but, speaking in Newbury, I must not fail to remind you, that in the neighbouring suburb of Speen we have the ancient Spinæ, one of the earliest and most important of those military stations by which Rome at once curbed and civilised her conquered provinces. That Spinæ was one of the earliest of those stations we know, because assuming its identity with Speen, on which I believe the great authorities are agreed, we find mentioned by name both it and the roads connected with it, in the Itineraries of the Antonines, which were not improbably compiled during the reign, if not under the especial instructions, of Hadrian. Occasionally, and in various parts of the country, the plough turns up some relic or memorial of Roman times in Britain —some vase or urn, some column or capital, or tessellated pavement, or shattered altar ; but to my mind the chief evidence of the power which Rome wielded, and the civilisation which she diffused, is to be found neither in camp nor temple, neither in coin nor pottery, so much as in those great military roads which were carried through the length and breadth of the land.   In them the real majesty and policy of Rome shine out; by them the progress of her arms and civilisation can be measured; and the more that their history is examined the more wonderful will they appear. It would be a paradox to assert that they were equal to the highways which existed in England towards the close of the last and the commencement of the present century; but it would not, I think, be too much to say that, for more than a thousand years after the abandonment of the island by the Romans, their roads were still the best, if not the only highways which deserved the name.   In connection with these roads, Spinæ—placed as it was on the northern edge of that vast tract of woodland which extended for one hundred and thirty miles along the southern counties of England, called by the Romans Anderida, and known to the Saxons by the name of the Andredsweald—occupied an important position, and by communications which pierced the forest was connected with Winchester, Southampton, Chichester, and probably, at a later period, with Silchester on the borders of Hampshire.   But Spinæ also, in its relation to the great western road, which pursued a similar line to that which it now follows, was a station enjoying perhaps no less consideration than that which, within our own memory, it claimed when it counted twenty-four coaches during each successive twelve hours.   Then, as now, that great highway started from London, the centre of traffic and power, probably crossed the Thames near Staines, and passing through Egham and Reading stretched onward to Speen. Thence it proceeded by Marlborough to the ancient city of Bath, the Waters of the Sun, known alike to British king and Roman soldier; whence bending northwards towards

Bristol it led the traveller, after an easy passage across the Severn, to the Welsh shores and to the bourn of his journey in the famous town of Carleon—the fabled Carduel of Arthur—whose glittering domes and stately buildings were recorded and admired even by the historian of the time of Henry II.

In speaking of the Roman roads in this part of England, I am reminded that I tread upon the verge of one of those long and learned controversies which has for many years divided archæologists, and of which perhaps a satisfactory conclusion is unattainable. I will neither venture to pronounce an opinion nor to enter upon a discussion of the details ; I merely note for the consideration of antiquaries present the fact of the controversy. Our object is to assign the Roman names, which have been preserved, to certain places known to have been the seat of Roman settlement, and, as far as may be, to identify certain Roman stations, which are recorded in the Itineraries, with existing towns. In Wallingford we have relics of Roman settlement and civilisation, but we can assign no name to it ; in Silchester we have large fortifications and municipal buildings, but there is scarcely the name of any Roman station in this part of England which has not been at some time, or by some learned antiquary, applied to it. On the other hand, in Bibrax, Calleva, and Vindomis we have names, but we are unable satisfactorily to determine the places to which those names belong, and to reconcile them as Roman stations with modern towns. Without venturing to express any definite view on this long-vexed question, I am inclined to think that the preponderance of argument leans towards the identification of Bibrax with Egham, Calleva with Reading, and Vindomis with some point between Reading and Winchester—possibly Basingstoke, though this last seems rather more open to doubt. This opinion has been taken and very ably sustained in a pamphlet published now some thirty years since by Mr. H. L. Long, an associate of our body, and if it be true, nothing, as that gentleman observes, remains but to identify Silchester with the old Segontium of Hampshire.

Be this however as it may, there is for the archæologist no mean field for inquiry and speculation in Silchester. There, on a bleak open moorland where four ancient roads meet, stands all that remains of the once wealthy and prosperous town. To me, the double character with which those ruins are invested, has always had a peculiar attraction. On the one side its easy access for the march of troops and the transport of stores ; on the other, its commanding position over the valleys and the lower country, its massive walls and even lines, its deep fosse and the rectangular streets, which to this day in dry seasons can be traced, remind us only of military defence and the stern features of war. On the other hand, the gentle slope towards the western sun, the fragments of architecture, the baths, the mosaic pavement, the shattered altar to the Segontian Hercules, the countless coins, the sweeping lines of the amphitheatre ; these all speak of peace, of refinement, of wealth and luxury. Strange place ! over whose origin and history, and end, there hangs a veil that has never yet been, perhaps never will be raised ; and which owes the preservation of its ruins to the utter desolation that fell upon it, and to the fact, that since its overthrow it has never been the dwelling-place of man. What was its origin ? It is a disputed point whether it was founded in the early part, or quite towards the close, of Roman rule in this country. What was its name ? Was it Calleva, or Vindomis, or Segontium, or one of the many other designations attributed to it ? What was its end ? There is a legend that it perished by wildfire, borne on the wings of the birds of the air. But how shall we interpret the tale ? Did it fall by the fiery arrows of the besiegers ? or can we identify the mode of its destruction with the stratagem of the pirate Hastings—the flight of sparrows with living coals attached to them against the thatch-roofed houses of the beleaguered town ? Did Silchester in fact perish solely by human agency ? When some years since the excavations were made, and a range of handsome baths was discovered, the skeleton of a man was found in one bath, as if he had been surprised by the sudden irruption of the enemy. Secure in their deep fosse and strong wall, and the prestige of the Roman name, the garrison recked little of the barbarous assailants, and perhaps Silchester fell in the midst of laughter and feasting, as ignorant of her approaching fate as the doomed city of old, which in the hour of unconscious revelry knew not even that the enemy was within her gates. Or was that wildfire the thunderbolt which fell from heaven consuming and rending a passage for the besiegers ? If so, in this, as it has been truly called in other respects, Silchester was the Pompeii of England. Perhaps too its doom was analogous. Who can tell whether its wealth— attested by the multitude of coins yet to be found on the spot—its luxury, indicated by its buildings, its baths, its costly pavements—its crimes shadowed out in the yet unbroken circle of the amphitheatre—called down in retribution upon it a supernatural fire such as that which overwhelmed the cities of the Italian plain ?

But Silchester is not the only enigma of the period. From the time of its overthrow, for many generations, we are surrounded with mystery. There is no study more interesting than to trace the curious darkening over of real history on the abandonment of the island by the Romans. During the four hundred years of their rule, Britain had made a vast stride in the development of her material resources, and even in the affectation of Roman elegance and luxury she had shown herself no incompetent pupil. Markets and temples and porticoes and banquetting halls had been built ; good government established ; roads created, public works constructed, military colonies planted, ninety-two great towns, it is said, founded, and villas and farms scattered throughout the country. She had become, in fact, an integral part of the empire, valued for something beyond the Kentish oysters, her chief title to credit in the eyes of the Roman epicures of the Augustan period. She had given, according to one story (of which we need not now discuss the truth), the founder of Constantinople to the Imperial purple ; she had towards the close of the Roman period, by the disbandment of her legions, formed the colony of Armorica : and in her " tyrants" as they were called, though they perhaps better deserved the name of national princes, she exhibited no inconsiderable vigour of policy and government. But when once we step across that boundary line in our early history, we walk in a cloud-land of strange events and mystic personages, which has been preserved and consecrated to romance only by the imagination and poetry of a later age. Here and there we may trace some one golden thread of real history, but so enwoven in an uniform web of fiction, exaggeration, and allegory, that at this distance of time, and with our imperfect materials, it is almost a hopeless task to unravel the true tale.

All along the western borders of Hampshire and Berkshire there extends a line of barrows and earthworks, which are generally supposed to indicate the struggle between the British and Saxon races : but it is not easy in many cases to assign their construction to this or to any other definite period ; it is difficult even to feel satisfied that they denote that obstinate and protracted conflict of which some have supposed them to be the memorials.

Again, the story of Aben the founder of Abingdon, and the weird circles of Stonehenge and Abury, looming across the borders of Wiltshire, raise many a dim, yet suggestive, legend. They recall the fearful but shadowy tale of the massacre of the British chiefs by Hengist and his Saxons— the " battle of the long knives"—the slaughter of the May feast, commemorated in the relics of bardic poetry which have come down to us, and bewailed for generations afterwards by the Welsh at the omen fires on All Saints' Eve,— in which the faithlessness of Vortigern, as the story runs, betrayed, for the love of Rowena the fair daughter of Hengist, his country and his race to the swords of the Saxon invaders. But was this really so ? Has the tale come down to us in its true characters ? Was it Saxon, or was it British perfidy ? We may well doubt, when, in the absence of any Saxon record to guide us, we are obliged to depend upon the British version, from which the learned have not hesitated in some cases to deduce inferences against British rather than Saxon good faith. Nor is it unimportant to inquire the precise scene of this desperate conflict, which, misrepresented as it may be, contains apparently a foundation of truth. Was it Stonehenge, or Ambresbury, or Old Sarum ? And if Stonehenge, was it in connection with the mysterious circle whose fragments are to this day the marvel alike of shepherd and antiquary ? Was the bloody drama enacted within its enclosure ; or, as some have contended, was that strange temple only then for the first time rising into existence ? Who were the builders ? Were they wanderers from the Phœnician coasts, or pagan Anglo-Saxons, or the aboriginal Cymry of Britain, or a later and a more skilful race ? Where they architects of a generation that preceded, or that followed upon, Roman rule in this country ? These are questions as yet unanswered, and perhaps unanswerable. None but those who, unrequited by public praise, have devoted years of patient study to a dark, a perplexed, and perhaps an uninviting subject, can pronounce an opinion ; and meanwhile we the uninitiated, bewildered and doubtful, wander in a trackless labyrinth, and tread a magic circle surrounded by the spectres and mocking phantoms of the past.

But it may be asked, Is no exception to be made in favour of Arthur, the legendary hero of Britain ? Did not a conclave of British chiefs at Silchester elect him the Basileus of Britain ? Was it not at Winchester that he built his castle, that he instituted his round table, that he installed his knights ? Were not the neighbouring downs the scene of his battles, and has not Stonehenge legends connected with his name ? Will none of these plead for his victories, for his adventurous exploits, or even for his existence ? Or must we, in spite of the monks of Glastonbury, say that king Arthur never lived nor ruled,—that his round table was but an allegory,—that the seat perilous, which none might take, was a mystic representation of the knowledge from which all but the wise hierarchy were excluded, and that his name was but a myth, under which was veiled a strange and monstrous revolution of religious faith, in which Christianity for awhile perished, and the mysteries of a semi-oriental magianism were enthroned ?

Who can tell ? The brazen head is thrown down and shattered, and none now knows the spell which may replace the oracle or bid it speak. And so we see the barrows, the mounds, the earthworks—monuments of successive races, records of successive struggles, which for the most part probably belong to the Saxon period, but which two centuries afterwards our Saxon ancestors attributed to the work of the giants—and we know of their origin or history nothing but what some vague legend may preserve, or some ingenious conjecture suggest. We see and we wonder ; we know that the men who constructed them have passed away, their lives of action and adventure unchronicled, their virtues and their faults unremembered, as our own will probably be with some future generation : and we sum up all that we can know or feel in the mournful saying of the preacher, as true now as it was three thousand years ago, "There is no remembrance of the wise more than of the fool for ever, seeing that which now is in the days to come shall be all forgotten."

But if Arthur and his round table are myths, what shall we say of the wild legends of Wayland Smith, which it will be our duty to examine and discuss ?   And first, by what name shall we know him ?   Shall it be the Weland who, in Scandinavian lore, plays the part which is assigned to the old Fire-god Ἡφαιστος in the classic tales of Greece, who learnt the art of working metals from the dwarfs, the supernatural indwellers of the mountain—the same, perhaps, as they who, in another northern tale, wrought the famous sword Tirfing, which was doomed to accomplish three of the most disgraceful acts—who forges the breastplates and the arms of the heroes ?—or shall we call him by his French and mediæval name of Galand ?—Galand, who enters into every tale of love and war and adventure, who tempered the blade of Sir Gawain of the round table, and who wrought the famous blades with which Charlemagne hewed his way through the ranks of paynimry, Durandal and Joieuse—historic Joieuse, which, when the great emperor of the west was entombed beneath the porphyry pavement of Aix-la-Chapelle, was placed in his lifeless hand, whilst the Bible was spread upon his knees ?—or shall we view him by the light of Anglo-Saxon legend as Wayland Smith, the cunning goldsmith, the magical farrier, whose name still lives in the stories of the White Horse hills, and whose cave has been consecrated by the genius of sir Walter Scott?

And here, however reluctantly, we must close allusion to these legends; not indeed that they are unworthy the attention of archæologists, or undeserving the study of the historian :

> " The mightiest chiefs of British song
>   Scorn'd not such legends to prolong :
>   They gleam through Spencer's elfin dream,
>   They mix with Milton's heavenly theme ;
>   And Dryden, in immortal strain,
>   Had raised the Table Round again."

But it is time to pass from this land of shadows into the region of assured and authentic fact.   Yet it should never be forgotten, that with us, as with every other nation, there lies a broad tract between the legendary and the historic ; a debateable borderland, in which legend and history meet, but in which myth prevails less and less and traditions have an evident and growing connection with actual men and events. That borderland is like the Hades of the ancient world. The hero descends into the shades below, and he meets the spectres of departed friendship and greatness ; he speaks to them of the things that were, and are, and are yet to be ; and it is only when, in the warmth of renewed intercourse, the present runs back into the past, and he seeks to embrace the form before him, that he sees the unsubstantial shadow flit from his grasp, and he knows that the cold stream of death has flowed between them, that the dead and the living cannot meet upon equal ground, and that things shadowy and real must be measured by a different rule. So is it with that borderland of ours, of which the Danish wars, and the siege and sack of Reading, with many other similar events, form the principal part. It is like mountain scenery seen through the mist of the morning. The hills, the rocks, the grand outlines are actually there, but the proportions are magnified and the effect is heightened by the broken light of cloud and sunshine which hangs over them. So, through the uncertain twilight of the ninth century, loom upon us the outlines of the Berkshire hills, the battle of Ashdown, the grave of the old Danish chief, and the grim figure of the Saxon Horse ; or, at no great distance, the villages of Denford and Engleford, marking by their names the positions of the rival nations ; or Charbury camp, which the royal harper penetrated by night, to learn the intentions of his enemies. But amidst all the men and all the events of his time, the name of Alfred rises foremost. In Wantage we hail his birthplace ; at Eddington we see him, in the true spirit of mediæval belief, sealing his victory by the baptism of his Danish captives ; at Oxford, in the foundation of the University—however doubtful the tale—we recognise that love of learning which gave England much of her early literature, and which, as the historian has well said, familiar-ised and endeared Anglo-Saxon Christianity, not as the religion of an educated priesthood, but as a popular and national faith. Historians may differ in this or in that detail of his life : but we know enough to be assured of this —that he was a great and good man, who, tempered in the

furnace of personal and national adversity, was raised by
God in an hour of the darkest difficulty to restore the
broken fortunes of his people, who checked the triumph of
the Northmen at a time when Christian Europe seemed,
for her faithlessness and her unholy quarrels, to be given
over to the arms of the heathen, and who lived long enough
to leave the signet-mark of his character upon the life and
the polity of his age.   What wonder if, at a later day, his
grateful countrymen attributed to him laws and institutions
which did not in truth belong to him, as naturally but as
groundlessly as, under the first pressure of Norman rule, the
Anglo-Saxon magnified the freedom which he enjoyed in
the golden times of good king Edward the Confessor?

I now approach to the period of the Norman Conquest.   Few periods of history can be more interesting;
few on which there has been a wider divergence of opinion
in the view to be entertained, and few on which the func-
tions of archæology can be brought to bear with greater
effect or advantage.

In the north of England the process of consolidation was
slower than in the southern provinces.   There were frequent
insurrections, harrying of country, sack of towns, pillage of
homestead and monastery, and in one case a bishop was
slain on his judgment-seat; for the invaders came into
collision with a fiercer and hardier race of men, who had won
the land at the point of the sword but one or two generations before, and who were in the vigour of their national
vitality.   They found a race kindred to themselves both in
blood and character—Northmen and Pirates as they had
been, and as resolute to hold Yorkshire and Northumberland
as they had been a century earlier to maintain the Duchy
of Normandy against the confederated assault of Carlo-
vingian and Saxon.   But in the south the process of the
Norman settlement was comparatively rapid.   A population
denser in number and milder in character, after a few
ineffectual attempts at resistance, acquiesced in the rule of
the conquerors.   And this probably is one of the reasons
why, for the first few centuries, the history, the policy, the
government of England seem to be concentrated in the
southern counties of the island—why, if it may be said
without exaggeration, our national history is for many
generations almost identified with the history of Hamp-

shire and Berkshire. Thus, from the day when Wigod, the great Saxon chieftain, tendered to the Conqueror after the battle of Hastings his submission, and his strong castle of Wallingford, which with his daughter—like a second Tarpeia—soon became the property of a Norman adventurer, royal marriages and coronations, wars and sieges, progresses, parliaments and palaces, seem all to be crowded into the history of the two counties. But here the Quarterly Reviewer, has been so full and particular that I will not incur the risk of repeating his words. Yet, whilst in deference to him I hasten onward with my task, I cannot, here in Newbury, forget to remind you of the story which attributes the possession of Donnington Castle to the father of English poetry, "Dan Chaucer, the first warbler, the morning star of song." It is, probably, but a story, though we need not pause now to discuss the argument on either side : but if it did not belong to the poet, it was certainly the property of the poet's son. And this recalls and illustrates the quaint saying of old Fuller as to the "skittishness" of the lands of Berkshire, and their tendency to pass from hand to hand ; for just as Donnington Castle and a very considerable property in the county came to Thomas Chaucer through a fortunate marriage, so it passed away in the next generation, and, by his daughter and heiress, was carried elsewhere, to swell the wealth and dignity of another family.

Nor can I omit to pay my tribute to the memory of a name for which Newbury may well feel respect—John Winchcombe—or, as he was better known among his fellow townsmen by the more popular designation—Jack of Newbury. A paper, I am glad to see, will be read on this subject. It will, I doubt not, do justice to his great qualities, his open-handed liberality, the hospitality with which he entertained Henry the Eighth and Queen Katherine ; it will not forget the homely stories of his wife sitting in her chamber with her two hundred maidens around her spinning all the day long, or of the hundred looms which were daily at work in his warehouse, or of the hundred bowmen whom he sent to Flodden, and who were, "as well armed and better clothed" than any other troops that stood on that bloody field. And that story well deserves a place in our

[1] No. 211 for July 1859.

local chronicles ; first, because it shows, to use again the words of Fuller, that " the broadcloth wherein the prosperity of England is folded up" was just as important then as now: and secondly, it is one of the thousand instances in which English history, and English history alone, abounds of the unvarying unanimity and devotion of all ranks and classes in time of national danger or difficulty. Our insular and exclusive character was as much acknowledged and sneered at in the sixteenth as now occasionally it is in the nineteenth century. But those who sneer would do well to remember that if we have been or are exclusive as regards our intercourse with other nations, we have never been so amongst ourselves. We have never known the grinding privileges or the long intervals of caste which alienate classes, and cramp the vigour of the State, but we do know in the public life hitherto of the nation, that whenever an emergency has arisen, party differences, which are inseparable from a free government, have been fused into common action, and that no class has ever hesitated to sacrifice life, or limb, or treasure, because none has ever had a monopoly of feeling in the honour or the interest of the country.

And so a long succession of kings and queens, nobles and knights, princes and prelates, men of commerce, of arts, of letters, and last, though by no means least, old county families—the very backbone of English strength, names intertwined in honourable association with national memories—pass across the stage of our local annals. In them is often to be found the clue to the real history of the time ; with them much of that history is identified. A modern historian has said with truth, " The history of any one noble or private family is often an essential portion of, and always a commentary on, national history. It gives a vertical section of the strata presented at one view. No other process affords an equally distinct disclosure of the chronological progress of human society." Nor do I know that this proposition can be better illustrated in the case of this county, than by a reference to the history of the Englefields, one of the oldest families in Berkshire, who claimed to have been settled for two centuries and a half before the Norman Conquest in the place which still bears their name, and to have enjoyed an uninterrupted possession of the soil for seven hundred years.

Take but a few illustrations, and these almost at random. We will not look back to the remote and doubtful honours which the Englefields may have enjoyed under Egbert, or Ethelwolf, or Alfred, or any of the Saxon kings ; but mark in the first instance the year 1307. That year was the last in the long and eventful reign of Edward I, who, as he gave, by his politic foresight, an early impulse to commerce, was amongst the first also to mould into rude but real form that parliamentary system, which has since been developed into those mighty proportions, which we now recognise as without precedent or rival. In that year sir Roger of Englefield was duly returned to parliament as a knight of the shire ; but in those days service in the Commons House was considered less as an honourable than a burdensome task, to which the elected member yielded with so much reluctance that, in the words of a modern historian, it was almost as difficult to execute a parliamentary summons in parts of England, as it has been of recent times to effect the execution of a writ of *capias* in the county Galway, and the sheriff was sometimes obliged to appeal to force to prevent the flight of the member to the Chiltern Hundreds, or to some other place of refuge. We may, however, in the absence of any special evidence against him, believe that sir Roger of Englefield was patriotic enough to assume the duty imposed upon him by his county without the application of such stringent inducements. Again, a few generations afterwards, in 1397, we find another of this family, Nicholas Englefield, comptroller of the household of Richard II. Pass over another two centuries, and the Englefield of the day becomes sir Thomas, at the hand of Henry VII, and on no less important an occasion than the marriage of prince Arthur and Catherine of Arragon ; whilst a few years subsequently, in 1509, we recognise in him the first speaker of the first of those important Parliaments which legislated during the reign of Henry VIII. His son, another sir Thomas, still maintained the position of the family in public life, as Justice of the Common Pleas ; but in his grandson the honours, the eminence, and the prosperity of the family attained their zenith. Sir Francis was a man of considerable distinction in his time. He was a privy councillor under Edward VI, and under Mary he united to that duty the office of master of the wards. But Mary's reign soon passed away, and the times of Elizabeth were uncongenial to those who had been the trusted ministers of her sister. Not that I believe there was any substantial difference in the loyalty and patriotism of Roman Catholic or Protestant. Difference, and often bitterness of feeling there was, but—setting aside the controverted question as to the religious faith of Lord Howard of Effingham—when the Armada appeared off the southern coast, there was neither doubt nor division in the country, and national honour and interests were equally safe in the keeping of Roman Catholic or of Protestant. But sir Francis Englefield trod a more slippery and dangerous path ; he was not only devoted to the Roman church, but he was a zealous adherent of the unfortunate Mary Queen of Scots. He became involved in the conspiracies which found their centre in Fotheringay castle, and, suspected by the English government, he was eventually forced to save himself by flight. He withdrew to Spain, and there he is said to have spent the remainder of his life, devoting the wreck of his fortunes to the endowment of the English college at Valladolid. Strong in attachment to his hereditary faith, and animated perhaps by generous impulse in the cause of an unfortunate lady and a captive sovereign, we may not lightly pass a censure upon him ; but we will hope that like the Athenian exile of old, forced to seek a refuge on the hearthstone of his national enemies, he would have courted death rather than take part in the invasion of the liberties of his country. His property was confiscated ; and though his nephew and heir, Mr. Englefield, disputed the title with the crown, the law courts decided against him, and the decision was subsequently confirmed by an Act of Parliament. Sir Francis Walsingham—who, as it may be remembered, was afterwards the chief agent in threading the mysteries of Babington's conspiracy ; who sat as a commissioner at Mary's trial, and whose clerk deciphered the secret letter on which the verdict was supposed mainly to turn—then became, by a grant from the crown, the fortunate possessor of Englefield. But the property stayed not long with sir Francis Walsingham, or any of his name. It passed to the Powlets, and when in the civil wars Loyalty House was burnt to the ground by Cromwell and his Ironsides, lord Winchester spent the remainder of his life at the old seat of the Englefields, and lies buried in the parish church ; his tomb graced by Dryden's Muse,[1] but his loyalty and fair fame his most enduring monument.

But the names of John Powlet, marquis of Winchester, and the sack of Loyalty house, lead us on to an eventful period in our local history. The nearer indeed that we approach the times in which we live, the more distinctly do we seem to see the forms, to recognise the principles, and to understand the motives of the great actors in public life. Two hundred years have passed since the great rebellion broke forth : the flame soon sunk down, but in the ashes there lived on for many generations a fire which divided men and kindled feeling, and which burnt so deep an impression into the national mind, that we seem even now to distinguish its effects.

It would be vain to enumerate the places around us which were signalised by the desperate struggle. On the borders of Hampshire and Berkshire, we live in a country every mile of which was fought over, every hamlet illustrated by some of the incidents of war. In Hampshire,—from the smoking ruins of Basing house, to Oliver's battery on the Winchester Downs,—there was many a severe conflict ; and in a recently published diary of Captain Symonds,[2] who was as good an antiquary as royalist, we have an interesting account of the march of the king's army along the top of the downs by Whitchurch, and Sydmonton, and Kingsclere. In Berkshire,—the Wantage and the Ilsley Downs, Aldermaston, and the valley of the Kennet, Shaw house, Donnington castle, Speen, and the battle-fields of Newbury, awake many a painful or heroic association. With the mere mention of these places, how many of the great actors seem to rise and to pass across the theatre of our county history! Here we have Prince Maurice—such as we may recall him from his pictures, with his colourless complexion of face, his dark brown hair, and the features expressive, if not of talent, yet of some force and will—better officer than diplomatist, better soldier than officer, defending the suburbs of Speen against the Parliamentarian forces. There we recognise sir John Boys, with his laconic messages, and his vigorous measures, vowing

[1] Dryden's Works, xi, 154.
[2] Published by the Camden Society, and edited by my friend and relative Mr. Charles Long.

that he will hold out Donnington castle while one stone but stands above the other, laughing at the fiction—and a monstrous fiction it was—of fighting for the king against his armies, and doing his duty cheerfully, fearlessly, and successfully against all odds. Here we might imagine the shadow of lord Falkland, the calm melancholy statesman, with his meditative, almost scholastic countenance, where once might have been detected the play of irony, but which now reflected only a wearied and careworn expression, as he rode into the battle, past the fatal hedge on Bigg's Hill, where he was shot. Or there we might fancy young lord Sunderland, redeemed from the meshes of the Parliamentarian intrigues, and riding as a volunteer in the king's troop, cut off in the spring and promise of his life. Or here the form of my namesake, the lord Carnarvon of his day, with his chivalrous bearing, and his long light hair falling on his shoulders, as he lives under the pencil of Vandyke, the perfect type of a cavalier—a gallant and accomplished gentleman, and an officer fast rising into distinction in that sad struggle, by capacity, judgment, and the strictest sense of honour[1]—slain by one of his routed foes through a too careless valour. And lastly, amid the names of many good and gallant gentlemen who fought on the king's side, and to close the royalist ranks with a great name, we may see the shade of Laud sweep by, the last of the ecclesiastical statesmen who have directed the government of this country— whose name will be a ceaseless source of discussion to men as they may chance to vary in opinion, but who excites an interest in, and claims a respect from us, as antiquaries, when we remember that he was a native and a benefactor of Reading, and no unworthy representative of the old munificence which satisfied private feeling by the foundation of church and college, the endowment of monastery and hospital.

Or turn we now to the list of Parliamentarian names, and we see the phantom of William Lenthall, the speaker of the Long Parliament, a man of too feeble a character to be either very good or very bad, and therefore ill-fitted to preside over the stormiest and most important Parliament that had ever been summoned to meet in the Commons' House; at one moment, after he had put to the House the resolution for the

---

[1] For an instance of this, see *Hist. of Rebellion*, vii, 192.

trial of the king, likening himself to Saul holding the clothes
of those who stoned the first marytr, and at another time
interceding in the plenitude of the Parliamentarian triumph
for the life of the heroic and unfortunate lord Derby.   Or
here the phantom of Blagrave, the brother of the mathematician and one of the king's judges, might seem to flit past
us.   Or there we might conjure up before our mind's eye
the witty look, the loose speech, the "rakehelly" air of
Henry Marten with his maxims of Greek and Roman
philosophy—the profligate spendthrift and the regicide. And
lastly, in the old Manor-house of Swallowfield, we are
reminded of the name of Clarendon, for ever associated with
the story of the civil war.   But Lysons[1] is in fault when he
supposes that the great lord Clarendon lived, still less that
he wrote any part of his history, here.   The closing years of
his life were spent in France, and like Thucydides, he composed his immortal work in exile ; but his son, who was
lord deputy of Ireland, and who played a considerable part
in the politics of his time, lived at Swallowfield, and Evelyn[2]
records both the charms of the place and the virtues of
lady Clarendon, through whom the property came to her
husband.

But ever as we draw nearer to our own times, local history
must of necessity lose in dignity and interest.   With the
civil wars the stir of action and the feverish conflict of
principles pass by, and insensibly we enter upon those
quieter paths of settled order and prosperity, unknown to
other nations, and wonderful even to ourselves. Yet, though
the stream of our history now runs smooth, there are
incidents to be found along its banks ; some projecting
headland breaking the current, some retreating creek
embosomed in shade and flowers, some reach of wilder
scenery, to remind us of the stormier and more eventful
course which its earlier waters ran.   Thus the Revolution
of 1688 is reflected in the subterranean vaults and the
midnight conferences of Lady Place, where the first lord
Lovelace and his political confederates opened communications with William of Orange at the Hague.   Thus, too,
when William had landed in Devonshire and was advancing
upon Reading, Hungerford was the scene of the negotiations
which were carried on between Halifax, Nottingham, and

[1] Mag. Brit. Berks., p. 384.   [2] Diary, vol. i, p. 615.   4to.

Godolphin, who were commissioners for the king, and the advisers of the prince of Orange, though he for the most part shunned the appearance of all personal interposition, and spent a great part of that critical period at Littlecot hall. Twyford again, at no great distance, witnessed a skirmish between the advanced posts of the two armies : and near Reading, where the Dutch guards came into conflict with an Irish regiment, the only officer who fell on William's side during this comparatively bloodless revolution lost his life.

But not even with the revolution do we in Berkshire take leave of all the great actors of that era. There are many who interest and who dazzle—for it has always seemed to me that scant justice is generally done to this period—but far above them all, above even the minister of more than twenty years' successful administration, rises one great and remarkable character. With enormous faults lord Bolingbroke, to my mind, far overtops all his political contemporaries and rivals ; greatest in ability and versatile genius, greatest in dignity both of thought and of expression, greatest in that rare art of mingling philosophy and statesmanship, greatest perhaps even in his enforced seclusion from public affairs, leading his party and conducting their policy when the doors of Parliament were closed upon him, wielding an empire of the pen to which few statesmen in England have ever aspired, and making king and court and minister feel insecure in the very hour of their triumph. If any man ever sought the character of an Alcibiades, none ever rivalled the prototype more closely. And in Berkshire we catch glimpses of that period of his eventful career which, because so rare among statesmen, perhaps possesses the greatest attraction,—the life of private and philosophic retirement. Whether amidst the labours of a government of which he was the mainspring, or, when driven from power and office, weaving a thousand webs of intrigue and policy, carrying on correspondence with every part of England and with many parts of the Continent, or in the intervals of speculation, of literature, of philosophy, we may picture him to ourselves in the Old Manor house of Bucklebury, as he is described by his friends and contemporaries, leading the life of a perfect country gentleman—handling and judging the samples of wheat, visiting his kennels and knowing every hound by name, entertaining his guests with a homely but courteous hospitality ; laughing, talking, drinking, smoking —for this is specially recorded—with his neighbours, and yet throwing into every word and action that grace of mind and that charm of manner which he possessed pro- bably above every man of his day. Here it was that Swift, who says that he was the only common friend whom Oxford and Bolingbroke at the time of their estrangement retained, laboured sincerely and industriously to bring about a reconciliation between the two great political rivals ; and it was only when convinced of the hopelessness of the attempt, that he retired to the neighbouring rectory of Letcombe- Basset and wrote his " Enquiry into the Conduct of the Queen's Ministry."[1]

With Bolingbroke it is almost time to bring my tale to a close. Did time permit, there are many other names and places which I could cite, rich in the associations of the past. The Loddon, and Pope's early days ; the epitaphs on his friends in Easthampstead church ; his *Essay on Man*, dedi- cated to Lord Bolingbroke ; Ufton court, with Arabella Fermor, immortalised as Belinda in the *Rape of the Lock*, all come before us. Atterbury, with his polished humour, his flowing periods and his graceful English is there ; Gay too is present in his house at Bray ; or we may fancy that through the tobacco-smoke, and after a long and jovial carouse, we catch snatches of a witty, if not always very decorous conversation with Swift in the parlour of the Rose inn, at Wokingham. Lastly, from her picture on the walls of Coombe abbey, attired in black, and with a melancholy countenance, looks down upon us the Electress Palatine, the exiled Queen of Bohemia ; she who, in the camp of Gustavus, was the idol and admiration of the youth of every nation, and who, through the romantic devotion of that fine old cavalier, the first lord Craven, ended her eventful life in peace and honour at Ashdown.

I would fain linger on amidst themes and characters such as these ; but it is time to draw the thread of a story, already too far prolonged, to its close. I have endeavoured to show how in our county history, the larger and continuous drama of national history is maintained and reflected by local scenes and circumstances ; but within the narrow

[1] Swift's Works, vol. xv, p. 51.

compass assigned to me, I have found it difficult to do justice
to so large a subject, or satisfactorily to give effect to the
scheme with which I started. I have, after the fashion of
the ancients, but drawn the plough around the ground where
our city is to stand : it is for those who hear me, to build
the walls and to fill up the details—to give in fact colour
and consistency to the outline which I have hastily and
lightly sketched.

For archæology,—it has had before now able champions,
and it needs no apology at my hands. But since this place
has been chosen for the centre of fresh operations (and it is
a subject which comes before us to-day for the first time), it
is perhaps right that, as briefly as may be, I should remind
you of the general objects which archæology professes, and
the character which it should assume. And first let me say
what archæology is not. It is not a curious dilettanteism,
which conceives a special virtue in the collection of quaint
and meaningless oddities ; nor is it, as some appear to think,
a devotion to the husk and chaff of the grain of literature—
a knowledge in which, as the Roman moralist says, there is
neither pleasure nor profit—but it is a study which in itself
constitutes one of the distinctive differences that contrast an
old with a new country—a study which sheds some gleams
of romance and poetry over a practical and perhaps a somewhat hard age,—which has chronicled many a legend and
ballad, which saved the Border minstrelsy, which inspired
alike Burton's *Anatomy of Melancholy*, and Southey's *Doctor*, and which culminates in that masterpiece of Sir Walter
Scott's writings—*The Antiquary*.

But archæology is not merely valuable for and in herself ;
she is valuable for the thousand suggestions which she
awakens. Take but one single instance. We are surrounded, north and west and south, by long swelling ranges
of open down, which stand out, like the beacons of earlier
times, from the tide of cultivation that is ever creeping up
and around their bases. They have been fought over inch
by inch. War has been there in all its forms of nobleness
and misery—*juvat ire, et Dorica castra Desertosque videre
locos,* and without believing that every Kaim of Kinprunes
is necessarily a camp of Agricola, we may often there learn
to read early history by a brighter and a truer light than
they who are content to spell it out only from the blotted

and crabbed manuscript. But these downs have also been lived over, and even on the ground where the soil is poorest and scantiest we can trace the signs of plough and enclosure, of human cultivation and industry. Who can say how far this suggests or confirms the theories by which some have contended for the historical existence of a larger population than that which the present soil can apparently support? Cobbett, in his *Rural Rides*, argues, more ingeniously than temperately, for the existence of a much larger population in the New Forest, at the time of the conquest, than that which can now be found there ; and Mr. Kemble shows reason for believing that the amount of land under cultivation, towards the close of the Anglo-Saxon dynasty, was equal to the area of arable land a quarter of a century since.

But archæology is not merely suggestive. She is essential to, she is the handmaid of, history ; and just as the knowledge of common things ranks before abstruser studies, or as topography should precede geography, so historians would sometimes have avoided errors, and have arrived at juster conclusions, had they made fuller allowance for local and personal details. Egypt and her early kings, Babylon and her mighty works, Persia with her satrapies and her countless hosts, would never have been pourtrayed in such living colours by the father of history, had he not been a wanderer and a sojourner in those lands. Nor would the records of the Peloponnesian war and of the great rebellion have been the masterpieces of history, which they are, had not their authors been also actors in the great events which they chronicled.

But a yet higher claim may be made for archæology. She is not only the handmaid to, but she is an indispensable part of, history. The existence of any nation is two-fold : there is an outer and an inner life. The outer life includes her wars and her diplomacy, her laws and her commerce : her inner life touches those subtle and more secret springs of action, which affect the habits of thought and the rule of faith, which govern the intercourse of man with man, and which descend into the minutest details of food and dress and daily life : for, as nothing is too high for history to grasp, so nothing which can aid or illustrate her teaching, is below her dignity. And thus the pattern of a chair, the fashion of a tapestry, the roll of a parchment, the turn of a letter, which are the specialities in the craft of the archæologist, become invaluable to the historian.   M. Thierry has left upon record the feelings with which he undertook the composition of the Norman conquest,—a work which, with some defects, is of great and unquestioned power—and his words seem so fully to express the relationship which archæology holds to history, that I think they deserve attention : " Details are of little interest in themselves, but they aid in forming an idea of the varied scenes of the conquest, and in investing with their original colours facts of greater importance. . . .   Through the distance of ages we must make our way to the then living men ; we must, as well as we can, realise them acting and living upon the land, where now not even the dust of their bones is to be found. . . .   The reader must fix his imagination upon these ; he must re-people ancient England with her conquerors and her conquered of the eleventh century ; he must conceive their various situations, interests, and languages : the joy and insolence of the one, the misery and terror of the other. . . . For seven hundred years these men have ceased to exist ; but what matters this to the imagination ? with the imagination there is no past, and even the future is of the present."

This then is history when it has incorporated archæology in itself, and when it is perfect in all its parts.   For history is not the dry bones of the past, the mere narrative of facts, or the hard logical reasoning on *a priori* grounds from those facts.   Still less is it the mechanical combination of events and circumstances rolling on within a fixed groove by irresistible laws, in which, as some have falsely contended, climate is the active agent, and society, not man, the responsible being ; in which expediency, like a second goddess of reason, is avowedly enthroned to the exclusion of religious faith or moral principle ; in which virtue and vice become mere names, and man himself " rolls darkly down the torrent of his fate."   The philosophy of history is not such a frigid, soulless, godless abstraction—an " ignoble circle of an iron necessity"—a theory in which the past is ever degraded to gain a fictitious triumph for the present, in which scientific considerations and material interests alone find a place, and from which great thoughts and noble actions are shut out.

But history is that great drama in which men and women like ourselves, with similar sympathies and motives, have lived and acted, blessing by their virtues, retarding by their sins, the fortunes of themselves and of their generation. And therefore, for our teaching and guidance, history is a fountain of living waters, from which we may draw inexhaustibly, and drink without satiety.

Happy are they whose serener leisure leads, and whose duty permits them to wander forth by these still waters, and along these quiet and flowery paths, where life steals noiselessly away, but where they have the consciousness that in every line they write, they are blending their names with the memory of the great and the good whose actions they are chronicling. For us,—whose avocations point in a different direction, to whom this cannot be, we may satisfy our less aspiring ambition by collecting the materials which the future historian may use, by gathering the flowers, though another weave them into his chaplet : and if in thus fulfilling our lowlier though useful mission we catch a breath of the true, loyal, chivalrous spirit which animated our forefathers,—if we learn the better to appreciate the inheritance which in the glorious history of England they have bequeathed to us,—we shall not be less likely, I think, to discharge the duties of our own generation with honour to ourselves, and with advantage to posterity.

ON THE HISTORY AND ANTIQUITIES OF BERKSHIRE.

BY T. J. PETTIGREW, F.R.S., F.S.A., V.P. AND TREASURER.

It has been justly remarked by a learned associate of our body, that "archæology, in these days, is no longer pursued for the mere gratification of curiosity, and the satisfaction of possessing some object prized merely for its antiquity. Archæology has fallen into the hands of able men, who have advanced it to the dignity of a science; and as such it is daily making a progress which gains us an accurate insight

4

into the history of mankind."[1]   The attainment of an object
so important is unquestionably in no little degree attributable to the establishment of our Association, and by its institution, in the year 1844, of annual congresses, to inquire
into the special antiquities of particular localities.   These
gatherings have been the means of creating, and calling into
action, many local societies, by the members of which considerable information has been collected together to constitute materials for more perfect inquiries and inferences to
be drawn by the antiquary and the historian.

One of the primary objects in the establishment of our
Association was to oppose the too prevalent spirit evinced
in the destruction of ancient monuments.   In many cases
the propriety of attempting their restoration may, perhaps,
be questionable; but as to aiding in their preservation, I presume, in an archæological association, there can be only one
opinion on the subject.   The extent to which this species of
conservatism has in some cases been carried, has, perhaps,
not unjustly exposed us to some degree of ridicule; but with
that admirable and quaint writer, whose works I never fail
to consult with delight, Dr. Thos. Fuller, I would say: "Con-
demn not this our diligence for needless curiosity, but know
that every meer-stone that standeth for a landmark, though
in substance but a hard flint or plain pebble, is a precious
stone in virtue, and a cordiall against dangerous controversies
between party and party."[2]   A Welsh antiquary[3] has also
well observed, that it shews a little soul, a narrow mind, as
well as bad taste, to pull down the walls of any sort of
ancient ruin; for

——" ' there is a power
And magic in the ruined battlement,
To which the palace of the present hour
Must yield its pomp, and wait till ages are its dower.' "

In entering upon the business of our Congress in the
county of Berks, it is necessary first to remark that no complete history of Berkshire is to be found.   It remains to be
written.   Elias Ashmole's work,[4] as far as it goes, is important; but the reader will, upon rising from its perusal, have

[1] H. Lawes Long's *Survey*, etc., p. 121.
[2] Pisgah-Sight of Palestine, lib. ii, c. 9.   [3] J. James (Iago Emlyn).
[4] The Antiquities of Berkshire, by Elias Ashmole.   Lond., 1719, 3 vols., 8vo.
History and Antiquities of Berkshire, with Appendix.   Reading, 1736.   Folio.

no distinct idea of the county, its monuments, or its products. Lysons has done much in regard to its antiquities; but an arrangement of the subjects is demanded,—the whole field, embracing primæval, Roman, Saxon, and mediæval, requires careful examination; and it is not, I trust, unreasonable to hope that the occasion of our present Congress may promote in some degree this desirable object. Hearne's researches were directed chiefly to the antiquities between Oxford and Windsor; and his notices of them were printed in *The Monthly Miscellany* for Nov. 1708, and subsequently in Leland's *Itinerary* (1744). In 1759, Mr. E. Rowe Mores circulated certain queries addressed to the rectors and vicars of the several parishes in the county; the replies to which are printed in the *Bibliotheca Topographica Britannica* (vol. iv). They, however, yield but scanty information: indeed, the rector of Newbury in 1759 (the rev. Thos. Penrose), in his reply says, " I do not know any person in this neighbourhood who is curious in matters of antiquity." Precisely a century after, and we have the gratification of holding a special Congress in the Mansion house of this town, the object being entirely devoted to the illustration of all matters of interest connected with the history and antiquities of the county.

My purpose at the present moment is simply, and, in conformity to the practice usually followed by us at these meetings, to endeavour, by a brief survey of the various places which time and convenience will permit us to visit, to direct attention to the particular subjects of our inquiries.

Like to the names of many other English counties, the origin of that of Berkshire is neither well nor completely settled. *Asser Menevensis,* an English historian, derives it from the word signifying a wood (*barroc*), which, he says, abounded with box. Barroc wood, we are told by Lysons,[1] is mentioned in a charter of king John as being the property of the nuns of Ambresbury. Leland follows Asser; derives Berkshire, or Barkshire, from *berrock* (a bare oak), beneath which the English Saxons held their assemblies. The *Saxon Chronicle* writes it Bearuscire and Barroscire, which became Beroscre or Barocscire. In the ninth century it was known as Berocscire; and in Domesday it is written Berroches-scire, Berroche-scire, Berche-scire, and Berchsire.

_____
[1] Magna Britannia. Lond., 1806. 4to.

Berkshire is an inland county of the southern part of England, picturesquely bounded by the aid of the Thames and Isis, by Surrey on the east, Hampshire on the south, Wiltshire on the west, Oxfordshire and Buckinghamshire on the north. In measurement it may be stated to be forty-two miles from Windsor to Hungerford, which constitutes its extent from east to west; and from Sunning hill to Buscot, the confines of Gloucestershire, it is upwards of fifty miles. In breadth, from Oxford to the edge of Hampshire, south of Newbury, it is more than twenty-eight miles. From these admeasurements (not to be regarded as actually precise) it will be seen that the county is distinguished in having an irregular shape. Fuller likens it to a lute, and it has also been deemed to resemble a sandal or a slipper. It only remains to add, that in circuit it comprehends two hundred and eight miles.

The ancient inhabitants of Berkshire, according to Camden and other authorities, are known as the Attrebatii, or Attrebates, a tribe migrating from Gaul anterior to the Roman conquest. Whitaker,[1] following Camden, has expressed an opinion that the south-eastern parts of Berkshire, including the hundred of Bray, were occupied by the Bibroci. The Segontiaci also constituted a portion of the ancient inhabitants; and the arrangement of these tribes may, perhaps, be fairly stated thus:

The ATTREBATES, occupying nearly the whole of the western part.

The BIBROCI, the south-eastern part.

The SEGONTIACI, a portion of the southern part.

Thus the Attrebates appear to have been the principal inhabitants; yet some have conjectured the county to have derived its name from the Bibroci mentioned in Cæsar,—Broc and Bark meaning the same. Bibroci is, however, derived from Bibrax, a place not far from Rheims.

The most interesting portion connected with probably the most ancient history of Berkshire, is that particularly known as "the Vale of the White Horse." It is scarcely necessary for me to remark that the name of the vale has arisen from a representation of a horse, three hundred and twenty-five feet in length, cut out of the turf upon a chalky soil; and that it has been usually regarded as a monumental record of

[1] History of Manchester, i, 92.

the great victory obtained over the Danes in 871 by Ethelred and Alfred. Ashdown is generally esteemed as the spot on which the conflict took place; and in the neighbourhood there are seven remarkable barrows of a circular form, and several others of a very irregular shape, in which bones almost innumerable have been found.

Wise[1] acquaints us that the Vale of the White Horse was known by that name in the reign of Edward III, occurring in an entry in a Close Roll (1368-9), where it is recorded,— " Gerard de L'Isle tient en la Vale de White Horse 1 fee"; but we are indebted to the research of sir Henry Ellis for an earlier notice, it being named in the Two Cartularies of Abingdon, written in the reign of Henry II,—" Prope montem ubi ad *Album Equum* scanditur," etc. And in relation to Sparsholt,—"juxta locum qui vulgo *Mons Albi Equi* nuncupatur," etc. Mr. Thoms, in a communication to the Society of Antiquaries,[2] esteems the monument commemorative of the ancient religion of the country, the worship of the horse having been common to the Celtic and Germanic as well as the Sclavonic tribes. This would render the memorial as of British origin, an opinion entertained by Lysons; and it must be admitted that the figure of the animal, as represented on the hill, and on the ancient British coins, bears a very strong and striking resemblance. Mr. Thoms has brought his familiarity with German literature to bear with advantage on this point; and he refers to "the sacred horses," which form no unimportant objects in the mythology of the ancient Saxons and other peoples of the Germanic race. "From these sacred horses," he says, "it is probable that many of the ancient heroes derived their names, of which Hengist and Horsa furnish a striking example, these names being nearly synonymous; although the former, Hengist, or Hengst, is, in the German and some other of the Teutonic tongues, more particularly applied to stallions."[3] Notwithstanding these expressed statements, Mr. Thoms coincides with Wise, and looks upon the memorial as formed by the Saxons; and, he thinks, at the time of their conversion to Christianity, and of the sacred white horse, which, in the

[1] Letter to Dr. Mead concerning some Antiquities in Berkshire. Oxford 1738. 4to. And, Further Observations upon the White Horse and other Antiquities in Berkshire. Oxford, 1742. 4to.
[2] Archæologia, xxxi, 291.
[3] Ibid., 292.

days of paganism, had depastured in the sacred grove of
Ashes. Mr. Akerman holds to the opinion that it is of Celtic
origin, and has given a cut of it from a drawing made by

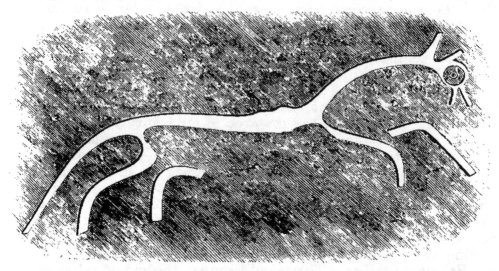

Mr. Christopher Edmonds.[1]   The horse, we must not fail to
remember, was equally a Celtic as a Saxon badge, and is
constantly found represented on Gaulish and British coins.
The subject is worthy of further discussion.

At about a mile and a half from the White Horse is another ancient memorial, known as Wayland's Cave, which the
more precise knowledge of the antiquaries of the present
day has shewn to consist of the remains of a cromlech. All
who attended our Congress at Rochester will at once perceive the similarity of material and structure with that of
Kit's Coty House in Kent, and hence be induced to abandon
the various conjectures that have been made in relation to
this monument of antiquity. It is a cromlech of the Celtic
period. Its several stones are in disorder, and thrown down.
They are what are commonly called *sarsens*, of which we
saw specimens on the occasion of our visit last year to the
grand monument of Stonehenge. Cromlechs are burial-
places formed of upright stones covered by a large slab or
slabs. Many of Wayland's Cave have been taken away to
serve a variety of purposes; but there remain sufficient to

[1] Archæologia, p. 298, kindly lent to the Association by the Society of Antiquaries.

denote its character. There is still also enough to shew that this cromlech had transepts or lateral chambers.

The tradition held in regard to this monument, is, that if a traveller's horse cast a shoe on his way, he had only to lead the animal to the cave, there leave him (at the same time placing a groat upon the capstone), and withdraw. After a short time, upon his return, he would find his horse shod, and his money removed.[1]

Barrows of various denominations, and belonging to various periods, are common in Berkshire. We shall have opportunities of inspecting several in the course of our excursions; and we have to thank the proprietors of several for having generously offered to us every facility for examining them, and which, I trust, it will be in the power of the Association, either during the Congress, or at some future time, to render available, and thereby advance the progress of archæological knowledge.

Belonging to the early period of Berkshire's history, we must direct notice to some antiquities which are recorded to have been found at Hagbourn Hill, of which Mr. Ebenezer King has given an account in a communication addressed to Mr. Samuel Lysons in 1808.[2] They consist of some horse furniture similar to that found at Polden Hill in Somersetshire,[3] now preserved in the British Museum; also an arrow head, celt with a loop, etc. They were obtained from a pit adjoining the Ickleton Way, about four feet from the surface. There were other articles, but they had been removed, and their restoration could not be effected. Coins were said to have been among these interesting relics.

We pass to the Roman æra; and here materials abound. No county requires more industry in the search for Roman roads than Berkshire. They appear to traverse in such various ways, that it would be difficult to define them with tolerable precision. The Roman town of Speen, or Spinæ, has, however, been determined, and will be visited by us on this occasion. Bibracte is another, the site of which is not quite clearly ascertained; and of a third at Wallingford, usually esteemed Calleva. There was also Pontes, named

[1] This subject will receive full elucidation from the learned labours of Mr. Thomas Wright.
[2] Archæologia, xvi, 348.
[3] Ibid., xiv, 90. See also examples found in Lincolnshire, and recorded in this *Journal*, vol. xv, p. 226, and plate 22, for September 1859.

in the seventh Iter of Antonine, thought to have been the peninsula formed between the Colne and the Thames, nearly opposite to Egham in Surrey. Whilst Spinæ and Bibracte may be regarded as recognized Roman stations, it is remarkable that but few Roman antiquities have proceeded thence; whereas from Wallingford many of various descriptions have been obtained, although its name is somewhat in obscurity. It was, however, an important place in the time of the Conqueror; and the coins of Posthumus, Gordianus, etc., have been found there.

A few years since, Mr. Hewett of Reading obliged us with a rough plan of the ancient roads in Berkshire, which is worthy of examination. Roman Watling-street enters the county at Streatley, and crosses in the direction of Marlborough. Another road enters from Hampshire, and passes to Newbury; one branch then going to Marlborough, the other to Cirencester. Two Roman milestones have been mentioned as standing between Streatley and Aldworth, but Lysons failed in his endeavour to find them.[1]

Of camps and earthworks there are many ancient ones in the county. It is possible that some originally British were subsequently used by the Romans. There is a circular camp, with a single vallum, on the western side of Ashdown park, commonly called Alford's castle. There is also a quadrangular camp near Wantage, and a fort at Lawrence Waltham. An account, together with a plan of a Roman encampment, have been given by Mr. John Narrien.[2] It is near East Hempstead, and the neighbourhood has afforded many specimens of Roman bricks and pottery. Various pavements have also been brought to light in the county. Our associate, sir S. Morton Peto, bart., and Mr. Grissell, exhibited to us drawings of tessellated pavements discovered in the vicinity of Shooter's Hill, two miles north of Pangbourne, on the road to Streatley, Moulsford, and Wallingford. They were found twelve or fourteen inches from the surface only. The first was eight feet in diameter, and formed the centre of a room; the second was of the same dimensions; and with them were found skeletons, a sword, portions of wall, pavements of large flints, red pottery, large tiles, and a coin of Lucilla, large brass. Other coins were reported, of Licinius, Con-

---

[1] Biblioth. Topog. Brit., v, 4.
[2] Archæologia, xix, 96, and plate vii.

stantinus, and Gratianus. An account of this discovery has been recorded by Mr. C. Roach Smith.[1]

Stukeley mentions a Roman altar dedicated to Jupiter, dug up at Frilsham, near Spene, in 1730.

Traces of Roman remains have been found in the parish of White Waltham, in Weycock field, and at Wickham Bushes on Bagshot Heath. Coins and urns have been dug up at Lawrence Waltham, St. Leonard's Hill, Wallingford, Bagshot Heath, and Wantage. A large urn was found, in 1756, on Spene Moor, in a tumulus one mile and a half west of Newbury.[2] It is to be regretted that this antiquity should not have been figured, as we might then have been able to judge of the period to which it belonged; but it was broken into fragments upon its removal, and it was not possible to ascertain what the nature of its contents may have been. It was dug out of a mass of peat, in which were also the bones of several kinds of deer, the horns of an antelope, the heads and tusks of boars, skulls of beavers, etc. Dr. John Collett, who communicated a notice of the discovery to the Royal Society, could not observe any human remains; but he was told that some had been found. Evidence, however, was wanting to prove the assertion. The urn is described as having been of a light brown colour, and large enough to hold a gallon. An artificial hill had been raised over it, about eight feet above the surrounding ground. The peat was therefore probably older than the urn.

Mr. Jesse King, in 1845, exhibited to our Association various Roman and Romano-British antiquities found in Berkshire. They consisted of a flint arrow-head from Sutton Courtney, two small cups, and an iron lamp-stand, from Wittenham Hills; a celt found in the Thames, near Sutton bridge; an iron axe on Pebworth farm, a bronze javelin from Highbourn Hill, accompanying a skeleton; an iron arrow-head from a barrow on Blewbury Down; a bronze dagger lying by a skeleton, at Sutton; fragments of light brown pottery full of black mould, lying by two skeletons, in Appleford fields; other fragments from Blewbury Down; part of a cap found near the shoulders of a skeleton in Culham fields; pale red and dark brown pottery from Sutton Courtney; fibulæ, brass ring, etc., and an urn of pale brown colour, by the side of a skeleton in Drayton field.

[1] Archæologia, xxviii, 447.   [2] Phil. Trans., l, 109.

Perforated baked clay weights, from three to five inches in diameter, from Abingdon, with other Roman remains, have been laid before the Association.   But it is unnecessary to particularize further.   The museum of Newbury offers to our notice many examples worthy of examination.

In plate 1 we have figured some Roman antiquities found in 1856, together with many skeletons (amounting to about one hundred, being probably the site of a Roman cemetery), upon making an excavation for ballast at the Newbury railway station.   The specimens of fictile ware obtained from this spot, and now deposited in the local museum, are very perfect, and consist of:—

1. An amphora of a globular form, having a narrow neck and double handle.   It is thirteen inches in height, and twenty-eight in circumference; of a pale ash colour.   It forms the centre figure in our illustration.

2. A cinerary vase of black colour, containing burned bones (broken).

3, 4. Two stands for cinerary vases, each nine inches in diameter.

5. A glass bottle (usually denominated *unguentaria*, as belonging to ointments or perfumes), on the bottom of which are the letters s p s, together with a figure conjectured to be that of Æsculapius, surrounded or enclosed within his usual emblem, the serpent.   (See fig. 2.)   Its height is six inches and a quarter.

6. A smaller bottle, of the same description, measuring only three inches and three-quarters.

7. A vase or cup, of a red colour, four inches in diameter and two inches and a half in height.

8. A patera, of a tazza form, with projecting handles.

9, 10, 11, 12, 13.   Five examples of the so-called Samian ware pottery.   They are pateras, and all of the diameter of seven inches.   Two are fractured; the others are perfect, and upon them the names of the potters are impressed.   As far as can be made out, they read, PECVLIAR . F . SEDATI . M . CINTVSMI . M . REGVLIN . F.

14, 15. Two Samian bowls or cups quite perfect, and each five inches and a half high.

In bringing this enumeration to a close, I must refer also to the urn described by the rev. J. Bagge, recently discovered in his garden at Crux Easton (plate 1, fig. 3), the

Fig. 1.

Roman Antiquities, Berkshire.

Fig. 2.

Fig. 3.

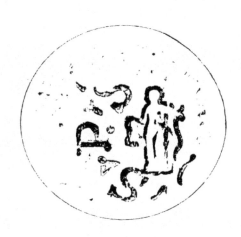

J.R.Jobbins

particulars of which exhumation are given in his communication detailed in the proceedings of Wednesday, Sept. 14th.

We pass on to Saxon times. Berkshire formed, during the Heptarchy, part of the kingdom of the West Saxons. The *Chronicle of Abingdon*, preserved among the Cottonian MSS. in the British Museum,[1] imparts to us the earliest authentic historical notice in relation to this county. It is to the effect that Offa, king of the Mercians, whose reign commenced A.D. 758, having conquered Kinewulf, king of the West Saxons, seized upon the county from Wallingford to Ashbury, which lay between the Ickeneld-street and the Thames.[2] In the succeeding century the irruption of the Danes constitutes the most remarkable incident; and their defeat by Ethelred, assisted by Alfred, has afforded scope for much ingenious conjecture. The site of the battle is still undetermined. The account given by Asser is the most circumstantial.

Berkshire had always a palace in the time of the Saxon kings. There was one at Abingdon, a town of great antiquity, "one of the glories of England, and reproaches of sacrilege";[3] a spot at which great councils of the nation were held; and a place of religious worship prior to the establishment of Christianity.[4] There was a magnificent cross of freestone, but, in the words of Ashmole, "triumphant rebellion has left us no remains of it." The cross would appear to have been connected with a guild established under the great seal, 20th Henry VI, as an association of "men and women to the honour of God and the holy cross, to make and ordain a brotherhood or gylde in the parish church of St. Eleyn (Helen) in Abingdon, which should be called the Master, Brethren, and Sisters of the Fraternity or Gylde of the Holy Cross of Abingdon."

Farringdon, Wantage, and Old Windsor, had also royal residences. Henry I removed from Old to New Windsor in 1110. It has ever since continued to be a royal habitation.

---

[1] Claudius, B. vi, and Claudius, C. ix; the latter half a century earlier than the former. See the rev. J. Stevenson's edition, published under the authority of the master of the Rolls (Lond., 1858), pp. 46, 47. Also Gale's *Hist. Angl. Script.*, ii, 162, et seq.; and *Decem Scriptores*, i, 125.

[2] "Quo mortuo ab Offâ rege Merciorum in bello victo, omnia quæ juridictioni suæ subdita fuerant ab oppido Wallingefordiæ in australi parte ab Ichenildestrete usque ad Esseburiam, et aquilonali parte usque ad Tamisiam, rex Offa sibi usurpavit." (*Chron.*, ed. Stevenson, p. 14.)

[3] Ashmole's *Berks*, i, 111. [4] See Dugdale's *Monasticon*, i, 99.

Wantage was the capital of the hundred, and the birthplace of Alfred, who, at his decease, bequeathed it to Alfrith. This town had a charter for a market one hundred and fifty years prior to the Conquest, which is reported to have been obtained by the interest of Fulke Fitzwarin with Roger Bigod the earl marshal. From the Fitzwarins this benefit descended to the Bourchiers, earls of Bath; thence to the Wrays, D'Oylys, etc. The Fitzwarins were great benefactors to Wantage; and they mainly, if not wholly, built the church, a Gothic structure in the form of a cross. In the roof are the royal arms, and also those of Fitzwarin. In the chancel is an altar-tomb with an effigy of one of the Fitzwarins, supposed to be sir Fulke Fitzwarin, as he has the order of the Garter; but sir Fulke, according to Lysons, was buried at Whittington, and he therefore conjectures it may have been sir William Fitzwarin, who was also of the order of the Garter. Round the old market cross was an inscription: " Pray for the good earl of Bath; and for good master Barnabe, the builder hereof, 1580; and for William lord Fitzwarren." This inscription was obtained by Lysons from Symonds's MSS. in the British Museum, who had taken a copy in 1644. Not a vestige of the old cross is now to be seen. Some portions were, however, preserved by a writer in the *Gent.'s Mag.* for 1821 (p. 13, under the signature of H. W. B.), who obtained them from a resident in a neighbouring village; the principal of which appears to have formed the upper portion of the shaft, and contains, within Gothic niches, rudely sculptured representations of eight of the apostles, the four evangelists having probably occupied some other and more imposing part of the cross. No part of the inscription was upon these fragments. Wantage is remarkable, as it has two churches in one churchyard. One is now used as a school. The north door is Norman.

There are brasses of interest in the church, of which accounts have been given in our *Journal.* One of Richard Davy, public executioner, who died in 1483. His wife is mentioned on the plate; which likewise contains a hatchet, the emblem of his office.

Many specimens of early Norman architecture are to be seen in several of the churches of this county, which will be duly pointed out by our architectural associates.

It was remarked by our great antiquary, Camden, that

the county of Berks had given title to no man; and it was not until 1620 that Francis Norris was created earl of Berkshire: he dying without issue, the title became extinct. In 1625, Thomas Howard was created earl of Berkshire: but upon Henry Bowes Howard, the fourth earl, succeeding to the earldom of Suffolk, on the failure of male issue in an elder branch, the titles became, and have ever since been, united. Various families, however, have obtained titles from different parts of the county. Thus, in 1616, William lord Knolles was created viscount Wallingford; in 1626, baron Craven, viscount Uffington. There were also baron Newbury, and baron Oakingham; the latter a title of prince George of Denmark, when created an English peer. Of these titles, several are now extinct. In 1682, James Bertie, lord Norris, was made earl of Abingdon.

There is no city in Berkshire. The county towns are Abingdon and Reading, where sessions are held, and also at Newbury. At the survey of Domesday, forty-six manors in the county were vested in the crown. The abbot and convent of Abingdon kept thirty-one in their own possession. There were also lay proprietors, the most considerable of whom was Henry de Ferrars, earl of Derby, who owned no less than twenty-two.

In ecclesiastical architecture and monastic remains, the county of Berks offers a variety of examples, many of which but too truly depict the ravages of time, and the still more destructive hand of man, in their present dilapidated, and, in some instances, almost annihilated, condition. We shall have the opportunity of examining a few that still exist, in the course of our inquiries; but there are others in different parts of the county which merit attention.

Avington church presents a fine specimen of what is commonly recognized as Saxon or early Norman architecture, and is in nearly its original condition.[1] Within, this building measures seventy-five feet in length by fourteen feet seven inches in breadth. The nave is separated from the chancel by an arch distinguished by zigzag mouldings and grotesque heads, with piers leaning outwards, worthy of observation. It has the originally groined roof of stone partly remaining. At the east end are three small round-

[1] Lysons, *Bib. Topog. Mag.*, i, 204. See also the rev. Mr. James's paper on the church.

headed windows. The font, a circular one with rude figures in *bassi-relievi* under arches, has been engraved by Lysons.[1]

Other churches in the county present somewhat similar features, among which may be enumerated, St. Nicholas at Abingdon, Aldermaston, Bucklebury, Cheddleworth, Charney, where there is a bas-relief in the chapel;[2] Childrey, having a circular leaden font with figures of an abbot;[3] Cholsey, Harmey, Halford, North Hinksey, Hurley, Kentbury, Lambourn, Padworth, Shelbourn, Shaw, Great Shefford, Shillingford, Sparsholt, Stamford-Dingley, St. Leonards at Wallingford, Sutton Courtney, Thatcham, Tidmarsh, Welford, and Windsor. Most of these present circular arches with zigzag mouldings and other ornaments denoting an early period. The church of Sunning Hill has been esteemed ancient Saxon.

Specimens of early Gothic may be seen at Uffington, Englefield, and Farringdon; also the chapel of Little Farringdon. But the most complete example of later Gothic is to be found in St. George's chapel, Windsor. At Marsham and Sutton Courtney there are wooden rood lofts. The churches of Berkshire abound with circular fonts, several of which are ornamented.[4] Stone stalls and piscinæ are also not unfrequent. There are two stone stalls at Aldworth.

Among monumental tombs, we have fine specimens of warriors of the fourteenth *sæc.*; particularly at Aldworth, where there are eight altar tombs with effigies of supposed members of the family of lord de la Beche. Of these, five are in armour, and cross-legged. Mr. Planché will doubtless enlighten us in regard to these and other monumental antiquities.[5] At Lambourn church are alabaster monuments to sir Thomas and lady Margaret Essex. Sir Thomas died in 1558. At Little Shefford, or East Shefford, there is a monument to Thomas Fettiplace, who is reported to have married an illegitimate daughter of John king of Portugal. Of this we may look for a refutation from Mr. Planché. In the chancel of Shottesbroke church is a monument to William Throckmorton, warden of the college, who died in 1535. His effigy is represented in alabaster, less than life, and it lies within

---

[1] Magna Britannia, i, 207, plate 21.   [3] Ib., i, 207, plate xix.
[2] Ib., p. 204.   [4] Ib., p. 207.
[5] See *Gent.'s Mag.* for May 1760, vol. xxx, p. 458. A plate of five of the effigies is (p. 149) in *Bibl. Topog. Brit.*, engraved from Ashmole's drawings.

an oblong stone hollowed out for its reception. At Speen church are the monuments of John Baptist Castillon, a Piedmontese, who died in 1597. His effigy is in armour. There is also a monument to dame Elizabeth Castillon, wife of his son, sir Francis, *ob.* 1603. She is habited in a fardingale and flowered gown, with a veil which almost covers her body.

At Aldermaston, Uffington, Speen, and other places, we shall also view various monumental effigies.

Many brasses belonging to this county have already received notice from our associates. I may specify those at Wantage[1] and those at Lambourn.[2]

It is sad to reflect upon the destruction of the most celebrated monasteries of Berkshire. Of that at Reading but little remains.[3] The Abbey Mills, however, exhibit Saxon arches. The gateway is not very ancient. The church of Grey Friars now forms the Bridewell. Of Abingdon abbey some remains will be found figured by Lysons.[4] They now constitute the premises of a brewer. The late Mr. Hudson Turner figured[5] a fireplace of the thirteenth *sæc.*, less massive in its construction than in the two preceding centuries. The flue consisted of a cylindrical shaft of masonry, and extended beyond the surface of the roof. Abingdon and Reading formed the two great monasteries of Berks, and they had mitred abbots. There was a priory at Sandleford, near Newbury. This has frequently been called Newton priory; and in the first edition of the *Monasticon* (i, 482), it was confounded with Sandford or Littlemore nunnery, in Oxfordshire,—an error corrected in the more recent edition. It was an establishment for Austin canons. In 1205,[6] Jeffrey or Geofrey, earl of Perche, and Maud his wife, founded and dedicated it to St. Mary and St. John the Baptist. For nearly three centuries it continued as a monastery, when it was, *circa* 1480, forsaken; and Edward IV, with the consent, and at the instance, of the ordinary of the place, Richard Beauchamp, bishop of Salisbury, and the dean of Windsor, annexed it to the collegiate chapel of Windsor; among the possessions of which, in 26th Henry VIII, it was valued at £10 *per ann.* Ashmole records the annexation (MS. 1114).

[1] Journal, viii, 61.   [2] Ib., p. 55.   [3] Ib., ii, 339, and xii, 84.
[4] Magna Britannia, i, 211.
[5] Domestic Architecture in England. Oxford, 1851, 8vo., p. 83.
[6] The confirmation charter of this priory by Stephen archbishop of Canterbury, assigns its foundation to have been prior to 1205.

William Westbury was prior in 1457. The abandonment of the monastery is endeavoured by Lysons to be accounted for by a difference existing between the prior and the bishop of Salisbury.[1] The second edition of Dugdale's *Monasticon* gives the charter of archbishop Stephen from the Cotton library, June 24, 1664, and also the charter of 21st Edward I. There were also cells at Henley and Wallingford. Benedictine nuns were located at Bromhale in Windsor forest; and there were various others, for which Tanner, Dugdale, Lysons, and other antiquaries, may be consulted. Several monasteries destroyed before the Conquest, are referred to by various writers. The royal chapel of St. George at Windsor still remains collegiate.

DONNINGTON, near Newbury, had a house of friars of the order of the Holy Trinity, founded by sir Richard Abberbury, knight (builder of Donnington castle), 16th Ric. II. It was valued, 26th Henry VIII, at £19 : 3 : 10 *per ann.* by Dugdale, and £20 : 16 : 6 by Speed. Leland gives an account of this house,[2] and calls them "Crossid Friers." Speed spoke of them as "ordinis Sanctæ Crucis." The surrender in 1539 denominates them "ordinis Sanctæ Trinitatis."[3] Their head is called minister, not prior, as the head of the Crossed or Crowched Friars generally was. At Donnington there is also a hospital, called God's house. This was also founded by Abberbury, though some have ascribed it to Thomas Chaucer, esq .(ob. 1434), and others to William de la Pole, duke of Suffolk, who married Chaucer's heiress. It was restored by the earl of Nottingham, in the reign of James I.

Appertaining to civil history we have several places of interest to visit. Who does not feel regard for Donnington castle, though little now beyond the ruins of a gateway, consisting of two towers, remain? These are of the fourteenth century, having been built in 1386, a valuable bit of information, derived from the patent rolls, 9th Rich. II, in which

---

[1] In the reign of James I it is reported that the rector of Newbury and the lessee of Sandleford had a dispute regarding tithes, and that, by an award of Chancery, Sandleford, consisting only of the priory house, was declared to be a separate and distinct parish. The owner of Sandleford was to have a pew in Newbury church, and to pay £8 *per ann.* to the rector in lieu of all tithes. In the old chapel belonging to the priory was the monument of a Crusader. The chapel was disused, and afterwards destroyed. (See Lysons, i, 353.)

[2] Itinerar., iii, 125.   [3] See Rymer, xiv, 613.

an entry appears, that license was given to a Richard Abberbury to build the castle of Donnington.[1] The castle was destroyed in the reign of Charles I, when besieged by colonel Horton.

NEWBURY, anciently *Newbir*, the seat of our present congress, is an ancient borough, and returned burgesses to Parliament as early as Edward I. I will not venture to say what the opinion of the reformers of the present day would be of that which was expressed by Elizabeth, in relation to this borough. Ashmole speaking of it, says, that it had formerly representatives in Parliament, but petitioned to be discharged of that expense, which had they kept to these days, they had not only been excused their salary, but enriched their town, as many others do by elections of this nature.

The church of Newbury dates from the reign of Henry VII. This place is of great renown, being in the neighbourhood of the two celebrated battles fought in the seventeenth *sæc.* during the civil wars. The first was in September 1643, when lords Carnarvon, Sunderland, and Falkland were killed ; and the second in October, 1644, the result of which is doubtful, as both parties claimed the victory. The bodies of those slain in the first battle were buried in two tumuli on the Wash ; those of the second were thrown into a pit near Newbury church.

Newbury is also renowned by one, who among those in this county who held great possessions, deserves to be mentioned with respect. He was the founder of the family of Winchcombe, and well known as Jack of Newbury. John Smallwood, *alias* Winchcombe, was a celebrated clothier, distinguished by his opulence, and no less by his patriotism. He entertained Henry VIII and queen Katharine at his house in this town. Henry Winchcombe, a descendant of the clothier, was created a baronet by Charles II. The title and family are extinct. Its wealth passed by marriage to the Packers, of Shillingford, at the commencement of the seventeenth century, and from them by another female heir to the Hartleys, now the representatives of both families.

Mr. Edward Roberts has favoured me with an admirable drawing of the almost only remaining portion of the house of

[1] Rot. Pat., 9th Ric. II : "Quod Ricūs Abberbury possit construere castrum in solo de Donyngton in com' Berk."

this celebrated clothier (see Plate 2), and has accompanied it with the subjoined remarks :—

"The remains of the residence and factory of 'Jack of Newbury' are very few, and still fewer are the parts visible; and since the congress, even these are diminished, and the rooms which were shown as the two parlours are now converted into a laundry and cart-horse stable; the carved chimney piece has found its way into a painter's workshop, and, true to his trade, the possessor is about to paint it. Some other remnants of the ancient timber structure and exquisite foliated carvings have been destroyed, and nothing now is to be seen except the gable end shown in the plate. This is at the north-west angle of the pile of buildings, adjoining the main street, the face next which has been rebuilt and a modern shop front inserted, the entablature showing sufficiently to mar the effect of the ancient work. The substructure is of quite new brickwork, the timber having been displaced; but with the exception of the plaster covering to the oriel window, all the remainder is of ancient construction, although not all of the same date or character: the verge-board, for instance, is of much earlier date than the other carvings, and may have been brought from some former building; and its comparative state of decay corroborates the suggestion. The whole framework is in oak, and in the main is still perfectly sound. The herring-bone brickwork is not coeval with the timbering; but it is quite clear that, as was usual, the timbers have always been exposed externally. There is no evidence forthcoming of the date of the erection of this remnant. It can hardly have been built by John Winchcomb; for on close examination it bears the impress of earlier years than Henry VII, and is most likely to be of about the middle of the fifteenth century. The oriel window cannot be seen in any way; the inside, although many of the old timbers are visible, having been carefully boarded or cemented in, and the oriel itself converted into a cupboard."

Newbury may be said to abound in almshouses, some of which will form objects for our visitation. There is,—1, St. Bartholomew's, or king John's, for fourteen poor men and women; 2, another, founded by —— Jemmett, esq., an alderman of London; 3, the church almshouse, of uncertain foundation; 4, Merry Hill almshouse, also of uncertain found-

PLATE 2.

Edward Roberts, del.

ation; 5, one founded by Mr. Pearce for two poor weavers; 6, by Mr. Hunt for three women; and 7, by Mr. Coxhead for two men.

Shaw House, a large building of the time of Elizabeth or James I, is also to be visited. It is a mile from Donnington, and was the headquarters of Charles. There is an inscription over the portico, which reads—

> " Edentulus vescentium dentibus invidet,
> Et oculus caprearum talpa contemnit."

The inscription may be looked upon in reference to the probability of envious feelings, on the part of his neighbours, upon the building of his house. It was erected in 1581, by one Dolman or Doleman, a clothier, upon retiring from business. Upon which occasion the following distich was made and circulated :

> " Lord have mercy upon us miserable sinners :
> Thomas Doleman has built a new house, and has turn'd away
> all his spinners."

Here also, in the old oak wainscot of a bow window in the library, is a hole formed by a shot said to have been discharged at Charles when dressing himself at the window. On a brass plate the following inscription is placed over the spot :

> HANC JUXTA FENESTRAM
> REX CAROLUS PRIMUS
> INSTANTE OBSIDIONE
> SCLOPPOPETRÆ ICTU TANTUM NON
> TRAJECTUS FUIT.
> DIE OCTOB. XXVII, MDCXLIV.

In illustrations of ANCIENT DOMESTIC ARCHITECTURE, the county of Berks may be regarded as rich. Mr. Hudson Turner has given us the representation of an entrance doorway, of the twelfth century, to the hall of a Norman house at APPLETON. It has been figured by Lysons[1] and also by Turner.[2] These serve to shew the arrangement of the hall, with small doorways opening into the kitchen and buttery, to be similar to that which we still observe in some of our colleges and inns of court. The house is of the close of the twelfth century, and stands within a moat. Mr. Turner

---

[1] Magna Britannia, i, 234.   [2] Domestic Architecture in England, p. 6.

esteems the walls, or at least the foundations remaining, as original.   The doorways, of which there are three, are interesting: the least, that which forms the entrance, is round-headed; but the mouldings are rather Early English than Norman, and the shafts on the jambs have round capitals with foliage.

SUTTON COURTNEY HOUSE, near the church, is of the latter part of the twelfth century, or the beginning of the thirteenth, and offers to our notice very substantial walls.   The doorway exhibits good mouldings, of transition Norman character and the tooth ornament.   There are signs of the house having originally been placed within a moat.   Mr. J. H. Parker[1] has given a striking illustration of the interior of the hall; and he has also represented other details, which, however, belong to the fourteenth century; together with a good plan of the hall, which is of the extent of forty feet, six inches, by twenty-three feet, ten inches.   The original open timber roof still remains;[2] and under one of the windows of the hall (now incorrectly denominated the chapel,— to which use, however, it is probable it may have been occasionally devoted) there is a low side window, which will bring to the recollection of such of us as attended the Congress at Manchester, a similar one at Cheetham's hospital, and there called the "dole window."   This, on the authority of Mr. Parker, is to be considered the first example of the kind that has been met with in domestic work.   It is nearly perfect on the inside, and has good decorated tracery; the hooks for hanging the shutter—glass not having at that time been fixed in them—still remain.

At CHARNEY BASSET there is a house of the thirteenth century, known as the "Monk's House."   It is in the parish of Longworth, and near to Wantage.   This building is furnished with a private chapel.   It was formerly a grange belonging to the abbey of Abingdon.   Mr. Turner suggests that it may formerly have been a residence of the Bassets, and have derived its name from having been given by a member of that family to the monks of Abingdon.[3]   A view of the west front is given, together with a plan of the house, the interior of the solar, the exterior and interior of the chapel, with fireplace of the south wing, and other details,

---

[1] Continuation of Mr. Hudson Turner's *Dom. Arch.*, p. 33.
[2] Domest. Arch., p. 272.   [3] Ib., p. 154, note.

all of considerable interest. The building is to be regarded as of the latter part of the thirteenth century, at the end of the reign of Henry III or the beginning of Edward I.

BISHAM ABBEY has an entrance porch of the time of Edward I, and the wooden door has the old iron work remaining upon it. The hall underwent many changes in the time of Henry VIII, and it is known that the princess Elizabeth was here confined. There is a good music gallery of the latter part of the fifteenth century, behind which are the kitchen and offices, and over them a solar, reported to have formed the chapel.

Of the fourteenth century numerous illustrations are to be found in WINDSOR CASTLE, but this building needs a separate consideration, and would of itself offer sufficient variety for an entire congress. In the castle, painting, as in the palace of Clarendon (the particulars relating to which, and embracing a notice of the examples at Windsor, together with observations as to the artists employed, I have already laid before the Association),[1] is abundant.

HENLEY PRIORY, in this county, offers some Norman work. It, however, underwent some alterations in the time of Edward II. According to Tanner,[2] it was a priory of Black Monks, a cell to the abbey of Westminster, and founded by Godfrey or Jeffrey de Magna Villa, in the reign of William the Conqueror.

At GREAT COXWELL there is a remarkably fine barn of the fourteenth century. It measures one hundred and forty feet in length, is forty feet broad, and thirty feet in height from the floor to the barn. A chapel which formerly stood at the back of the ancient manor house, was pulled down, and the vicarage built with the materials. The chapel is conjectured to have been the *Capella infra capital mess* in the grant of Henry VIII. Here was a cell of Cistercians (tradition says Cluniacs) from Beaulieu abbey.[3]

BRIMPTON presents a chapel, formerly a domestic one, standing in a farmyard near to the church, and attached to a house, round which are still portions of a moat by which

---

[1] Journal, vol. xv, for September 1859, pp. 246-264.
[2] Notitia Monastica.
[3] See *Bibl. Topog. Brit.*, iv, 1-26; where also will be found plates representing the manor house, king John's stable, now used as the barn, the church of St. Giles, and brasses of William and Johane Morys, with three children in the background,—of the sixteenth century.

it had been surrounded. It is also of the fourteenth century. Tanner makes mention of a house of Knights Hospitallers of St. John of Jerusalem, of the time of Henry III, which we propose to visit and examine.

CUMNER, COMNOR, or CUMNOR, in the north of the county, is an ancient place, being named in a grant to the abbot and monks of Abingdon, by Ceadwalla, in the seventh century. The manor house was of the middle of the fourteenth century, and ultimately came into the possession of the Abingdon family. These ancient buildings have been conjectured to have belonged to a place of retreat which might be rendered available during the occurrence of plague or other contagious or severe visitation, and such as would be urgently required in the neighbourhood of an abbey of the magnitude of that at Abingdon.

The parish of Cumnor, upon the suppression of the religious houses, came into the possession of the crown, and we find that on the 9th Feb., 1538, Thomas Rowland, the last abbot, ceded the property, which was retained by Henry VIII for eight years, as appears from letters patent dated Windsor, Oct. 8th, 1546, by which the lordship, manor, and rectorial tythes of Cumnor, with all its rights and appurtenances, and particularly the capital messuage, Cumnor-place, and the close adjoining called the Parke, and the three closes adjoining called Saffron, Plottye, etc., in consideration of two closes in St. Thomas parish, Oxford, the site of Rowley abbey, and the sum of £310 : 12 : 9 in money paid into the court of augmentations, were granted to George Owen, esq., physician ("in re medicâ nobis a conciliis"), and John Bridges, doctor in physic. It must have been very shortly after held by Anthony Forster, and made to constitute the manor house, his residence, as here, in 1560, he had under his roof the lady Robert Dudley.

During the civil wars, Cumnor was in the possession of a family named Pecock or Peacock, of which Richard Pecock compounded for his estate at £140. The following letter appears in the *Mercurius Academicus*, p. 100 :

"Thursday, Feb. 26 (1644-5).

"To present you with as honest men as those of Evesham;[1] and honeste you will not deeme them to be, when you heare they came from

[1] Surprised by sir W. Waller's horse in June 1643.

Cumnor Church, Berks.

1

Abingdon to a place called Cumner, in no smaller a number than 500; where their chieftanes view the church, goe up into the steeple, and overlook the country, as if they meant to garrison there; but finding it not answerable to their hopes and desires, they descend, but are loath to depart without leaving a marke of their iniquitie and impiety behind them. Some they employ to take downe the weathercock (that might have been left alone to turne round); others to take downe a crosse from off an isle of the church (and this you must not blame them for,—they are enemies to the crosse); others to plunder the countrymen's houses of bread, beare, and bacon, and whatsoever else was fit for the sustentation of man."

The burialplace of the Peacock family is at Cumnor; and against the eastern wall is a tablet to the memory of Alicia Peacock, who died May 21, 1715, æt. 50; and on the north side another of Whorwood Peacock, gent., who died August 11, 1759, æt. 72. There is also another monument, to a child, Frances daughter of Charles and Alice Peacock, who died March 12, 1688-9, aged eleven months. The school of Cumnor is mainly supported by a legacy from Mrs. Peacock. From the Peacocks, I presume, Cumnor Place passed to the Abingdon family; and it is but justice to the noble earl who directed the demolition of this interesting place, to state that the utmost care was taken to preserve every vestige of antiquarian interest connected with the building. In addition to some remains now preserved in Wytham church and its churchyard, and to representations of other fragments to be found in the *Gentleman's Magazine*,[1] I have to acknowledge my obligations to Miss Kymer, of Beenham Lodge, Reading, for various drawings, with some of which I am enabled to illustrate this paper. These illustrations are exceedingly interesting, and fully establish their claim to the middle of the fourteenth century. They consist of :

The remains of the base and portion of the shaft of a cross in Cumnor churchyard.

A window and portion of an arch, with the capitals of three columns belonging to the same, from Cumnor.

A corbel of elegant workmanship.   (Plate 3, fig. 1.)

Another corbel.   (Plate 4, fig. 1.)

Two arches in St. Catherine's chapel, attached to Cumnor church, formerly containing monumental effigies.

[1] For 1821, Part I, pp. 34, 201, 310, 403, 489, and Suppl. 598. See also Lysons in *Magna Britannia*, vol. i, p. 213 et seq.

A carving in the chancel representing the sacred mono-gram, I.H.S. in a shield; and in another the feet, hands, and heart (the five stigmata). These are surmounted by a shield on which is a cross.   (See plate 3, fig. 2.)

The reverse of the preceding, having also three shields, on one of which are figured the emblems of the crucifixion, namely, the ladder, the spear, and the rod or staff, to which is affixed a sponge; on another, the hammer, pincers, and three nails; whilst upon the upper shield are the vestments, crown of thorns, and the bag of money.   (Fig. 3.)

A bold carving, from the north aisle, representing a figure, probably that of St. Michael, standing upon the heads of two monsters or dragons; and the reverse, exhibiting the body and limbs of the animals.   (Plate 4, figs. 2 and 3.)

By time and neglect then, it appears, Cumnor place had fallen into decay, and was patched up for the abode of a farmer; the chapel was converted into a stable, and the hall into a granary.   Soon afterwards (as we learn from a writer in the *Gent.'s Mag.* for 1821, part 2, p. 35) the upper story of the southern side fell down, and on the departure of the farmer, the residue of the pile was parcelled out into smaller tenements, and let by the lessee at Abingdon to the poorer classes.   The entire place was demolished in 1810. In Wytham church, however, the beautiful windows which had belonged to the hall are employed in embellishing that edifice, and that which has been called the outer gate of Cumnor-hall, and erected by Forster, made to form the en-trance to Wytham churchyard.[1]   The doorway, erected by Forster, was copied by the rev. Benj. Buckler, D.D., vicar of Cumnor, a fellow of All Souls, and keeper of the archives in the university of Oxford (ob. Dec. 24, 1780, æt. 64.)   This bore the date of 1575, and the inscription upon it is suitable to an ecclesiastical building, JANVA VITÆ VERBVM DOMINI. It seems scarcely probable that this doorway could have formed the principal gateway to Cumnor park, and it has been suggested that it may have been merely the postern, and that the carriage entrance to which it was appended had been totally demolished.   It measures only eight feet in height, and is three feet four inches in width.   It is formed by an elegant pointed arch, enclosed by an archi-trave of a square form, the spandrils holding trefoil panels.

[1] These are engraved in *Gent.'s Mag.*, 1821, p. 201.

Cumnor Church. Berks.

Passing on to the fifteenth century, it remains to notice two fine and remarkable remains in this county : Ockholt and Ufton court.

OCKHOLT is an ancient manor, the property of the ancestors of the lords Norreys of Rycote. In 1267, Henry III gave it to Richard de Norreys, cook to queen Eleanor, subject to a fee farm rent of 40s., and according to the grant it was constituted by an encroachment from the forest.[1] Sir W. Norreys died, seized of this estate, in 1507, and it went to the Fettiplaces. The next century occasioned a change of owner, for about 1679 it was in the family of Finch of Hertfordshire, who in 1786 sold it to P. P. Powney, esq. The manor house formed the residence of the Norreys family, and the stained glass gives illustrations of the heraldic bearings of the family with their motto " Feythfully serve," and also of the arms of the abbey of Abingdon with the mitre. Lysons[2] has given a good representation of the house, a general plan of the building, the glass windows with the bearings of Norreys, Beaufort, king Henry VI, and his queen.

UFTON had two manors, Ufton Nervets and Ufton Greyshall. The former is conjectured to be that which in the time of the survey belonged to Wm. Fitz-Anscalf, ancestor of the Paganels, held in 1316 by Wm. de Ufton. The manor of Ufton Greyshall belonged to the abbey and convent of Reading. In 1603 they were united. In process of time they passed into the possession of the Parkinses, and the parish church has monuments of this family. The most interesting is, perhaps, that of Arabella, wife of Francis Perkins, the Belinda of the *Rape of the Lock*, which was dedicated to her by Pope, under her maiden name of Fermor. She died in 1738. The present Ufton court is of the time of Henry VII, Henry VIII, Elizabeth, and, as I believe, also of James I, and is of great extent. It now belongs to Richard Benyon, esq., by whom it has been kindly placed for our examination on this occasion, and merits particular attention.[3]

[1] Pat., 52nd Hen. III.   [2] Magn. Brit., i, 247.
[3] In the hope of obtaining information in regard to the history of this mansion, the illustrations of it are deferred to a future opportunity.

ON THE LEGENDARY HISTORY OF WAYLAND SMITH.

BY THOS. WRIGHT, ESQ., M.A., F.S.A., ETC.

ON the western limits of this county, in an interesting district which borders on Wiltshire, a county so celebrated for its early barrows and earthworks, there is, in the parish of Ashbury, a monument which has obtained more individual celebrity than most similar remains. It has suffered great dilapidation, but enough remains to show that it has consisted of a rather long rectangular inclosure, with two lateral chambers, formed by upright stones, roofed with large slabs, and the whole was probably once covered with a mound of earth. There can be no doubt, indeed, of the sepulchral character of this monument, and it belongs to that class which are commonly called Celtic; but it is not my intention, on the present occasion, to inquire how far this denomination may be correct. It is in another point of view that I claim your attention to it—its connection with the remotest traditions of our race, I mean of the Anglo-Saxons.

It was the local popular tradition, known to have existed during several ages, that these chambers, or, as the peasantry denominated the monument, this cave, were inhabited by an invisible smith ; and it was believed, that if the horse of a traveller passing that way happened to cast a shoe, he had only to take the animal to this "cave," and, having placed a groat on the capstone, withdraw to a distance from which he could not see what was going on ; on his return, he would find that the horse had been well shoed during his absence, and that the money had been taken away. The invisible workman was called by the peasantry Wayland Smith ; and the monument of which I have been speaking has been known from time immemorial as Wayland Smith's cave.

It is a curious—and in this instance an important—circumstance, that this Berkshire monument happened, in Anglo-Saxon times, to lie upon the line of boundary of an estate, and that on this account it is mentioned in an Anglo-

Saxon charter of the land, made long before the time of the Norman conquest. It is there called Welandes smiððe, which means literally Weland's Smithy, or Weland's Forge ; and there cannot be the slightest doubt that the modern name of Wayland Smith is a mere vulgar corruption of this Saxon name. We thus find that this identical monument has continued to bear the same mysterious name since the Anglo-Saxon period—we trace it by written documents nearly a thousand years, and it had borne the same name probably during a much longer period, namely, from the earlier ages of the Anglo-Saxon occupation of this island, and we discover also that that name belonged to one of the most ancient mythic legends of the Teutonic race. Such legends were located extensively throughout Saxon England, but this is almost a unique case in which we can trace the connexion directly without having recourse to conjecture. There is another circumstance in which this early occurrence of the name is interesting. I have said that, like all similar monuments, this "cave" was, no doubt, originally covered with a mound of earth. It is evident that, at the time of this Anglo-Saxon charter, and indeed at the moment when the name was first given to it, the mound must have been already cleared away, and the traces of sepulchral interment so far removed that the Saxons could not take it for a grave, or they would hardly have called it a smith's shop. It would thus appear that many of our "cromlechs" may have been uncovered at a much earlier date than we suppose—perhaps in the later Roman period, or in the period of transition between Roman and Anglo-Saxon.

But to return to our more immediate subject, the legend, it will perhaps be not uninteresting to many of you if I tell you briefly Weland's story. This story is found in its earliest form, but briefly and imperfectly, in one of the songs of the elder Edda, composed about the end of the eleventh century, but compiled no doubt from the popular Scandinavian songs of a much earlier date. In a considerably later composition in the northern literature, this story is dilated, and has received additions which probably do not belong to the older story, but the latter is in some parts explained and completed by it. It is from this latter compilation that we derive the history of Weland's parentage.

There was, we are told, a king in Sweden named Wilkin,

who, in one of his expeditions formed a connection with a
sea-woman—in fact, with one of the spirits of the sea, the
result of which was a son named Wade, who was a giant,
one of the Alfs, or supernatural personages of the ancient
creed. Wade, who lived in Iceland, had three sons, named
Slagfid, Egill, and Vælund. The father entrusted his son,
Vælund, to the dwarfs in the mountains, in order that they
might impart to him their wonderful skill in forging metals,
and in making weapons and jewellery. We now take up
the story from the Edda. In the course of their hunting
expeditions, as they pursued their game on skates, the three
brothers came to Ulfdal, where they took up their abode not
far from a lake called Ulfsiar. One morning they found on
the bank of the lake three Valkyrier, who I need not tell
you were also supernatural beings—sitting together and
spinning, with their alf-garments lying beside them. They
were king's daughters, two being sisters, and their names
were Hladguth Svanhvite, or white as the swan ; Hervoer
Alvite, or all-knowing ; and Alrun, which latter name may
perhaps be interpreted All-learned. The three brothers
liked the damsels, took them home with them, and made
them their wives, Egill taking Alrun, Slagfid Svanhvite, and
Vælund Alvite. During eight winters the Valkyries remained with their husbands, but on the ninth year their
desire to return to their old habits of hovering over battlefields overcame their other feelings, and they flew away, to
return no more.

When the brothers returned from the chase and found
their huts empty, two of them, Egill and Slagfid, immediately went off in search of their wives, but Vælund remained
alone in Ulfdal, and employed himself in his forge, making
rings of gold, which he strung upon a twig of willow to
keep them together, waiting patiently his wife's return.
There lived at this time a king of Sweden named Niduth,
who had two sons and a daughter named Baudvild. Niduth heard that Vælund was alone in Ulfdal, and he set off
secretly one night with a troop of his armed followers, and
visited the hut of the skilful smith, while he was absent in
the chase. They entered, and saw his rings and other
works, and Niduth took the rings off the twig, and then
restored them all except one, which he carried away and
gave to his daughter Baudvild. When Vælund returned,

he made a fire to roast a piece of bear's flesh for his supper, and when the flames rose and gave light to his chamber, he saw the rings, counted them, and perceived that one was missing ; but he thought that his wife, for whom it was intended, had returned during his absence and taken it, and he laid him down to sleep. When Vælund awoke in the morning, he found himself securely bound hand and foot, and Niduth and his men standing over him. They carried him to Niduth's palace, where, at the suggestion of the queen, they ham-stringed him that he might not be able to escape, and placed him in a forge in a small island called Sævar-Staud, where he was compelled to work for the king, and where all individuals except the king were forbidden to approach him under the severest penalties.

Vælund, as he worked over his anvil, brooded constantly on revenge, and an opportunity soon presented itself of carrying his vengeance into execution. The king's two sons came secretly to visit him ; they were led by the desire of obtaining possession of some of the wealth which was understood to be contained in the forge, and, demanding the keys, they opened a chest which was filled with rich and beautiful jewelry. Vælund knew their thoughts, and he told them that all this treasure should be theirs, if they could come to him next day in perfect secrecy. Early in the morning the two princes, without the knowledge of anybody, repaired to the forge of Vælund, who shut the door and immediately cut off their heads. He buried their bodies under the marshy ground on which his forge was built. With the skulls, plated with silver, he made drinking cups for Niduth's table ; with their eyes he made fine gems, which he sent to the wicked queen ; and with their teeth he made a collar of pearls which he sent to the princess Baudvild. All these different presents were received with the greatest satisfaction.

But the revenge of Vælund was not yet complete, and he waited for another victim.

Baudvild had broken the ring given her by her father, and, fearful of his anger while she was emboldened by Vælund's present, she applied to him secretly to mend it. The wily smith promised to do it in such a manner that her father should never discover the accident, but he required that she should come with it secretly to his forge. She had no sooner entered it, than he made fast the door, and effected his designs upon her person.

Having thus completed his vengeance, while the princess left the scene of her dishonour in tears, Vælund made his escape in a manner which seems never to have been anticipated—he flew away. But he halted for a moment on the wall of an inclosure of the palace, where he called for the king and queen, and told them every circumstance of the murder of their sons and of their daughter's shame, adding that the latter was with child. The princess was questioned and confirmed his story, and in process of time she gave birth to a son, who also in due time became a hero of Northern and Teutonic romance. Vælund continued his flight and was heard of no more. He seems to have pursued his labours in secret places, and was believed from time to time to forge weapons, especially swords, which it was granted only to the greatest of heroes to possess.

Such is the legend of Weland. In his capacity of a supernatural maker of equally supernatural weapons, his name was popular through many centuries in the romantic and poetic literature of western Europe. The Germans spoke of him as Wieland, the Latin writers as Wielandus and Guielandus, and the French as Galand, while the English writers used the pure Anglo-Saxon form of Weland. It would be abusing your patience, without any particularly useful result, to enumerate now the various passages in which the name of Weland occurs in the medieval writers in these various languages. I will only speak of our own native literature, because the allusions to Weland we find in Anglo-Saxon are much older even than the Scandinavian mythic legend in the oldest form in which it is preserved.

It might very justly be asked, how do we know that the Weland alluded to in Anglo-Saxon writings, is the Vælund of the Scandinavian legend ? We have accidentally—for all our remains of Anglo-Saxon popular literature have been preserved accidentally—a very direct answer to this question. Among the fragmentary poems in the now well known *Exeter Book*, there is one which has every appearance of being of very early date, and to which the editor (Mr. Thorpe) gives the title of "The Complaint of Deor the Scald" or bard. The poet, in his misfortunes, calls to mind the examples of others who had passed through disasters of

various kinds, and overcome them, in order to encourage
himself in bearing his own with patience. The first name he
quotes is that of Weland :

" Weland in himself the worm
Of exile proved ;
The firm-souled chief
Hardship endured,
Had for his company
Sorrow and weariness,
Winter-cold exile,
Affliction often suffered,
After on him Nithhad
Constraint had laid
With a tough sinew-band,
The unhappy man.
That he surmounted ;
So may I this."

His next example is the victim of Weland's vengeance, here
called Beadohild, which is the Anglo-Saxon form of the
Norse Baudvildi, the daughter of king Niduth, or in Anglo-
Saxon, Nithhad :

"To Beadohild was not
The death of her brothers
In thought so grievous
As her own mischance,
When she certainly
Had become conscious
That she was pregnant.
She might never
Think confidently
How it could be as to that.
That she surmounted ;
So may I this."

We have here distinct references to several of the prominent
circumstances of Weland's history as told in the *Edda;* and
they not only shew that the Anglo-Saxon legend of Weland
was identical with the Scandinavian legend, but they prove
that in this form the legend belonged to a very remote
period. The name and adventures of Weland were so familiar to the Anglo-Saxon mind, that when king Alfred, in
translating Boethius, came upon the line—

" Ubi nunc fidelis ossa Fabricii manent ?"

interpreting the name Fabricius by deriving it from *faber,* a smith, the name of Weland immediately presented itself to his thoughts, and he gave an Anglo-Saxon paraphrase which may be literally rendered into English, " Where are now the bones of the celebrated and wise goldsmith, Weland ?...Where are now the bones of Weland ? or who knows now where they were ?"

But we may look much further than the middle ages for forms of this curious legend. There can be no doubt that the original myth on which it was founded, gave birth also to that of the lamed smith of the more refined mythology of Greece and Rome; called in the former Hephaistos, and in the latter Vulcan; as well as to another character of this mythology, Dædalus, which had become separated from the other character of the original mythic personage in the course of refinement. In fact, the type, or the germ, of this myth existed before the various peoples separated from the great branch of mankind to which we belong, and was carried away by each, and modified in the course of transition. As the races separated into divisions and subdivisions, each, taking these primeval legends of the race with it, believed them to be its own, located them in the country in which it settled, and gave them a nearer date. Perhaps in some primeval period, the myth of Weland may have belonged to the peoples of the Caucasus; but it belonged afterwards, at various periods, to various peoples and countries; and the Scandinavians believed that its scene was Sweden, and that it belonged to the beginning of their own historical period; while the Germans must have brought it to a still later date, and perhaps to another country, as they introduce Weland's son by the princess Beadohild, among the heroes at the court of Diderich of Berne, or, in more correct historical and geographical language, of Theodoric of Verona.

This process of locating legends was one of constant occurrence in the movements of races and nations; and it is important, for many reasons, that it should be well observed. It explains the legendary character of the earlier periods of our national history, and it helps us to the true interpretation of a host of local names and legends which are otherwise inexplicable. The Anglo-Saxons pursued unconsciously this practice of locating their older legends in their new country to a much greater extent than might by many be supposed; and we have evidence of this in the particular legends I have been relating to you. A local legend in Yorkshire is not yet forgotten, according to which the giant Wade—Weland's grandfather, according to Scandinavian story—resided at Mulgrave castle, and made the Roman road which runs near it, and which is popularly called "Wade's Causeway." The remains of a cromlech, or rather what some would call two Druidical stones, in the immediate neighbourhood, are called "Wade's Grave." There once existed an English romance of Wade, which is alluded to by Chaucer; but it now seems to be irrecoverably lost. Other names connected with Weland's history might be pointed out in those of different localities in England, and generally in connexion with some remarkable monument of remote antiquity which exists, or has existed, there. The name of Weland himself is, as we have seen, attached to the monument which has given rise to these, I fear, too hastily drawn up remarks.

This irresistible tendency of people to carry about from country to country, and locate wherever they settled, under successive modifications, their primeval legends, may be remarked in other branches of the great stock of nations. It appears among the Greeks and Romans to quite as great an extent as among the German tribes; for we perceive, through the works of writers like Pausanias and the Scholiasts, that the original mythology of those races continued to exist among the peasantry, as in England, quite independent of and untouched by the process of refining under which what we call classical mythology was formed, and that its legends had been located in a similar manner. The discordance between the local legends and the grand system of mythology, greatly puzzled the professed writers on the subject, and led them into various theories, one of the most common of which was that of supposing a number of mythic personages of the same name. Thus even Cicero, in his treatise on the Nature of the Gods, finding a Vulcan located in so many places, came to the conclusion that there was not one but many Vulcans, and he enumerates four, one of whom he seems to locate in Attica ; another, he says, lived in Egypt ; a third exercised his craft at Lemnos ; and the fourth dwelt in the Vulcanian islands near Sicily. Vulcan was, as already observed, no doubt, originally the same personage as Weland,

and I will conclude with a local legend relating to the last
of the localities mentioned by Cicero, which has been preserved by the Greek scholiast upon Apollonius Rhodius,
and which is particularly illustrative of the similarity which
these localized legends take in far distant lands. " Vulcan,"
we are informed by this scholiast, " appears to have taken
up his abode in the islands of Lipara and Strongyle;" and
he adds, " it was formerly said, that whoever chose to carry
there a piece of unwrought iron, and at the same time deposited the value of the labour, might, on the following
morning, come and have a sword, or whatever else he desired,
for it." It is the very story of our Wayland Smith's cave ;
and furnishes, if it were wanting, a new proof of the extreme
antiquity and of the extreme durability of such local legends
in general. In the changes of society, these ancient legends
have been degraded in their transitions, and it can hardly be
doubted that, in the earlier ages of Anglo-Saxon rule, the
Weland of Berkshire was supposed to supply swords or jewels
to the warrior, and not horse-shoes to the peasant.

AVINGTON CHURCH, BERKS.

BY THE REV. JOHN JAMES, M.A.

THIS church is a Norman structure, of the earlier part of
the twelfth century, and of the very simplest type. On a
ground plan in the form of an elongated parallelogram, four
walls are raised, enclosing an area seventy-five feet by fifteen
feet, or five widths in length. Of these five square spaces,
one forms the sanctuary, another the choir, leaving three for
the nave, of the church. The nave is divided from the choir
by an arch originally semicircular, but now very considerably depressed. (See plate 4.) The choir is divided from
the sanctuary by pilasters with cushioned imposts, that were
evidently meant to sustain another semicircular arch,—
which arch seems, however, not to have been even commenced. From either side of these pilasters there springs
the foundation of a groined arch, corresponding to a more
advanced structure of the same kind at the transverse angle,
formed by the east and west end of the chancel with the

Pl. 5.

AVINGTON CHURCH. BERKS.

J.R.Jobbins

north and south wall thereof respectively. So far, therefore, it is clear that the original design of a vaulted ceiling to the chancel lacks completion.

How this came to pass, and how the existing chancel arch came to be depressed, are moot questions; but they seem best to be explained by another remarkable feature in this church, namely, the out-leaning, or declination from the perpendicular, of the lateral walls, both internally and externally, along their whole line. This out-leaning, or deflexion of the side walls, is greater the nearer to the chancel arch; and it is reasonably accounted for by the fact that, along their whole line, there was originally no external buttress, not even where the lateral pressure of the chancel arch demanded counteraction; neither is there internally, to make up for this external defect, any adequate projecting pier. By an obvious law of mechanics, no semicircular arch so placed between two bare, unsupported walls, could do otherwise than exert a powerful lateral pressure on them, proportioned to the weight of wall upon its superincumbent architrave. Fortunately for the arch itself, the wall over the architrave, in this instance, was never meant to rise beyond a very moderate height; and it seems clear that it could not have risen far before the depression of the arch commenced. When once it had commenced, it would have been madness, either to proceed with the erection of the groined arches already begun, or to attempt the construction of the uncommenced sanctuary, or second chancel arch. From that moment, indeed, the whole skill of the workmen employed would be demanded for the safe completion of the wall, which was to be borne up by the already depressed arch. This difficult work they accomplished; but seemingly not without resorting to the expedient of supporting the arch by means of some sort of substruction, whether of wood or flint. Most probably a strong wooden framework was constructed for this purpose; and, having been so constructed, was made to serve the further purpose of a temporary east end to the church, until the mode of ceiling the chancel should be decided on.

This conjecture is strengthened by the existence of two pointed arches westward of the chancel arch, which were evidently opened after the original completion of the walls, and which served—the one on the south side, beyond a doubt, as the piscina to an altar erected westward of the chancel arch,—the other, in all probability, as the opening to a north transept, whose purpose was to supply that space for the clergy and the choir, of which they had been deprived by the temporary non-completion of the chancel choir. That this latter archway was opened subsequently to the completion of the original wall, is evident, not only from the awkwardness of its form and workmanship, but from some remaining traces of a round-headed window (corresponding to the one opposite, which still exists) having been blocked up in order to make room for the required transept; and that the arrangement was only temporary, appears from the transept itself having disappeared, and from the archway being now closed up, with a lancet window inserted in the wall. This lancet window thus indicates the period at which the church, in its present form, was finally completed, and at which the altar was removed from the east end of the nave to the east end of the chancel. It was probably at the same period (viz., "circa temp. Richardi primi") that another smaller lancet window was inserted in the south wall of the chancel, for the greater convenience of the officiating priest at the vesper or matin services.

With these three exceptions, and that of the north doorway in the nave (long since blocked up), every[1] opening in the walls is semicircular, and belongs to the period of the original erection. This remark applies not only to the south doorway, but also to the beautiful sedile and piscina on the south side of the sanctuary, and to the eleven original windows still existing, of which seven are in the chancel and four are in the nave. All these semicircular arches are faced internally with freestone of excellent workmanship; and all the windows are splayed, but otherwise entirely unadorned.

The remarkable chancel arch is supported on either side by one large and one small round pilaster; of which the surface was at some time stained with a diaper pattern in red, and of which the capitals are adorned, some by rich perpendicular chasings, others by rude angular faces with eyes of omniscience; while the spacious arch itself is ornamented by manifold zigzag work on its western face, surmounted by floriate studs, and by a circular soffit underneath, with

---

[1] The priest's doorway was, indeed, originally square-headed, and the aumbry is a perfect square. The existing priest's door is quite recent.

twenty-nine grotesque heads[1] on either side along its whole semicircular extent, their elongated beaks or tongues meeting in the centre.

The south door way, by which the church is usually entered, is ornamented by disengaged shafts with diverse capitals, also by bead and manifold zigzag mouldings, surmounted by open leaf-work; which last has been ruthlessly damaged by the insertion of ridgebeam and wall plates for a sixteenth-century porch. The precise date of this porch is indicated by the letters R. C. sculptured on its front entrance, and corresponding to letters which appear, together with the date (A.D. 1574), on slabs over the south door of the ancient manor house, and which are the initials of the then existing lord of the manor, Richard Choke.[2] The stone coping or ridgetile of this church porch, and also the pretty quatrefoil windows in its side walls, were evidently transferred from some of the old walls and detached buildings of the then family mansion.[3]

Perhaps the most curious, if not most interesting, object in this church presents itself at the first entrance into it, viz., a Norman font of considerable circumference and depth, with the usual cable ornament round its upper edge, and an arcaded series of thirteen figures round its perpendicular sides. Of these figures, eleven are vested ecclesiastically, some with copes, some with chasubles, some with dalmatics, nearly all with stoles; one of them has both hands raised in act of benediction, one carries a crook or pastoral staff, another a crozier

---

[1] These grotesque beak-heads appear also on the springings of the groin arches of the unfinished choir vault.

[2] Lysons tells us that Richard Choke married the heiress of the Coventrys of Avington, and that his grandson, Francis Choke, was knighted in 1643. Before the Coventrys, this manor belonged to the lords Strange of Knockit, to whom it had passed, by marriage, from the Lacys earls of Lincoln; who had also, in their turn, inherited it by marriage from the Longspées earls of Salisbury. The Longspées appear to have held it from the reign of Henry II. It now belongs to sir Robert Burdett, bart., whose father, sir Francis, inherited it from his maternal relative, the heiress of the family of Jones of Ramsbury.

[3] The traditionary idea is, that these out-buildings are parts of a monastic residence,—possibly the cell of some two or three brothers of a monastery proper, situated at Old Sarum or elsewhere in Wiltshire. And this idea seems favoured,—1, by the fact of the earls of Salisbury having been early possessed of the manor; 2, by the seeming provision for a plurality of clergy in the choir, as well as in the temporary north transept, of the church; 3, by the extraordinary zeal of the founder of the church, which seems implied in its erection so near to Kintbury,—for so small a territory cut out of the midst of that parish, and with no example of a like provision being made for any other of the numerous hamlets in that extensive parish.

or mace surmounted by a cross; one holds in his hands his own head decollated; while two of them are grouped, each with another figure, under the same arch respectively, and embraced by that other figure—in the one case, apparently, with the kiss of peace—in the other case, with that of a tempter or accuser. In this last case cloven feet and pointed ears are very distinctly sculptured.

The only sepulchral monuments and escutcheons of importance in this church, are those of the Berkshire family of James,[1] at this time represented by sir Walter James, of Langley Hall in this county, baronet. The existence of these memorials is readily accounted for by the fact of the neighbouring estate of Denford having been the residence of this family down to the commencement of the present century, from the time of the first Tudor sovereign, during whose reign its previous possessor, lord Lovell, was attainted of high treason. In Henry the Eighth's reign this family was further aggrandized by the grant of other lands in the townships of Eddington, Hidden, and Newtown, made to them in token of their loyal support of the reformation of religion, which was then going on. Of these last named possessions they were indeed temporarily deprived on the accession of queen Mary. One of the monumental inscriptions briefly notes the womanly virtues of the lady who, in the sixteenth century, brought with her a further accession of property, as heiress of the family of Head of Langley hall. Unfortunately little or no light is thrown on the parochial history by its registers, as they do not ascend higher than to the beginning of the eighteenth century. The earlier records are supposed to have been destroyed by fire.

ALDERMASTON.

BY T. J. PETTIGREW, F.R.S., F.S.A., VICE-PRESIDENT AND TREASURER.

ASSEMBLED at Aldermaston, it may be interesting to some of our members and visitors to listen to a few words in relation to its history. From Domesday Book we obtain

---

[1] The town of Wallingford appears from Lysons to have been represented in parliament by a member of this family as long ago as Richard II.

the information that it was a manor of some importance at the time of the Norman conquest. Its name is unquestionably Saxon—Alderman or Eldermanstown, and was probably derived from having been the possession of some individual who held that rank in Saxon times. Leland uniformly writes it *Aldermanton*. It is a parish in the hundred of Theale, and lies south of the river Kennet on the borders of Hants. It was anciently in the hundred of Redinges, as we find in Domesday :—

"In Redinges. Rex tenet in dominio Helder-manstune Heraldus tenuit. Tunc se defendit pro 15 hidis. Modo pro nichilo. Terra est 30 carucate. In dominio sunt 2 carucate et 36 villam et 12 bordarii cum 18 carucis. Ibi 2 servi et molinum de 20 solidis et 2 piscarie de 5 solidis. Ibi ecclesia et 124 acre prati. Silva de 30 porcis. Tempore regis Edwardi et post et modo valet 20 libras et 10 solidos. Tamen de hac et de hocfelle que subter est reddit qui tenet 26 libras.

"In Eldiemanestune jacet Hocfelle Brieswardus tenuit de dono Heraldi. Tunc se defendit pro una hida et dimidio, modo pro nichilo. Terra est 3 carucate. Ibi 3 villam et 6 bordarii cum 2 carucis. Ibi 2 servi et 6 acre prati. Silva de 50 porcis precium ejus superius."

The mention of Thele hundred occurs in 1275. (Rot. Hund., iv, Edw. I.)

The history of Aldermaston can be traced from the time of Henry I, when the king granted the manor to Robert (not Richard, as given by Leland) Achard, who in the grant is styled "magister meus," and he, perhaps, held some high office at court at that time, or he may have been a professor of civil law, to whom that designation was frequently applied. One of the witnesses to the grant of Henry I was no less a personage than the queen Matilda ; the instrument therefore dates from the commencement of the twelfth century. The manor, including five considerable estates, was held by the service of one knight's fee. The original grant does not appear to be now in existence ; but it is referred to and confirmed by a charter of Henry III. At this time, according to the Coll. Rot. 13th Henry III (1229) the manor was in the possession of the same family, who indeed held it to the close of the fourteenth century.

There are but few and short notices on record in regard to the Achards ; but from some MS. notes written by the reverend Mr. Bellas, formerly minister of Aldermaston, a friend of the last Mr. Congreve, (for which I am indebted to the kind attention of Mrs. Higford Burr,) I find that in the reign of Henry I, Richard Achard, son and heir to the grantee, enfeoffed three persons of the estates Fyncham-stead, Silhamstead, and Colethorp, the former two held by two knights named Banastre, the latter by Hugh de Bru-tinol, and those were held under Achard by the service of one knight's fee, though, as we have seen, he himself held the whole property of the king *in capite*, by the service of one knight's fee only. This system of enfeoffment was abolished in the 18th Edward I (1289-90), by statute *Quia emptores terrarum*, commonly known as the Statute of Westminster the third. William Achard, son of Richard, succeeded to the property, and his name occurs in the Liber Niger Scaccarii, A.D. 1166 (12th Henry II). He gave the church of Aldermaston and other property to the priory of Shirburn in Hampshire, and this donation was confirmed by his son, also named William, either in the reign of Richard I, or in that of king John, by a deed which is without date, but is said to be still in existence.

Robert Achard succeeded William, and had a confirma-tion of the original grant (Rot. Chart. 13th Henry III). Peter, who appears to have been the son of Robert, died seized of Aldermaston in 1277 ("Inquis. post mortem 6th Edward I"). And in the same year Robert, son and heir of Peter, did homage to the king for his lands (Rot. Orig. 6th Edward I). In 1292 he had a grant of a market and fair at Aldermaston, and free warren for Aldermaston, Spersholt, Eastmarton, Westcote, Silhampstead, Banastre, and Challow (Rot. Chart. 20th Edward I). He died in 1298 ("Inquis. post mortem 27th Edward I").

In 1312, another Robert, who is styled sir Robert Achard, presented to the church of Sparsholt; and two years after we find a Peter Achard lord of the manor. (Rot. Pat., 8th Edward II.) Sir Robert Achard, the last male heir of the family, died in 1353, leaving a daughter and heir, who mar-ried to sir Thomas Delamare.

Thus Aldermaston passed through the female line, *circa* 1358, to the Delamares, sir Thomas Delamare marrying the daughter and heir of sir Robert Achard, who died in 1353. Agnes, widow of sir Robert, died in 1358. ("Inquis. post mort. 32nd Edward III.") Leland[1] confirms this, and tells

---

[1] Itinerar., vi, 37.

us that there was a younger brother of the house of the Delamares, who, by preferment of marriage, had, about the time of Edward III, the daughter and heir of one Achard, "a man of faire landes in Barkeshire." The first of the Achards, Leland records, was preferred to seven lordships in Berkshire by Henry the First's gift, whereof two of the principal were thus married, Sparshold...and Aldermanton.

"At Sparshold lyith one of the Achards, honorably byried in a chapel annexid hard to the side of the paroche chirche, having a chauntery; and on eche side of hym lyith a wife of his. There is a commune saying that the one of them was a duches, and the other a countes; but this saying hath little appearance of truthe."[1] Sir Thos. Delamare, into whose possession we have thus, by marriage with the daughter of sir Robert Achard, traced the holding of Aldermaston, served the office of sheriff of Berkshire in 44th Edward III, and was knight of the shire, 2nd, 5th, and 6th of Richard II. A Robert Delamare was knight of the shire in the 1st and 5th Henry V, and sir Thomas Delamare in 12th Edward IV. He was sheriff also in 38th Henry VI, 16th and 21st Edward IV, also 5th Henry VII. Between those two, Robert and Thomas, there must have been a generation, of which I can find no notices.

From the family of the Delamares, Aldermaston passed by the marriage of Elizabeth daughter of John Delamare, son and heir of sir Thomas[2] (who died during the life of his father), to sir George Forster, knight; and when Leland wrote (*temp.* Henry VIII), he records that "v of the vii lordshippes of Acharde above spoken of, be yet in syr Humfrede Foster's handes, that now most duellith at Aldermanton. The house of syr Humfrede Foster in Barkeshire, cam oute of the house of Foster of Northumberlande, of whom one of late tyme was caullid syr Thomas Foster, and was mareschal of Barwicke."

Sir George Forster, who espoused Elizabeth Delamare, was sheriff of Berks and Oxfordshire in 1516; his father, Hum-

---

[1] Itinerar., vi, 37.

[2] "Syr Thomas Delamare, knight of the Sepulchre, the last of this house, had a sun caullid John, and he dying afore Thomas his father, left 2 doughters; whereof one was maried to Humfre Foster, father to syr Humfre that now lyvith; the other to Morton of Dorsetshire, kinesman to cardinal Morton; but she had no childern, and so the landes of this Delamer cam totally to Foster." (Leland, *Itin.* vi.)

phry Forster, having filled the same office in **1475**. Sir
George had a son, sir Humphry Foster, who was one of the
equerries of the body to Henry VIII, was sheriff in **1545**,
of whom Fuller says: "He bare a good affection to Protest-
ants, even in the most dangerous times, and spake to the
quest in the behalf of master Marbeck, that good confessor;
yea, he confessed to king Henry VIII that never anything
went so much against his conscience, which under his grace's
authority he had done, as his attending the execution of
three poor men martyred at Windsor."[1] Sir H. Forster was
one of the judges on this occasion. The sessions were held
at Windsor, whither these poor men had been, after examination, sent.[2] His descendant, Humphry Forster, esq., served
the office of sheriff of Berks in **1579** and in **1592**, and was
honoured by a visit from the queen Elizabeth in **1601**. A
sir W. Forster likewise was sheriff in **1608**; and he had a son,
Humphry, who was sheriff in **1619**. In **1620** he was created
a baronet. The title became extinct in **1711**, and the manor
passed to Ralph Congreve, esq., who married Charlotte the
only surviving child of lord Stawell, by Elizabeth only
daughter of William Pert, esq., the sole heiress in right of
her mother. From the family of Congreve it passed in **1846**,
by sale, to D. Higford D. Burr, esq., the present proprietor.

The erection of the old Aldermaston house was by sir
Humphry Foster in **1636**. Scanty remains of this building
are now to be seen. Mr. Burr has, however, most judiciously
introduced into his library windows portions of painted glass
representing the armorial bearings of the Achards, the Delamares, and the Forsters, obtained from the former building;
and he has also preserved the handsome oak roof and carved
staircase, which may be a subject of interest to those who
are versed in heathen mythology. This staircase has been
figured by Nash in his *Mansions of England in Olden Time,*
and together with the fine wooden roof constitutes an object
worthy of examination.

The park of Aldermaston, which in the reign of Edward VI

[1] Fox's *Acts and Monuments*, vol. ii, p. 461 et seq. Folio ed.; London, 1684.
John Marbeck, Henry Filmer, Anthony Pearson, and Robert Testwood. The
latter three were burnt: Marbeck, the author of the *Concordance*, received the
king's pardon. The examination took place before the council on the Monday
after Palm Sunday in 1544. In the edition of Fox referred to, there is a plate
representing the trial and execution of the martyrs, and above these is an extended view of Windsor Castle.
[2] Fox's *Acts and Monuments*, p. 1221.

comprised two hundred and eighty-six acres, amounted in 1721 to four hundred and thirty-six acres. It received subsequent enlargements, and at the present time consists of seven hundred and fifty acres.

The church of Aldermaston is not of much interest in regard to its structure. With its wooden spire, however, it is somewhat picturesque. It has frequently, but erroneously, been called a vicarage; but it is neither vicarage nor rectory. There is a peculiarity in regard to it which is worthy of notice, as I believe there are very few similar cases. It was included in the grant of Henry I to Robert Achard; and, as I have told you, was in the reign of Henry II, by the donation of William Achard, given to the prior and monks of West Shirborne, together with land and the advowson of the chapel. His son confirmed this grant; and in return for this donation, the prior and monks were bound to find a chaplain, for whom the said William Achard engaged to provide a lodging, and to give him maintenance in his house, and also for his palfrey and a domestic. The priory of Benedictine monks was dissolved, and at this time was a cell to the alien monastery of St. Vigor, at Cerasy in Normandy, dedicated to St. Mary and St. John. It had been seized into the king's hands by Henry V, and there remained until the time of Edward IV, when the chapel of Aldermaston, together with the estates of the priory, were given to Queen's College, Oxford, by Edward VI. In 1567, however, William Forster obtained from the college a lease of the rectory and vicarage for the long term of five hundred years, at a small quit-rent; and thus acquired a right of nominating the minister, to whose office no stipend was annexed, and who was appointed without institution from the bishop. William Congreve purchased from the college all their interest in the rectory; and in this state it remained until a few years back, when arrangements were made by which institution by the bishop is provided for, and to which the present minister has been subjected.

In 1852 our associate, Mr. F. J. Baigent, visited Aldermaston church, and gave to us a short description, together with a few remarks on some painted glass, of which he took a tracing. Those will be found in the eighth volume of our *Journal.* The church consists of a nave with a tower at the west end, having a broach spire, a chancel and chantry, on

the south side of the nave.   The chancel is early decorated
with some debased windows, as also is the nave.   The east
window consists of three lights, and in the lower part of the
centre light is the piece of glass to which Mr. B. directed
our . attention.   The figures are placed within a circle of
blue glass surrounded with a white beaded border.   The
glass belongs to the decorated period : the figures are stiff.
The inscription on the scroll was concealed with a coat of
dark colour which has been partly cleaned off.   In the
tracery of the window is a fragment of glass of the same
time, representing the coronation of the Virgin.   In the
lights of these windows are circular pieces of glass, of the
time of Henry VIII, containing armorial bearings and
quarterings of the Forster family.   There is a niche about
a foot high and six inches deep in jamb on either side of
the chancel arch, to the probable purpose of which I would
direct the attention of our architects.[1]

The monument of sir George and lady Elizabeth Forster
is in this church.   It consists of a fine alabaster tomb.   Lady
Elizabeth died in 1522, the decease of sir George is not inscribed on the tomb.   It is in the Forster chapel or
chantry on the south of the church, which now forms the
family pew of Mr. Higford Burr.   The tomb presents to us
recumbent figures of sir George and lady Elizabeth.   The
lady is much taller than her husband, and the artist, we
may presume, being unable to introduce the usual emblem
of fidelity, the dog, at her feet, has ingeniously sculptured a
diminutive animal as playfully biting at her robe by the
side.   Her head is on a pillow supported by angels at the
side.   The knight reposes with his head on his helmet, at
the top of which is a hind's head springing out of a crown,
his feet rest upon a fawn.   He wears the collar of SS. with
a portcullis pendant.   Around the slab on which the
figures lie is the following inscription :—

𝕳𝖊𝖗𝖊 𝖑𝖞𝖊𝖙𝖍 𝖘𝖎𝖗 𝕲𝖊𝖔𝖗𝖌𝖊 𝕱𝖔𝖗𝖘𝖙𝖊𝖗, 𝖐𝖓𝖞𝖌𝖍𝖙, 𝖘𝖔𝖓 𝖆𝖓𝖉 𝖍𝖊𝖞𝖗𝖊 𝖔𝖋 𝕳𝖚𝖒𝖋𝖗𝖆𝖞 𝕱𝖔𝖗𝖘𝖙𝖊𝖗,
𝖊𝖘𝖖𝖚𝖎𝖗𝖊.   𝕮𝖔𝖘𝖔𝖓 𝖆𝖓𝖉 𝖔𝖓𝖊 𝖔𝖋 𝖙𝖍𝖊 𝖍𝖊𝖞𝖗𝖊𝖘 𝖔𝖋 𝖘𝖎𝖗 𝕾𝖙𝖊𝖕𝖍𝖊𝖓 𝕻𝖔𝖕𝖍𝖆𝖒, 𝖐𝖓𝖞𝖌𝖍𝖙, 𝖆𝖓𝖉

[1] Mr. E. Roberts has favoured me with the following memorandum relating
to Aldermaston church : "The exterior is exceedingly plain, principally rough
cast.   There is an early English buttress on the south side.   The west doorway
is Norman.   The interior contains scarcely two parts of the same period ; and
the moulded and more decorative parts range from the Norman to the latest
period of mediæval work.   There are two recesses of plain Early English work,
opposite each other, in the nave, which appear to have been shrines, probably
for the Virgin Mary and the patron saint of the church."

𝕰𝖑𝖎𝖟𝖆𝖇𝖊𝖙𝖍 𝖜𝖎𝖋 𝖔𝖋 𝖙𝖍𝖊 𝖘𝖆𝖒𝖊 𝖘𝖎𝖗 𝕲𝖊𝖔𝖗𝖌𝖊, 𝖉𝖆𝖚𝖌𝖍𝖙𝖊𝖗 𝖆𝖓𝖉 𝖍𝖊𝖎𝖗𝖊 𝖔𝖋 𝕵𝖔𝖍𝖓 𝕯𝖊𝖑𝖆𝖒𝖆𝖗𝖊, 𝖊𝖘𝖖𝖚𝖎𝖊𝖗, 𝖘𝖔𝖓 𝖆𝖓𝖉 𝖍𝖊𝖎𝖗𝖊 𝖔𝖋 𝕮𝖍𝖔𝖒𝖆𝖘 𝕯𝖊𝖑𝖆𝖒𝖆𝖗𝖊, 𝖐𝖓𝖞𝖌𝖍𝖙; 𝖜𝖎𝖈𝖍𝖊 𝕰𝖑𝖎𝖟𝖆𝖇𝖊𝖙𝖍 𝖉𝖎𝖊𝖉 𝖙𝖍𝖊 𝖇𝖎𝖎 𝖉𝖆𝖞 𝖔𝖋 𝕯𝖊𝖈𝖊𝖒𝖇𝖊𝖗 𝖎𝖓 𝖙𝖍𝖊 𝖞𝖊𝖗𝖊 𝖔𝖋 𝖔𝖚𝖗 𝕷𝖔𝖗𝖉 𝕲𝖔𝖉 m°ccccc°xxii, 𝖆𝖓𝖉 𝖜𝖎𝖈𝖍𝖊 𝖘𝖎𝖗 𝕲𝖊𝖔𝖗𝖌𝖊 𝖉𝖞𝖊 𝖎𝖓 𝖙𝖍𝖊 𝖞𝖊𝖗𝖊 𝖔𝖋 𝖔𝖚𝖗 𝕷𝖔𝖗𝖉 𝕲𝖔𝖉

On the north side of the monument are represented eight of his sons in armour, and at the foot three more. On the south side are eight daughters. At the west is a shield which formerly contained the armorial bearings of the Forsters, but they are now obliterated. The shield is supported by a son and daughter of the deceased kneeling.

The church contains other funeral inscriptions of the same family. That of William Forster is on a brass plate thus :—

" Here lyethe Wiłłm Forster, esquyer, lord of Aldermaston, sonne and heyre of sir Humffraye Forster, knyght, and Jane his wyffe, one of the daughters of syr Anthony Hungerford of Downeamney, knyght, wᵒʰ Wiłłm deceased the xᵗʰ daye of January anno D̄M 1574, and his said wyffe the .... daye .... anno M̄D."

On the floor of the chapel is also inscribed : " Dedicated to the precious memorie of four virtuous sisters, daughters of sir Humphry Forster, bart., and of Anna his wife, viz., Anna, who dyed May the 16th, 1638, aged 18 yeares 5 monthes ; Mary dyed September the 9th, 1638, aged 14 yeares and 10 monthes ; Bridgett dyed May the 29th, 1637, aged 10 years and 1 moneth, and Margarett, who dyed February the 19th, 1623, aged one yeare and 6 monthes.

LIKE BORNE, LIKE NEW BORNE, HERE LIKE DEAD THEY LYE,
FOUR VIRGINE SISTERS DECK'D WITH PIETIE,
BEAUTIE, AND OTHER GRACES, WHICH COMMEND,
AND MAKE THEM ALL LIKE BLESSED IN THEIR END.

A still later one records the death of John Forester, December 12, 1674. There are other memorials of the Forsters, of the hon. W. Stawell, son of lord Stawell and Elizabeth his wife, only daughter of William Pert, of Arnold's hall, in the county of Essex, esq., and sole heiress, in right of her mother, to sir Humphry Forester, of this place, baronet, and of some members of the family of Congreve.

ON THE ROMAN STATION OF SPINÆ.

BY THE REV. J. ADAMS, M.A.

IT has been remarked by the writer of the article on Roman roads and stations in Lysons's history of this county,[1] that although there were not less than three undoubted Roman towns within the limits of Berkshire, the site of one only has been ascertained, and that not without some difficulty. The town thus alluded to was known by the name of Spinæ, and is generally supposed to have stood somewhere between Newbury and Speen, and covered part of the site of the town. That Newbury sprung from the ruins of an older town, its name no doubt indicates, and that Spinæ stood at no great distance does not, I think, admit of question ; but whether Spinæ was ever of sufficient importance to be designated a Roman town, or whether it was merely a military station, are points which have not yet been made clear. I propose, therefore, to give a brief account of the traces of Roman occupation which now exist in and around Newbury, and in doing so, my aim is rather to invite discussion and to call forth the opinion of others, than to introduce any new theories of my own.

First—With regard to the locality of the Roman station of Spinæ. The fact that an old Roman encampment stands near a village, which has been known from time immemorial by the name of Speen, would naturally lead one to expect that it might be identified with the ancient Spinæ. I am aware that there is nothing in the earthwork itself to prove a distinctively Roman origin. On the contrary, the irregularity of its outline would perhaps make it appear to many persons more like a British or Danish than a Roman encampment ; for it is well known that the Romans generally made their camps perfectly square or oblong. But there must have been frequent exceptions to this rule, especially in the later days of the empire ; for we are told by Vegetius, a writer who lived in the fourth century, that camps were made in his day square, round, or triangular, to suit the nature of the ground. This appears to have been the

[1] Magna Britannia.

case with the camp in question ; for its rampart seems to have been accommodated to the outline of the hill-top on which it stands. On the sides overlooking the valley of the Kennet, it was formed by an escarpment of the brow of the hill, and about 450 yards of it still remain ; on the north and east sides there was no doubt a deep fosse, hardly any traces of which are now apparent. It seems to have crossed the Bath-road near the eastern and a little beyond the western entrance to Miss Wyld's grounds, and to have extended some thirty or forty yards into the field on the north of the road. The extreme width of the encampment was not less than 1,250 feet, and its area is nearly double that which Dr. Stukeley assigns to the neighbouring station Cunetio, that being according to his computation 500 feet square. But that which stamps the Roman origin of Speen, and gives it the strongest claim to having been a Roman station of great importance, is the convergence of several undoubted Roman roads at some point within the parish. Richard of Cirencester and Antonine both mention Spinæ as a station midway between Cunetio and Calleva, and the course of the old road from the former place to Speen can still be distinctly traced. The upper or Baydon-road is, I believe, constructed upon it, and to this circumstance the travellers on that road are indebted for its unusual freedom from angles and twists. In two or three places, the modern road-makers, as if impatient of a straight line, have made a variation from the old beaten path. One of these windings may be noticed on the east side of Lambourn Woodlands, with the trace of the old road in the field adjoining, pursuing its direct course. Another instance may be seen at Wickham, where the only object of the divergence seems to be to encounter a steep hill, and there, too, a bank may be seen, which, if I mistake not, marks the straight course of the old road.

It is interesting to find, in many places, the actual material which the Romans had still in use. Compact layers of flint in some places underlie the green sward which here and there fringes the wide parts of the road, and these are frequently dug out to repair the way, so that not only the same line of road, but the very same stones are now being used, over which the haughty Roman legions were wont to travel some fourteen centuries ago. The traces of this road, eastward of Speen, are quite obliterated, and as the locality of Calleva, the station to which we know that it ran, is by no means settled, it is no easy matter to point out its course. But whether Silchester be the Calleva of the *Itinera* as Dr. Doyle thinks ; or Farnham, as Dr. Stukeley affirms ; or Reading, according to Dr. Beke ; or Streatley, as Mr. Hewett, with much better reason in my opinion, argues ; we may fairly conclude from the importance and contiguity of those places, that there were direct Roman roads which radiated from Speen to all of them.

The only one, however, of which I can find any traces, is that which connected Streatley with Speen, and the discovery of this one is due to Mr. Hewett, who thus describes its course in his book on the hundred of Compton :—"Leaving Aldworth church, it pursued the same course as the present footpath and road to Turville coppice, where, in the shape of a high embankment in a hedge road, it may still be traced. Hence, passing by Beech wood, and Hampstead Norreys, over Wayley Hill, it continued on to Hermitage and Shaw" (p. 119).

The road from Speen to Silchester, not a vestige of which remains, is supposed by the bishop of Cloyne and Mr. Leman to have proceeded some miles in the direction of the present turnpike-road towards Reading, and to have fallen into the road from Streatley to Silchester, near Thatcham ; but as the discovery of a Roman cemetery near the Newbury railway station shows that the Romans had, in all probability, a bridge across the Kennet at this place, I have no doubt that the Silchester road from Speen crossed the river just where the present bridge stands, instead of going out of its way to cross a ford and a swampy valley at Thatcham.

Seeing, then, that Speen must have been a Roman station of some importance, it might naturally be expected that traces of Roman occupation, more generally interesting than those which I have mentioned, would be frequently brought to light. I will now show that this has been the case, although not perhaps to the extent that might have been expected. From time to time Roman coins in considerable numbers, fragments of pottery, and pieces of tessellated pavement, have been dug up in and around Speen. Amongst the most noteworthy of those relics, I may mention a copper coin of the empress Faustina, found on the site of the encampment : a vase, containing a great number of silver coins, at a place called Hangman-stone-lane, near Boxford ; and another vase, full of copper coins, at Stock-cross. Unfortunately the vases were at once broken, and thrown away as worthless, and their contents sold as old metal. But the most interesting discovery was made about three years since, near the goods station of the Great Western Railway at Newbury. In removing a bed of gravel, the workmen came upon ground that had clearly been part of a Roman cemetery. There were found a great number of human bones, ashes, amphoræ, some perfect and beautiful specimens of Samian ware, and two glass bottles of the kind generally designated unguentaria.[1] The marks of graves could be distinctly traced by the dark colour of the soil, and in every case they lay north and south. Most of the bodies appeared to have been consigned to the ground without cremation, a fact which has led some persons to suppose that the burials were of a date subsequent to the Roman occupation of this country. But I would remark that cremation never appears to have prevailed universally amongst the Romans. According to Pliny, it was not an ancient custom,[2] but was introduced when they found that the bodies of their fellow-citizens which were buried in distant lands in time of war, were sometimes dug up again, and exposed to insult.

The largest of the glass bottles above mentioned and shown in plate 1, is, by precise measurement, $6\frac{1}{2}$ inches long by $3\frac{3}{8}$ in diameter, and is quite perfect. The other bottle is about half this size, and is slightly chipped. The figure with flowing robes, stamped on the bottom of the larger bottle, has been conjectured to be Æsculapius holding his usual symbol of a serpent.

[1] See *ante*, p. 34, and illustrations on plate 1.
[2] "Ipsum cremare apud Romanos non fuit veteris instituti : terra condebantur." (*Hist. Nat.*, lib. vii, § 55.)

British Archæological Association.

SIXTEENTH ANNUAL MEETING, NEWBURY, 1859.

SEPTEMBER 12th TO 17th INCLUSIVE.

PATRONS.

THE MARQUIS OF WINCHESTER, *Lord Lieutenant of Hants.*
THE MARQUIS OF DOWNSHIRE.
THE EARL OF ABINGDON, *Lord Lieutenant of Berks.*
THE EARL OF CRAVEN, *High Steward of Newbury.*
THE RT. REV. LORD BISHOP OF OXFORD, D.D., F.R.S., F.S.A.

PRESIDENT.

THE EARL OF CARNARVON.

VICE-PRESIDENTS.

EARL SEFTON
LORD BOSTON
LORD BRAYBROOKE, F.S.A.
HON. P. PLEYDELL BOUVERIE, M.P.
SIR FORTUNATUS DWARRIS, F.R.S., F.S.A.
SIR HENRY SINGER KEATING, M.P.
SIR CHRISTOPHER RAWLINSON
SIR J. GARDNER WILKINSON, D.C.L., F.R.S.
REV. JOHN ADAMS, M.A.
JOHN ALEXANDER, ESQ.
C. J. ANDREWES, ESQ., Mayor of Reading
EDMUND ARBUTHNOT, ESQ.
RICHARD BENYON, ESQ.
EDWARD B. BUNNY, ESQ.
D. HIGFORD D. BURR, ESQ.
BENJ. BOND CABBELL, ESQ., F.R.S., F.S.A.
WILLIAM CHATTERIS, ESQ.
GEORGE C. CHERRY, ESQ.
ARCHER J. CROFT, ESQ.
REV. J. CROOKALL, D.D.
ALFRED S. CROWDY, ESQ.
FRANCIS CROWDY, ESQ.
EDMUND CURRIE, ESQ.
REV. GEO. FRED. EVERETT, M.A.
CHARLES EYRE, ESQ.
HENRY RD. EYRE, ESQ.
WILLIAM FOX, ESQ.
GEORGE GODWIN, ESQ., F.R.S., F.S.A.
HENRY GODWIN, ESQ., F.S.A.
NATHL. GOULD, ESQ., F.S.A.

ROBT. FULLER GRAHAM, ESQ.
JAMES HEYWOOD, ESQ., F.R.S., F.S.A.
HENRY HIPPISLEY, ESQ.
REV. THOS. ARCHER HOUBLON, M.A.
G. E. HUGHES, ESQ.
THOMAS HUGHES, ESQ.
REV. JOHN JAMES, M.A.
HENRY KEENS, ESQ., Mayor of Newbury
WILLIAM KINGSMILL, ESQ.
JOHN LEE, LL.D., F.R.S., F.S.A.
MAJOR ROBERT LOYD LINDSAY.
JOHN MATTHEWS, ESQ.
MAJOR J. A. MOORE, F.R.S, F.S.A.
WILLIAM MOUNT, ESQ.
J. T. NORRIS, ESQ., M.P.
THOS. J. PETTIGREW, ESQ., F.R.S., F.S.A.
THE VEN. ARCHDEACON RANDALL, M.A.
REV. JAMES LESLIE RANDALL, M.A.
REV. NICHOLAS J. RIDLEY, M.A.
REV. J. ELLIL ROBINSON, M.A.
CHARLES SLOCOCK, ESQ.
S. R. SOLLY, ESQ., M.A., F.R.S., F.S.A.
R. C. TULL, ESQ.
ROBT. H. VALPY, ESQ.
WILLIAM VANSITTART, ESQ., M.P.
CAPT. LEICESTER VERNON, M.P.
THOMAS WAKEMAN, ESQ.
REV. GEORGE WALLACE, M.A.
JOHN WALTER, ESQ. M.P.
H. F. WINTERBOTTOM, ESQ.

Treasurer—THOMAS JOSEPH PETTIGREW, ESQ., F.R.S., F.S.A.

Honorary Secretaries { J. R. PLANCHÉ, ESQ., Rouge Croix.
H. SYER CUMING, ESQ.

Secretary for Foreign Correspondence—WILLIAM BEATTIE, M.D., Member of the Historical Institute of France.

Palæographer—W. H. BLACK, ESQ., F.S.A.

Curator and Librarian—G. R. WRIGHT, ESQ., F.S.A.

Local Secretary for the Congress—SILAS PALMER, M.D.

GENERAL COMMITTEE.

George G. Adams, Esq.
George Ade, Esq.
Charles Ainslie, Esq.
John Alger, Esq.
Thomas Allom, Esq.
B. Blundell, Esq., F.S.A.
Alfred Burges, Esq., F.S.A.
H. H. Burnell, Esq.
George A. Cape, Jun., Esq.
James Copland, M.D., F.R.S.
Charles Curle, Esq.
C. E. Davis, Esq., F.S.A.
Roger Horman-Fisher, Esq.
James O. Halliwell, Esq., F.R.S., F.S.A.
George Vere Irving, Esq.

Rev. Edmund Kell, M.A., F.S.A.
T. W. King, Esq., F.S.A., *York Herald*
C. H. Luxmore, Esq., F.S.A.
W. C. Marshall, Esq., R.A.
Joseph Mayer, Esq., F.S.A.
William V. Pettigrew, Esq., M.D.
J. W. Previté, Esq.
David Roberts, Esq., R.A.
Edward Roberts, Esq.
John Savory, Esq.
Alfred Thompson, Esq.
Albert W. Woods, Esq., F.S.A., *Lancaster Herald*
William Yewd, Esq.

LOCAL COMMITTEE.

H. R. EYRE, ESQ., *Chairman.*

Messrs. Adey
" Barnes
" Blacket
" Bodman
" Brown, F., M.D.
" Bunny, J., M.D.
" Cave
" Corbould
" Cowper
" Davis, F.
" Deller
" Fidler

Messrs. Fielder
" Flint
" Gore
" Gray
" Gurney
" Hall
" Hannington
" Hickman
" Jackson
" Lack
" Lucas
" Martin

Messrs. Mason, H. H.
" Mason, G. H.
" Randall
" Roake
" Royston
" Shelley
" Simmons
" Somerset
" Talbot
" Turner
" Vines
" Wilson

Proceedings of the Congress.

THE general and local committees assembled at the Mansion House at two o'clock, and made arrangements for the reception of the patrons and president. Upon the arrival of the earl of Carnarvon and the lord bishop of the diocese, the proceedings commenced by an address from the PRESIDENT, an abstract of which will be found at pp. 1-25 *ante*. At its conclusion—

The BISHOP OF OXFORD moved the thanks of the meeting to the earl of Carnarvon, and observed that he had been desired to undertake the task of returning thanks to lord Carnarvon for the essay which he had been good enough to pronounce to them. He was happy to think that it needed no words of his to induce them to acquiesce in that proposition. Heartily did he thank the noble earl himself for the hour's good instruction and good entertainment which had been afforded them. It seemed to come with peculiar gracefulness from lord Carnarvon, the inheritor of a name than which no name was brighter in the English annals ; for where, and on what part of that old English history on which they had been dwelling in thought, could they look and not see the name of Herbert holding an honourable and distinguished position ; shining in literature, in arts, in war, and in all those gentle acquirements which belonged to the old English country gentleman? And there was another feature which made it peculiarly apposite. It was one of the favourite reproaches thrown at archæology, that it had no practical good in it, or that it had no practical ground to stand upon ; that it was a sort of dusty, dry, and uninteresting study. Now their president was a nobleman standing forward as a practical business man in the state, winning the position he held from his business-like qualities in that state. He was the very man above others to come forward in his hour of relaxation, and show that the affairs of the present time could be better administered by those who were not afraid of looking back into the past. Indeed, he (the bishop of Oxford) believed it was no little boon that a person like the earl of

Carnarvon conferred on society when he addicted himself to these pursuits, and came into public to declare or show the good that was to come from their study. It was, indeed, man-study—that which man should study—the study of man himself. The study of archæology, as the noble earl had well expressed it, was not mere *dilettanteism.* When a good archæologist or a good antiquary studied the minutest details of things belonging to past ages, what was it for? Not for the things themselves, but to obtain from them results which should be useful to future generations. It was a linking together of the past with the present generation. Was it not a great thing to study the fragments,—not the broken fragments of the lower animals, but of human life,—that enabled them to contemplate man again in a new aspect, and link together the old and the new man; and so to prophecy better about the future? So was it with archæology. They looked into the things of the past with the view of ascertaining their meaning, and the causes which brought the appearances that presented themselves, in order to guide them in their actions for the future. And this was a study which man should pursue. It was man's high attribute, given to him by God, to be far back-reaching and far on-reaching. It was his high attribute to prevent his being swallowed up and baffled by the apparent magnitude of things which came upon him, to converse with that which was past, and to have his eye open to illuminate the future. They should all strive to learn practical lessons of usefulness from the history of the past, which had been opened up to them by the earl of Carnarvon; and he was sure they would heartily unite with him in thanking his lordship.

H. R. EYRE, esq., of Shaw House, seconded the motion, and remarked that, all residing in that neighbourhood must think themselves fortunate in occupying a district so associated with historical incidents, and abounding with such local interests, as to attract the Archæological Association. They were equally fortunate in having a nobleman as a neighbour, well qualified, by his great scholastic attainments, to fill the chair on the occasion. He was sure they would all join in wishing to lord Carnarvon that of which he had given promise, a long life of honour and usefulness.

The proposition was carried by acclamation, and the meeting then adjourned for the inspection of Newbury, making, in the first instance, examination of the church of St. Nicholas, the only parish church of Newbury. Its erection dates from the close of the reign of Henry VII.

Mr. C. E. DAVIS remarked that the general plan was that most usual in ordinarily sized churches, but had been here applied to a building of unusually large dimensions, which gave an effect not so satisfactory as would have been produced had the church had the addition of transepts or another aisle. The chapels, which are on either side of the chancel, are used, the one to the north as a vestry room, and that to the south (until lately) as the town school, from which purpose it has fortunately been rescued. The style of the whole building is that of the late Perpendicular period, with the usually depressed arches of the style, but with exceedingly good and well articulated caps to the attached columns supporting architraves composed of mouldings singularly deficient in shadow. Mr. Davis expressed a hope that, at a future time, the organ and gallery would be removed in order that the western arch might be better seen ; although, unfortunately, it would disclose a modern Perpendicular window of bad design, which of late years has been inserted in the tower. This alteration might be effected without removing the Jacobean screen, of a date corresponding with the arcade of the old Market House. The western is the principal point : the tower, rising well in the centre, is of three stories, with octagonal turrets at the angles, which appear never to have been completed; indeed, the battlements between them are so poor and ineffective, that they clearly do not belong to the original design, and seem the addition of an age in which the true principles of Gothic were still less understood.

John Winchcombe, better known as "Jack of Newbury", lies interred in this church ; and a brass to his memory and that of his wife, Alys, stands on the east wall of the north aisle, near to the vestry, with the following inscription :

Off go charitie pray for the soule of John Smalwode, als Wynchcom & Alys hys wyfe. John dyed the xv day of February A° m°cccc°xix.

Their effigies are depicted on the plate, which, it was stated, had been long since removed from their tomb.

There are several monuments and tablets with inscriptions of interest in the church, among which may be mentioned an elegant memorial in Latin, to a former rector, the rev. Thos. Penrose, M.A., who held the living for twenty-four years : a brass plate of an earlier rector, the rev. Hugh Shepherd, who died A.D. 1596 ; and whose epitaph offers a good example of monumental inscription of the close of the sixteenth *sæc.* :

> " Full eight and twentie yeeres he was your pastor,
> As hee was taught to feede by Christ his maister ;
> By preaching God's Word, good life, good example,
> (Food for your soules, fitt for God's house or temple).
> Hee loved peace, abandoned all strife,
> Was kinde to strangers, neighbours, children, wife ;
> A lambe-like man, born on an Easter Daye,
> So liv'd, so di'de, so liv's againe for aye :
> As one spring brought him to this world of sinne,
> Another spring the heavens received him in."

Another, which may be cited as an instance of unfrequent occurrence, being without a name, (which is considered by some authorities as absolutely essential to an epitaphial inscription), on a diamond-shaped white marble gravestone :

" It is
Earnestly
Desired
That the remains
Of the
Pious persons
Interred
Under this stone
May not
Be
Disturbed.
1768."

The tomb contains the remains of the family of the rev. —— Davies, rector of Highclere, and also of St. Nicholas, Newbury. Ashmole has recorded several inscriptions which are not now to be seen. One of the family of Winchcombe : " Here lyeth HENRY WYNCHCOMBE, gentylman, and ANNES his wife : whyche HENRYE deceassyd the 3ᵈ day of October, in the yere of our Lord 1562, & was of the age of 40 yeres." On the exterior of the church, against the southern wall of the chancel, a large stone monument is affixed, and erected upon three Ionic columns, presenting in one compartment a statue of a man in armour, kneeling ; and in the others, the figures of three females, said to be those of his wives ; and of six sons and five daughters, all sculptured in the costume of the time, which is expressed on the ledge of the monument, under the man, which reads :

" Hic jacet Griffinvs Cvrteyes, armiger. Nov . xxx . MDLXXXVII."

The remains of the house occupied by John Smalwode, *alias* Winchcombe, and commonly called " Jack of Newbury" (now known as a publichouse bearing that denomination), was then visited, and Mr. E. Roberts pointed out its various ancient portions.[1]

From the house the party proceeded to the chapel of St. John, at which, common report says, Jack of Newbury was married. Tradition reports this edifice to have been founded by king John, but no documents are known to be now extant in support of this statement. It is, however, not improbable, as in the account of charitable donations in Berkshire, furnished by Mr. Parry, is the grant of a fair to Newbury for the support of the hospital of St. Bartholomew, (Rot. Chart., 17 John, i.m. 8, N. 51), which is in close alliance with this chapel, situated at the end of Bartholomew-street. No regular service is now performed in this chapel ; but a triangular piece of ground is attached to it, and is called the " Litten," and may, therefore, have constituted a burial ground belonging to it. The discovery of some skeletons upon digging at the spot a few years back, gives support to this conjecture.

[1] See description and illustration, p. 42 *ante*, and plate 2.

Thence to the gateway and almshouses of St. Bartholomew, which invited attention; but no part was found to be of earlier date than the commencement of the last century. The estates belonging to this hospital yield a good revenue, and the charity maintains and clothes seven men and six women, with a nurse to attend upon them, and relieve their necessities. Grants by John for the foundation of this hospital were made in 1204 and 1216. It is now vested in the corporation, a member of which, styled a proctor, receives the rents and disburses the expenses to the recipients of the bounty, the chaplain, repairs of the houses, &c. In the reign of Henry VIII an inquisition was taken of " Seynt Bartylmeas," and the lands were valued at £23 1s 8½d " to the intent to have one prest to synge in the said hospitull, and two pore men to pray there contyneually," etc., and the gross income is stated in 1816 to have amounted to £744 18s 3½d, from the savings of which, three years previously, ten new almshouses were built.

Many interesting brick houses were remarked in the town, one particularly in North Brook-street, where pilasters and mouldings, with egg ornament, are most skilfully rendered. A stack of chimneys near Newbury church was also much admired for its peculiar form, though unpicturesque as to its effect. In a house occupied by Mr. Paine, a chair maker, which formerly was the residence of Mr. Head, who received the Viscount Falkland as a guest the night before the first battle of Newbury, in which that distinguished and beloved nobleman was slain, there is an ancient and remarkable cupboard in a recess concealed by a panel. The cupboard is of mahogany, and the shell like ornament at the top, as well as the mouldings, are gilt. The cupboard measures five feet eleven inches in height, and at the bottom was a board, which, upon being drawn out, serves the purpose of a writing table.

Having made the tour of the town, the meeting assembled at the table d'hôte, presided over by the Treasurer.

The evening meeting was held at the Mansion House,

James Heywood, F.R.S., F.S.A., V.P., in the Chair,

who called upon Mr. Pettigrew to deliver his paper on the History and Antiquities of Berkshire. (See pp. 25 to 49, *ante*.)

Mr. Heywood then read a communication from J. O. Halliwell, F.R.S., F.S.A., "On the Popular History of Jack of Newbury, its Origin and Literary Curiosity," of which the following is an abstract:—

"Warwick is not more popularly associated with the adventures of the celebrated knight, sir Guy; nor Southampton with those of the equally renowned sir Bevis; than is Newbury with the name of the prosperous clothier, John Winchcomb, who for nearly three centuries, if not for a longer period, has been distinguished by the familiar appellation of

Jack of Newbury. There is, however, this distinction peculiar to the history of the last named personage, that, whereas, even the names of Guy and Bevis are fictitious, the popular novel of Jack of Newbury concerns not merely a real individual, but details circumstances founded partially on well ascertained facts, and partially on details derived from traditional sources. Jack's real name was John Winchcombe *alias* Smalwoode, an eminent clothier of Newbury during the reigns of Henry VII and Henry VIII. He realised a large fortune, and, amongst other benefactions to Newbury, is said to have built the church vestry. In his will, dated in January 1519, the year in which he died, he is described as 'John Smalwoode the elder, *alias* John Wynchcombe, of the parisshe of Seynt Nicholas in Newbery.' He gives ' to the parisshe churche of Newbery, towards the buylding and edifying of the same, £40,' besides donations to the various altars. He directs that he should be buried ' in our Lady chauncell within the parisshe churche of Newbery, afore- said, by Alice, my wif, and a stone to be leyde upon us boothe.' His wife, Alice, had been long dead at the date of this will, as he had again married, and left a widow named Joan, who is mentioned, and liberally provided for. There are also legacies to numerous individuals, and to every one of his servants. Amongst the former may be mentioned forty shillings to sir John Waite, parson of Newberry, 'for the recom- pens of my tithes, necligently forgotten,' the ' sir,' it is hardly necessary to observe, not being the title of knighthood, but the ordinary Angli- cised one from *Dominus*, the scholastic denomination of clergyman, as we have the parson Evans termed sir Hugh Evans in the *Merry Wives of Windsor*. The will was proved on March 24th, 1519, by the testa- tor's son, John, who was residuary legatee.

"John Winchcomb died within a few weeks after the date of this will, as appears from a brass effigy in Newbury church bearing the following incription :—' Off your charitie pray for the soule of John Smalwode *alias* Wynchcom and Alys, his wife. John dyed the xv day of February, A.D. 1519.' This memorial, as is noted by Mr. Pettigrew, must be distin- guished from a stone monument of a man in armour, with three wives, six sons, and five daughters, which is sometimes vulgarly stated to re- present Jack and his children, but which really belongs to another family. Winchcomb died at an advanced age, six years after the battle of Flodden, so that the tradition that he was present at that celebrated contest is probably an error, though it was very possible that he may have furnished a company for the service of his country. There is also a tradition that he entertained Henry the Eighth and queen Catherine at Newbury. The site of his house is believed to have been partly the ground upon which the inn bearing his name now stands, and it is said, that his workshops extended to the marsh. Certain it is that ancient carvings, some of which undoubtedly belonged to the Winchcomb family in the sixteenth century, were discovered some years ago in pulling down old buildings in that locality. Jack's family attained to some social distinction; for his eldest son John obtained a grant of arms, and one of his descendants was the owner of Donnington castle. A portrait of this son, taken in 1550, when he was in the 61st year of his age, is, I am told, still preserved at Newbury. Supposing, therefore, that Jack himself married very early in life, this fact of the son's age in the year 1550 would incline us to place the father's birth in 1470 at the very latest; but he probably first saw the light some years before the date last mentioned.

"Some of the principal facts in the life of Winchcomb were unquestionably in traditional circulation at Newbury at the close of the sixteenth century; for when that prolific pamphleteer and novelist, Thomas Deloney, made him the subject of a romance, the leading circumstances of his history were faithfully adhered to. Deloney's novel of *Jack of Newbury* was licensed to T. Myllington on March 7th, 1596, and it was undoubtedly published soon after that period; but no copy of so early a date is now known to exist, the earliest one I have met with being the ninth edition, published by Cuthbert Wright in 1633. This is, no doubt, with the exception of the orthography and perhaps some little of the idiomatic language, a faithful reproduction of the earlier copies. This complete version was several times republished; but in the last century abridged editions of it were sometimes issued, and the modern chap-book copies are generally mere fragments of the original. The romance, although highly illustrative of old manners and customs, is of very small literary merit. It chiefly consists of a number of desultory stories, some of which have no relation to the subject of the history, and ends, like *Rasselas*, with a conclusion in which nothing is concluded.

"The hero of this ancient historical romance is thus described:—'In the days of king Henry the eighth, that most noble and victorious prince, in the beginning of his reign, John Winchcomb, a broad-cloth weaver, dwelt in Newbury, a town in Berkshire, who, for that he was a man of a merry disposition and honest conversation, was wondrous well beloved of rich and poor, especially because in every place where he came, he would spend his money with the best, and was not any time found a churl of his purse; wherefore, being so good a companion, he was called of old and young, Jack of Newbury, a man so generally well known in all his country for his good fellowship, that he could go in no place but he found acquaintance; by means whereof Jack could no sooner get a crown, but straight he found means to spend it; yet had he ever this care, that he would always keep himself in comely and decent apparel, neither at any time would he be overcome in drink, but so discreetly behave himself with honest mirth, and pleasant conceits, that he was every gentleman's companion.'

" Whilst Jack was in his apprenticeship to his predecessor in trade, his master died, and the widow entertained a strong affection for him, noting his orderly habits. Our hero, although, as the author quaintly observes, 'guessing by the yarn it would prove a good web', received her advances very reluctantly, and even recommended her to accept the hand of either of several other suitors, speaking in praise of each. The widow, however, gives plain reasons for rejecting all; but thinking to induce an offer on the part of the independent apprentice, she invites them to dinner ; a banquet which is quaintly described by Deloney.

" The author's intention in all this, and much more discursive writing of a similar character, is to show that the widow is determined to marry John Winchcomb. At length she carries her point by a stratagem, marrying him almost against his will at the chapel of St. Bartholomew. This union, according to the novelist, was not a very happy one. His wife is given to gadding about, and staying out late at night, a practice which gives the author the opportunity of introducing the following anecdote :—

" Thus the time passed on, till on a certain day she had been abroad in her wonted manner, and staying forth very late, he shut the doors, and went to bed. About midnight she comes to the door, and knocks to come in, to whom he, looking out of the window, answered in this sort, 'What! is it you that keep such a knocking? I pray you, get hence, and request the constable to provide you a bed ; for this night you shall have no lodging here.' 'I hope,' quoth she, 'you will not shut me out of doors like a dog.' 'All is one to me,' quoth he, 'knowing no reason but that as you have stayed out all day for your delight, so you may lie forth all night for my pleasure.' The woman, hearing this, made piteous moan, and in very humble sort entreated him to let her in, and to pardon this offence, and while she lived vowed never to do the like. Her husband at length, being moved with pity towards her, slipped on his shoes, and came down in his shirt. The door being opened, in she went quaking, and as he was about to lock it again, in very sorrowful manner she said, 'Alack, husband, what hap have I ? My wedding ring was even now in my hand, and I have let it fall about the door; good sweet John come forth with the candle, and help me to seek it.' The man did so, and while he sought for that which was not there to be found, she whipped into the house, and quickly clapping to the door, she locked her husband out, and treated him with the same sauce he had before given to her.

" A similar anecdote is related by much earlier writers, one example of it occurring, if I recollect rightly, in the exceedingly curious and valuable collection of medieval Latin stories published by Mr. Thomas Wright. John Winchcomb was not, however, long troubled with these kinds of adventures, his wife dying, leaving him great wealth. Shortly

afterwards, he marries a servant, a daughter of an old farmer of Ayles-
bury, whose consent to the match is given in language which affords an
early and curious example of the humour of mistaking words, a kind of
joke very much relished by our ancestors, and carried to perfection by
Shakespeare.

"When the old man had seen this great household and family, then
he was brought into the warehouses, some being filled with wool, some
with flocks, some with wood and madder, and some with broad cloths
and kersies ready dyed and dressed, beside a great number of others,
some stretched on the tenters, some hanging on poles, and a great many
more lying wet in other places. 'Sir,' quoth the old man, 'I wis che
zee you be bominable rich, and cham content you shall have my daughter,
and God's blessing and mine light on you both.' 'But, father,' quoth
Jack of Newbury, 'what will you bestow with her?' 'Marry, hear you,'
quoth the old man, 'i-vaith, cham but a poor man, but, I thong God,
cham of good exclamation among my neighbours, and they will as zoone
take my vice for anything as a richer man's. Thick I will bestow; you
shall have it with a good will, because che hear a very good condemna-
tion of you in every place, therefore chil give you twenty nobles and a
weaning calf, and when I die and my wife, you shall have the revelation
of all my goods.'

"This second marriage turns out very happily, and the remainder of
the novel is occupied with an account of Jack bringing to queen Catherine two hundred and fifty men equipped for Flodden; with a tedious
and silly narrative of Jack's interview and bantering with Henry the
eighth at Newbury, interspersed with pointless anecdotes of Will Somers,
the celebrated jester; with an account of Jack getting up a monster
petition of clothiers to the king, and of his being imprisoned for a short
time for perpetrating an unpleasant quip on cardinal Wolsey; a notice
of his being chosen burgess in parliament for Newbury; and a long
account of his relieving the necessities of a London draper who had
become bankrupt.

"Beyond these slight particulars here noticed, there are no details of
Jack's personal history. The novel, or romance, is in itself at best a
literary curiosity, possessing no intrinsic value either in respect to facts
or composition; but, like many other of the minor remains of the literature of the Elizabethan æra, it is valuable as containing those illustrations of the manners and phraseology of the time, which are so necessary
to the complete appreciation of much which is found in the pages of the
great authors of the period, especially of Shakespeare. In reference to
this, there is scarcely any contemporary production of the same extent
which offers so much of importance as the apparently frivolous compilation of *The Pleasant and Delightful History of John Winchcomb.*"

A short conversation ensued, in the course of which the rev. Charles

Kingsley, of Eversley, expressed an opinion that "Jack of Newbury" was not a Berkshire man, but an apprentice named John Smalwoode, of Winchcombe in Gloucestershire, who had brought from that place to Newbury the woollen trade; and that Winchcombe was not his surname, being only attached to Smalwoode to shew the place whence he had come, and to distinguish him probably from others bearing the same name. He also expressed a doubt as to "Jack of Newbury" having been actually present at Flodden Field with his hundred bowmen. The rev. gentleman, however, gave to Deloney's works the merit of presenting, with all their absurdities, as complete and accurate a picture of our forefathers as we possessed.

The meeting was continued to a late hour, when the proceedings for the next day were announced.

TUESDAY, SEPTEMBER 13.

A large party congregated at the Pelican inn, at 10 A.M., and proceeded to the battlefields, where Dr. Palmer, Mr. alderman Gray, and Mr. R. H. Valpy, discoursed upon the course and position of the contending armies; that of Charles I commanded in person by the king, and the parliamentary army by the earl of Essex. The first engagement was on the 18th of September, 1643; the victory at which was claimed by both sides. In this battle fell the noble Falkland; but the precise spot at which he was killed, still remains a matter of dispute. There are three large mounds on the field where the slain are said to have been interred; and at different times swords, helmets, cannon balls, and various other implements of war, have been found. Several of these are to be seen in the Newbury museum. The second battle was on the 27th of October, 1644; the king being at Newbury from the 17th, residing in a house of a Mr. Hoar, a wealthy clothier, on the west side of Cheap-street. This house has been completely modernized, but was mentioned as having been a very ancient mansion.[1]

Thence the Association proceeded to the countess of Craven's park at Hampstead, to view the mounds; the rev. J. Adams and Mr. Vere Irving making observations upon their character and description. The largest of the tumuli is of very considerable elevation, with a deep excavation round a large portion of its base. It was probably a fort, or the site of some chieftain's house. The others bear the appearance of places of sepulture; but as they have not been opened within the memory of any

---

[1] The particulars of these conflicts were detailed in an elaborate paper (a portion of which was read at an evening sitting) by Mr. B. Blundell, F.S.A., which has since been published by Simpkin and Marshall, and to which our readers are referred. Mr. Blundell kindly proffered to supply the place of Thos. Hughes, esq., F.S.A., who was prevented from fulfilling the task by a severe domestic calamity.

resident, and as objections had been made to their being touched upon the present occasion, accounts as to their origin and purpose must be mere conjecture.

Kintbury church, an ancient Norman structure, unfortunately nearly divested of all antiquarian attractions by the process of so-called renovation which it is now undergoing, was then visited; and Mr. Roberts remarked that the foundations of this church were Norman, if not even ante-Norman; but that, like almost all structures of those ages, repeated alterations had been made, the effects of which were to change the aspect. Much of the original Norman walling remained recently; but the openings for arches and windows are all of later date, some of them being of the transitional period of the later part of the twelfth century, and others of the earliest Pointed period; of the latter, the lancet-window of the tower, deeply splayed, offered an example. The church has just been restored, and in such a manner as to leave very small remnants of the ancient work. The roof has been taken down, and replaced by a new one; and the walls have been almost rebuilt. Of the interesting remains, the piscina on the south side of the chancel, and an aumbry on the north side, are of the end of the twelfth century. The upper part of the tower is of about the time of Henry VIII. There is a monumental brass in the church to John Gunter, 1626.

Avington church was the next place visited. Here the associates were received by the rector, the rev. John James, M.A., who detailed the history of the church, and called the attention of the architects present to its peculiarities. (See pp. 58-62 *ante*.) The church was particularly examined by Mr. C. E. Davis and Mr. E. Roberts, who made some observations regarding it, being probably as interesting a church as any within a very large circuit; indeed, the Association had rarely met with so good a specimen of early Christian architecture, for it had suffered little from the modernizing of succeeding ages. It is simply a church, consisting of a nave, chancel, and south porch, the bell-turret being attached to the western gable. The remains of the chancel of this church, internally, are either of very early Norman, or of a period slightly anterior; and those of the nave of nearly a hundred years later. The exterior does not exhibit signs of antiquity corresponding with the interior; and the porch is of very late work of the sixteenth century. The chancel has attached to its walls capitals of columns, shafts, etc., which clearly shew that it was the intention of the original builders to groin it in two bays: a design which appears never to have been carried out, either in consequence of an undue settlement of the walls, the result of a thrust from the chancel arch; or in consequence of the expense. It is difficult to speak with certainty as to the precise nature of the original plan; but Mr. Davis suggested that it was probable the most western bay was to have formed the area of a low tower, as the groining ribs were evidently purposely made to differ from those in the eastern. This arrangement would divide the church into the three divisions usual in the twelfth century. The chancel arch is unfortunately very much distorted, from the settlement before mentioned; but it is well moulded, and displays a considerable amount of skill in the arrangement of its parts; and in many respects shews that its architect, in designing this and the southern doorway, was anxious to introduce a style he must have studied, where the Romanesque was far more classical than in Britain. The depression of the chancel arch, its great peculiarity, seen in plate 4, may be described as being formed by two segments of circles instead of one semicircle, the centres being outside the middle line; and, but for the walls inclining outwards, would appear to have been built in that manner. The probability, however, in the opinion of Mr. Roberts, is that the vaulting, of which the groin-shafts and part of the ribs remain, was too heavy for the walls, and therefore was taken down. The appearance of the later nave walls, which also incline outwards, would seem to bear out this supposition, the inclination being less at both ends than in the centre; the walls being, in fact, curved in the plan.

The party now proceeded to Wickham church, and were met by the rector, the rev. William Nicholson, to whose munificence the present magnificent structure principally owes its existence.

Mr. ROBERTS undertook the description of this interesting edifice, and commenced by observing that, within a year or two the old church, with the exception of the tower, had been demolished, and that some of the very beautiful Early English remains were now being preserved in a conservatory, and other buildings adjoining, in the course of erection by the rev. Mr. Nicholson. The tower he regarded as one of the rarest monuments in this country; and the peculiar windows, ascribed to the Saxon æra, have been repeatedly illustrated. If the windows are Saxon, the masonry of the tower is also of that date; but of the "long and short" work of the groins, much, he thought, was undoubtedly modern. The whole bears the impress of more recent facing; but the windows with their peculiar central pillar and bracketed abaci, are unquestionably very ancient, and most likely more than eight hundred years old, and may be upwards of one thousand. The newly built church itself deserves remark as being an attempt to reproduce a number of the best portions of various buildings of the thirteenth century, and still to make a congruous whole. The materials used are of expensive and good kinds, and the work is creditable to the energy of the proprietor, but valueless as regards archæology.

In the course of a very interesting examination, the worthy rector directed the attention of the Association to a variety of particulars which were especially deserving of attention in the old and in the new structure. Of these, it may be sufficient here to specify the *Saxon* work in the tower the west window, which should be examined from the inside; the band or tone of the column of the south window; the long and short Saxon work of the North-west corner; the tower, originally terminated at the string-course with a four-sided gabled roof, the upper part being an adaptation of Mr. Cottingham's restoration of the great gateway, Bury St. Edmund's. The chancel arch (Saxon) became ruinous, and was taken down in 1845. Mr. Nicholson stated that it was built of small stones. The two early Decorated windows (north side of chancel) are original; so also is the piscina. The reredos is copied from the Cologne altar. Under a straw shed, attention was directed to a very beautiful triplet. Some few remains of this were found built in as rubble in the walls of Welford church, detached from each other. It has been carefully restored. In the same place also is a mutilated sedile from Welford, and fragments of others: all had been built in to rubble walls, and the fragments were entirely detached from each other. Under a tree south of the house, and on a wall north, are various remains from Welford church; in front, two of its nave pillars, one bearing a gablet and Early English cross; the other, the ball from the spire. The tower of the house (i.e., the detached part) is an exact copy of the tower of the house of Jacques Cœur of Bourges (1454). On the site where a pond is now being made, close to the house, there have been found a very large quantity of broken remains of British pottery, and some Roman, but all much broken.

Returning thanks to the rev. Mr. Nicholson, and quitting Wickham, the Association proceeded to view Shaw House, the residence of H. R. Eyre, esq., whose attentions to the society were most zealous, and of whose splendid hospitality the members and visitors most heartily partook. The house is approached by a magnificent avenue of trees, and is of the Elizabethan period; well known in the history of the county, not only by the circumstances attending its erection, but also by its having been a place where, during the civil wars, Charles I usually sojourned when on his journeys westward. It was noticed in Mr. Pettigrew's paper, "On the History and Antiquities of Berkshire." (See p. 43 *ante*.)

Having duly acknowledged the truly English hospitality of Mr. Eyre and the courtesy of his lady, the party proceeded to inspect the remains of Donnington castle. This building, of such importance in its day, is now a mere ruin, little beyond the two towers being visible. The general plan of the castle is, however, apparent; and as far as the weather, which had become unpropitious, would admit, was viewed by the Association.

The *table d'hôte* at the Pelican, was presided over by the noble president.

At the evening meeting, which was numerously attended,

THE EARL OF CARNARVON IN THE CHAIR,

Thos. Wright, esq., F.S.A., read his paper, "On the Legendary History of Wayland Smith", (see pp. 50-58 *ante*), which led to some discussion on the part of the president, the rev. Chas. Kingsley, rev. Mr. Milton, and others; after which Mr. Pettigrew read a paper entitled "An Inquiry into the Particulars connected with the Death of Amy Robsart (lady Robert Dudley) at Cumnor-place, Berks, Sept. 8, 1560; being a Refutation of the Calumnies charged against sir Robert Dudley, K.G., Anthony Forster, and others."[1] A discussion ensued, in which the principal speakers were Mr. Thos. Wright, Mr. Planché, Mr. Gould, and Mr. Blundell.

The meeting was at a late hour adjourned.

WEDNESDAY, SEPTEMBER 14.

The Association assembled at 9 A.M., and proceeded to inspect Greenham camp and the barrows in the neighbourhood, which are numerous. Thence the members departed for Brimpton church and chapel, which were viewed under the superintendence of Mr. C. E. Davis and Mr. E. Roberts, accompanied by the rev. Mr. Caffin.

Brimpton church consists of a nave, chancel, and south aisle. The nave is of the twelfth century; the south aisle is separated from it by small Decorated arches very picturesquely grouped; the chancel has been in some degree restored, and a Decorated window inserted. In the north wall is an ambry of the usual simple form, but which is in part built with a large Roman flue-tile. The window on the north side is of Norman work, with strong evidences of colour on the jambs, probably of the twelfth or thirteenth century. In the south wall is a piscina of early date, with an attached column supporting the shaft. This, as well as the font, is Norman; but the recess of the former is of the Early English period. The font is lined with heavy lead, and bears every appearance of being the original lining. In this church an arrangement has been very cleverly made to aid the deaf in hearing the discourse from the pulpit; the window over which contains some remains of ancient stained glass with coronets in the borders, surmounted with the Greek initials, Ω and X, the character being that of about the year 1260 or 1270. There have been some repairs to the exterior of the church; and judging from the accumulated heap of moulded stonework in the churchyard, much decorative work has been taken down. The buttresses have been rebuilt. The tower dates only 1749. In the corner of a garden, at the churchyard gate, are the stocks with the original ironwork of mediæval workmanship.

---

[1] This "Inquiry" being too long for the *Journal*, and in some respects not sufficiently archæological for its pages, has been separately printed, but uniformly with the *Journal*, and may be had of the librarian.

Brimpton chapel, in the neighbourhood of the church, is an early building, of one bay, having little of any architectural character remaining, save one square-headed Norman doorway with a very pretty enrichment in the architrave. The Knights Templars are esteemed to have had a preceptory here in the reign of Henry III.

Quitting Brimpton, the party proceeded to Silchester, where the members were met by the lord bishop of Oxford, the provost of Eton, Mr. Higford Burr, rev. C. Kingsley, and others; and the following paper on this Roman station, from the pen of the rev. Beale Poste, was read:

" Silchester is a subject on which a volume of inquiry, discussion, and description, might easily be written; which is a sufficient reason for me to be extremely brief on the present occasion. I have chiefly to advert to two points: its scale of importance among the cities of ancient Britain and Roman Britain; and its position as a Roman station,—relinquishing all matters of detail to others.

" The earliest name of Silchester was *Segontium*, or, in the British language, *Caer Segeint;* and I shall allude further presently to the subject of the various names which this place bore. Segontium was the capital of the Segontiaci, a people who formed part of the race of Belgic Gauls of the Continent, who, coming over to this country, possessed themselves of a rather limited extent of territory lying along the banks of the Thames, of about forty miles in length, and ten or eleven in breadth. It is true they are not mentioned by Ptolemy in his *Geography*, or inserted in his *Map*, among the native states of Britain; but this is more than compensated by their being enumerated by Julius Cæsar in the fifth book of his *Gaulish Wars*, as forming part of the confederacy which resisted him in his second invasion. Subsequent to this, their importance is notified by three types of ancient British coins which were struck, each severally inscribed with the name of their capital city, Segontium; and two of them jointly so with the name, or titular designation, of Cunobeline, who was king of Britain in the reigns of Augustus and Tiberius,—they forming, at that time, a part of his dominions. On this point, let it be remembered that there are only so many as three other cities of ancient Britain, of which there are an equal number of types remaining. Those cities are, Camulodunum, Verulam, and Uriconium or Wroxeter, where the excavations are now going on.

" In Roman British times the importance of Silchester, or Segontium, is sufficiently indicated by its forming, under its name Vindonum, or Vindomum, the commencement of two *iters*, that is, of iters XII and XV. It was, then, of ancient renown in British and Roman-British times; but it was after the Romans were departed that its fame became still more celebrated. It is mentioned by the well known ancient British historian, Nennius. Ralph Higden, the old historian, includes it in his list of eminent cities; and the various old chronicles, one and all, speak of it as

the centre of the principal public acts in this part of the kingdom,—
namely, of kings crowned, public councils held, and the like.

"We thus see the rank which this city held at the time the walls,
considerable ruins of which still remain, were built. The date of the
said walls is evidently towards the end of the Roman occupation of Britain; and there is no difficulty in surmising that, as we find by the
History of Ammianus Marcellinus, the Saxons began to harass the Britons
as early as the year 364, so that many of the wealthiest and most influ-
ential of the inhabitants retired for security from Londinium to this place,
and made walls and fortifications here, as being a place not only higher
up the river, but as being some little distance from its banks, and not so
likely to be surprised on the side of the water by a fleet or squadron suddenly arriving with a hostile armament.

"As to another point, scarce any place had ever so many names as
Silchester. With the ancient Britons it was *Caer Segeint*, as we have
the testimony of *Ralph Higden* and *Henry of Huntingdon*, conjoined with
an *inscription* found in the place many years since, dedicated to Hercules
of the Segontiaci. In the ancient British *Chronicles* it is called *Caer
Vaddau* or *Caer Vaddon;* in the *History* of Nennius, *Mirmanton*, that
is, *Mawr-ventum;* and in the *Itineraries* of Antoninus, *Vindomum, Vindonum*, or even *Vindinum;* and in the work of Ravennas, *Ardaoneon.*
The Saxons, when they came, shewed their disregard for all these names,
and called the place *Silchester*, that is, literally, the 'great Chester', or
fortified city or camp. There is but little doubt that, as concerning the
etymology of the other names, Mawr-ventum means the 'great thorough-
fare'; while Vindonum, the form preferred by Camden, or Vindomum,
is a composite of the well known, though little explained, British term,
'Venta', which is affixed to various towns, as Venta Silurum, Venta Icenorum, and Venta Belgarum.

"There has been some dubitation expressed in comparatively late
times, whether Silchester be Vindonum or Calleva; and this point, before
I conclude these brief remarks, requires to be adverted to. If any one
will take the trouble to refer to *iters* XII and XV of Antoninus, bearing
in mind the relative position of Silchester, the proof will appear very
clear and satisfactory; but again, if *iters* VII, XIII, XIV, and XV, be
examined, in which Calleva is mentioned, whether from incorrectness of
the text or otherwise, the matter appears not so certain; and a tolerably
fair case can also be made out for Calleva being Silchester, as the text
of Antoninus at present stands. In this dilemma it will be best to distrust the correctness of the text of certain portions of those *iters*, and to
concur in the formerly universally received opinion,—the one held by
Camden, Gale, and other great names,—that Vindonum or Vindomum
is Silchester; which will also have this advantage, of agreeing far better
with the known Roman-British topography of this part of the kingdom."

The site of the amphitheatre, the remains of the walls, etc., were examined, and various remarks offered in relation to, and in description of, them by the rev. Mr. Wills, Mr. T. Wright, Mr. Vere Irving, the bishop of Oxford, Mr. Pettigrew, and others.

. The walls of Silchester are nearly three miles in circuit; examination, therefore, of only a portion could be made, and proved, contrary to a generally reported statement, that tiles were not, as usual in other Roman buildings, to be found. Their presence, however, the rev. Mr. Wills pointed out on a portion of the original face; and he has, since the Congress, examined other portions more particularly as to this point, and has ascertained their presence more generally; bricks he has found less common; but on the south side in particular are small flat stones, in layers, as nearly as possible of the shape of the Roman brick, but some-what larger and thicker, *i. e.*, each stone interspersed with the cement is about four inches in thickness.[1] The walls, at the present time, are about twenty feet in height, and twenty-five feet in thickness; what they were fifteen hundred years since it would be difficult to say. There is a large deep ditch surrounding them, and it is partly filled up with the *débris* of the face. Beyond the ditch, in the external vallum, Mr. Wills has traced round the whole city, and found it to be about sixteen feet in height; and on the outside of the ditch is the pomœrium, which extended to the outward vallum, and is still easily to be discerned. Constructed, as these must have been, for defence, they serve to shew that Silchester was a place of no mean strength and intended for more than a temporary purpose. The walls are of an irregular form, and of nine sides; the city had four gates.

In a garden near to the site of the amphitheatre there are two large portions of a fluted column, each about three feet in height, and nearly two feet and a half in diameter; and in another garden adjoining there is a large flat piece of stone found upon digging. It is seven feet four inches high and two feet thick, probably weighing nearly a ton. When discovered, Mr. Wills states, it was flat, on a setting of brickwork and rubble; but the men turned it up on its side, where it now remains. Mr. Layard and Mr. Pettigrew had made an inspection of these remains and conceived they may have constituted portions of some erection for civil or sacred purposes.

In 1833 some excavations were commenced at Silchester, but dis-continued, by order of the late duke of Wellington, who owned the property. Baths were, however, discovered a short distance west of the church, the walls of which were covered with fresco of a honeysuckle

[1] This construction did not escape the notice of Mr. T. Wright, who specifies it in *The Archæological Album* (p. 151); in which work the reader will find a good view of the site of the amphitheatre, and a portion of wall shewing the herringbone-like arrangement of flints in the Silchester walls.

pattern. Upwards of two hundred Roman coins in brass were also then found in a leaden pipe, and a skeleton was likewise discovered in the bath. Evidences of fire distinctly presented themselves. There were flue tiles with inscriptions scratched upon them before being baked. In addition to what has been enumerated, there was also brought to light a portion of a sculptured marble capital, measuring four feet by three, probably part of the remains of a temple. It is much to be regretted that further excavations are not permitted to be made; many very interesting remains are doubtlessly concealed beneath the surface of the ground. As far back as 1732 a votive inscription was dug up, and proved to be a dedication to the Hercules of the Segontiaci. It reads—

DEO . HER
SAEGON
T . TAMMON
SAEN . TAMMON
VITALIS
HONO

which may be read Deo Herculi Sægontiacorum Titus Tammonius Sænii Tammonii Vitalis filius ob honorem, *i. e.*, Titus Tammonius, the son of Sænius Tammonius Vitalis, dedicated this in honour of the god Hercules of the Sægontiaci. Another inscription, nine years later, was taken up dedicated to Julia Domna, the second wife of the emperor Severus, who deceased about A.D. 217. It reads—

JVLIAE . AVG
MATRI . SE
NATVS . ET
CASTROR
M. SABINVS
VICTOR . OB.

i. e. Juliæ Augustæ matri senatus et castrorum M. Sabinus Victorinus ob honorem posuit. Marcus Sabinus Victorinus placed this in honour of Julia, the empress, the mother of the senate and the army.

In a house adjoining, occupied by Mr. Barton, numerous coins, fibulæ, and other Roman remains, dup up or discovered at various times, are deposited. These had been previously examined by Mr. Pettigrew and Mr. Layard, and the following may be stated as the results obtained.

Gold coins of Nerva and Valens.

Silver of Vespasian, Nerva, Trajan, Hadrian, Faustina, Marcus Aurelius, Verus, Caracalla, Julia Domna, Posthumus, Julianus, Severus, Constantius, Julius, Gratianus, Honorius.

Brass of Domitian, Nerva, Antoninus Pius, Commodus, Faustina jun., Lucilla, Alexander Severus, Maximinus, Decius, Gallus, Valerian, Posthumus, Valens, Tetricus, Salonina, Gallienus, Claudius II (Gothicus), Quintillus, Tetricus jun., Carus (Spes Publica), Carausius (Roma Eterna and Salvs Avg.), Allectus (Providentia Avg.) Constantius, Constantine, Licinius, Crispus, Constantine jun., Constans, Magnentius, Gratian.

Mr. Pettigrew deposited during the Congress for inspection, at the Museum at Newbury, a selection of coins in his possession, also obtained from Silchester, which embrace those of other emperors than are recorded in the preceding list. They are ninety-three in number, eighty-nine of which are of silver, and four of brass.

Of the *silver* there are of

Nero	. . . .	1	Marcus Aurelius . . .	9
Vitellius	. . . .	1	Lucius Verus . . .	2
Vespasianus	. . . .	5	Faustina Junior . . .	2
Domitianus	. . . .	4	Barbia Orbiana, wife of Alex-	
Titus	. . . .	3	ander Severus . .	1
Nerva	. . . .	3	Gordianus	1
Trajanus	. . . .	21	Gratianus	1
Hadrianus	. . . .	10	Victor	1
Sabina	. . . .	1	Eugenius	2
Antoninus Pius	. . .	16	Arcadius	1
Faustina Senior	. . .	4		

Thus ranging from A.D. 54 to 395.

Of *brass*—

Gallienus	. . . .	1	Victorinus	1
Valerianus	. . . .	1	Valentinianus . . .	1

Many objects found at Silchester at various times have been reported to the Association, and are deserving of being referred to on this occasion. In the *Journal* (vol. i, p. 147), Mr. Barton, the tenant of the farm, exhibited, through Mr. Fairholt, some fibulæ, bronze ornaments, etc., of which it is sufficient here to notice and repeat two fibulæ, fig. 1 being of its full size, fig. 2 half ditto. On the former specimen traces of enamel may be observed in the upper ornaments, and the compartments of the latter are filled with matter of a red and blue colour alternately. The æquipondium, or steelyard weight, is of bronze, and offers a good piece of workmanship. (Fig. 3.)

Fig. 3.   Fig. 1.   Fig. 2.

In the *Journal* (vol. iv, p. 383) Mr. C. Havell, of Reading, is recorded to have exhibited some medieval rings and other antiquities obtained from this locality. Among them a small metal figure of an eagle with expanded wings, reported to have been Roman, but considered medieval by the council of the Association. C. J. Andrewes, esq., mayor of Reading, entrusted for exhibition to the Society the pommels of two swords, said to have been dug up at Silchester. (See *Journal* for Dec. 1859, p. 357-8, and illustrations on plate 30, figs. 6 and 7.)

SILCHESTER CHURCH was inspected, and the ancient door of early English style admired. It has a simple dog-tooth moulding. There is now little to demand attention in the church, but the wooden screen of the chancel, apparently of the fifteenth century, is worthy of inspection, being richly carved with figures of angels bearing scrolls, interspersed with representations of the pomegranate. There is also a monument to a lady who lies beneath a low pointed arch, as early, perhaps, as the reign of Edward I. Her head is supported by angels, and a dog is at her feet. Whitewash has done its usual mischief, and the tomb is much mutilated. At the back of the recess, however, by careful examination, the figure, in distemper, of a lady may be observed. She is in an attitude of prayer and borne up by angels.

Two sepulchral slabs in the churchyard attracted notice. They belong to the latter part of the thirteenth, or the beginning of the fourteenth, century, and have been figured in Cutts's *Manual for the Study of the Sepulchral Slabs and Crosses of the Middle Ages*, pl. lxix; Boutell's *Christian Monuments in England and Wales*, p. 135; and in the *Archæological Album*, p. 171. On one of the slabs (the most perfect) are the busts of a man and woman, beneath which is a cross flory placed within a quatrefoil, around which is a circle resting upon a tall stem. The busts (probably of man and wife) surmount the cross. The other slab presents the much mutilated head of a lady placed within a cross calvary. It is to be regretted that these interesting monuments are not removed into the church for their preservation and security. They were dug up when a portion of the churchyard was lowered.

From Silchester the Association proceeded to UFTON COURT, the property of Richard Benyon, esq., who had most kindly given facilities for particular examination of a most interesting but neglected specimen of domestic architecture in this country. As it is desirable to obtain further knowledge in regard to the history and building of the mansion, and to have the same illustrated, a more particular notice of it is deferred to a future opportunity.

The Association now proceeded to ALDERMASTON HOUSE, whither they had been specially invited by D. Higford Burr, esq. The company were received by Mr. and Mrs. Burr, and conducted over the mansion, which is modern, but contains the fine staircase and some other portions of the old house, and the members of the Association and visitors enjoyed the opportunity of inspecting the beautiful drawings of Mrs. Burr, which, at the solicitation of the Treasurer, had been placed in the library, drawing room, and study. These are of rare value and great excellence, and form a series of the principal frescoes copied from the originals in various parts of Italy. The company quitted the mansion to assemble in a marquee which had been most tastefully erected in the grounds, and to enjoy the elegant hospitality of their host. Mr. Pettigrew returned thanks to Mr. Burr, and the Provost of Eton proposed the health of Mrs. Burr, after warmly responding to which the Association again assembled in the hall, where Mr. Pettigrew read a paper on Aldermaston. (See pp. 62-69 *ante*.)

This concluded, a visit was paid to the church adjoining the mansion, and particular inspection made of the monument of sir George Foster and lady; for an account of which, see paper referred to.

On the way back to Newbury, a visit was paid to THATCHAM CHURCH; upon which Mr. Edward Roberts made some remarks. This church has been recently under extensive alteration in such a manner as to have utterly destroyed the greater part of the antiquarian remains; indeed, with the exception of the south porch, north aisle, and part of the roof, all is new. The church now consists of a nave with aisles, and a chancel with a south aisle, formerly a chapel called the *Fuller chapel*. It is over this portion that the only old piece of roofing exists, which Mr. Roberts assigned to the date of 1450 or 1460. In the archway between this chapel and the chancel, is an altar-tomb, locally attributed to William Danvers, a justice of the Common Pleas; but as that official died in 1504, and the character of the tomb is a century earlier, some other person must have lain beneath it; and most likely it belonged to some of the Fuller family, from whose chapel it was displaced. The Fullers are not known to have had property here, nor to have been connected with Thatcham. The manor appears to have been given by Henry I to the abbot and convent of Reading; and after the dissolution of that establishment, it was granted (in 1539) to John Winchcombe, the son of "Jack of Newbury." There were, in 1620, two persons, father and son (Nicholas Fuller), who died seized of the manor of Crokeham; but there is no inscription, or sign of armorial bearing, remaining on the tomb to shew whether it belonged to any of the ancestors of these Fullers. It may likewise be remarked that the large Purbeck marble slab on the tomb clearly did not originally belong to the paneling beneath. The south porch is of the date of about 1160, and has been taken down and replaced stone by stone, but has been somewhat carelessly cut away in the course of cleaning. In the floor was found an inscription on brass, which has been screwed against the wall of the tower arch. It appears to be of the time of Richard II :

> "Here lythe John Godfroman [on]
> Whos sowlye God have mercy."

An evening meeting was held at the Mansion House.

T. J. PETTIGREW, F.R.S., F.S.A., V.P., IN THE CHAIR.

The business of the evening commenced by the reading of a paper by the rev. John Adams, M.A., "On the Roman Station of Spinæ. (See pp. 70-73 *ante*.) After a short discussion, in which Mr. Vere Irving expressed his satisfaction that Mr. Adams had disproved the theory that Roman encampments must be either square or oblong; and remarking that the Romans adapted their camps to the situation in which they were placed, and that they were therefore to be seen in almost every possible shape, a short notice transmitted by Mr. B. B. Woodward, descriptive of a map of Roman Berkshire and Hampshire,[1] was read. The map, of which a large diagram was exhibited, gave rise to many remarks and suggestions; and the chairman, agreeably to the author's desire, requested those local antiquaries well acquainted with the several places, to add in pencil such spots as they, of their own knowledge, could vouch for as having been the sites of discoveries of ancient British, Roman, or Saxon, antiquities.

The chairman read the following memorandum he had received from Mr. Hewett of Reading, a resident in the county for thirty-four years, and an attentive archæologist. It has reference to the Roman roads of Berkshire:

"There are many ancient roads to be seen. The first is the Old-street road, which, in my opinion, runs from Silchester to Cirencester, etc. It passes from the river Kennet to Cold Ash common, and runs near the White House in Ferne wood; and from thence down the hill for Fair-cross pond, and along Sandy-lane to the New inn, Langley, and on to Bredon common; then turns to the right, and on to a green lane where four roads meet and cross, viz., one from Ilsley to Peasemore, and another from Bredon common to Catmore farm; it turns to the left between Red-lane barn and the cross-roads, and in a hedgerow which parts Witten-ham's farm in Peasemore and the farthest extremity of Bredon parish, it is overgrown with briars and hazel. The road here is small (a *British* one); then it runs by the Catmore farm side of a wood called High Robbins, through the furze-ground, Knapp's wood, and Grey field, which it surrounds; but goes on again to West Ilsley kiln, pointing for the ridgeway, which no doubt it joins, and runs to Wanborough in Wiltshire and Cirencester. It passes several encampments, viz., the White House, Fence wood, Wittenham's farm, where clinkers are found, etc.; and Grey field, on the east corner of which, at the Poor's wood, is a deep well, which is scarcely ever without water; and some few years ago, the

---

[1] This is intended to form a portion of an archæological map of England and Wales, to be published by Mr. Woodward. The names of subscribers to the map should be addressed to Mr. Woodward, 20, Eton Villas, Haverstock Hill, London.

late Mr. Dewe, when tenant of Catmore farm, had it cleaned out, and found it bricked at the bottom.

"Another road (British) passes by the north side of Bennett's wood, and near Wood's farm, Streatley, and appears to have run from the Grotto, or near where there was, since my time, a ferry called Hose Mill; and it strikes me it joined the Ickneild-street, where Dr. Plott traced it to Goring, Oxon, two hundred years ago. This road, on leaving Bennett's wood, runs through College wood, Streatley, Portabello wood, Aldworth, to Beech farm; and from thence to Compton Cowdown, and from Compton Cowdown through Ashridge wood, Ilsley, Stanmore, Bredon, and joins Old-street road by Red-lane barn, in the hedgerow which parts Bredon parish and Wittenham's farm.

"Another road runs from the village of Streatley to Aldworth, and crosses the Ickneild-street near Turville farm, Compton. Many parts are worth seeing, as the road runs through woods, and sunk, every three or four miles there are ponds, as if they were made to water cattle at in ancient days."

In another note, Mr. Hewett remarks:

"The country, no doubt, was thickly inhabited in ancient times by Britons, and afterwards by the Romans. I have taken some pains to find the ancient roads, encampments, etc., for fifty years, and have seen nearly all in Berkshire. I have sent you an account of a Roman road from Allcester to Dorchester, Oxon. I strongly suspect Thamesis was at or near Dorchester, as the Thame river joins the Isis there; and that the road from Allcester passed on to Streatley farm, which was *Calleva* (*vide* sir Richard Colt Hoare's *Ancient Wiltshire*). From Streatley and along the Thames, branches of the Ickneild-street seem to have passed into Berkshire: one to Wallingford, another at Little Stoke ferry, a third at Mulesford (now called Moulsford). Down to this village the Thames, before pounds, locks, weirs, etc., was fordable, excepting in times of floods, as the names of places imply, viz., Appleford, Shillingford, Wallingford, and Monks*ford* (now Mulesford, or Moulsford), being in ancient days on the road from London to the west of England. Probably goods were conveyed on mules by pack-roads; for to this day, publichouses are called the ' Pack-Horse,' ' Pack-Saddle,' etc., on the line to London through the extreme southern end of Oxfordshire, or rather the east from the west of England.

"There is a road which has been used for ages, and is to this day, from the Isle of Anglesey into Kent, for Welsh cattle, viz., from three hundred to four hundred miles, and yet no turnpike gate to pay, or a bridge. It runs through Berkshire from Wonborough, Wilts, to the ridgeway on the downs, and to Farnborough near Wantage; and from thence to Lilley, and on to Jack's Booth on the river Kennet, and on to Mortimer, Mattingley, in Surrey, and into Kent. That road is a branch one from Silchester on the north-west."

The rev. JAMES BAGGE, of Crux Easton, Newbury, made the following communication :—

" In the month of December 1856, a labourer was employed in preparing the ground for planting a tree in the garden of the rectory of Crux Easton. Having dug down to the depth of about eighteen inches, he reported, that he had thrown up a few bones, which seemed to him not such as were commonly met with. Attention being thus drawn to the circumstance, the greatest care was taken in pursuing the investigation ; and, as some fragments had been carted to the glebe, the soil was carefully looked over, and they were brought back.

" In prosecuting the work, many other bones were found ; and at last a human skull presented itself, lying, to all appearance, in the very spot and position of its original interment, and in its natural globular form. On touching it, the different parts separated ; but the sutures were distinctly marked, and so well defined, as to admit of their being re-fitted to each other. The spot, on which it had lain for ages, exhibited the corresponding concavity. Portions of the upper and lower jaws were brought forth. In the upper jaw, four teeth remain in their sockets, but so loosely as to require the most delicate handling. In the lower, there are five. There are nine others, in all eighteen, with their enamel perfect. A London dentist has given it as his opinion, that the individual was about forty-five years of age ; which opinion might possibly receive some confirmation from the well defined edges of the sutures of the cranium. It is said, that the skulls recently exhumed at Wroxeter exhibit strange conformations, unlike any that we are acquainted with. The one discovered in the lawn at Crux Easton presented no distortions of that kind ; whatever peculiarity of formation may be discovered by careful ethnological scrutiny and comparison. There was sufficient evidence to shew, from the position of the cranium, and the bones, that the body, when buried, was placed with its head to the west and the feet to the east. This circumstance, however, cannot be safely regarded as an indication of the progress of Christianity.

" Archbishop Potter,[1] quoting from the scholiast on Thucydides, shews, that the heads of deceased persons were so placed in the grave that they might look toward the rising sun, and consequently the head must necessarily lie toward the west ; the position in which this subject was found. There were no signs of decayed wood, or fragments of stone, to indicate the existence of a coffin ; but there was a bent iron nail, perhaps not connected with the body, the preservation of the bones of which may probably be attributed to the chalk.

" Closely contiguous to the cranium lay a small vase. It attracted the attention of the labourer as something curious in the side of the excavation ; and, bringing it out with his finger and thumb, asked, ' What's

[1] Potter, *Antiq.*, vol. ii, 236.

this?' None but a lover of antiquity can tell how great the satisfaction is of recovering such a specimen without fracture from the pickaxe. It was nearly full of the adjacent chalky soil, but contained nothing more. Whether flour and honey, rarely omitted, had been originally deposited within, it is, of course, impossible even to conjecture. (See plate 1, fig. 3.)

"Some years ago numerous fragments of pottery were discovered in the New Forest. Specimens of these may be seen in the British Museum. Some are larger than the one here spoken of; but there is one precisely similar in form, colour, and dimensions. All exhibit the well known depression on the sides made with the thumb. They appear to have been formed upon the wheel of the potter, as there are concentric ridges or lines drawn upon the surface internally and externally.

"With regard to the two modes, of interment and burning, the latter, generally speaking, was adopted by the Romans. This is a fact attested by innumerable cinerary urns dug up in this country, as well as by direct testimony. The historian, in recording the death of Nero's wife, says that, although burning the deceased was the regular custom, she, on the contrary, was interred.[1] But though interment is here declared to be exceptional, others maintain that it was the most ancient mode; and that the place where the dead was buried was held sacred, but not where it was burnt.[2] The instance of Numa is adduced in proof of interment.[3] Of him it is expressly recorded that he prohibited burning his body after death, and left directions that it should be interred; and it was interred accordingly under the Janiculan Mount, in a stone coffin.[4] This coffin, we are told, was discovered long after; its dimensions being eight feet by four.[5] The quotations thus cited must be regarded as authorities for the statements here advanced."

The Rev. Edmund Kell, M.A., then gave a minute description of a late discovery of a Roman villa at Carisbrooke, in the Isle of Wight, and produced drawings of the several antiquities discovered. This paper will be printed and illustrated in a future number of the *Journal*.

---

[1] "Corpus non igni abolitum, ut Romanus mos; sed......conditur, tumulo-que infertur." (*Tac.*, *Ann.* xvi, 6.) "Et tamen ipsam quoque ictu calcis occi-dit, quod se, ex aurigatione sero reversum, gravida et ægra, conviciis incesserat." (*Suet. in Neron.*, s. 35.)

[2] "At mihi quidem antiquissimum sepulturæ genus id fuisse videtur...locus ille, ubi crematum est corpus, nihil habet religionis," etc. (*Cic. de Legibus*, ii, 22.) "Ipsum cremare apud Romanos non fuit veteris instituti: terrâ conde-bantur." (*Plin.* vii, 54.)

[3] "Regem nostrum Numam conditum accepimus." (*Cic. ib.*)

[4] Πυρι μεν ουκ εδοσαν τον νεκρον, αυτου κωλυσαντος, ως λεγεται· δυο δε ποιησαμενοι λιθινας σορους, υπο τον Ιανοκλον εθησαν, την μεν ετεραν εχουσαν το σωμα, την δε ετεραν τας ιερας βιβλους· κ. τ. λ. (*Plut. in Num.*)

[5] "Duæ lapideæ arcæ octonos ferme pedes longæ, quaternos latæ, inventæ sunt." (*Liv.* xl, 29.)

THE JOURNAL

OF THE

British Archaeological Association.

JUNE 1860.

ON

THE ROCK-BASINS OF DARTMOOR, AND SOME BRITISH REMAINS IN ENGLAND.

BY SIR J. GARDNER WILKINSON, D.C.L., F.R.S.,
VICE-PRESIDENT.

THE attention of those who have visited Dartmoor has often been directed to the numerous "rock-basins in the granite" of that district; and some interesting observations have lately been made by Mr. Ormerod on the subject, in the *Quarterly Journal of the Geological Society* for February 1859.

Intimately acquainted as he is with certain portions of Dartmoor, any remarks made by Mr. Ormerod must be received with great respect; and his memoir is a valuable contribution to our knowledge of that part of the country. He is of opinion that all these rock-basins are of natural formation, and that they are not, as some have been disposed to think, artificial. He produces many arguments to shew that the natural disintegration of the granite accounts for their presence, and for their general appearance; and the number he has examined proves the diligence with which he has conducted his inquiry. But it does not appear that *all* the instances he brings forward bear out his inference. In their form and appearance some of the large basins differ essentially from the smaller ones; and I shall presently shew that similar rock-basins are found in *other rocks,*—a fact which at once negatives the conclusion that they are owing simply to the peculiar decomposition of *granite*.

He states that Mistor Pan, the *only* basin on Mistor, " has been supposed to be artificially formed," and describing it, says, " The sides are nearly perpendicular, leaning slightly back : at the south and easterly side, the highest bed of rock projects slightly, and under this a hole reaches through to the eastern side of the Tor, about two inches above the bottom of the pan.   The only other places where similar perfora- tions have been observed, are at Fur Tor and Willistone Rocks.   From the northerly side, a lip or channel runs for about five inches in a northerly direction, and then irregu- larly.   At the basin it is about five inches wide, and there reaches nearly to the bottom of the basin.   The diameter from north to south is thirty-six inches; from east to west, thirty-five inches; and the longest diameter is from north to south.   The depth (at the lip) on the north side is four inches; on the easterly, six inches; on the southerly, five inches; and on the westerly, six inches.   The bottom is nearly level, but slopes slightly towards the centre, where it is about half an inch deeper than at the sides.   The bottom was covered with small, sharp gravel, consisting chiefly of felspar and quartz, formed by the disintegration of the granite.   With the exception of the perforation, and that a lip is not of very frequent occurrence, the above description is also applicable, the dimensions being altered, to nearly every rock-basin with a flat bottom; and there seems to be no reason for considering the origin of this basin different from that of the other basins."   (Page 17.)

He then mentions the holes worn in rocks exposed to the direct action of falling water in a river, which has the well- known effect of hollowing out and perforating stone; but which does not appear to be relevant to the question of rock-basins.   And he afterwards states (p. 19) that no basins exist on many of the most remarkable Tors to the north of the Teign, nor on Hounter Tor, and some other of these lofty rocks.   But he very properly refutes the notion of Dr. M'Culloch, that " the friction of quartz and felspar frag- ments, not unfrequently found in rock-basins, may have con- tributed to deepen them, being set in motion during high winds,"—those fragments not being round, but " angular"; and he justly observes, that " the cause suggested by Dr. M'Culloch could not affect the deep basins, as in these cases the particles would be undisturbed by the motion of the water from wind." He states, however, that the contents of the basins "generally consist of a small angular fragment of quartz and felspar, as above mentioned, and schorl, which sometimes cover the bottom of the basin." (p. 21.) He afterwards observes (p. 22), "During the inclement part of the year these basins are full of water; that, during part of the time, often rapidly alternating with ice. When the warm weather comes on, the water evaporates, and the basins are dried up. From the frequent showers there is then a constant change between the rock being saturated with wet, and being warm and dry"; and he shews the effect which the "alternations of heat and cold, wet and dryness," must have in decomposing the granite; but when he attributes the whole formation of the deepest basins to this action of the weather, and when he supposes that "the eye will discriminate between the Tors where rock-basins would probably be found or not," and that "they are scarcely ever met with where the action of the water has not that particular effect upon the rock," he appears to have been led to generalize too hastily.

I cannot, however, give an opinion in opposition to that of Mr. Ormerod, without expressing my admiration of the fairness with which he makes all his statements; and I feel sure that he will pardon my differing from him respecting the formation of one particular kind of deep circular rock-basin. First, then, I must observe that the fact mentioned by him, of the holes in some of them having been perforated through the rock, is strong evidence of human agency in their formation; 2° the lip, or channel, to let off the water from the basin, mentioned above, also appears to owe its origin to the hand of man; 3° the very *small quantity* of "angular fragments" he noticed at the bottom of the deepest basins, suffices to shew that this is not the accumulation of all the detached particles of the granite, the decomposition of which formed the basin, but merely of those of its sides and bottom, which had become detached by a subsequent disintegration of their surface long after the basin itself had been formed; for the decomposition of all the stone which occupied the space of that basin would not have produced a small, but a very large, mass of decayed granite, even allowing for the lighter particles having been blown away by the wind; and in some of the large basins very little decay of the sides and bottom has taken place,

neither do they contain the necessary fragments or particles
proceeding from decomposition of the stone.   4°· The presence of one or more large circular basins on *some one rock
remarkable for its form, size, and position*, and the absence
of similar basins on other large rocks close to it, of granite of
the *same quality*, and liable to the *same action* of the atmosphere, are strong presumption of a *selection* having been
made by *man* in the former case; and it would certainly be
difficult to explain why a particular rock, as at Carn Brea,
near Redruth, in Cornwall (placed, too, as it is within an
ancient walled town of British time), should be the *only one*
hollowed out by the action of the atmosphere, with upright
cavities more than two feet in depth, while so many other
rocks in the same locality are destitute of such remarkable
basins.   I do not pretend to say that a small *natural* cavity
may not have been occasionally formed by man into a larger
basin: indeed, this is highly probable; and the *idea* of the
basin may have been derived, in the first instance, from
some of the smaller and ruder natural ones.   A parallel case
is mentioned by Sir J. Emerson Tennent in Ceylon, where
the famous sacred footprint on Adam's Peak has been formed
by enlarging a *natural* hollow in the gneiss rock; and neither
Buddhism nor Druidism appear to have neglected natural
phenomena when they could be made subservient to a religious, or superstitious, purpose.   5°· The circular, or slightly
oval form of basins which have their sides nearly *perpendicular*, and a flat bottom, cannot be satisfactorily explained
by, or attributed to, decomposition of the stone; and so
regular are the sides of Castor basin (which was discovered
by Mr. Ormerod in September 1856), that the diameter
decreases gradually from the rim to the flat bottom, the
depth being two feet seven inches.   "The opening at the
top" (he observes, p. 18), "as marked by the line to which
water stands when it is full, is oval, measuring eight feet
from north to south, and six feet eight inches from east to
west.   A few inches below this level, the basin is nearly circular; the diameter half way down is fifty inches; at the
bottom, twenty-four inches; the perpendicular depth is
thirty-one inches.   The bottom is flat, rounding up at the
edges to the sides, which curve outwards in the form of the
mouth of a trumpet; and two indentations, caused by decay,
run round the basin."   It had "not many stones, nor the

small fragments of quartz and felspar usually found in rock-basins"; but a quantity of *spagnum,* or bog moss, and peat, the presence of which was explained by the statement of the old moor man, that "the basin was filled with peat between a hundred and a hundred fifty years ago, to prevent accidents to the sheep." From this, then, it is evident that the disintegrated fragments of the stone were not found even in a basin two feet seven inches in depth; and it is certain that if filled with peat, to prevent accidents to sheep, the shepherds would not have cleared out the decomposed stone in order to supply its place with peat. There is, therefore, neither in this, nor in any similar deep basin, the evidence of that decomposition of the *whole mass* which is supposed to have formed them; and the *small quantity* occasionally met with in those of large size may be readily accounted for by the *subsequent* decay of the inside of the already existing basin.

Mr. Ormerod admits, with his usual candour, that his observations of rock-basins are confined to a portion of Dartmoor; and, I think, if they had extended farther, that he would have found reason to alter his opinion respecting the formation of some of the larger ones, like those in a mass of granite rock at Carn Brea, near Redruth in Cornwall, which have every appearance of being artificial, and made for some particular purpose with great care and labour. They consist of a succession of deep basins uniting into one at the lower part, where a lip, or opening, is formed to enable the collected water to flow off to the ground below. The sides, which are nearly perpendicular, are about two feet high, varying according to the position and surface of the stone; and the bottom of each is smooth and even. The mass of rock, in which the basins are cut, has an inclination towards the lower end where the lip opens; so that the slope of the bottom of each basin follows that of the rock itself, and being on the summit of a hill it is in a position where no fall of water could have worn the rock, or hollowed it into these cavities. From all these facts we have strong evidence against their being solely the result of natural agency.

But what is still more conclusive against the opinion that they are attributable to the peculiar action of the weather on *granite,*—and that, too, on granite of a particular structure,—is, that they are formed in other kinds of stone; and if, as Mr. Ormerod states (p. 22), "the eye will in a short period discriminate between the Tors where basins would probably be found or not," being " scarcely ever found where it is the character of the Tor to have the perpendicular joints clearly developed," this might be owing to their makers having selected such rocks as were capable of holding water, and not subject to fissures.

They occur also on the Peak of Derbyshire,[1] and in Staffordshire, in *gritstone;* and the numerous granite rocks I have examined in other places, where similar deep circular basins do not occur, offer a strong argument against the selection supposed to be made by nature for their position in *some few* places.   Besides, the deep circular basins in the gritstone of Derbyshire and Staffordshire not only resemble those of Dartmoor in their form and general appearance, but are, in like manner, in the neighbourhood of ancient remains; and here, as on the granite Tors, they are evidently placed on certain rocks selected for the purpose, and not indiscriminately *throughout* the hills of the Peak and of the Staffordshire moors. In the gritstone near Hathersage are numerous rock-basins; mostly, it is true, natural, yet some few are evidently made, or enlarged, by man; and to these alone it is my object to direct attention.   One of them is on Stanage Edge.   It is circular, with upright sides and a flat bottom, having a diameter of four feet by three feet nine inches, and a depth of twenty-one inches (varying to twenty-five, from the unevenness of the upper surface of the rock); and another is at the highest part of Eyam Moor (on the summit of one of three isolated rocks that rise conspicuously above, and about a third of a mile to the west-south-west of a sacred circle), and has, in like manner, upright sides[2] and a flat bottom, and measures two feet six inches by two feet two inches diameter, and nine inches in depth (varying to fifteen, according to the height of the surface of the rock), with a channel on the east, evidently cut to let off the water when it reached the brim on that side.

In Staffordshire, too, the basin on the Ramshaw rocks, called the " Devil's Punch Bowl," is in gritstone; and is

---

[1] It was while writing this paper, that, having accidentally heard of them, I paid a visit to the Peak in order to examine the gritstone basins.

[2] These, which were evidently once perfectly upright, have since been slightly worn or hollowed below the brim by the action of the wind on the surface of the water contained in the basin, but could not have assumed their present shape had they not been *first* upright.

worthy of notice from its being the *only one* in that locality, which abounds in British remains; and a 'still more remarkable one, about three paces in diameter, is met with in the British fort of Old Bewick in Northumberland, which is now called by the peasants " the bloody trough" (from a tradition that human sacrifices were made over it by the Druids), and which is of importance from its obvious bearing on the question respecting the natural formation of deep circular rock-basins from the decomposition of the granite in which they are found,—since it is not in granite, nor even in gritstone, but is evidently hewn in a sandstone rock. I may also mention another basin of elliptical form, chiselled out of the solid rock, on the common called *Maes-y-dref*, near Rhyader castle in Radnorshire (see *Archæolog. Cambrensis*, Series III, vol. iv, p. 566), where the rock is neither granite nor gritstone, but of the silurian formation.[1]

Rock-basins, then, are evidently not confined to granite of a particular structure; and though it is sometimes difficult to decide, in granite or in gritstone rocks, whether basins of a certain form and appearance are natural or artificial, there seems to be little doubt respecting the deep round ones with upright sides, even in those cases where they have been corroded by a subsequent decomposition of the stone, which has sometimes worn two or more into one, and given them an irregularity of shape quite at variance with their original circular or slightly oval outline. And this decay seems to have been frequently promoted by the presence of a small channel by which they were made to communicate with each other when originally cut in the rock. This union of several basins into one, may be observed in those at Carn Brea and other places; and in one or two which I have seen, the spout or channel to let off the water is so clearly defined, and so evidently the work of human hands, that it might almost be attributed to the accidental caprice of some much more modern stone-cutters, did we not feel sure that modern labourers look for more profitable employment than adding lips or channels to old rock-basins. And though the junction of two basins is sometimes the result of natural causes, I think we may generally determine which are attributable to human agency, and which to atmospheric influence.

[1] In N. Wales, Adam's and St. Tydech's foot-prints are basins in slate rock.

There is also another fact connected with the large rock-basins, which is pertinent to the question respecting their origin; and this is their presence in localities marked by the vicinity of sacred circles, avenues, and other monuments connected with the religious or funereal rites of the Britons; and in all cases, whether in Cornwall, on Dartmoor, in Staffordshire, the Peak of Derbyshire, in Northumberland, or in Wales, they are always in the neighbourhood of ancient remains. I may also notice one in an isolated rock of granite within the camp of Treen, or Trerhyn ("town of the cape"?), behind the Logan rock in Cornwall, which has evidently been *brought* there, whether natural or artificial.

It is true, as I before observed, that by far the greater proportion of rock-basins are natural; but I think we may distinguish most of those formed by human agency : and to infer that none are the work of man, because so many are naturally formed, is almost tantamount to the conclusion that, because many rocks resemble buildings, all buildings are of natural formation.

I cannot, in so limited a space, enter into all the details of the subject, nor point out the various reasons which enable us to distinguish artificial from natural basins; but after having examined so many in different parts of England, I have no hesitation in saying that even in those which, from subsequent decay of the rock, have lost their original form, there is generally a clue to the distinction between them. And it would certainly be difficult to explain why so large a sediment of decomposed rock is found in the shallow basins; and little, or more frequently none, in the large deep ones which have upright sides and flat bottoms; unless we admit that the former are natural, the latter artificial. The water they hold may evaporate; not so the decomposed stone.

It has been a very general opinion that the large basins were used for some religious purpose, and I do not perceive any improbability in the suggestion. If they are artificial, they could only have been intended for that purpose; being useless for holding potable water in places where springs are close at hand;[1] their spouts shew that the object was not to keep within them more than a certain quantity of water;

---

[1] At Carn Brea, near Redruth, and on Eyam Moor, are abundant natural springs close to the ancient remains and the basin.

and this, when lying long in them, becomes impure. And if intended for a religious purpose, we can only attribute them to the priests of the religion professed by the people near whose monuments they are found.

The question may not be one of very great importance; but there is another which ought to interest us, and this is the name and religious rites of the people by whom the many ancient monuments in Britain were erected; and as some have doubted the very existence of Druids and their religion in this country, it may not be irrelevant to inquire on what authority those doubts have been raised. It is the tendency of the day to call in question whatever has been hitherto credited: some, therefore, not satisfied with doubting the antiquity of every ruin of early times, have affected to disbelieve the accounts handed down to us by Roman writers concerning the Britons, their priesthood, and their customs; though I must confess that such doubts amount to something more than mere scepticism, when we have numerous records of a people whose ortholithic circles still remain at Stonehenge, Abury, Stanton-Drew, Arbe-Low, and many places in Cornwall, Devonshire, Cumberland, and various parts of this country, as well as in Wales and Scotland, together with cromlechs and various monuments; and when similar records are found in France and other countries once inhabited by tribes professing the same religion, and offsets of the same race, as the early Britons. If we are not to trust to the authority of Roman writers who mention the Druids, what is to be our guide? And if history is to be unceremoniously put aside, on what are we to depend for any information respecting the inhabitants, the manners, and the religion of Britain and Gaul, or the state of any other country of antiquity? We may at once cease to read history, if mere speculations are to take its place. We have circumstantial accounts of the existence of Britons and of Druids in our island, of the stand they made in defence of their sacred retreats, and of some of their ceremonies: at all events they were in Britain when the Romans first landed, and when they afterwards conquered the country. And if not to them, to whom are these strange monuments to be attributed?

Passing in retrospective review the different populations who have inhabited this island, both Christian and

Pagan, let us inquire to whom they can have belonged. 1°· Are they the work of the Saxon race since the introduction of Christianity? Certainly not.   2°· Are they of the same people when pagans? There is evidence of their being of greater antiquity than any monuments in this island; and their occurrence in Brittany and other parts of France, as well as in Savoy, will not admit of their being attributed to the Saxons.   3°· Are they Danish?   The localities where they are generally found being those least accessible from the sea, and their position upon the remote hills of the interior, which were so secluded and unapproachable that none but people long accustomed to those retreats would have selected them as the sites of what are most precious in their estimation,—their sacred monuments,—suffice to disprove this.   There is also other evidence of their builders having sought protection from enemies coming from the coast, when they selected those spots; and we have ample proof of their not being the work of a people who, if their visits were not quite confined to plundering excursions from the coast, never possessed the remote fastnesses on the hills of Derbyshire, Staffordshire, Wales, Dartmoor, and other parts of the country, in which those monuments are most abundant. 4°· Are they Phœnician? Unquestionably not; as that trading people never sought to settle or penetrate into the interior, visited only a small portion of our coast, and cannot be claimed as the ancestors of any tribe of people either in Britain or in Ireland. 5°· Are they of the Trojans who came under Brût, latinized into Brutus? We only treat this fable with a smile, or suppose it to be corrupted from some fact no longer recognizable. 6°· Are they Roman? Certainly not: and the occasional discovery of "Roman interments" in circles and cromlechs will not prove either of these to have been made by a people who had no such monuments elsewhere; as the age of Egyptian tombs is not altered by the discovery of Greek and Roman bodies within them.

It would be curious, then, to learn from those who doubt their being of the pagan Britons, and who question the existence of Druids in this country, to what people they are to be ascribed; and it would also be satisfactory to know on what plea the authority of the Roman writers, who mention the Druid priesthood of the pagan Britons in this island, is to be set aside.   To stop to argue the point would be as great a loss of labour as to refute the notion of some that cromlechs are natural formations !

We may not be able to state the exact object of all these monuments; nor is it necessary to decide whether the rock-basins were intended for lustral ceremonies, as some have supposed, or for any other rites; and it is far more reasonable to admit our inability to decide upon this and other questions connected with the remains of the ancient inhabit-ants of our island, than to offer speculations upon them, such as have led to the well known but fanciful theory respecting the serpent-worship, and the arkite ceremonies, of the Druids.

In support of this theory, classical writers have been quoted to shew that the worship of the serpent was an ac-knowledged part of the religion of Egypt, Greece, and other ancient countries; and certain indications of respect or aver-sion for it have been both produced for the same purpose. But even if serpent-worship, *properly so called*, were really a part of the Egyptian, Greek, or Roman religions, how does it follow that it was also part of the religion of the ancient Britons ? The conclusion in the former case has been too hastily formed from certain expressions of old writers, and from the fact of the serpent being a type, an emblem, or a character in a fable; all which are very different from actual serpent-worship; and though the cross is an emblem among Christians, it is not worshipped by them. Moreover, in the case of the Druids, the fact of the serpent being a type or an emblem has not even been established; and the *angui-num* mentioned by Pliny (xxix, 3) is no more connected with serpent-worship among the Druids, than is the similar nur-sery tale among the Moslem Arabs, of the snake having a jewel in his head, a proof of serpent-worship in Arabia. It would be as easy to prove that the Druids worshipped the bull Apis; and the oxen of Hû Gadarn (who is said, like Osiris, to be Noah) would be as plausible a groundwork for the existence of arkite ceremonies among the Druids,[1] as any put forth by its advocates. On such conditions, what theories might not be broached? And the assumption that, because some people of antiquity were *supposed* to have worshipped the serpent, the British avenues and temples were *therefore* Dracontia, is both gratuitous and illogical.

[1] Even the learned Bryant only states: "I *make no doubt*......that the arkite rites prevailed in many parts of Britain." (Vol. ii, p. 471.)

I feel the greatest respect for the ingenuity and industry of those who have maintained it; but it must be confessed that the same learning and extensive research might have been better employed upon a more reasonable hypothesis; and inextricable confusion has been caused by pressing into the same category the most opposite principles, and by confounding together serpents, some of which were types of sin, and others of the good genius; for which the distant Egypt has been ransacked, as well as other systems of ancient superstition. Not only has fancy been resorted to, in order to make the various statements conform to this theory; but in the case of avenues, those most rectilinear in form have been adopted without the least scruple, in support of it, as well as the most irregular and ill defined. Whether an avenue extends from one circle to another, or is unconnected with any circle; whether it terminates in a *cist* (or sepulchral *chest*), or in a long upright stone (*maen-hîr*), or in a cromlech, it is equally pronounced to be an indication of serpent-worship. And yet the inconsistency of attaching the same meaning to every avenue, whatever the monument may be to which it leads, ought to be sufficiently obvious; and though nobody has ever ventured to suppose that *every* road or avenue to a temple, a tomb, or other monument, was in any country connected with *one peculiar* worship, or *one solitary emblem,* a claim is here put forth in *all cases;* without any authority to prove a connection with it *even in a single instance.*

I will not stop to notice all the improbabilities of this hasty conclusion, nor point out the many reasons against the assertion that avenues were indications of the worship of the serpent, or were intended to imitate its form; but I must offer this simple suggestion, that they afford stronger evidence of having served for sacred or funereal processions, like the *dromos* of an Egyptian temple, the avenues to Egyptian tombs, and the long nave of a Roman Catholic church; and were more likely to have been devised by a priesthood in order to impose upon a superstitious people, and to display their own importance, than to shew their respect for serpents. At the same time, I invite attention to the avenues on Dartmoor, below Castor[1] (plate 6), and to

[1] In making a plan of this curious town, I find it contains twenty-five circular houses or huts, supposed to be British; and many similar hut-circles are found in the neighbourhood.

The Avenues near Castor, Dartmoor.

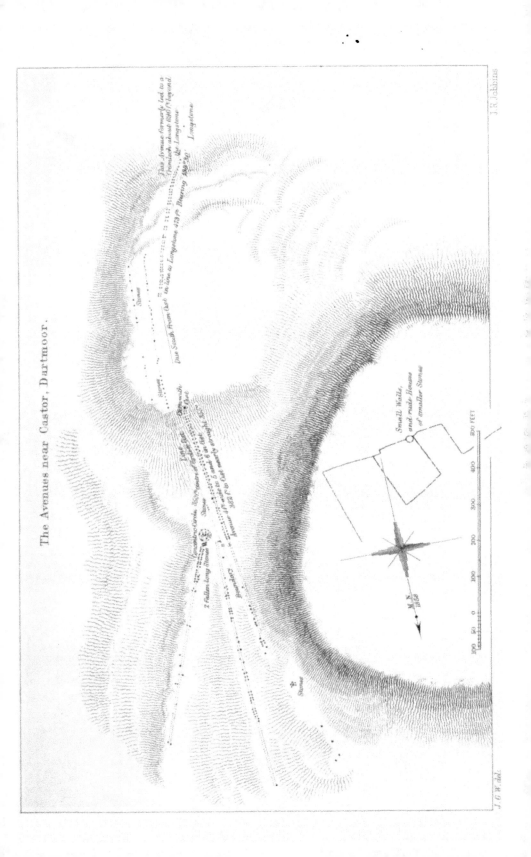

J.G.W del.

J.R.Jobbins.

those near Merivale bridge (pl. 7), to prove by their rectilinear direction how little they accord with the form of a serpent; and the double avenue on Chillacombe Down, near Grimspound,[1] as well as the two straight avenues below Black Tor, are equally at variance with it.

One of the avenues at Castor formerly terminated, at its southern extremity, in a three-pillared cromlech (of which, as Mr. Ormerod informs me, the three stones called the "Three Boys" have long been the only remains); and in its straight course to the northward, and about six hundred and ninety feet from the cromlech, it had a long stone (or *maen hîr*), which is still standing.[2] The avenue extends northwards from this long stone about four hundred and seventy feet, and there ceases; but whether it originally ended there, or once continued to the *carn*, which is about three hundred feet farther to the northward, it is difficult now to determine. If so, it changed its direction from N. 16° 20′ E., to due north (by compass). This *carn* contains a *cist*; and from it another avenue descends the hill, in the direction of N. 5° W.; but though at a distance of nearly seven hundred feet all traces of it are lost, it evidently runs in a straight line throughout its existing course. About three hundred and fifty feet from the same *carn*, but without any connexion with it, and bearing from it about N. 2° 30′ E., is a circle, twenty-eight feet in diameter, composed of stones with intervals between them, arranged in three concentric rows round other central stones, which probably belonged to a more important kind of tomb, or sepulchral cromlech; and from this circle another avenue extends in a straight direction, N. 21° 30′ E., to the distance of nearly five hundred and seventy feet, where two large stones seem to mark its northern limit. At its southern extremity also are two long stones (now fallen), one, 7 ft. 4 in.; the other, 11 ft. 4 in. in length: which separate it from the circle. Between these two avenues is a third, which being imperfect at both ends, does not appear to be connected with any monument; but

---

[1] I regret that the present paper will not admit of my introducing plans and descriptions of this, and other monuments in the neighbourhood of Castor, Merivale, and other parts of Dartmoor.

[2] Mr. Wright, in his most useful work, *The Celt, the Roman, and the Saxon,* (p. 53), seems to think that the *maen hîr* is the solitary remaining stone of a ruined cromlech; but in some places, as in an avenue, there is no room for the other stones. In the three-pillared cromlech, too, the three stones are often so placed as not to admit of a *fourth*, which he thinks necessary to complete it.

as it may be traced for about seven hundred feet, running very nearly due south, and has, like the other two, no semblance of a serpentine form, its evidence on this point is equally satisfactory.   From its direction pointing exactly to the position of the sacred circle on Gidleigh Common, some have supposed it led to that monument; though from the great distance (between four and five thousand feet), and the fall of the ground, as well as the interference of the river and its rugged banks, this conclusion is more than doubtful.

Indeed, it is by no means necessary that avenues should be connected with sacred circles.   They are so at Stanton-Drew, at Abury, at Throwlsworthy, and in some other instances; but at Merivale bridge they lie parallel to, and at a distance of three hundred and eighty feet from, the sacred circle.   They each terminate in a large upright stone; and one has in its centre a *carn* composed of earth and upright stones in two concentric rows.   Other instances also occur of avenues terminating in *circle-carns*, as below Black Tor and in other places.   Indeed, at Black Tor one avenue ends with a *carn* surrounded by upright stones placed at intervals, with concentric rows within it; and the other in a *carn* destitute of any circle of stones around it;[1] while a similar *carn* of earth and stone stands in the same locality, unconnected with those avenues, and not to be claimed as the serpent's head by either of them.

Having made careful plans of different avenues, some of which I lay before the reader, I leave him to decide whether any resemblance to the serpent's form can there be traced; and I shall introduce another plan (see pl. 8) of the avenue at Stanton-Drew in Somersetshire, which has been brought forward in so decided a manner as an evidence of serpent-worship among the Druids; where it will be seen that the line A, B, is perfectly straight; and that the other, C, D, if it really joined the avenue A, B, did so at a direct angle instead of a curve.   What the other avenue may have been, which is supposed to have connected the large with another small circle at Stanton-Drew, I will not pretend to say; as no vestige of it remains, if it ever existed.   At Abury, again, though little remains of the avenue leading from the great sacred enclosure towards Kennet, the only portion of it, in

---

[1] The outer stones may have been removed.   The *carn* surrounded by upright stones placed at intervals, I call a *circle-carn*.

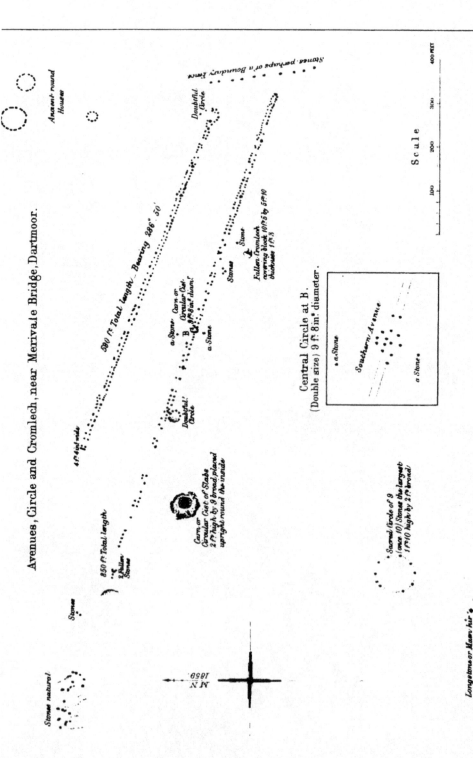

Avenues, Circle and Cromlech, near Merivale Bridge, Dartmoor.

Central Circle at B.
(Double size) 9 ft. 8 in. diameter.

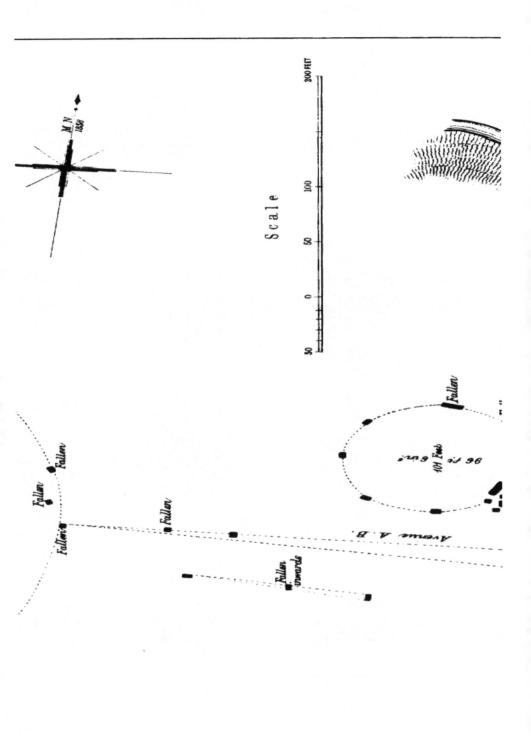

Scale

50 0 50 100 300 FEET

M N
1859

Fallen
Fallen
Fallen
Fallen
Fallen

Fallen

Avenue A. B.

Fallen
onwards

Fallen

104 ft by 96 ft

which its real course can be traced, indicates a perfectly straight direction for the distance of about two thousand and seventy feet; and if the outlying stone to the east, between the great enclosure of Abury and the remaining part of the avenue just mentioned, did really once form a portion of the same avenue, this deviation from the straight line was far more probably connected with a desire to avoid the steepness of the intervening hill (an example very wisely followed by the present road), than with any respect for the serpent, or its form. This may be seen from the plan of the temple and avenue at Abury, given by Mr. W. Long,[1] which being very accurate enables me to omit a copy of my own which I had made to accompany this paper.

Even the winding avenue of Carnac, in Brittany, so carefully delineated in Mr. Deane's *Serpent-Worship*, is very unlike the *form* of any serpent; for mere *sinuosity* does not necessarily imply the *imitation* of a serpent, as undulation does not imply *imitation* of waves.

The same plan of Abury will also fully demonstrate the fact that its *agger* and ditch are not made for defence, like those of fortified places where the fosse is on the outside of the vallum, but rather for separation and exclusiveness, serving to keep the *profanum vulgus* from the sacred area on which the priests performed the ceremonies, which the *laity* were only permitted to contemplate from without.

The same disposition occurs in a circular enclosure known as "Arthur's Table," near Penrith in Cumberland; where the central platform is surrounded by a ditch, and by an agger on the *outside* of the ditch; and a still more remarkable instance occurs at Arbe Low[2] in Derbyshire. (See pl. 9.) This has two entrances. The inner platform is 167 feet in diameter, and the ditch is 18 feet broad at the bottom. The stones are small compared to those of Abury, the largest belonging to the circle measuring 13 feet by 7; while one of the largest at Abury measures from 14 to 18 feet in length, 12 feet 3 inches in height, and 7 feet (varying to 2 feet 4 inches) in thickness : and the platform of Abury has an average diameter of 1,130 feet. The agger of Arbor Low is still about 15

---

[1] In the *Journal* of the Archæological Institute, No. 59, and in the *Wiltshire Arch. and Nat. Hist. Magazine*, vol. iv, 1858.

[2] Called Arbe or Arbor Low. *Lowe* or *low*, a Saxon word signifying a hill or mound, is the *law* of Northumberland. (See plan.)

to 18 feet high, or from 20 to 24 to the bottom of the ditch;
and the circumference at the top of it is nearly 820 feet.

It has been stated that the narrow end of the stones points
to the centre of the circle; but as Mr. Bateman[1] justly remarks,
it points as often towards the ditch; and instead of radiat-
ing to or from the centre, as if to imitate the sun's rays,
they lie in the direction in which they have fallen : for it is
evident that they originally stood upright, as in other sacred
circles; and the notion of those who doubt it is evidently
erroneous, as some are even now in an oblique position, the
upper end not having yet reached the ground; confirming
the statement of an old man, mentioned by Mr. Bateman,
who declared that he had seen them standing obliquely on
one end.   The entrances open towards the north and south,
and the two passages leading from them to the platform
measure each about 27 feet in breadth.   Here the advocates
of the ophite theory see in the wall, or dyke of stone and
earth, which runs from the western side of the agger, near
the southern entrance, the form of the wished-for serpent,
and connect it by a proper curve with a large barrow or
tumulus, called Gib Hill, standing about three hundred paces
to the westward, which is conveniently made into the rep-
tile's head; but as the dyke heedlessly continues its course
even beyond the line of the tumulus, and there terminates
in some broken stones, it plainly shews that it has no connexion whatever with the tumulus, or supposed serpent's
head,—if, indeed, the dyke is of equal antiquity with it.

At Arbe Low, as in some other sacred circles, are certain stones in the centre which have the appearance of a
sanctuary, or a cromlech,[2] as some imagine ; and one of

---

[1] Vestiges of the Antiquities of Derbyshire.

[2] Cists have been found in sacred and other circles, as well as in the walls of
forts; and also a certain kind of *cromlech* covered with two or more flat slabs.
The *cromlech proper* has only one massive cover-stone, generally *convex* on its
upper surface, or sloping at one end ; whence some suppose the name "cromlech" has been derived,—*crom* (or in Irish *cro&m*) signifying bowed or bent, and
llech, a slab. The *cromlech* has been confounded with the *subterraneous chamber*,
which frequently has a long covered passage leading into it; especially in
France and the Channel Islands. I divide the cromlechs into five: 1°, the
cromlech proper, or *three-pillared cromlech*, supported on three stones; 2°, the
four-pillared, or *cist-cromlech*, supported on four slabs enclosing a square space
like a *cist* or *chest*; 3°, the *many-pillared cromlech* with more than four slabs or
piers, as Arthur's Stone in Gower, and Trevethy and Zennor Quoits in Cornwall ; 4°, the *chamber-cromlech* with high walled sides composed of several upright slabs (the Dolmen of France), sometimes with several large cover-stones ;
and 5°, the *subterraneous chamber* (*cromlech*) above mentioned. But this last is

ch ;

nts
rks,
iat-
lys,
t is
red
tly
the
ing
an,
on
th,
rm
tes
nd
ear
nt,
or
ces
ep-
rse
tes
on-
t's

er-
f a
of

s of
abs.
its
om-
and
ber,
in
the
the
ace
s or
oru-
up-
ies ;
it is

J.   obbins.

them measures 14 feet by 8 feet 7 inches, being larger than any of those forming the circle. The agger had a counter-scarp towards the ditch, fronted with stone, and was itself composed of small stones and earth. At the south-east corner, about fifty feet from the southern entrance, is another barrow or *tumulus*, projecting from the exterior of the agger, in which a vase was found, of British time; and in the large tumulus called Gib Hill, a cist was discovered, consisting of a slab placed on upright stones; both which are in Mr. Bateman's valuable collection at Youlgrave. (See vol. xv, p. 152, pl. 12, of this *Journal*, 1859.)

The number of stones composing this circle exceeds that of many others remaining in the country, which seem very often to have had nineteen or twenty,—the former being also the number in the inner part of Stonehenge, supposed to have reference to the Metonic cycle. At Arbe Low the number of stones was probably between forty and fifty, few of which now remain in their proper position; and as the two entrances do not accord with the centre of the circle, they were more numerous on one side than on the other. The old or inner circle of Stonehenge appears to have consisted of about fifty-six or fifty-seven : the larger circle, of more massive, and well-hewn stones, which is of a later date, having apparently thirty or thirty-one; and the five contemporary trilithons, outside the nineteen enclosing the sanctuary, consisting of ten. The number nineteen is certainly worthy of notice; and I cannot read the account given by Diodorus (ii, 47) on the authority of that greatest and earliest traveller, Hecatæus, of the circular temple of the Sun, and of the belief of the Hyperboreans (or Britons), that the god visited their island every nineteen years, during which the revolutions of the stars were completed (when great ceremonies were performed by their priests and bards, from the vernal equinox to the rising of the Pleiads), without considering that this account connects the cycle of nineteen years with the number of those stones at Stonehenge. It must, however, be confessed that the number of stones in sacred circles is far from being always nineteen, or multiples of it; nor is twelve a "number more frequently found than any

not properly a cromlech. Some think *cromlech* a later name, and that it was originally merely *llech;* but *cromlech* is the name among the peasantry, who do not derive names from books. They are probably all sepulchral.

other"; nor are they confined to the range "from twelve to twenty-seven." But I will not now enter into this question; and I shall only observe that the three remaining stones, in the circular platform round Stonehenge, shew their position to have been fixed by the length of the radius of the circle, and that their original number, six, divided it into six parts.

Many other remarkable mementos of our British ancestors might be noticed; but I shall be satisfied for the present to invite attention to certain rude concentric rings carved upon stones, which, as far as my observations carry me, only occur outside the *enceinte* of ancient forts, or of sacred circles. They appear to be confined to the north of our island, and chiefly to Northumberland. I have also met with one on the long upright stone outside the sacred circle near Penrith in Cumberland, known by the name of "*Long Meg* with her Daughters"; but they are not found in Devonshire and Cornwall. They generally consist of three or four concentric rings, the outer one measuring from about seven inches to twenty-four in diameter; the innermost one, or centre, being a single dot, from which a line, more or less straight, runs directly through the successive rings, and extends beyond the circumference of the outermost one. (Pl. 10, figs. 2, 3, and 4.) The first that I observed was that on the stone called "Long Meg" near Penrith. (See pl. 10, figs. 1*a*, *b*.) This was in 1835, at which time, I believe, they had never been noticed;[1] and though I continued to search for them in many places, it was not till 1850 that, in visiting the double British camp called Old Bewick, in Northumberland, I met with other instances of these concentric rings. (Figs. 3 and 4.) I there found several, carved upon two large blocks respectively thirty and a hundred and thirteen paces beyond the outermost vallum of that camp; the positions of which, as well as the curious and unusual form of the encampment, will be seen in plate 11.

Though I had found at length, after so many fruitless inquiries, that the one in Cumberland was not a solitary instance of this device, I was unable to hear of any more, until, in 1851, the attention of the Archæological Institute, during their meeting at Newcastle, was directed to them by the discovery of others at Rowtin Lynn,[2] near Ford in

---

[1] I should not have mentioned this, had I not been told that others have laid claim to their first discovery.

[2] Rowtin Lynn is so called from a small cascade on one side of the old camp,

Pl. 10

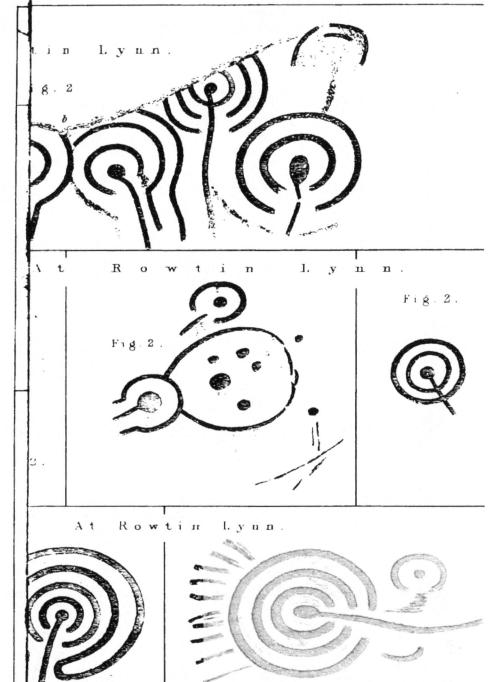

in Lynn.

g. 2

b

At Rowtin Lynn.

Fig. 2.

Fig. 2.

At Rowtin Lynn.

Fig. 2.

Fig. 2.

J.R.Jobb

Britsh Camp of Old Bewick in Northumberland in 1850.

Northumberland; and I was gratified by the sight of a copy of them. But nothing was then, nor has since that time been elicited, to shew their object or their meaning; and I am not disposed to maintain the opinion which at first suggested itself to me, that they related to the circular camps, and certain dispositions connected with them, such as are traced in times of danger by the Arabs on the sand, to guide the movements of a force coming to their rescue.

I afterwards visited these of Rowtin Lynn also, and found that the rock on which they were cut, stands, as usual, outside the camp; the agger of which is still traceable, though there are remains of other mounds beyond it, which may have surrounded the external enclosure in which it stands. The rings are very numerous, amounting to between twenty and thirty; and the rock is rather more than seventy feet in length. Some are more varied in form than those of Old Bewick, though they seem mostly to be designed on the same principle, with the exception of some small rings, and one of a semi-elliptical figure. (Pl. 10, fig. 2a.) This last measures twelve inches in breadth and ten in height. The largest of the other rings are, respectively, of 2 ft. 0½ in., 2 ft., 1 ft. 10 in., 1 ft. 8 in., and 1 ft. 3 in. diameter.

On one of the blocks at Old Bewick are about five rings; and the other bears from ten to twelve, some of which are double, like others at Rowtin Lynn (fig. 2b), as may be seen in fig. 3k and l, plate 10. Other rings are said to be found in Northumberland, at Dowth, and at Fordwestfield; and another occurs on a stone in one of the cells of a tumulus opened in 1853 at Pickaquoy, near Kirkwall, in Orkney.[1] Some at

and is supposed to signify "the roaring fall," though the smallness of its stream scarcely justifies such an appellation. Lynn, though properly the *pool* formed by falling water, seems often to occur in the sense of " cascade," as in Cora Lynn, one of the falls of the Clyde, and elsewhere; and its general use as a British word is confirmed by its occurrence in Cornwall also; where, the language being Celtic, the meaning of local names is often explained by words from the Welsh and Gaelic dialects. Of this I recently met with a singular illustration. Walking with some friends in Cornwall, in quest of British remains, we passed a valley the name of which, as I learnt from them, was *Lyn-her*, or *Lynn-hir.* " There must, then, be a cascade in the river," I observed. " Yes" was the reply. "And," I added, " it must be a *long fall:*" when the answer, " It is a succession of falls half a mile in length," shewed how appropriate was the name *Lynn-hir*, " long fall," and how the two words bore the same meaning in the northern and southern dialects. The custom of giving similarly descriptive names is common to other early languages. *Llyn* in Welsh means " lake."

[1] See the *Proceedings* of the Society of Antiquaries of Scotland, vol. ii, pt. 3, p. 61. Those in the walls of a Pict's house in Holm of Papa Westray, in Orkney, have not the same character.

New Grange, near Drogheda, in Ireland (on the upright slabs forming the entrance-passage to the sepulchral cell), representing a scroll-shaped design, may be thought to present a similar character;[1] but others, at the same place, which are convoluted, and consist of several spiral folds turning in opposite directions, differ essentially from the concentric rings here alluded to; and are more like those at Gavr Innis,[2] in the Morbihan,[3] which I shall have occasion to mention presently. Others are found on what are called the Calder-Stones, near Liverpool; but the principal one being convoluted, while two others consist each of a central and outer ring, with another device below one of them, of elongated and pointed form like an animal's nose, these may also be considered distinct from the concentric rings of Northumberland;[4] though they may assist in establishing the fact of circular devices having been common in the northern parts of the country. Those, which are of the very complicated character before mentioned, bear some analogy to the mazes or labyrinths met with in Cumberland, Yorkshire, Bedfordshire, Hampshire, Wiltshire, Dorsetshire, and other parts of England, cut in turf, and varying from about thirty to sixty, or a hundred and ten feet, in diameter; and to others formed of stone which are found in Italy.[5] But it may be doubted whether these mazes bear any relationship to the concentric rings; and if, as I before observed, these ring-devices are confined to the north, and are unknown in the south, of England, there is less reason to feel surprise or regret at this circumstance, as it appears to be consistent with the fact of stones inscribed with various emblems being common in Scotland. Indeed, one of those figured in Wilson's *Prehistoric Annals of Scotland* (p. 322), which was once the cover-stone of a cist found at Coilsfield, in Ayrshire, has concentric rings carved upon it, not very unlike some at Rowtin Lynn and Old Bewick; and that it is of British time, is proved by the pattern on the urn containing the burnt bones buried

---

[1] Others are *reported* to exist in some chambered cromlechs in Brittany.

[2] Innis, "island," is the νῆσος and *ins(ula)* of Greek and Latin. *Mor* is "*mare*."

[3] See below, p. 121; and Higgins, *Celtic Druids*, p. xxxix, pl. No. 19-20.

[4] I am indebted to the kindness of Mr. H. Duckworth for very careful rubbings and an admirable sketch of the stones; and though I cannot offer any opinion respecting them, I am enabled, by these satisfactory copies, to compare them with the other markings already alluded to.

[5] See the *Journal* of the Archæological Institute, No. 59, 1858, p. 216, "On Ancient and Mediæval Labyrinths," by Mr. Trollope.

in the tomb. There is also one given in plate 123 of Mr. Stuart's *Sculptured Stones of Scotland*, which was found at High Auchinlay by Wigton Bay, and has similar rings;[1] though the other sculptured stones contained in that interesting work are of Christian time, and have the western, or papal, cross ; with the fish, the mirror and comb, and various fanciful devices of a much later period than the pagan æra.

The introduction of emblems such as the concentric rings, in which the monuments of the north differ from those of Devonshire and Cornwall, and other southern parts of Britain, may be owing to some diversity in the habits of the two people; for though similar in their general customs, and in their erection of sacred circles, cromlechs, and other monuments, the Celtic tribes of the north and south had some peculiarities, which may be traced in their tombs and dwellings, and in certain points where a difference might reasonably be expected from their being far removed from each other; and above all, from their belonging, in most cases, not merely to different *tribes*, but to two distinct *branches* of the Celtic family. It must, however, be admitted that those who lived still further to the south had the custom of engraving stones with various devices ; and some found at Gavr Innis, in the Morbihan, are covered with most complicated patterns. (See *Journal* of the British Archæological Association, vol. iii, pp. 272, 275, 278.)

It is well known that the Celts[2] of Scotland, Ireland, and the Isle of Man, are of the older branch of that race, who immigrated to these islands from the east; and that the Welsh and Cornish, like the Armoricans, and like all the

---

[1] My friend, Mr. Rhind, whose name is so eminently connected with British antiquities, tells me of others " on a small slab dug up in the fortified enclosure on a hill-top near Dundee."

[2] Despite Cæsar's assertion that the people called by the Romans Gauls (*Galli*), were by *some of themselves* denominated Celts (*Celtæ*), there is little doubt that *Gauls*, or *Gael*, *Galli*, *Galatæ*, and Celt (Kelt, Κελται), are forms of the same word (properly *Gael*) ; and there is every reason for applying the same to the names *Welsh* and *Wales* (*Pays de Galles*), and to Corn*wall* (*Cornubia*). *W* for *gu* is a common mutation in many languages, as *guad* (Spanish), and *wad* (Arabic), a river; *gwirid*, *viridis;* *Gwent* and *Venta;* and *gwint* and *ventus* "wind," in Welsh and Latin; *gwr*, a man, and *gwir*, true (Welsh), and the Latin *vir* and *verus;* *guastare* (Italian), to waste; *guard* and *ward;* *Walter* and *Gualterus;* *Wilhelm* and *Gulielmus*,—with many more; and the Teutonic *Wael*(sch) is equally a form of *Gael*, whatever difference may have taken place in its application, as often happens with borrowed words in other languages. The name may be a Saxon corruption; but when Wälsch is said to have been *given to the Welsh* because they were "*foreigners*" this is unreasonable, for they were not more so to the Saxons than were other Britons.

Celtic population of Gaul described by Cæsar, were of the later immigration,[1] which swept from Gaul and from eastern Britain the older Celtic occupants, and confining them to the west and north, occupied the plain and most eligible parts of Britain in their stead,—a proceeding which was afterwards partially imitated by the Belgæ,[2] who some time before Cæsar's invasion of Britain made themselves masters of the "maritime part," or the districts lying south of the Thames, and of a line drawn from thence westward to the Bristol Channel ; though they did not, as some suppose, extend their dominions to the north of the Thames ; Cæsar distinctly stating that it separated the "maritime parts" from the dominions of Cassivelaunus, and from the interior.

It is also sufficiently obvious that, in the case of immigration from the east (whence the stream flowed westward over Europe), the last invading wave was that which fixed itself in the most easterly position; the older immigrants having been pressed onward by it, and forced to retire before it to the westward. This was probably the case also with the early races which peopled Italy and Greece; and we may, on the same grounds, conclude that the parents of the Latin were an earlier immigration than those of the Hellenic race. Each found an earlier people in possession of the country ; and the Latin and Greek races, in like manner, dispossessed older occupants of the soil when they first arrived in Italy and Greece. Among these, their immediate predecessors, were the Celts ; who were driven westward by them, as by the Teutonic race in the north; and Celtic names, indicating the nature of the

---

[1] This was comprised of different tribes whose dialects varied slightly, but not to the same extent as those of the two main and distinct branches of the Celtic race ; and the division of each branch into three or more tribes is confirmed by tradition (as by the Welsh *Triads*), by their various names (as Cymry and others), and by difference of dialect. Some of these Triads may be of late date ; but Sir Samuel Meyrick has shown that one is given by P. Mela (iii, 2), and another by Diogenes Laertius. (See *Journal* of the Brit. Arch. Assoc., 1846, p. 103 ; see also Camden, p. xxxvii.)

[2] If the Belgæ had held central as well as southern Britain, Winchester would scarcely have been called Venta *Belgarum*, and Wells, *Fontes Belgarum*, by way of distinction. Nor would Cæsar have said " Britanniæ pars interior ab iis incolitur quos natos in insula ipsa memoria proditum dicunt ; maritima pars ab iis qui prædæ ac belli inferendi causa ex Belgis transierant" (*Bell. Gall.*, v. 12) ; and the Wansdyke is evidently the agger and fosse made by the Belgæ against the inland Britons, being intended against an enemy from the north, and being backed by forts behind it to the south. A curious custom still prevails there when a man is about to marry a wife beyond the dyke ; in accordance with which the neighbours pretend to drive him back across the dyke, as if from a hostile land.

former occupants of the country, may still be traced there. Thus the rock of Scylla bears the Celtic appellation, *scill*, a rock (found also in our Scilly Isles); and Quintilian (*Inst. Orat.*, i, 5) thinks that, of Latin words derived from a foreign source, those from the Gaulish or Celtic are the most numerous ("Plurima Gallica valuerunt.") It is not, therefore, surprising that many of the so-called aboriginal languages of Italy should have an affinity to Celtic; and its relationship to Etruscan may readily be explained by an intermixture of the Celtic element. But it is an error to suppose Latin to be a mere *compound* of other languages of Italy, formed by the accidental union of several people in Rome. It was an original tongue, like Greek or any other of the Indo-European family; and in its adoption of some foreign words, it only followed the example of other languages.

Though, in so limited a space, it is not possible to enter fully into this question, I cannot refrain from mentioning certain variations in these cognate languages, the Latin and the Greek, the Irish and the Welsh, which, like the Sanscrit and the Zend, follow fixed laws; and in which a striking analogy is observable in the use of the *s* in one case, and of the *h* in the other. Thus in words common to Latin and Greek, those which in Latin *begin* with *s*, in Greek begin with н: as, for instance, the Latin *sol* (sun) is ἥλιος (*helios*) in Greek; *sal* (salt) is ἅλς[1] (*hals*); *sex* is ἕξ (*hex*); *semi* is ἥμι (*hemi*); *septem* is ἑπτα (*hepta*); *salix* (willow) is ἑλικη (*heliké*); and the same interchange of *s* and *h* is found in Erse (as well as in Gaelic) and Welsh: the sun, in Erse or Irish, *sam*, or *sail* (*sajl*), "beam," being in Welsh, *haul* (*hàil*); the Erse *sajle*, Gaelic *saill* (salt), being in Welsh *halen* (the *halan* of Cornish); and the willow in Erse, *sajleog* (Gaelic, *seileach*), being in Welsh *helyg*, as in Cornish, etc. Analogous to this is the change in Sanscrit and Zend,

---

[1] We are always taught that in Greek minuscules the *alpha* should be written from right to left (ɑ); and a distinguished archæologist has actually been accused of ignorance of Greek because he writes that letter like our English *a*; but all ancient inscriptions on papyri, pottery, etc., shew that it was written by the Greeks like our English *a*, from left to right (a). It is high time that our custom so at variance with Greek usage, and the offspring of scholastic pedantry, should be abandoned. We may hope also that θεος will no longer be derived from θεω, τιθημι (to place), or from θεω (to run); and that *deus* of a cognate language, and an older form of the word (like the Sanscrit *dev, divas*), will cease to be derived from θεος. It might be pardonable in the Greeks and other tyros in etymology to fancy such derivations; but not so to adopt them in the present day.

the Sanscrit *sahasra* (thousand) being in Zend *hazanra*; the Sanscrit *swar*, in Zend *hvare* (heaven or sun); and the Sanscrit *soma* (an intoxicating beverage) in Zend *homa*.

Nations have at all times prided themselves on their antiquity. Some have assumed it on very slender grounds; others have been more open to inquiry, though their method of conducting it was as ridiculous as their conclusion. The Egyptians are reported to have sought for the oldest language by observing what children would say if debarred from hearing any spoken words; and a similar experiment was tried in Scotland by order of James IV; but by some unaccountable accident, the Egyptian children used an Egyptian word, which strangely enough led to the conclusion that Phrygian was the oldest language; while the Scotch children are reported to have spoken (instinctively) pure Hebrew! In the present day, though autochthonous claims are no longer set up, many pride themselves on their excessive antiquity; and it has been considered by the Welsh almost an affair of national honour to maintain it, and to rank themselves as the oldest of the very ancient Celtic family. But a people of high spirit should rather be satisfied with the greater honour of having belonged to the victorious race which dispossessed the older occupants of a country, and established itself in their stead; and the fact of the greater portion of the inhabitants of Britain, south of Scotland (settled there long before the period of Cæsar's invasion), having belonged to the later Celtic immigration, is proved by the dialect they used, and by that almost invariable law which, as already stated, causes the later settlers to occupy the most fertile, and to confine those they displace to the less desirable and more mountainous regions. Of that later race were the Britons, of whom the Welsh formed a part; and if, in after times, a foreign conquest of Britain has obliged them in turn to remain satisfied with their mountain land, this is a question irrespective of their original occupancy of the country, and of the inroads of their ancestors on the earlier Celtic race in olden times.

This question is also one of too great extent to be fully discussed in a limited space; but I may state, in a few words,—1°, that it is evident *the whole* island of Britain was once possessed by those earlier Celtic tribes whose descendants still occupy Scotland and Ireland as well as the Isle of

Man, together with a few other settlers. 2°, that already, in the time of Cæsar, the greater part of Britain to the south of Scotland had long been possessed by other tribes of the later Celtic stock, who, as before observed, had dispossessed the earlier cognate race; and 3°, that before the same period, Gaul had been long inhabited by some of the same later Celtic tribes. Of this relationship, between the Gauls and Britons of that period, there is sufficient evidence; not merely from the former, as Cæsar tells us,[1] having derived the Druidical rites from Britain, and from the fact of those who, in his time, wished to become acquainted with them, coming over to this island in order to complete their religious education at the fountain head of Druidism; but from the similarity of the two dialects. And as the Armorican, to this day, resembles the Cornish and the Welsh (the former the remnant of the Gaulish, and the latter two of the British tongue), so also the names of places in the two countries, Gaul and Britain, mentioned by the Romans, fully bear out the identity of their dialects;[2] for both in Gaul and Britain the word *dwr, dûr,* or *dour*[3] (water), which belongs more especially to the later Celtic dialect, is applied to rivers in preference to *usk* or *uisg*[4] (water) which occurs rarely in Gaul, and which is the word so long employed for water (instead of *dour*), in Scotland and Ireland, where it is found in *whisky* and *usquebaugh* (strong water).[5] Even in the north of

[1] He says the Druidical "disciplina in Britannia referta, et inde in Galliam translata esse existimatur, et nunc qui diligentius eam rem cognoscere volunt plerumque illo discendi causa profiscuntur."

[2] Armorica, afterwards called Brittany, derives its name (as did the Morini of the present department of Calais) from *môr* (sea), being on the sea shore. It was to Gaul what Wales was to Britain, the westernmost corner where the Celtic race found a refuge when the eastern parts were overrun by later invaders. Armorica bears no relationship to Aquitania.

[3] The word, in another cognate language, is ὕδωρ, as *Avon* is *amnis* in Latin. *Dwr* is still the usual Welsh word "water," as *Dwr twym* "warm water;" *cf* Sanscrit, *uda*, "water;" the Latin *udus*, "moist;" and the Sclavonic *voda*, water.

[4] It may, perhaps, be traced in the Sequana; in Uxellodunum on the Duranus or Dordogne; in the Axona; in two towns called Axuenna; in Axcisum on the Lot; and in Aix; but these are rare instances, and may be, like Usk, Esk, Exe, and others in Britain, the names given by the *older* Celtic inhabitants.

[5] *Wysg* is not used in Welsh for "water," nor for "river," though in that dialect *wysg* does signify a current, or a stream. *Wys*, or *Ys*, means "flowing," or a "current," as in *Isère*. *Wy* (*wee*) is used for "running water," and is applied to rivers, as the *Wye, Tâwë, Tâwy*, etc.; *Ta*, as in *Tamar, Tay*, etc., signifying "wide spread." *Ai* also is "water," as *Menai* (straight), is "narrow water," and not from *Mona I.*

England, as well as in Scotland and Ireland, *dour* is rarely met with in the ancient or modern names of rivers; and though traced in some, as Derwent[1] (*dur gwent*) and a few more, and in the ancient Duris (Ptolemy's Dour), near Tralee in Ireland, a preference seems to be given to the oldest name, *uisg*. And if some streams in Wales, and at the south-west extremity of England, have retained this name, as in *Usk*; and if it may be traced in *Exe*[2] and some others, both in central and southern England, this is at once explained by the fact of the older appellation having been given to them in the time of the earlier, and retained by the later,[3] Celtic inhabitants. This I believe to have been the case also with the name of the Severn, which, in accordance with the rule in the Welsh dialect, already noticed, is called *Hafren* (*Havren*); and the Roman Sabrina was evidently borrowed from the *earlier* name of the river, which until that time had been retained, as that of *Usk* still is for one river by the Welsh. But neither *usk* nor *dour* appear to have been used in the sense of " river."[4] They both signified " water." It is also certain that though the word *usk* may exist in the later dialect, it occurs much more rarely than *dour* or *dur* in the names of rivers, and towns[5] on their banks, mentioned by the Romans, both in Britain and Gaul; and some instances of the frequent occurrence of *dur* may be seen from the following lists :

---

[1] In Cumberland it is easily accounted for.

[2] Exeter was Isca Damnoniorum; and in Damnonii we trace the origin of Devon, the Welsh Dyfnant,—*v, f, b,* and *m,* being transmutable letters. The older race remained most probably in Wales and Devonshire longer than in central Britain.

[3] In the same manner, old British names of rivers and mountains were retained by the Saxons. They change less than the names of towns.

[4] The term " water" for a river, is older than the term " river;" and *wysg,* or *usk,* was used in the former sense, not as " stream." In Aix it evidently had the sense of " water." Thus, too, *avon,* or *afon,* which in Welsh is " river," really means " flowing." But it was not a common term, as it seldom appears in Roman names; and if *aufona,* or *avona,* is an exception, it is of rare occurrence. And we see how much more usual was *dur* at that time both in Britain and in Gaul. Nor is *avon* common in Scotland. Cf. *penj-ab,* " five waters," for " five *rivers.*" The next term is " the river," and lastly a *name* for it, as " the Rhone" and others; though most of these are only taken from the idea of " flowing," or from some old word meaning water or stream. Cf. βεω, " to flow, *rièka* (Slav.), " river," *Rhean* (Welsh) a " rill," etc. Some were called from their supposed appearance, as Dee (*Dhu,* " black"); Nile (*Nil,* " blue"), a colour given to the god Nilus. Could the Latin *aqua* have been originally *asqua?*

[5] Which are *later* names than those of rivers.

IN GAUL.	IN BRITAIN.
Antissiodurum. *Auxerre.*	Derventio. *Derby* and *Derwent,*
Atur, the *Adour.*	i.e., *Dur-gwent.*
Augustodurum, in the present Nor-	Dorvatium, the *Dart.*
mandy.	Durnovaria. *Dorchester.*
Brivodurum. *Briare.*	Durobrion. *Breg Casterton.*
Divodurum. *Metz.*	Durobrium. *Hertford.*
Divodurus, to the west of Paris.	Durobriva. *Castor.*[2]
Duranium, the *Dordogne.*	Durobriva. *Rochester.*
Durocasses. *Dreux.*	Durocobriva. *Stony-Stratford.*
Druentia, the *Durance.*	Durocornovium. *Cirencester.*
[Durias, the *Dora* at Susa.[1]]	Durolenum. *Lenham.*
Durocatalaunum. *Châlons* sur Marne	Durolipons. *Cambridge* or *God-*
Durocortorum (afterwards called	*manchester.*
Remi). *Rheims.*	Durolitum. *Leyton.*
[Ganodurum on the Rhine, near the	Durovernum. *Canterbury,* i. e.,
West end of Lake Constance.]	*Dur-gwern,* "water" or "river
[Octodurum. *Martigny.*]	of the alder."
[Salodurum. *Soleure.*]	The modern *Adur* at Shoreham
[Vitodurum. *Winterthur.*]	displays the same name.

Many other names of towns, of individuals, and of tribes, might also be mentioned in Gaul and Britain to prove the similarity of the two dialects; but my space forbids my noticing these and other facts in support of this opinion; and I also refrain from attempting to trace the migrations of the two main Celtic races which first peopled Gaul[3] and this island, the earlier of which was supplanted, as I have before stated, in Gaul and eastern Britain by the later branch found by the Romans, together with the Belgæ, in these countries. But I cannot conclude without observing that the occupation of Wales by foreign settlers, after the departure of the Romans, is neither probable, nor necessary in order to account for the destruction of Roman towns in that part of Britain; and though I give my opinion with great deference when it differs from that of so distinguished an archæologist as Mr. Wright, I must be permitted to doubt that the Armoricans from Gaul *conquered* and *peopled* Wales

---

[1] In Portugal and Spain also, as the Durius, now Douro, and in the extreme south, at Granada, etc. Can *Atûr,* or *Adûr,* an ancient name of the Nile, be related to *Dur?*

[2] *Dubris, Dover,* is from *dau brê* (two hills).

[3] Ortholithic remains are found in Savoy. At Regnier I have seen a three-pillared cromlech, called Pierre des Fées; and others are found in Germany, North Friesland, and Norway. They are also met with in very different parts of the world, in Persia and India, in Malabar, Sweden, Malta, Syria, and Northern Africa, etc. I may also notice the frequent occurrence of names in Savoy which are still common in Wales, as *nant* (a brook), *e.g.,* Nant d'Arpenes, Nant de Bor-geat, etc.

"in the fifth century," or that there is any necessity for attributing the destruction of the Roman towns there to a *supposed* event which is at variance with the traditions and history of the country. Indeed, there seems to be no more reason for considering the Welsh a colony from Armorica, or the Armoricans a colony from Wales, than for supposing, in the case of any other two countries where the same language is spoken, that one was necessarily peopled from the other, rather than offsets from the same stock; and the occasional passage of any number of settlers from one to the other does not imply colonization.

Relations of amity and frequent intercourse had long before been established between Wales and Armorica. Britons from Wales had migrated to it A.D. 383; and about 456, Samson, one of the Welsh priests who passed over to Gaul, became bishop of Dôl. It was also to that country that many fled from Wales when alarmed by the Saxon invasion; and there seems reason to believe that the Armoricans, who retained their Druidical rites as late as 458 A.D., were converted to Christianity through this intercourse with, and this influx of, the Christian Britons. And if Armorica, in after times, received the name of Brittany, it is more reasonable to conclude (even if no other evidence were present to assist us) that a *greater* influx of settlers had taken place from Britain to Armorica, than from the latter to any part of Britain.

It cannot certainly be supposed that the Britons in Wales had lost their language, and received the present one, *after* the Romans had left Britain, from Armorica. Still less could they have derived it from Scotland,[1] as some have imagined, the dialects of Wales and Scotland being a *different branch* of the Celtic; and though Wales was occupied by the Romans, the language and race were not destroyed. Even if the

---

[1] This modern name of the ancient Caledonia is derived from the Scoti, a Celtic tribe which passed over from Ireland to Cantyre (*ceantir*, "headland"), A.D. 503. They are supposed to be Dalriads who had originally migrated from Scotland to Ireland; and as the Hellenes of Phthiotis gave their name to all Greece, so the Scoti gave theirs to all Scotland. But the name Scoti, or Scotch, which is that of a small fraction of the Celtic population of the country, when applied to the Lowland Scotch is really a misnomer, as they are not Celts, but descendants of the Anglo-Saxon invaders who confined the Celtic race to the west of a curved line extending from Nairn to the North Esk and Dunkeld, and thence to Dumbarton, which may be readily seen in the map of Browne's *History of the Highlands*. The Highlanders are Celts, but the Lowlanders are of the Anglo-Saxon race, as are the Anglo-Saxon English.

peasants of a conquered country become serfs, still they remain, and retain their language. Nor are the women destroyed; the invaders intermarry with them: so that half the community preserves the old language and customs, and their influence on the children has its effect. The natives also exceed in numbers the powerful minority by whom they have been conquered; and the invading race fails to constitute the *population* of a country. In this a conquest differs from an immigration, where a whole tribe dispossesses, and sometimes sweeps off, the entire native race. Nor is the character of the original race changed by an infusion of foreign blood; and it is curious to observe in how many particulars the character of the Gauls, given by some ancient writers, resembles that of their successors at the present day. This, too, is remarkable, that the mixture of races has an effect upon the face long after all foreign blood has been absorbed; and in like manner the peculiar features of some remote ancestor occasionally reappear in a late descendant, and are sometimes confined to this single repetition.

It would require more than an invasion, or a conquest, by a body of Armoricans, to change the language of a country like Wales, and impose their own; and experience abundantly proves that even the *occupation* of a country by a foreign race frequently fails to have this effect. On the contrary, conquerors adopt the language of the country they invade, whenever they do not establish themselves there in preponderating numbers; and thus the Normans abandoned their own, and that, too, at a time when the language of France was in embryo, and in a state of formation. French was only forming in the first half of the 900 A.D., and the Normans settled in Neustria in 911. Forty years after this, "the Danish language struggled for existence"; and according to Palgrave, it was in Normandy that the *langue d'oïl* acquired its greatest polish.

The English, again (whom history proves to have had a power in Wales, to which the Armoricans have no claim either from history, or any authorised conjecture) never changed the language, which to this day continues to be spoken, and is in many parts the only one known to the Welsh, notwithstanding the many advantages which might be derived from a knowledge of English; and if a language continues unchanged under such circumstances, it is not easy to credit its entire displacement by the irruption, or the temporary settlement, of any body of Armoricans.

The language of Wales, as of Cornwall, was the same, or a dialect of the same, which was spoken in the south of Britain by the Celtic tribes who constituted that branch of the Celtic population of the country; which is proved by the names of places and persons at the period of the Roman conquest, as I have already stated; and the frequent occurrence of the marked word *went* or *gwent*, as Venta Silurum (Caerwent), Venta Belgarum (Winchester or Caerwent), Venta Icenorum (Norwich or Caistor), Derventio (Derby and Derwent), and others, and that of *gwin* or *vin*, in the names of places and individuals, shew the common use of words still well known in Welsh,—the modern remnant and representative of the Celtic language of the southern portion of our island.[1] As the *Cymry*, or Welsh, continue still to be un-Anglicized, so the same people of old, as well as those of *Cumberland* and Cornwall, continued to be un-Saxonized Britons; and two of them have retained their peculiar appellation of "the conlinguar," or compatriot race, indicated by the word *Cymbro* or *Cymro*, which is still traced in the modern names *Cymro*, *Cymru*, and *Cumberland*.

If the Armoricans had gone over to Wales at the time of the Saxon invasion of Britain, their visit could only have had for its object the assistance and support of their kinsmen, and they would have had no reason for destroying the Roman towns. Such a visit will not, therefore, account for their destruction; and it is far more reasonable to suppose that when the Romans left those parts of Wales, which they occupied chiefly for mining purposes, the towns being deserted fell into decay; the people of the country, who then lived for the most part as an agricultural and shepherd race, not caring to inhabit them.[2]

The occupation of a country, of sufficient duration to change its language, would rather argue the possession than the destruction of the towns, which would have also served as strongholds; and their entire demolition would not only

---

[1] Aristotle (*De Mundo*, c. 3) mentions the "Bretanic Isles" under the names of "Albion" and "Ierné" (Erin), shewing that Albion is not from the Latin *albus* and the whiteness of its cliffs. Alban, applied to Scotland, signifies the "*highest*" part.

[2] They were very different in *olden* times, when they had their strongholds, as at Carn-Goch and other fortified places.

have been an Herculean task, but a neglect of the very advantages they offered to a people holding military possession of a country; for they were towns, not cities; and if these towns were fortified by walls, they would have been better adapted than mere entrenched camps for its permanent occupation.   Again, if the towns were suddenly and completely destroyed, this is more likely to have been the work of the Welsh, to prevent their serving as strongholds for the Saxons; from whom they could protect themselves more effectually in their hilly retreats than in towns, which they had not the means of defending against such powerful adversaries.

By doing this they freed themselves from any formidable aggression of the Saxons; and the fact of these invaders not having occupied the country is in accordance with my view of the state of Wales at that period. It is, however, far from certain that all those towns, as towns, were strongly walled; and judging from the unfortified condition of some of them,[1] even in the most secluded mining districts, we may conclude that they were not generally furnished with defences of the same strength and durability as those in other parts of Britain. Moreover, where the remains of towns fortified with strong walls, like Caerleon and Caerwent, still exist, it is evident that even these were not occupied by the Britons on the retirement of the Romans; and this convinces me that the Welsh, feeling more secure in the natural fastnesses of their hilly country, did not require artificial defences, to which they had been unaccustomed; and that the circumstance of other Roman towns being no longer traceable may be attributed to the effects of time, rather than to their forcible demolition by a foreign invader.

In olden days, before the Romans had broken down the martial spirit of the old Britons of Wales, they might have willingly occupied any towns whose sites were calculated for defence; and we know, from the extensive remains of the walled and entrenched camps they once possessed, that the habits of themselves and their neighbours required those strongholds. But long before the Roman occupation had ceased, they had abandoned warlike pursuits; and the nature of their country enabled them to dispense with walled towns, persuaded, as they doubtless were, that greater security was

[1] " Tre-coch" (the red town,—doubtless from the bricks of the ruins), at the gold mines of the Ogófau, in Carmarthenshire, had evidently no wall.

afforded them in their mountain districts which offered no attractions to an invader.

In this they differed from the generality of the eastern Britons of England, to whom towns had become a necessity, and who could obtain no other refuge, except in a few distant hilly regions; and this sufficiently explains the occupation of the Roman towns by the eastern Britons, and the disregard of them by the Britons of Wales. The subsequent settlements in the *neighbourhood* of the old sites, as at Caerleon and other places, is a different question, and quite irrespective of any *occupation* of the Roman towns; and we know that these were not at once transformed into Welsh towns, which are of a later date.

A general migration of the eastern Britons did not certainly take place into Wales with a view of escaping from the Saxon invasion, which in reality was not a sudden one; nor was this influx of fugitives required in order to people the country. It was not till then uninhabited; and though many who lived on the borders did very wisely avail themselves of the refuge offered by that hilly and secluded country, they did not constitute the population of Wales. But to deny that any fled thither, is to suppose them incapable of following the ordinary dictates of self-preservation. If, however, it is unnecessary to introduce refugees from eastern Britain, in Saxon times, to account for the population and language of Wales, it is still more unnecessary to introduce them from Armorica, or any other country.

ON CÆSAR'S PASSAGE OF THE THAMES,

AND THE DIRECTION AND EXTENT OF HIS SUBSEQUENT ROUTE THROUGH BRITAIN.

BY THE REV. H. JENKINS, B.D., F.G.S.

——— "A kind of conquest
Cæsar made here; but made not here his brag
Of 'came' and 'saw' and 'overcame': with shame
(The first that ever touch'd him) he was carried
From off our coast, twice beaten."
Cymbeline, ACT III, Sc. 1.

CONCERNING the landing-place of Julius Cæsar in his two invasions of Britain, much has been written, and many theories have been advanced. But whilst our scholars[1] and men of science have vied with each other in their efforts to determine the spot where Cæsar first moored his fleet, little attention, comparatively speaking, has been paid to his military movements inland; and the two main achievements of his second campaign, his passage of the Thames, and the direction of his march on the northern side of the river, have not been investigated with the care which their importance deserves. On these points, indeed, our information must be drawn from Cæsar's own narrative; and every minute circumstance which he mentions should be brought, as far as it is possible, to bear on the inquiry. Here our English writers, for the most part, have failed. In their description of the second campaign,[2] the great majority of them have pursued a far easier but most unsatisfactory plan. Instead of keeping wholly to Cæsar's *Commentary*, and working out from it their own details, they have made Camden, as it were, their polar star; and, under his guidance and dictation, they have crossed the Thames at the Coway Stakes,[3] and proceeded

---

[1] An interesting little work on the two campaigns of Cæsar has lately been published by Longman & Co. Its author, Mr. T. Lewin, with great research and ability, claims for Boulogne and Lymne the honour of being the ports on each side of the Channel, at which Cæsar embarked and landed his army.

[2] Vide *Cæsarem De Bello Gallico*, lib. v, cap. xviii–xxiii.

[3] Some of our archæologists have fixed on other parts of the Thames for the supposed passage of Cæsar; but their number is small in comparison with the multitude who have adhered to Camden's opinion. One of them, Mr. Daines Barrington, is certain that Cæsar never passed the Thames at all, but only the Medway, which Cæsar called by mistake the Thames (see Lewin, p. 102.)

onward from thence to Verulam. In the present paper it is intended to shew that neither of these statements corresponds with Cæsar's account, and to submit to the judgment of the reader a more conformable interpretation.

Cæsar thus describes the ford of the Thames:[1] "*Tamesis uno omnino loco pedibus, atq. hoc ægre transiri potest......* *Ripa autem erat acutis sudibus præfixis munita, ejusdemq. generis sub aquâ defixæ sudes flumine tegebantur.*" [The Thames could only be passed in one place on foot, and that with difficulty......The bank was planted with sharp stakes, and others of the same kind, fixed under the water, were concealed by the stream.] We cannot doubt but that these obstacles to the free use of the river would at once have been removed by the victorious Romans for their own convenience; or, if they had been suffered to remain, that in process of time they would either have perished through age, or have been swept away by the stream. Yet Bede,[2] who lived more than seven centuries after Cæsar, tells us that "the remains of the stakes were to be seen in his day, each apparently about the thickness of a man's thigh; and, being cased with lead, were fixed immovably in the bottom of the river." He, however, does not mention the locality; but Camden, by identifying them with the Coway stakes at Shepperton, affords us the means of proving they could not be those that had been laid down for the hinderance of Cæsar. The latter were fixed both on the bank and in the bed of the river, and were concealed beneath the water. In order to obstruct and overspread the whole ford, they must have been very numerous, and have been placed obliquely, so that their sloping points might molest and injure the advancing foe; and being designed only for a temporary purpose, would not need an additional weight of lead to strengthen them in their position: whereas the Coway stakes were not fixed in the bank, neither were they sloping or pointed, but broad at top, and plain to view, and placed upright in the stream. They were also few, consisting merely of two rows; and their casements of lead seemed to adapt them for permanent guide-posts, or aids, rather than for obstructions to the ford. May they not have been the supports of a wooden bridge, or served to form a weir? As

---

[1] De Bello Gallico, lib. v, c. 18.
[2] See Bede's *History*, chap. ii.

philologists derive the word *Coway* from the Saxon *cyning-way* (*i.e.*, the king's way), it probably had been a ford for ages; but assuredly it is not the one which Cæsar mentions, because he crossed the Thames where it first became ford-able, and there are several fords lower down than Shepper-ton or Chertsey, where the Coway stakes once stood. Amongst others, there is one at Old Brentford,[1] which we are certain was used as early as the Saxon days; for according to the *Saxon Chronicle*, king Edward passed it twice with his army in the year 1016.

Here, on many accounts, I am inclined to place the passage of Cæsar. Its British name, Brentford (*i.e.*, Brenin-ford, the king's road or way), favours this supposition; for the name, even should it not apply personally to Cæsar, establishes the fact that this part of the Thames was known to, and used by, the Britons as a ford. The height of the banks also at this place is an important consideration, since it allowed the Britons more space to fortify them with stakes, and at the same time afforded the Romans a fairer oppor-tunity of plying their engines over the heads of their own men as they entered the river, and of striking the enemy posted on the topmost verge of the opposite side. Thus, whilst the cavalry,[2] sent in advance to cross higher up the stream, were threatening the flank, the main body of the legions pressing forward in front, and sheltered, as it were, by the military engines, made good the passage of the river.

A brief review of some of the principal events which had just occurred, will best explain the direction of Cæsar's sub-sequent route on the farther or northern side of the Thames, and his reason for taking it. Since Cæsar's departure from Britain in the preceding year, Imanuentius, king of the Tri-nobantes (a powerful tribe inhabiting the district now called Essex), had been murdered, and the sovereignty seized by Cassivellaunus, who ruled over the Cassii, and whom the

---

[1] At Old Brentford the Thames was anciently forded with great ease; and was so still in bishop Gibson's time, there being then, at low ebb, not above three feet of water. (See Gibson's *Camden's Britannia*, p. 327.)

[2] "*Præmisso equitatu*" are Cæsar's words. By them I understand that the cavalry were sent in advance to attempt a passage higher up the stream, at Kingston, Walton, or elsewhere, in order to distract the enemy's attention and draw off a part of his forces, whilst the infantry pressed forward to the ford directly in their front. The cavalry and infantry did not cross the stream together, and in the same place. Such a plan would have caused inextricable confusion.

confederate tribes of the Britons had chosen to be their commander-in-chief. Mandubratius, son of the murdered monarch, fearful for his life, fled for safety into Gaul to Cæsar, and had returned with him to Britain, and was then in the Roman camp. The Trinobantes, impatient of their wrongs, sent ambassadors to Cæsar, and proffered their submission to him, and engaged to give hostages and supply his army with corn, provided that he would restore to them Mandubratius, the son of their late king, and promise to protect him from the violence of Cassivellaunus, and also to secure their own people from all injury and insult on the part of the Roman soldiers. Cæsar at once assented; and in order to fulfil the terms agreed on (which, he informs us, he afterwards did), his first and chief object, after he had crossed the Thames, must have been to lead his army into Essex, and form a junction with the Trinobantes. In anticipation of this movement, the British general commanded the region which he knew the Romans were about to traverse, to be cleared of its population,[1] and the flocks[2] to be driven from the fields and farms into the woods. Through the defection of some of the tribes, he was sensible of his inability to contend any more openly with the whole force of the Romans; nevertheless he abated nothing of his hostility towards them, and continued to prosecute the war with the same vigour and daring under a new system of operations. Having dismissed the main bulk of his forces, he retired with a choice reserve of four thousand charioteers into the deep woods. From thence he watched the march of the Roman legions, and eagerly availed himself of every opportunity that offered to sally forth and cut off their straggling parties and foragers. These woods were so extensive that Cassivellaunus, though occasionally changing his position, continued in them during

---

[1] "*Iis regionibus, quibus nos iter facturos cognoverat pecora atq. homines ex agris in sylvas compellebat.*"

[2] The word here translated flocks, is *pecora.* When Cæsar previously mentions the produce of Britain, he writes "*pecorum magnus numerus.*" All our historians have rendered these words by *cattle,* which is not their meaning, for in the plural number they apply only to sheep and goats. When speaking afterwards of the *oppidum,* or pah, of Cassivellaunus, he uses the word *pecoris* in the singular number,—"*magnus ibi pecoris* numerus." Our old writers also render this word by *cattle;* whereas, in the singular number, it means sheep only. From Cæsar's narrative we collect that sheep, in those days, were as much the staple produce of Britain as they were in after times, when a woolsack was made the seat of the lord high chancellor of England. Even the celebrated Merino sheep of Spain were imported from Britain.

the rest of the campaign; and so intricate were they, and difficult of access, that Cæsar could neither force his way into them after repeated attempts, nor even discover where the British chief had ensconced himself, until he was betrayed by his own countrymen. They could be no other than what was afterwards called the forest of Essex, which extended into Hertfordshire and Middlesex, and of which Epping forest, Hainault forest, North Weald and South Weald,[1] are the scant and scattered relics.

In the depth of these woods, and at a due distance from the Roman camp, Cassivellaunus chose and fortified a stronghold, or trysting-place, for his select warriors. Cæsar gives it the name of *oppidum*, and his description[2] exactly tallies with the *pah* of a New Zealander.[3] The British *oppidum*, or *pah*, could of course be relinquished, and a new position be taken up, according to the relative change and site of the Roman encampment. But as the Britons moved within a much narrower compass than the Romans, fewer changes would be required for them. Now, within the recesses of the old forest of Essex may still be seen two British entrenchments which bear the character of *oppida*, and may possibly have been thrown up at the time of Cæsar's invasion. The first of these, commonly called Ambresbury Banks, is situate on the south-east side of Copped Hall park, in the parish of Epping, and was thus noticed in the last century by Mr. Letheuillier:[4] "This entrenchment is now entirely overgrown with old oaks and hornbeams. It was formerly in the very heart of the forest, and no road near it till the present road to Epping was made, almost in the memory of man......It is of an irregular figure, rather longest from east to west, and on a gentle declivity to the south-east. It contains nearly twelve acres, and is surrounded by a ditch and a high bank much worn down by time, though where there are angles they are very bold and high. There are no regular openings like gateways or entrances. As I can find no

---

[1] *Weald* signifies a wood or forest.   [2] Lib. v, c. 9, and lib. v, c. 21.
[3] The New Zealanders displayed their genius for war in building, attacking, and defending stockades, which they call *pas* or *pahs*. Such strongholds stood on headlands jutting into the sea, on mountains, and in forests. Their shape and size depended much on the nature of the ground and the strength of the tribe. Previously to a siege, the women and children were sent away to places of safety. (See Dr. Thomson's *Story of New Zealand*, vol. i, p. 131.)
[4] Mr. Letheuillier. See Wright's *Essex*, vol. ii, p. 467.

reason to attribute this entrenchment either to the Romans, Saxons, or Danes, I cannot help concluding it to have been a *British oppidum;* and perhaps it has some relation to other remains of that people, which are discoverable in the forest of Essex." Mr. Letheuillier therefore held the same opinion as myself with respect to the origin of Ambresbury Banks. I conjecture it to have been the first *pah* or *oppidum* raised by Cassivellaunus as soon as the Romans had crossed the Thames and were proceeding onwards. The second (of which I shall presently speak more in detail) is situate in a different part of the forest, and was probably fixed on and fortified after the Romans had arrived amongst the Trinobantes.

We will now return to Brentford. Whether Cæsar passed the river at this place, or above it, it matters not as to his future line of march. In either case he had, during the whole of his subsequent route, the impenetrable barrier of the forest on his left, and on his right the full enjoyment of a free communication with the Thames. London as yet was not.[1] The space over which our metropolis now stretches its giant bulk, was then studded with farms and homesteads, though denuded for a time of its flocks and its population. These, and all the country on the outside of the forest, the Romans laid waste with fire and sword. Two rivers, however, the Lea and the Roden, fordable only in particular places, were still to be passed; and the laborious task of raising a firm road through the low intervening meadows was still to be accomplished before Cæsar could form a junction with his allies. He must have crossed the Roden at or near the modern bridge of Ilford, because above it the thick woods, defended by the Britons, debarred his advance, and below it the marshes were impassable. Previous to Cæsar's arrival, miry trackways, difficult and dangerous, and known only to the natives, intersected the low grounds adjoining the Lea and the Roden. But rather more than a century later, a grand military road connecting London,

---

[1] When Aulus Plautius, in the winter of A.D. 43, quartered his army on the southern bank of the Thames, at Keston (*i.e.*, Cæsar's town), London had no existence; but at the great British insurrection under Boadicea, A.D. 61, it had become a great town for shipping, an emporium of commerce,—*Long-din* (the town of ships). Within these seventeen years, therefore (between 44 and 61), it had risen, like one of our mercantile towns in Australia, from nothing, to become a town celebrated for its wealth and its commerce.

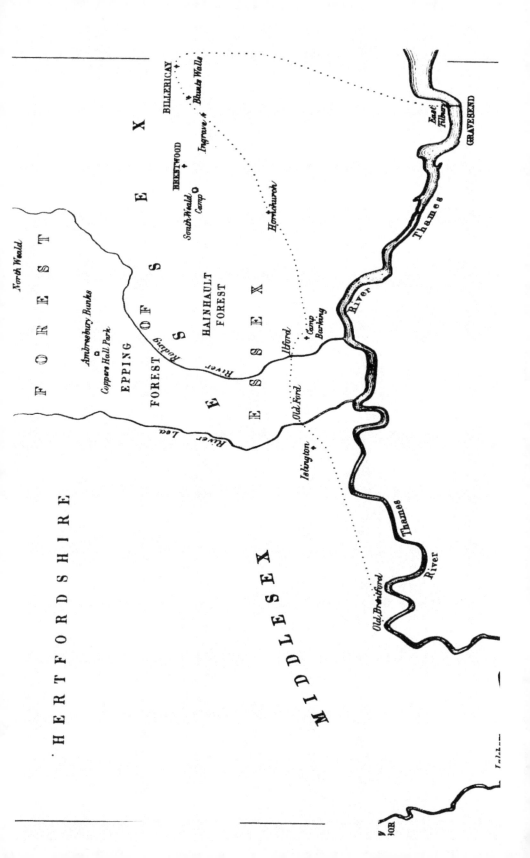

the emporium of commerce,[1] with its more dignified rival, Colonia, swept across these meadows; and the future conquerors seem to have trod, as far as they could, in the footsteps of the first. About midway between London and Colonia (Colchester), and in the midst of the Trinobantes, stood the Roman station Cæsaromagus,[2] *i.e.*, the town of Cæsar. The name imports much; and what better explanation of it can be given than that it is derived from the great Julius,[3] and commemorates a site occupied by him in his second campaign? In the same locality, and at a similar distance from London, now stands Billericay,[4] a very ancient town, which though only a hamlet, still bears its British name, and also gives its Saxon name to the parish in which it is situate, Burgstead, *i.e.*, the seat of the fortress. Coins and urns, and other Roman remains, continually dug up at the place, and Roman roads traceable to and from it, plainly betoken the town to have once been a Roman station; whilst the conformity of its distance both from London and Colchester entitle it to the peculiar claim of having been Cæsaromagus. Thus far then Cæsar led his invading legions into Britain; and thus far, by help of his own narration, and Antonine's ninth *Iter*, we will attempt to trace his route, and explain the transactions which took place whilst he was stationed at Billericay.

A straight line drawn on the accompanying map (see plate 12), from the bend of the Thames at Brentford to Ilford bridge, will nearly touch Old Ford, where Cæsar pro-

---

[1] " Londinium, cognomento quidem Coloniæ non insigne, sed copiâ negotiatorum et commeatuum maxime celebre." (*Taciti Lib. Annal.*, xiv, cap. 33.)

[2] Vid. *Antonin. Iter* 5 and *Iter* 9.

[3] Camden, in his *Britannia*, has a long and learned note on the derivation and position of Cæsaromagus; but he deprived himself of the possibility of deriving its name from Julius Cæsar, by conjecturing that he marched to Verulam in Hertfordshire, and not into Essex.

[4] *Billericay* is a compound British word. Its affix, *cae*, in its primary meaning, signifies a fence or enclosure; and in its secondary, an entrenchment or rampart. *Cae* in *Billericay* answers to *magus* in *Cæsaromagus*. The prefix, *Biller*, therefore, must have reference to Cæsar in the name of the Roman station. *Bel* was a title given to many of the British chiefs, as *Bell*inus, Cunobeline, Cassivell*aunus, i.e., bell*aunus. And again in the promontory, Belerium (the Land's End), so called from the name given to the first Phœnician captain who visited their coast. Milton, in his *Lycidas*, alludes to it as "the fable of Belerius old." According to Owen Pugh (see his *Dictionary*), *Bel* was the British name of Mars, and *wyr* is the descendant; so that *Biller*, or *Belwyr*, means the descendant of Mars. The letter *y* changed here into *i*, is the same as the article *the* in English; and *cae*, or *cay*, is equivalent to the word camp, so that Billericay signifies in English, *the camp of the descendant of Mars.*

bably crossed the Lea, and where the road of Antonine's ninth *Iter* first falls into, and follows, his previous route. Our archæologists of the last century make mention repeatedly of a Roman camp at Islington. Would it be an idle theory, or might we be allowed to conjecture, that the earthworks of this camp were thrown up for the security of the legions whilst they were employed in the toilsome task of macadamizing a way (so to speak) through the fens of the Lea and the Roden ?

Cæsar, when he had passed the last stream at Ilford, still continued to keep the main wood on his left, and marching along the skirts of it, came to a point of land where the Roden discharged itself, in those days, into a tidal creek of the Thames. There he fixed his camp,—a strong position, and most advantageous; since on the water side he could maintain an uninterrupted intercourse with his fleet on the Kentish coast, and by a reinforcement of a few ships could totally prevent Cassivellaunus from circumventing him, or attacking either his rear or his right. On the land side he would be supported by the whole strength of the Trinobantes, into whose territory he had now entered. The circumference of this camp can still be traced.[1] It comprises an area of forty-eight acres, and lies in the parish named from it Barking, *i.e.*, *burg*, a fortress, and *ing*, a valley,—the fortress in the valley. During the Romano-British period it became the military station Durolitum,[2] so called from *duro*, the Latin rendering of the British word *dwfr* (water), and *litum* (mud), *i.e.*, the muddy water station,—a very appropriate name, because in those days the southern bank of the camp was washed by the tidal water of the Thames. It is also worthy of notice that the manor adjoining the camp is still called Dover, and seems by its name to identify its contiguity to the station,—Dover and Duro being synonymous words.

All discussion of Cæsar's route from Barking, through Ingrave and Blunt's Wall, to Billericay, will on this occasion be avoided :[3] suffice it for the present to say that the ground

---

[1] For a full description of this camp, see Lysons' *Environs of London*, vol. iv, p. 58.

[2] It is also variously written *Durositum*, *i.e.*, situate at the water.

[3] In my paper on Antonine's itinerary roads in Essex, I enter into a more minute detail of the course of the Roman military way through the various parishes from Barking to Billericay. For an account of Blunt's Walls, see Wright's *Essex*, vol. ii, p. 544.

over which he passed is for the most part high and open, and suited for the movements of an invading army. Billericay itself stands in a noble situation. On the south it commands a fine view of the windings of the Thames, and on the north looks over a wide extent of the forest of Essex. Here, probably, Cæsar fulfilled the stipulations of his treaty with the Trinobantes: here, too, he received embassies and offers of submission from several of the neighbouring tribes, the Cenimagni, the Segontiaci, the Ancalites, the Bibraci, and the Cassii,[1]—"*Ab his cognoscit non longe eo loco oppidum Cassivellauni abesse, sylvis paludibusq. munitum, quo satis magnus hominum pecorisq. numerus convenerat. Oppidum autem Britanni vocant, quum sylvas impeditas vallo atq. fossâ munierunt, quò incursionis hostium vitandæ causâ convenire consueverunt.*" [From them he learns that the town of Cassivellaunus was not far off, protected by woods and marshes, and occupied by a good number of men and sheep. The Britons call by the name of a town, a place in the fastnesses of the woods protected by a rampart and a fosse, and calculated to afford them a retreat from hostile incursions.]

Camden totally mistook both the character of Cassivellaunus' *oppidum* and its locality, when he pronounced it to be the chief town of the Cassii, and on that account to have been Verulam. It might be objected to Camden's theory, and with little fear of contradiction, that Cassiobury was at that time the seat of royalty, and that Verulam had not yet risen into existence. Apart, however, from these objections, if the British *oppidum* had been the metropolis (so to speak) of a tribe, it would have contained a numerous population, their wives and children, their goods and chattels and stock of every kind, and its situation would have been known far

<hr>

[1] The *Cenimagni* dwelt at, and around, Manningtree in Essex, *i.e.*, Mannitrè (the town of the Manni). It is worthy of especial notice that Manningtree retains its original British name, notwithstanding the utmost efforts of the Saxons to supersede it by a name of their own. They called it Sciddinchou, *i.e.*, the tumulus or grave of Sciddinc, a Saxon chief, slain and buried there; and the manor is called Sciddinchou in *Domesday*. But the Saxon innovation soon sank into disuse, and the original British name, Manningtree, regained the ascendancy, and still survives. The *Segontiaci* most probably lived on the borders of the Thames, adjoining Essex. The *Ancalites* lived in the Hundred of Ongar, or Aungar, Essex, *i.e.*, Hên-gar-les (the place or palace of the old fortress.) The *Bibraci* lived in Babrig Hundred, Suffolk, on the borders of Essex. The *Cassii* lived in Caysho Hundred, Hertfordshire; and if Cæsar had marched into Hertfordshire, the Trinobantes, and not the Cassii, would have sent ambassadors to him.

and wide through all that part of Britain; whereas, on the contrary, we understand from the *Commentary* that it was a strong stockade constructed on a sudden emergency in the midst of the woods, and with such secresy that Cæsar was unable to discover it but through the information of traitors. It contained only a garrison adequate to its size, and a supply of sheep for their sustenance; even the chariots and horses of these chosen warriors seem to have been driven off to a place of safety before the Romans made their attack. As to its locality, the whole tenour of Cæsar's previous narrative points to Essex.   An advance into the state of the Cassii (the modern Hertfordshire), so far from offering him any advantage, would have removed him to an inconvenient distance from the Thames; and in the presence of a dauntless and active enemy, have endangered his commissariat.   But into Essex he was bound to lead his legions by his treaty with the Trinobantes; and his performance of the conditions agreed on, proves that he actually did lead them thither :[1] nay, the very spot which he and his army occupied whilst he was present amongst the Trinobantes, and negotiating with the surrounding tribes, became in after years the Roman station Cæsaromagus; a name commemorative of him, and of which Billericay is the modern equivalent and representative.

Not far, therefore, from Billericay (*non longe eo loco*), and within the forest of Essex, the traces of Cassivellaunus' *oppidum*, if any are extant, must be sought for.   Many, who are not aware of the great durability of earthworks, may deem visionary any search for the site of a British hold after the lapse of nineteen centuries.   Its abbatis of felled trees, indeed, through exposure to the weather, would, in ages long gone by, have mouldered into dust; but its raised rampart, and its wide and deep fosse, if uninjured by plough or spade, would withstand the ravages of time; a thick vesture of turf would gradually overspread the surface, and year by year renew with fresh strength its protective verdure.

Now, amidst the range of woods visible from Billericay, and at the distance of eight miles, an old entrenchment stands on the summit of the south-western verge of South Weald park, near the church.   It is circular, single-trenched, and contains about seven acres.   Our Essex historians con-

---

[1] "*Trinobantibus defensis atq. omni militum injuria prohibitis,*" are Cæsar's words, and they certify to the presence of Cæsar and his army in the territory of the Trinobantes.

cur in calling it *castra exploratorum*, a camp of observation, —a strange name for an earthwork embosomed in the dark obscurity of woods, and having no communication with the military roads. This entrenchment, however, so far from being Roman, is evidently British by its form; and not only does it harmonize with the general description of the site of a British *oppidum*, but almost appears, from its locality, to have been the one thrown up by Cassivellaunus. The position is lofty and very strong, especially on the side next unto Billericay, where a deep ravine rendered the approach to it more formidable. Here then, I conjecture, stood the *pah* against which Cæsar led his legions. Neither should it be thought unreasonable to suppose that the catastrophe from which the adjacent hamlet, Brentwood (*i.e.*, burnt wood), received its name, was occasioned by the method which the Roman soldiers took to clear a way for themselves and their engines through the thick jungle. Little praise to the victor, that, with legions more numerous than they which afterwards fought and conquered for him at Pharsalia, and with traitorous tribes as his auxiliaries, he forced four thousand Britons to quit their forest *pah*, and slew every one he could lay hold of! (*Multi in fuga sunt comprehensi atq. interfecti.*) His boasted trophies, too,—what were they? A number of captured sheep! (*Magnus ibi numerus pecoris repertus.*) The British chief, though forced to retreat, had still the indomitable spirit to continue the war; and by his enemy's own confession, could have protracted it through the winter. But urgent matters demanded Cæsar's presence in Gaul and Italy; and rather than prolong the contest with a man undeterred by defeat, he at once entered into a treaty with him, and led back his army to the sea. (*Exercitum reducit ad mare.*)

Thus ended the active operations of Cæsar's second invasion of Britain. A march of twelve miles would bring him from Billericay to East Tilbury, and across the Thames to Higham in Kent; and from thence, in three days, he would reach his fleet on the sea coast. Here, at a place where the old Roman road from Canterbury to what was once the shore, terminates; and in the parish of Lymne (which D'Anville, and Philipot the Kentish topographer, and our ablest archæologists, suppose to have been the port where Julius Cæsar landed) lies a hamlet called Billerica. It is situate

about a mile N.N.W. from Lymne.   As its name is all but
the same with that of the modern representative of the station Cæsaromagus, in Essex, may not this in Kent have been
given, like the other, to memorize the presence of the mighty
Julius ?   Within this hamlet, according to the common voice
of tradition, a large town once stood, and on its southern
side several old entrenchments and high banks still attract
the view.   Although they are now at a considerable distance
from the sea, yet they face seaward; and beneath them, in
a line with the Royal Military Canal, the tidal waters of an
estuary formerly flowed.   Here, then, I venture to fix the
landing-place of Cæsar; and would fain regard those high
banks as the ramparts thrown up by him for the twofold
purpose of protecting his soldiers and his ships.   After his
final departure from Britain, the merchants who frequented
this part of the coast, still continued to use the roadstead
where the Romans moored their fleet, as their harbour, till
it silted up, and then they opened the celebrated haven of
Lymne, a mile S.S.E.; and the Romans, during their occupation of Britain, there built the strong fortress of Stutfall.
The change had probably not been effected till about the
time of Ptolemy the geographer; for he calls Lymne Καινὸς
λιμήν (novus portus), i.e., in English, Newport.   Its late
occupation can also be shewn from the Roman coins dug up
there, none of which are of an earlier date than Antoninus
Pius : many of the stones also at Stutfall castle are supposed
to have been brought from older buildings at Billerica.   Billerica at first stood on the margin of the sea, and can be
identified in a remarkable manner with the double camp of
Cæsar.   In the British language, its affix, ca,[1] is the plural
of the noun cae or cay, which in Billericay is equivalent to
magus in Cæsaromagus, and signifies one entrenchment;
ca, therefore, in Billerica, being plural, must denote more
entrenchments than one.   They can be no other than the
earthworks by which Cæsar, after ten days incessant toil,
united his fleet to his former camp.   Though the beach upon
which they were thrown up, now yields pasture to nibbling
sheep; though the British town, which from them received
its name, has disappeared; yet the name Billerica survives
every change unaltered, and, like a talisman, marks the spot
where the great Julius, first and last, trod the British soil.

[1] See Owen Pugh's Welsh Dictionary.

ON THE MONUMENT OF A SUPPOSED PRINCESS OF PORTUGAL IN EAST SHEFFORD CHURCH, BERKSHIRE.

BY J. R. PLANCHÉ, ESQ., ROUGE CROIX, HON. SEC.

ELIAS ASHMOLE, in his *Antiquities of Berkshire* (published in 1723), describing the church of East or Little Shefford, says : "On the south side of the chancel is a fair, raised tomb, whereon lyes the statue of a man in armour; much like that once upon John of Gaunt's tomb in St. Paul's cathedral, London. On a wreath on his helm, lying under his head, is his crest, viz., an eagle's head, and his feet resting on a lion. His lady lyes by his right side, drest in the habit of the times in which she lived; without any inscription by which any discovery can be made to whom it belonged." (Vol. ii, p. 259.) Lysons, as late as 1806, describing the same church, speaks of " a handsome monument, with figures in alabaster of a man in armour, and a female without any inscription or arms." (*Mag. Brit.*, vol. i, p. 360.) And even the industrious author of the *History and Antiquities of Newbury* (published in 1839) contents himself with repeating almost *verbatim* the brief notice of Lysons. There can be no doubt, however, that the late sir Nicholas Harris Nicolas was correct in assigning it to Thomas Fettiplace of East Shefford, and his wife Beatrice ; the latter of whom died on Christmas day, 26th Henry VI (1447). And it appears by the will of their son, John Fettiplace, citizen and draper of London, dated 22nd of August, in the fourth year of the reign of king Edward IV (1463), and proved 3rd of September, 1464, that he bequeathed £40 to repair the church of Shefford, to build new pillars, erect a " little steeple" of timber, and make " a closure" round the tomb of his father and mother buried there. (Will in Prerog. Off. Godyn. 5.) By an inquisition taken at Wilton, co. Wilts, on the 22nd day of April, in the 26th of Henry VI (*i.e.*, 1448, according to the present style), we learn that this Beatrice had been previously the wife of sir Gilbert Talbot, baron Talbot of Blake-

mere; that she was seized, at the time of her death, of the
third part of the manor of Swindon in the said county of
Wilts; and that she held that third part in dower of the
inheritance of John earl of Shrewsbury, and of the gift of
her former husband, the said Gilbert Talbot; and the jurors
also found that William Fettiplace was the son and heir of
the said Beatrice, and was then twenty-four years of age.
Dugdale, in his *Baronage* (vol. i, p. 328), has stated, apparently on the authority of a document of the 11th of Henry VI,
that Beatrice lady Talbot " was an illegitimate daughter to
the king of Portugal, who surviving him" (*i.e.*, sir Gilbert
Talbot), " became the wife of Thomas earl of Arundel"; and
he has been followed without question by Lysons and others;
while Collins, in his *Peerage*, states that Beatrice was first
married to the earl of Arundel, then to Gilbert lord Talbot;
after his decease became the wife of John Holland, earl of
Huntingdon; and finally married *John* Fettiplace of Childrey in Berkshire.[1] The author of the *History of Newbury*,
before mentioned, follows Collins, correcting only the Christian name of the last husband, which was Thomas, not John;
but, singularly enough, does not associate him or his lady in
any way with the monument which he describes in the same
page.   It is evident, therefore, he was not aware that five
years previous to the publication of his valuable volume,
sir Harris Nicolas, with the assistance of sir Frederick Madden, had clearly demonstrated that Beatrice, the illegitimate
daughter of John king of Portugal, who was first countess
of Arundel, and then countess of Huntingdon, was a perfectly distinct personage from Beatrice lady Talbot, afterwards wife of Thomas Fettiplace, esq., of East Shefford, Berkshire.   This notice is to be found in the first volume of the
Collectanea Genealogica et Topographica (8vo., London,
1834, pp. 80-89), to which I must refer those who desire
more detail than I can be allowed to enter on at the present
moment, while I limit myself to a brief statement of the
principal facts collected by these eminent antiquaries; and
which will be sufficient to satisfy my auditory that we may
dismiss from our present inquiry all other material bearing
on Beatrice countess of Arundel and Huntingdon.
   That lady was undoubtedly the daughter of John, first
king of Portugal, by donna Agnez Pirez, or Perez, by whom

_____
[1] Vol. iii, p. 11, ed. 1812, under "Talbot earl of Shrewsbury."

he had also a son named Alphonso, who "was legitimated by his father on the 20th of October 1401; created count of Barçellos, and afterwards duke of Braganza, and was the immediate ancestor of the present royal family of Portugal." His sister, donna Beatrice, was contracted to Thomas Fitz Alan, earl of Arundel and Surrey, whom the Portuguese historians properly describe as "do sangue real da Inglaterra," as he was great-grandson of Edward I of England, and second cousin to Philippa daughter of John of Gaunt, the queen of John king of Portugal, his father-in-law. By his descent also from Eleanor of Castile, queen of Edward I, he was fourth cousin once removed to the king of Portugal himself. "It can scarcely admit of a doubt," observes sir H. Nicolas, "that similar letters of legitimation to those accorded by king John to his son Alphonso, were granted to his sister Beatrice; but however that may be, she was solemnly contracted to the earl of Arundel, by proxy, at Lisbon in April 1405, the earl's representative being sir John Wiltshire, first gentleman of his household; and about October in the same year she proceeded to England, accompanied, it appears, by her brother Alphonso count of Barçellos. Her marriage took place at Lambeth, with great splendour, on the 26th of November following, in presence of Henry IV and his queen, the king himself giving away the bride." The earl of Arundel died without issue on the 13th of October, 3rd Henry V (1414), and on the 11th of Henry VI (1433), his widow, Beatrice countess of Arundel, married John Holland earl of Huntingdon, afterwards duke of Exeter; the licence for which marriage is dated 20th of January in that year. This match is neither mentioned by Sandford, Brooke, nor Vincent; but the latter has made a manuscript note of it in the margin of his own copy preserved in the College of Arms, London. The countess died at Bordeaux, without issue, on the 13th of November 1439, and was buried with her first husband, in the College of Arundel. Her effigy, affording a fine example of the horned headdress of that period, has been engraved by Stothard and Blore; and that portion of it which illustrates the headdress, in my own and other works on costume. Her seal, exhibiting the arms of Fitz Alan, quartering Warren, and impaling the royal arms of Portugal as borne by king John her father, without any mark of illegitimacy, is circumscribed "Sigillum Beatricis comitissæ Arundeliæ et

Surriæ." It was engraved for the volume of the *Collectanea* before mentioned, from an original impression affixed to an instrument in the Harleian Collection (MS. 4840, f. 650.)

These dates and facts, supported by the most authentic collateral evidence, having been fully set forth in the *Collectanea*, and the distinction between the two Beatrices clearly established, it remains for us still to discover who was Beatrice lady Talbot, so many years confounded with the daughter of John king of Portugal, and around whose last resting place we are now assembled in, I trust, no irreverent spirit of curiosity. That she was also a Portuguese is proved by the Close Roll of the 7th of Henry V, No. 6, which states that Gilbert lord Talbot is dead; that Beatrice, his widow, was born in Portugal; and that during the time his wife was an alien, he became seized of the manor of Blakemere, *alias* Whitchurch, to the use of himself and the said Beatrice and the heirs of the said Gilbert," etc. The absence of all allusion to royal birth in this official document, would of itself be a sufficient answer to the assertion that she was actually the daughter of John king of Portugal; but that she was in some way descended from, or connected with, the royal family of Portugal, appears probable from her seal affixed to a grant dated 8th of Henry V, exhibiting a shield of the arms of Talbot quartering Strange, and impaling quarterly, first and fourth, the ancient arms of Portugal, and second and third, five crescents in saltire, surrounded by the inscription, "Sigillum Beatricis Talbot d'ne de Blakemere"; of which a drawing is preserved in the Cottonian Collection of MSS., Brit. Mus., Julius, C. vii, f. 193, and has been engraved for sir H. Nicolas's essay in the *Collectanea*. To this portion of the evidence we will return presently.

Gilbert lord Talbot, K.G., elder brother of sir John Talbot afterwards the great earl of Shrewsbury, had been first married to Joan Plantagenet, one of the daughters and heirs of Eleanor de Bohun, wife of Thomas of Woodstock, duke of Gloucester, who died in 1400, and is buried at Walden in Essex.[1] The date of his second marriage with Beatrice has not been ascertained; but on his death, in 7th of Henry V (A.D. 1419), their only child, Ankaret, was about three years old, so that it could not have been later than 1415. This

---

[1] Rot. Claus. 2nd Henry IV, 1401. Dugdale, *Bar.*, vol. iv.

Pl. 13

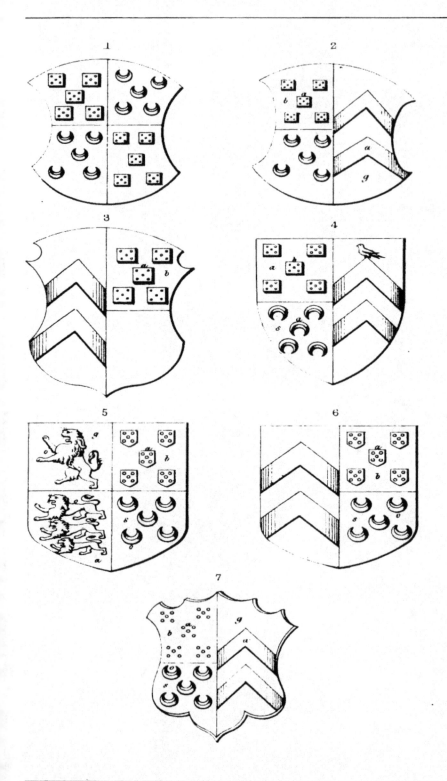

Ankaret is incorrectly stated by Sandford (*Gen. Hist.*, p. 234) to have been the daughter of Gilbert lord Talbot by his first wife, Joan Plantagenet; but it is clear by the escheat of the 9th of Henry V, No. 44 (A.D. 1421), that she was the issue of Beatrice; and was, at the time of her death, about five years old, her father's brother, sir John Talbot, being then found to be her heir.   Before the year 1423, lady Talbot married her second husband, Thomas Fettiplace, who had been appointed by lord Talbot, on the 17th of September, 1413, steward of the manor and hundred of Bampton; and seems to have obtained, in 1421, the grant of a house at Caen in Normandy.   The date of his death has not yet been discovered; but it must have been subsequent to 1433, as in that year I find him as "*sir* Thomas Fettiplace of Childrey," sheriff of Oxford and Berks.   His widow, as I have already stated, died on Christmas day A.D. 1447; and the remains of both undoubtedly repose beneath this still beautiful though dilapidated example of the monumental sculpture of the fifteenth century.   Unfortunately, however, nothing remains, in the way of heraldic decoration, to afford us any further clue to the family of the lady than we already possess in her seal, which I have just described; for although twelve escutcheons are still extant on the tomb, supported each by an angel, the arms with which they were no doubt originally charged have been completely effaced.   On a similar monument, however, erected, it would seem probable, by sir Gilbert Talbot to the memory of his mother Ankaret, at Whitchurch in Shropshire, where he himself was buried (and also in the east window of the chancel of the church there), the arms of Talbot and Strange, impaling Portugal ancient and the five crescents in saltire, are, or were, to be seen, exactly corresponding with those on the seal of lady Beatrice; while in the hall windows of the ancient manor house of East Shefford, in the kitchen window of the same edifice, in the south window of Childrey church, in the hall windows of the manor house at Childrey, in a lower window on the south side of Marcham church, and on several wooden shields nailed to the ceiling in the parlour of Compton House, Compton Beauchamp, there existed in the seventeenth century, and may still perhaps be found, the same arms variously displayed, and occasionally incorrectly painted, if we can rely on the copies of them preserved amongst the heraldic manuscripts in the

British Museum, and the church notes of Ashmole appended to the *Visitation* of Berkshire (marked C. 12) in the College of Arms.

At Shefford, the five blue shields of Portugal, each charged with as many silver roundels or plates, as they are technically termed, are transformed into figures resembling dice, the colour being white or argent, and the field in which they are displayed blue. (Plate 13, figs. 1 and 2.)   At Childrey they are still in the form of dice; but in the church window they are white (fig. 3), and in the hall window blue (fig. 4), the colours of the field being reversed accordingly.   At Compton House they have resumed the form of shields, but the colours are still the exact reverse of the royal arms of Portugal (figs. 5 and 6); while at Marcham the lines of the cubes, or the escutcheons, have disappeared entirely, and five groups of five white or silver spots, arranged in saltire, are seen on an azure field, utterly destroying all similarity whatever to the coat they were intended to represent. (Fig. 7.) The same perplexing variety extends to the quartering with the crescents, which are in some instances *or*, and in others *argent;* and in the hall windows at Childrey drawn with the points downwards,—an evident blunder of the painter or the glazier (fig. 4); and to make "confusion worse confounded," the arms of Beatrice, in this and in two other instances, are displayed on the dexter side of the impalement, and those of Fettiplace on the sinister. (Figs. 2, 4, and 7.)

To return, therefore, to the seal of Beatrice, about which there can be no mistake as far as the form and disposition of the armorial bearings are concerned. We cannot doubt that the first and second quarters of her family coat exhibit the arms of Portugual as borne by some of the sovereigns of that country previous to the reign of Alphonso III, A.D. 1248, viz., *argent*, five escutcheons in saltire *azure*, each charged with as many plates in saltire also. That monarch is reported to have surrounded them with a bordure *gules* charged with nine castles *or;* in commemoration, according to Portuguese heralds, of his acquisition of the kingdom of the Algarves, A.D. 1267.[1]   His descendant, John I, is said, upon the same authority, to have been the first to dispose the five escutcheons in cross in lieu of in saltire; and at any rate so we

---

[1] I venture to question the authority for this assertion; but it is unnecessary to discuss that point at present, as it does not affect the one before us.

perceive them in the seal of his daughter, our other Beatrice countess of Arundel.[1] Alphonso III died in 1279, and was succeeded by Dionysius or Denis, his eldest son by his second wife, Beatrice de Guzman, natural daughter of Alphonso king of Castile; but he had also two illegitimate sons, Alphonso Denis and Martin Alonzo Chiccorro, the first of whom married Maria Perez de Ribeyra e Souza, daughter, and finally heir, of Constance Mendez de Souza, coheiress of Mendez Garcia de Souza and his wife Theresa de Ribeyra, and became the progenitor of one branch of the great family of Souza, whose ancient arms were, *gules* five crescents in saltire *argent*, derived, as the historians of that family tell us, from the Moorish standards taken by Gonsalo Mendez at the siege of Seville in 1178. The second son married Agnes, the only daughter of the other co-heiress, Maria Mendez de Souza; and from them descended the branch of Souza Chiccorro, who seem to have discarded their family crescents in favour of a lion rampant.

The particular combination occurring on the seal of lady Talbot, led naturally to the inference that she must have been born a Souza, although the colours and metals of the arms in the painted examples could not be completely reconciled with those of any of the many different coats of that family. The researches of sir F. Madden and of sir H. Nicolas, both here and in Portugal, were productive, however, of no proof of her descent, although they led to a suggestion that she was, perhaps, of the family of Pinto, who also bore five crescents in saltire; but are certainly not " the only house in Portugal" displaying such a charge, as it is rather too positively stated in the *Addenda* to the first volume of the *Collectanea*, p. 405, and repeated in *Notes and Queries*, vol. ii, p. 478; see also *Notes and Queries*, vol. iii, p. 10. Some notes and correspondence on this subject were kindly placed in my hands by my friend Mr. C. E. Long, who had interested himself with sir Harris in the pursuit of this inquiry; and I can only regret they were not in my possession in the early part of last year, when, during my official visit to Lisbon, I might have personally examined the records in the

---

[1] They appear, however, in cross as early as the thirteenth century, on the seal of Matilda countess of Flanders and queen of Portugal, first wife of Alfonso III (1235), and *without* the border of castles. (*Vide* Olivar. Vredius, p. 25.)

Torre do Tombo, imperfect as I understand they have the misfortune to be.

From such information, nevertheless, as I have been able to obtain, and a careful study of the various pedigrees of the Souza family, both in print and in manuscript, together with a genealogical notice in Portuguese, with which I have also been favoured by Mr. C. E. Long, I am in hopes of bringing you a degree or two further in our voyage of discovery; and if not actually to land you safely, at least point out the course we must continue to steer to arrive at the desired haven.

The issue of the marriage of Alphonso Denis and Maria de Souza appears to have been five sons, who all took the name of Souza. Garcia Mendez de Souza was prior of Alcaçona; Gonzalo Mendez de Souza died without issue; Pedro Alphonzo de Souza was the ancestor of the marquises of Guadalemar and other noble families in Spain, and seems to have borne party per saltire *argent* and *gules;* the first charged with the five escutcheons of Portugal, and the second with a castle *or,* omitting altogether the family coat of Souza. Don Rodrigo Affonzo does not appear to have married; but left illegitimate issue, who became ancestors of several families both in Spain and Portugal. The fifth brother, Diego Alphonzo de Souza, living 1344, married Yolande or Violante Lopez, daughter of Lope Fernandez Pacheco, by whom he had two sons, Alvaro Diaz de Souza and Lope Diaz de Souza. Now Imhoff, in his *Genealogical History of the Kings of Portugal,*[1] most provokingly furnishes us with the descent from Alvaro, but does not even condescend to name the wife of Lope Diaz. The *Livro des Linhages de Portugal,* by Antonio de Luna Pereria (Lansdown MS., No. 189, Brit. Mus.), is equally silent; but père Anselm, in his *Histoire Genealogique de la Maison de France,* says her name was Beatrice; and the proof is given by Antonio de Souza in the twelfth volume of his *Historia Genealogica* (Part I, p. 264), where she is described as the wife of Lope Diaz de Souza in an instrument dated Lisbon 1369, in the reign of king Fernando: "Dom Fernando, etc., Faço saber que Lope Diaz de Souza, Rico Homen, meu vassallo et D. Brites (Beatrice) *suo mulher,*" etc. Of what family she was, however, does not appear; and père Anselm states that Lope died in 1373,

---

[1] Stemma Regium Lusitanicum. Amstelodami, 1708. Fol.

without issue by Beatrice his wife; but a Portuguese antiquary, who favoured Mr. Long with the genealogical notice I have referred to, assures us that the learned Francisco Antonio Roussado and Jose Faria de Monteiro had inspected certain muniments of the Souza family, which proved that Lope had by his wife Beatrice two sons and two daughters;[1] and suggests that one of the latter was in all probability the person we are in search of. The date of the death of Lope renders this, however, questionable; as, taking the latest year of his existence, or presuming her even to have been a posthumous child, would make Beatrice at least thirty, perhaps forty-two, at the time of her first marriage. She might, however, have been his grandchild.

The arms displayed on her seal, and in the other examples cited, do not correspond with those attributed to this particular branch of the Souza family, who are said by the Portuguese antiquary before-mentioned to have borne what may be termed Portugal modern, that is, the escutcheons in cross with the border of castles, quarterly, with a variation of the coat of Souza, viz., *gules*, four crescents in cross the points to the centre, *argent* (blazoned a *quaderna* of crescents in Portuguese) in which form it is still borne by the English descendants from the family of Souza de Aronches. (MS. Coll. Arm., L. 39, pp. 141.) In the coloured examples of the arms of lady Talbot, the field is sometimes *azure*, sometimes *sable*, and the crescents in saltire sometimes *argent*, sometimes *or*. Still I do not think this circumstance alone would be fatal to the conjecture, as Don Lopez, the youngest son of five, may have so differenced his arms, or some mistake may have been made in the colour of the field by the English painters, who have evidently been at issue also as to the metal of the charge. Indeed both Anselm and Imhoff blazon the field *azure* and not *gules*. But another hypothesis, to which I have already alluded, has been started by a Portuguese gentleman, the chevalier de Moraes Tarmento, who became so much interested in the subject, that he has actually written a novel, of which he has made Beatrice the heroine, and asserts that she was of the family of Da Pinto, who bore *argent* five

---

[1] Sandford also, in his *Genealogical History of the Kings of Portugal* (Lond., 1662), says: " From which Lope descend those of Souza, which *at present* are called Diabos." (p. 24.)

crescents in saltire *gules*. Here, again, the colour and metal are at variance with the suggestion : another question, however, arises on it. Alphonso the third had an illegitimate daughter, whom he names in his will, and who appears in the pedigrees as Leonora Alfonza. She married before 1271 Don Estefan Annez de Souza, son of John Garcia de Souza, who was Senhor D'Achuna e *Pinto*. Upon his death, she married in 1273 Gonsalvo Garcia de Souza, uncle of her first husband. There is no mention of issue by either marriage ; but the fact of one branch of the Souzas being lords of Achuna and *Pinto*, may reconcile the conflicting assertions of our Portuguese colaborateurs, and account for the arms of Pinto being identical with one of the coats of Souza. Much speculation has been wasted on the circumstances under which lord Talbot first became acquainted with his bride. Some, confounding him with his father Richard lord Talbot, who visited Portugal in the train of the duke of Lancaster. At that time, however, Beatrice, if born, must have been an infant, and still of tender age in 1381, when Edmond duke of Cambridge led an English force to Portugal to assist king Ferdinand in his claim to the crown of Castile : but I find that there was another occasion on which the chivalry of England made a conspicuous figure at Lisbon, and the date of it most happily corresponds with that which I have already given as the probable one for the marriage of Beatrice. In 1414, a grand tournament was held at Lisbon by king John I, to which he had invited some of the most illustrious Spanish, French, and English knights. They again assembled in the same capital in 1415, and joined the king of Portugal and his nobles in that memorable expedition against the Moors which terminated in the taking of Ceuta. The latter year, as I have shown, is the latest in which the marriage could have taken place, the only issue of it, Ankaret, being three years of age in 1419, and I am therefore strongly inclined to believe that sir Gilbert Talbot was one of the English present at the tournament, if not also in the expedition. Supposing Beatrice then to have been between the ages of fifteen and twenty, it would give us the dates of 1395-1400 to choose between for her birth. According to the same calculation, she would have been from twenty to twenty-five at the time of her marriage with her second husband, and from

Effigies of Sir Thomas and Lady Fettiplace, East Shefford Church, Berkshire.

.

forty-seven to fifty-two at the period of her decease in 1447, when William Fettiplace, aged twenty-four, was found to be her heir, which places his birth in 1423.

The features of her effigy before us, corroborate in my opinion, this portion of my suggestions.   They have no character of advanced age.   Small and delicately chiselled, they convey to my mind the idea of a female of much personal beauty, and not exeeeding the age of fifty ; while those of her husband, sir Thomas Fettiplace, are characteristic of a veteran soldier considerably her senior.   We know that such memorials exhibit, as far as the skill of the artist could accomplish the task, faithful portraits of the individuals represented and accurate copies of the costume they wore ; and the sculpture of this monument is a sufficient guarantee to us that no ordinary talent or labour has been employed to perpetuate the features of the deceased warrior and his, perhaps, royally descended lady.

A few words on the costume of these effigies (*vide* pl.14,15.) The male one presents us with a fine example of the armour worn in the reign of Henry VI, and certainly not much like that formerly displayed on the effigy of John of Gaunt, in St. Paul's cathedral, as stated by Ashmole, the latter, according to the engraving in Dugdale and Sandford, being, as we should expect, the military equipment of the time of Richard II, when the hauberk of chain was covered by a jupon of silk, and the neck defended by a collar of mail.   The effigy before us is in the complete plate of the fifteenth century.   The hauberk and jupon had then been generally abandoned, and to the breast and backplates, steel skirts were appended, composed of six or seven overlapping horizontal pieces, to which again were attached, by straps and buckles, plates called tuiles, to protect the thighs.   The fan-shaped ornaments of the knee and elbow-pieces are remarkably elegant, and highly characteristic of the period.   Over the hips was still worn the military girdle which had previously encircled the jupon.   The camail, or neck piece of chain, was now exchanged for a defence of plate called the hausse col.   The bascinet of this effigy is surrounded by a fillet which not only embellished the head piece by its ornamental character, but served to steady the heaume, or tilting helmet, occasionally worn over it, and which, in the present example you perceive, with its crest, a *griffin's*, not an *eagle's* head, and its mantling with escalloped edges and tassel, placed as usual under the head of the recumbent warrior.[1]

The costume of the lady is in perfect accordance with the date of her death, the middle of the fifteenth century. It consists of an under-dress closely fitting the bust and arms, called the kirtle, and over it the sideless garment (a sort of surcote), of which we have not as yet discovered the proper name; the skirt, exceedingly full, descending to the feet; and over her shoulders a mantle of state, fastened with cord and tassels. Her headdress is of that description known amongst antiquaries as the mitre-shaped, a fashion much seen *in monuments and illuminations of the reign of Henry VI and Edward IV.

The right arm of the effigy having been broken off has given rise, I am told, to a ridiculous story, still current amongst the peasantry, that lady Beatrice had but one arm.

I feel that on this occasion, as on many preceding ones, I have added little to the stock of information respecting my subject already in the hands of antiquaries; but at the same time I consider it my duty to assist in clearing away the mass of confusion, error, and unauthorised assertion with which an object of great local interest has been so long surrounded. If any thing can be more extraordinary than the complacency with which our predecessors received assertions as facts, and then wasted all their time and learning in arguing on them, it is the vitality they have imparted to the erroneous conclusions necessarily arrived at. To root up such weeds in the path of progress is the first duty of the antiquary, but the task is an arduous one. A celebrated French author has truly said, "we must fight incessantly. No sooner have we destroyed an error, than some one is always found ready to resuscitate it." It has been for years as clear as noon day that Beatrice countess

---

[1] Near the altar I found hanging up a fine bascinet, à *bavierre*, of the fifteenth century, the immediate precursor of the close helmet of the sixteenth (*vide* plate 15, figs. 1 and 2). It was thickly covered with whitewash; and Mr. Long informs me he saw it, several years ago, in the same condition. I should be inclined, from its undoubted date (compare it with that on the effigy of Thomas Plantagenet, duke of Clarence, who died A.D. 1421), to consider it as having been actually the property of Thomas Fettiplace; but Ashmole, in his church notes, speaks of "a helme" existing in his time in this church, with a sickle, the crest of Hungerford, upon it. He gives a drawing of the crest; but unfortunately not of the helm. The question arises, was this the bascinet that he calls "a helme", or was there another head-piece at East Shefford, which has disappeared?

of Arundel, and Beatrice lady Talbot, were two distinct individuals, but intelligent writers still continue to confound them. It is positive that the former was the natural daughter of John I, king of Portugal. It is obvious, from the quartering of the crescents by the latter, that she could not have been the daughter of any king, though it is probable she was a collateral descendant of one. Yet the royal crown of Portugal and the Algarves stands at the head of the pedigrees of Fettiplace, and sheds a false glory round that of Talbot, which surely needs no fictitious lustre, and although I do not despair, now that my attention has been seriously called to the subject, of eventually un-ravelling the mystery that still surrounds it, I am by no means sanguine in my expectation that any humble efforts of mine will prevent the fresh dissemination of an error which has been viewed as a truth for upwards of two centuries.[1]

I trust to be able to lay before our readers, in the next number of the *Journal*, two pedigrees,—one shewing the descent of certain branches of the Souza family from the illegitimate children of Alfonzo III, and the other containing more information respecting that of Fettiplace than has yet been published. It is also worthy of notice, that Beatrice is said, in one or two early pedigrees, to be " the daughter of Alphonsus" (not John) " king of Portugal," which, though equally untrue, seems to indicate the existence of a tradition supporting the suggestion of a descent from one of the branches above mentioned.

[1] This observation most singularly met with an immediate illustration. In the report of this very meeting, which appeared in a local print, and afterwards found its way into the London journals, I was said to have read an elaborate paper at East Shefford, proving that lady Fettiplace *was a princess of Portugal*,—the whole object of my paper being to prove that she *was not!*

URICONIUM.

BY THOS. WRIGHT, ESQ., M.A., F.S.A., ETC.

THIRD ARTICLE.

I RESUME the account of the excavations at Wroxeter, continuing the description published in the *Journal* of the Association for September 1859. Since that time so much work has been done that I may now give a plan of the whole; and in explanation of it I will briefly sum up what was said on the former occasion. In this plan (see pl. 16), the darkly shaded mass marked A, B, is the portion of building remaining above ground, which is known by the name of the Old Wall. The figures 1, 2, 3, 4, mark the different parts of the building to the north of the Old Wall, now covered up, which are fully described in my former article. C, C, are portions of the pavement of the street which was traced to the north of this building, running nearly east and west. Two doors (5 and 6 on the plan) were found in the southern wall of this building; and it was through the first of these that the workmen proceeded with their trench, and came upon the great mass of buildings to the south. The greater part of these buildings has now been cleared of earth, and presents a series of rooms, of different sizes, stretching from east to west, and most of them furnished with hypocausts. Two of these (7 and 8) communicated with each other by a passage in the partition wall, and were entered from without by a staircase at 9. On the western side a complicated arrangement of walls has been found (10), which evidently served some purpose connected with the heating of the hypocausts. The next hypocaust to the east (11) had been entered from an internal court, through an aperture in its southern wall. The skeletons, with the coffer of money, were found in the north-west corner of this hypocaust. Other similar apartments (12 and 13) carry us to what was evidently the eastern extremity of the building. The latter is the room, a view of the northern wall of which accompanied our first article on Uriconium, and which has been conjectured to be a *sudatorium*. There is a certain degree of uniformity of plan in the arrangement of these last three hypocausts, and the two small apartments with herringbone pavements (14 and 15). Extensive buildings have also been traced to the southward, opposite the

Pl.16.

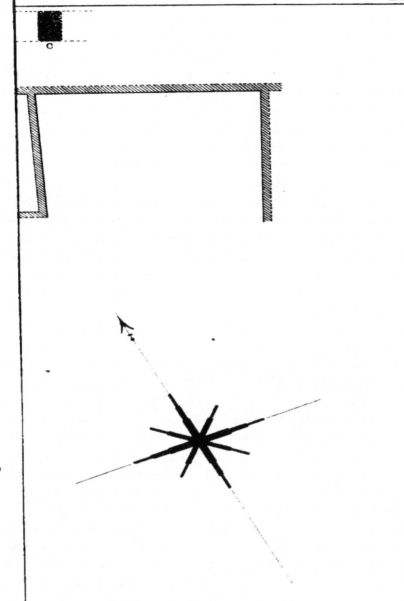

C

Watling Street Road

⊃NIUM OF THE ROMANS.

120   140   160   180 FEET

; del.

J.R.Jobbi

Old Wall, by their boundary walls; within which, at D, was found a floor paved with large tiles, apparently the bottom of a reservoir of water, or perhaps of a cold bath. To the west of this building, and to the south of the range of hypocausts, there was evidently a large but very irregularly shaped open court, in which there had also been a large tank of water (E), the floor of which was similarly paved with large flat tiles. A breach in the eastern wall of one part of this court (at F) had been newly repaired with much inferior masonry at the time the city of Uriconium was taken and destroyed; and it is a curious circumstance that some large pieces of stone lie here on the floor of the court, left unfinished by the stonemasons; as though repairs and alterations in the buildings were going on at the very moment of the final catastrophe.

Between the range of hypocausts and the Old Wall there were five apartments (16, 17, 18, 19, and 20), the southern parts only of which will be at present excavated, in the fear of endangering the stability of the Old Wall itself. The room to the east (20) has had the interior surface of its walls ornamented with tessellated work instead of fresco painting; and the lower edge of it, consisting of a guilloche border, still remains. The floor below has a plain pavement of small white tessellæ, and is apparently that of a bath. Remains of tessellated work on the wall were also found in the room numbered 16.

A comparison of the character of these various buildings left no room for doubting that they belong to the public baths of Uriconium; and further excavations to the south and west shewed that they formed an extensive square (G, H, I, K), the northern side of which was formed by the Old Wall and its continuation westward; and the southern side of which bordered upon another street running east and west, the pavement of which, similar to that of the street at C, C, has been uncovered at various points along the line L, L. The western and southern sides of the square were formed by a wide gallery or cloister (H, I, K), no doubt the ambulatory, which was considered as an important part of the public baths of the Romans. The ground to the eastward, in which no buildings could be traced, may have been gardens, which were also usually attached to the Roman baths.

Having once decided that the building we have thus explored, is the public baths, another equally interesting ques-

tion arises out of it. The public baths of the Roman towns
in Britain are not unfrequently mentioned in inscriptions
commemorating the repairing or rebuilding of them; but it
is a circumstance of some importance that this building is
combined with the basilica, or town hall. Both seem
to have participated in the same accidents, and to have
undergone decay together. Thus an inscription found at
Lanchester in Cumberland (supposed to be the Roman town
of Epiacum) speaks of the baths and basilica (BALNEVM CVM
BASILICA); and at Ribchester, in Lancashire, the baths and
basilica (BALINEVM ET BASILICAM) were rebuilt after having
fallen into ruin through age. We are therefore, I think, justified in concluding that the two great public buildings, the
baths and the basilica, usually joined each other; and I
think we may venture further to assume that the large building to the north of the Old Wall, the remains of which are
now covered up, was the basilica of Uriconium. The proportions of this building are rather extraordinary, and cannot be easily explained; but it is probable that in a provincial town the basilica served a variety of purposes. An
inscription found at Netherby, in Cumberland, speaks of a
basilica for practice in riding (BASILICAM EQVESTREM EXER-
CITATORIAM.)

We may now proceed a little further in identifying the
topography of the ancient town. The line of the buildings
we have traced parallel to the Watling-street road is at some
distance within the hedge of the field; and I believe that,
when the farm buildings were erected on the opposite side of
the road, what appeared to be the front of buildings facing
the opposite direction, were found likewise at some distance
within the field. This, with the road, would make a very
wide space; very much wider than either of the two transverse streets. Moreover, a glance at the plan will shew that,
beyond the transverse street to the south, this wide space
became considerably narrowed; and, in fact, it seems to have
been reduced to the width of an ordinary street. It is my
belief that this wide space was the forum of Uriconium; and
in that case it is rather remarkable that the basilica held
here exactly the same place, in regard to the forum, as at
Pompeii.

We have thus already brought to light a very interesting
portion of the ancient Roman town, and have learnt something more than we knew before of the character and eco-

nomy of the Roman towns in Britain. The basilica, as we have seen, came up to the front of the street, and formed the side of a transverse street; but this was not the case with the baths, for a space of some width between them and the forum is occupied by buildings which have the appearance of having been independent of the building of the baths. One of these (M) has been, in our former article, supposed to have been a marketplace, or an establishment of storehouses and shops. It was entered by a large doorway, approached by an incline plane at *d*; and by a foot entrance, with worn steps, at *e*. On each side of the court within was a series of square rooms (*g, g, g*); and on the eastern side a sort of gallery with recesses (*f, f, f*), the floor of which was lower than the level of the court, with which it communicated by steps at *h*. Another building (N) is now undergoing exploration, and has presented some rather singular features, which I will proceed to describe.

This room is nearly a square, and is about thirty feet in its longest dimension. The side towards the street seems to have been open, or at least the masonry of the wall presents the appearance of having had wide folding doors, or a framework of wood of some kind, in two compartments (*c, c*). In the centre of the room is a large pier of masonry (1), perhaps a table for workmen. More towards the north-western corner, a sort of furnace or forge (2) was found, built of red clay, with a hole or cavity in the upper part sufficiently large for a man to thrust his head in. As the surface of the cavity, internally, was completely vitrified, and as there was much charcoal strewed about, there can be no doubt that the cavity had been occupied by a very fierce fire. A low wall (*a, a*) has been traced, running across the room east and west, in a line with this furnace; and a transverse low wall of similar character (*b, b*). Upon the low wall (*a, a*), a little behind the forge (at 3), the excavators came upon what was supposed to be the lower part of a column with its base; but it is formed roughly, and I think it more probable that it was a stone table for the use of the workman at the furnace. It was at first supposed that this might belong to a colonnade running along the wall (*a, a*); but no trace of such a colonnade has been found, although a large piece of a shaft of a column lies in the middle of the room. This column, however, is of larger dimensions than the supposed base (2). Had such a colonnade existed, it seems so little in accordance with

the existence of a forge, that we might be led to suspect
that the room had, at some late period, been diverted from
its original purpose, and occupied by a worker in metals, or
even in glass, as fine specimens of glass were found scattered
about, and also many fragments of metal. But objects of
all kind seem to have been thrown about in such a manner,
when the town was plundered, that it would be unsafe to
argue upon the purpose of any particular building, merely
from movable articles found in it. Among other things
found in this room were nearly a dozen hair-pins, two of
which were much more ornamental than any we had found
before; a much greater quantity of fragments of Samian
ware, and of higher artistic merit, than had previously been
met with in one spot; a portion of a large bronze fibula; a
number of coins, and other things. One of the vessels of
Samian ware is a fine bowl, with figures in high relief, representing a stag-hunt. Upon the low wall of the sill (c), a
number of copper Roman coins (about sixty) were found
together; and near them the fragment of a small earthen
vessel, in which probably they had been carried by some one
who dropped them here as he was hurrying out of the place.

Other apartments surrounding the one just described, have
yet to be explored; and then we shall, I think, be better
acquainted with the character of the whole of this line of
buildings which looked upon the open space which I have
supposed to be the forum. I have already said that this
open space contracts to the south of the transverse street
(L, L), in what has been no more than the breadth of an ordinary street, which ran down towards the river. A gutter (i, i)
very well made, of carefully squared stones, and remarkably
well preserved, runs near the houses on the eastern side of
the street; the only side which at present can be explored,
as it is near the hedge of the Watling-street road. It runs
very near the walls of the houses, is a foot wide, and about
a foot deep, and from place to place square stones are laid
in lozenge-fashion, apparently intended for stepping-stones,
but they must have stopped the current of water down the
channel. The buildings at this corner consist of small rooms,
and were probably private houses. The existence of walls
running parallel and transverse to the street (L, L), has been
ascertained along the whole length of its southern side; but
they have not yet been sufficiently explored even to be laid
down in the plan.

(*To be continued.*)

Proceedings of the Association.

ANNUAL GENERAL MEETING.

APRIL 11.

Nathaniel Gould, F.S.A., V.P., in the Chair.

Mr. Previtè, one of the auditors for 1859, was called upon, and read the following report, communicating also the balance sheet of the treasurer's accounts for the year.

"We, the auditors elected at the Annual General Meeting in April 1859, having, in pursuance of our appointment, duly examined the treasurer's accounts, have now the gratification of reporting to the Association that, during the year the sum of £573 : 1 : 6 has been received, and £493 : 6 · 2 expended; leaving in favour of the Society, £79 : 15 : 4. This added to £17 : 6 : 9 of the preceding audit, renders a balance on behalf of the Association to the amount of £97 : 2 : 1.

"In 1859, sixty-two associates have been elected, eight withdrawn, and seven deceased. Seven have also, in pursuance of the vote at the General Meeting in 1859, been removed from the list of members, for non-payment of their subscriptions.

"The condition of the Association is highly satisfactory. There are no liabilities; not a debt undischarged; and the associates are increasing at every meeting. Thirty have already been added upon the present year. The Newbury Congress, under the presidency of the earl of Carnarvon, has been very successful and productive to the Society's funds; thus enabling the council to extend their illustrations of the antiquities of the county. The *Journal* has met with the entire approbation of the associates; and notwithstanding the strict economy necessarily pursued in regard to the expenditure of the Association, has fully sustained its high character.

"We regret to find that several subscriptions are still unpaid; and as regularity in their discharge is the only means of carrying on satisfactorily the business of the Society, we concur with the council in recommending the removal of seven names, which have been submitted to us, of members four and five years in arrear, and neglecting to attend to the frequent applications they have received.

"We cannot close our report without adding one to the many acknowledgments made by previous auditors, of the satisfactory manner in which the accounts of the Society are kept, and of the undivided attention paid to its interests by the treasurer; to whose exertions the present very prosperous condition of the Association is mainly attributable.

WILLIAM RUTTER }
 J. W. PREVITÉ } Auditors."

"9th April, 1860."

DONATIONS IN AID OF NEWBURY CONGRESS.

	£	s.	d.		£	s.	d.
The earl of Carnarvon (president)	10	0	0	D. Higford Burr, esq.	3	0	0
Messrs. Bunny and Slocock	10	10	0	Henry Hippisley, esq.	2	2	0
H. R. Eyre, esq.	5	5	0	John Alexander, esq.	2	2	0
Charles Eyre, esq.	5	5	0	Thomas Hughes, esq.	2	2	0
H. F. Winterbottom, esq.	5	5	0	N. Gould, esq., F.S.A.	2	2	0
The earl of Abingdon	5	5	0	Rev. N. J. Ridley, M.A.	2	2	0
Admiral sir J. W. D. Dundas, G.C.B.	5	5	0	Rev. J. Bagge, M.A.	2	2	0
				R. Tull, esq.	2	2	0
The venerable archdeacon Randall, M.A.	5	5	0	Rev. J. W. Randall, M.A.	2	2	0
Hon. P. P. Bouverie, M.P.	5	5	0	Sir P. Hunter, bart.	2	0	0
Edward Wilson, esq.	5	5	0	R. Sherwood, esq.	2	0	0
H. Keens, esq. (mayor of Newbury)	5	5	0	T. Hubbard, esq.	2	0	0
				W. H. Cave, esq.	1	1	0
J. H. Mason, esq.	5	5	0	C. W. Doe, esq.	1	1	0
John Walter, esq., M.P.	5	0	0	— Harrington, esq.	1	1	0
Sir Christopher Rawlinson	5	0	0	— Somerset, esq.	1	1	0
Mrs. Stacpoole & Miss Wasey	5	0	0	— Blacket, esq.	1	1	0
William Mount, esq.	3	3	0	C. Royston, esq.	1	1	0
J. T. Norris, esq., M.P.	3	3	0	T. Talbot, esq.	1	1	0
Joseph Bunny, esq.	3	3	0	W. J. Cowper, esq.	1	0	0
J. Blythe, esq.	3	3	0	Various smaller sums	4	9	6
Lord Boston	3	3	0				
					£142	7	6

RECEIPTS.

1859.

	£	s.	d.
Balance due to the Association at the audit of 1858	17	6	9
Annual and life subscriptions	276	3	0
Donations:			
S. R. Solly, esq. £1 0 0			
W. Yewd, esq. 1 1 0			
J. R. Jobbins, esq. 2 2 0	4	3	0
J. G. French, esq.—Eight plates to illustrate his paper, "On Ancient Sculptured Stones."			
Thos. Wakeman, esq.—Two plates to illustrate his paper, "On Pembridge Castle."			
Donations collected by Local Committee at the Newbury Congress (as per list)	142	7	6
Balance received on account of Congress	129	13	6
Sale of Publications	20	14	6
	£590	8	3

	£	s.	d.
Balance brought forward	£97	2	1

WILLIAM RUTTER } Auditors.
J. W. PREVITÉ }

9th April 1860.

PAYMENTS.

1859.

	£	s.	d.
Printing and publishing Journal for the year	185	0	6
Illustrations on account of Journal	79	14	2
Binding of Vol. XIV, Journal	5	0	0
Miscellaneous printing	20	0	10
Rent of room for public meetings	13	13	0
Delivery of the Journals	20	0	0
Postage, advertisements, notices, etc.	22	0	0
Stationery	4	18	0
Petty expenses, gratuities to servants, carriage of antiquities, etc.	12	15	0
Expenses defrayed by the Local Committee at the Newbury Congress	130	4	8
Balance in favour of the Association	97	2	1
	£590	8	3

WILLIAM RUTTER } Auditors.
J. W. PREVITÉ }

9th April, 1860.

The treasurer communicated the following lists of associates elected, withdrawn, and deceased, during 1859:

Associates Elected, 1859:

John Alexander, esq., Newbury
Thos. Allom, esq., Buckingham-street
J. H. Belfrage, esq., New Inn
W. D. Bennett, esq., Weedon
Richd. Benyon, esq., Grosvenor-square
T. Brand, esq., East Sutton, Sledmere
Wm. Bridges, esq., Kensington
John Joseph Briggs, esq., King's New-ton, Swarkeston
Edward Bullock, M.D., Chelsea
Cornelius Carter, esq., Grosvenor-street
William Cockeram, esq., West Coker
Thos. W. Davies, esq., Barnes
Right hon. C. Tennyson D'Eyncourt, F.R.S., F.S.A., Bayons Manor, Lincolnshire
Geo. Doubleday, esq., Soho-square
William D. Field, esq., Shrewsbury
H. Godwin, esq., F.S.A., Speenhill
R. Fuller Graham, esq., Greenham
George Greenhill, esq., Barnes
George Gubbins, esq., Soho-square
C. Ashley Hance, esq., Alexander-sq.
Henry Hill, esq., Hammersmith
Henry B. Hodson, esq., Guildford-st.
D. D. Hopkyns, esq., Weycliffe, St. Catharine's, Guildford
George Hughes, esq., Luton
T. Hughes, esq., F.S.A., Lincoln's Inn
R. Hutchison, esq., Cape Coast Castle
Rev. W. Jackson, M.A., Westen-super-Mare
Swynfen Jarvis, esq., Barleston Hall, Staffordshire
Henry Lee Jortin, esq., Maidenhead
Henry Keens, esq., Newbury
W. Landon, esq., Hammersmith

Rev. T. B. Levy, M.A., Knight's En-ham Rectory
D. Littler, esq., Pump-court, Temple
Luke Lousley, esq., Manor House, Hampstead Norris
Rev. John M'Caul, LL.D., Toronto
Francis B. Macdonald, esq., Brompton
R. R. Madden, esq., M.R.I.A., Dublin Castle
Parker Margetson, esq., Maddox-street
Jas. Heywood Markland, esq., D.C.L., F.R.S., F.S.A., Bath
Henry M. Mason, esq., Newbury
J. H. Mason, esq., The Firs, Newbury
H. S. Mitchell, esq., Great Russell-st.
A. Murray, esq., Enoch-sq., Glasgow
Right rev. lord bishop of Oxford, D.D., F.R.S., F.S.A., Cuddesdon
Silas Palmer, M.D., Newbury
Geo. Patrick, esq., Loughborough-road
J. C. Pawle, esq., New Inn
Thomas Read, M.D., Kensington
Rev. N. J. Ridley, M.A., Newbury
Charles Rooke, M.D., Scarborough
Lady F. Russell, The Chequers, Bucks
J. Savory, esq., Sussex-pl., Regent's Pk.
John Scott, esq., King William-street
Charles A. Scott, esq., Wharton-square
N. E. Stevens, esq., Fenchurch-street
James Sullivan, esq., Stamford Villas
J. Walter, esq., M.P., Upper Grosvenor-st
Henry Walker, esq., Blomfield-road
Geo. Edw. Wentworth, esq., Woolley Park, Wakefield
T. Wright, esq., M.A., F.S.A., Brompton
Rev. C. F. Wyatt, M.A., Forest Hill, Oxon
Joseph Wyon, esq., Regent-street

Resignations, 1859:

T. Jones Barker, esq.
J. C. Cumming, M.D.
Sir Arthur H. Elton, bart.
G. M. Hughes, esq.

Samuel Lepard, esq.
C. G. Lewis, esq.
William Allington Long, esq.
Henry Youens, esq.

Deaths, 1859:

Pudsey Dawson, esq.
John George Patrick, esq.
Mrs. Percival
William Henry Rolfe, esq.

Robert Stephenson, esq., M.P., D.C.L., F.R.S.
William Stradling, esq.
Colonel Thomas Wildman

Upon the recommendation of the council the following names were erased from the list of associates for non-payment of their subscriptions:

Coutts Arbuthnot, esq.	.	5 yrs. due	Samuel Heywood, esq. .	4 yrs. due
Charles Egan, esq. .	.	5 ditto	Charles Edward Jenkins,	
Lieut. Morrison, R.N.	.	5 ditto	esq., K.M. . .	4 ditto
Henry Dearsley, esq.	.	4 ditto	S. Isaacson Tucker, esq. .	4 ditto

The thanks of the meeting were voted to the auditors for their report

Thanks were also voted to the president, the earl of Carnarvon, for his lordship's great attention to the Association, and to the advancement of its interests, especially at the Congress held at Newbury.

Thanks were also voted to the treasurer for his continued exertions in support of the Association; to the vice-presidents, officers, and council; to the authors of papers, and the exhibitors of antiquities, during the past year.

A ballot was taken for officers and council for 1860-61; and upon examination of the lists, the following were declared to be elected:

PRESIDENT.

BERIAH BOTFIELD, M.P., F.R.S., F.S.A.

VICE-PRESIDENTS.

JAMES COPLAND, M.D., F.R.S.	JAMES HEYWOOD, F.R.S., F.S.A.
SIR F. DWARRIS, F.R.S., F.S.A.	JOHN LEE, LLD., F.R.S., F.S.A.
GEORGE GODWIN, F.R.S., F.S.A.	T. J. PETTIGREW, F.R.S., F.S.A.
NATHANIEL GOULD, F.S.A.	SIR J. G. WILKINSON, D.C.L., F.R.S.

TREASURER.

T. J. PETTIGREW, F.R.S., F.S.A.

SECRETARIES.

J. R. PLANCHÉ, *Rouge Croix*. | H. SYER CUMING.

Secretary for Foreign Correspondence.—WILLIAM BEATTIE, M.D.

Palæographer.—W. H. BLACK, F.S.A.

Curator and Librarian.—GEORGE R. WRIGHT, F.S.A.

Draftsman.—HENRY CLARKE PIDGEON.

COUNCIL.

GEORGE G. ADAMS	MAJOR J. A. MOORE, F.R.S.
GEORGE ADE	J. W. PREVITÉ
CHARLES AINSLIE	EDWARD ROBERTS
THOMAS ALLOM	SAMUEL R. SOLLY, M.A., F.R.S., F.S.A.
J. O. HALLIWELL, F.R.S., F.S.A.	ALFRED THOMPSON
GORDON M. HILLS	CHARLES F. WHITING
GEORGE VERE IRVING	ALBERT WOODS, F.S.A., *Lancaster*
THOMAS W. KING, F.S.A., *York Herald*	*Herald*
WM. CALDER MARSHALL, R.A.	THOMAS WRIGHT, M.A., F.S.A.

AUDITORS.

W. E. AMIEL | JOHN SAVORY.

The treasurer then read the following notices of associates deceased during 1859, and the thanks of the meeting being voted to him for the same, and to the chairman for his attention to the business of the meeting, the associates adjourned to dine together, and celebrated the seventeenth anniversary, at St. James's Hall.

Obituary for 1859.

BY T. J. PETTIGREW, F.R.S., F.S.A., V.P. AND TREASURER.

It is a practice esteemed by the Association, and gratifying alike to its members and the friends of those who have departed from us during the year, to record in the pages of our *Journal* the connexion their relatives maintained with us, to detail the interest they felt in the researches in which we are engaged, and to receive the expressions of our sympathy for the loss they have sustained.   We have during the past year to register the death of seven of our associates.

JOHN GEORGE PATRICK, esq., was born on the 4th of June 1803, and died the 20th of February 1859, at the age of fifty-five years. He had been a member of our body from 1847, and occasionally favoured us with exhibitions at our public meetings.   He was of a good family, and a descendant of the celebrated Simon Patrick, bishop of Ely, whose writings shed a lustre in the latter part of the seventeenth century, and whose Commentaries are frequently consulted and referred to at the present day.   On his mother's side, Mr. Patrick was descended from the De la Fontaines, an ancient and noble family of France.   A member of this family, John De la Fontaine (no less than the bishop already mentioned on the paternal side), was remarkable for his defence and support of protestantism, and indeed suffered martyrdom in 1563 for the maintenance of his faith.   Our deceased associate was distinguished by the refinement of his taste, and his attachment to letters and the fine arts. He was passionately fond of music, and in his earlier days composed several songs and ballads which have been greatly esteemed, and which I have heard him execute with great taste on his favourite instrument, the piano. He had a small but choice collection of paintings, and he possessed a good mineralogical collection.   His library contained several rare works, tracts and pamphlets of curiosity, and MSS. with choice illustrations and illuminations.   In 1851 he exhibited to us a pax of the fifteenth century, and also a medal of Ignatius Loyola, which had been picked up on the bank of the river near Lambeth palace, and appeared, from a loop hole with which it was furnished, to have been made for suspension round the neck.   In 1855, he presented to us another medal of the celebrated

[1] Journal, vii, 83.

Jesuit, in brass and of a circular shape, which had the legend s. IGNAT.
s. i. f. *(Sanctus Ignatius Societatis Jesu Fundator)*. The reverse bore the
sacred monogram within a rich circle.[1] In the previous year, Mr. Patrick
submitted to us a massive gold betrothal ring, which was said to have
belonged to lord Southampton. The ring is of the time of Elizabeth, and
bore the initials H and S united together by a true lover's knot.[2] In 1856
he laid before the Association an interesting memento of the celebrated
circumnavigator sir Francis Drake. It consisted of his clasp or pocket
knife, and has been described by Mr. H. Syer Cuming, and figured in our
volume for the past year.[3]

Our late associate has been succeeded in our body by his son Mr. George
Patrick, who has already exhibited to us some good rubbings from
brasses in Bexley Church, and will, I have no doubt, by treading in the
footsteps of his father in the love of Archæological subjects, secure
to himself that respect and attachment which were held by the Association to his deceased parent.

WILLIAM STRADLING, esq., of Roseville, Chilton Polden, Somersetshire, a deputy lieutenant of the county, joined us as an associate at our
Congress at Bridgwater in 1856. On this occasion he threw open his
museum at Polden Hill to our inspection, and received us with that
amiability and cordiality by which he was distinguished, and which
secured for him so many friends. In the pride of ancestry, he would
refer to his descent from the Easterlings or Stradlings of St. Donat's
castle, Glamorganshire; a castle given by William the Conqueror to
sir William Esterling, one of his twelve knights, whose great grandson
married the lawful heiress to the castle and manor. Mr. Stradling's
attachment to the study of antiquities was displayed at an early age, and
in the cause of his favourite pursuit he was fortunate in being associated
with his neighbour and connexion Robert Anstice, esq., with whom he
collected numerous British antiquities from the turbaries or peat moors
in the neighbourhood of his residence. These are deposited in the British
Museum. With another friend, Samuel Hassell, esq., he was associated
in the discovery of Roman tessellated pavements at Littleton, Hurcot and
Pitney; and by his zeal, he obtained the approbation of sir Richard
Colt Hoare, bart., the historian and antiquary of Wilts, who designated
him " a true spade and shovel antiquary", and associated with him in his
most valuable labours. Having particularly specified these in my introductory address at the Somersetshire Congress,[4] it is unnecessary here
further to allude to them.

Mr. Stradling's printed contributions in furtherance of archæology, will
be found chiefly in the *Proceedings* of the Somersetshire Natural History

[1] Journal, xi, 158.
[2] Ib., x, 177.
[3] Ib., xv, 348, and plate 30, figs. 4, 5.
[4] See *Journal*, xii. 310 and 382.

and Archæological Society, in addition to which, may however be mentioned, as proceeding from his pen, a small volume called *Chilton Priory*, in which many particulars relating to the duke of Monmouth and his rebellion, derived from the recollections of aged persons in Bridgwater and its neighbourhood, may be met with. Mr. Stradling was in latter years much afflicted with gout, which disabled him from carrying on his favourite researches, and he died at Chilton Polden, on the first of April 1859, at the age of seventy years, deeply regretted.

PUDSEY DAWSON, esq., of Hornby Castle, Lancaster, is a name of note in the county of Lancashire. He was a deputy lieutenant, and justice of the peace of the West Riding of Yorkshire, being the possessor of Langcliffe and Great Stainforth, and served the office of high sheriff in 1845. He was born October 2nd, 1778, and died April 12th, 1859, having therefore attained the age of eighty years. He was twice married; first, September 19th, 1808, to Sarah, eldest daughter of George Bigland, esq., of Bigland Hall, who died in December 1816, and by whom he had issue a son, Hugh Pudsey, B.A., Oxon., deceased at the age of twenty-two, unmarried, at Madeira in 1831; and secondly, May 9th, 1821, to Jane Constantine, second daughter and co-heir of rev. Richard Dawson of Halton Gill, and rector of Bolton by Bowland, Yorkshire. Mr. Pudsey Dawson succeeded to Hornby Castle under the will of his kinsman admiral Sandford Tatham, January 24th, 1840.

The Dawsons' was an old Yorkshire family, connected with the Pudseys by the marriage of William Dawson to Jane Pudsey, who eventually became the sole heiress of her father and brother Ambrose Pudsey, of Bolton hall in Craven. The nephew of Richard de Bolton, bow bearer of the forest of Bowland (*temp.* Edward I), John de Pudsey, inherited the manor of Bolton. Other branches succeeded, and many members of the family distinguished themselves by military exploits. Sir Ralph Pudsey concealed Henry VI for several weeks at Bolton Hall, after the battle of Hexham. Mr. Pudsey Dawson, on occasion of our visit to Hornby Castle in 1850, exhibited to us a pair of boots which had been presented to sir Ralph Pudsey by the king, together with other presents, and among the rest a box on which is this inscription:—" The gift of king Henry VI of England to sir Ralph Pudsey, of Craven Hall, Yorkshire; his boots, spoon, and gloves—the only gifts in his power to bestow on a faithful and loyal adherent, having remained under his hospitable roof for several weeks after the fatal battle of Hexham".

Another member of this family, Thomas Pudsey, received a letter from the earl of Surrey on the march of the English army to Flodden Field from Newcastle, May 31st., 1513, which was exhibited to us at the Congress.

The late Pudsey Dawson was the issue of Pudsey Dawson and

Elizabeth Ann Scott, daughter of James Scott of Amsterdam, who died at the age of eighty-six, in February 1837. His father was mayor of Liverpool in 1779 and 1780, and is benevolently known by having been one of the founders of the school for the Indigent Blind in that town, the first of the kind, I believe, instituted for the relief of that unfortunate class. His motto " *Penser peu de soi* ", appeared to be very applicable to him. His arms were quarterly eight :—Dawson, Pudsey, Bolton, Laton, Strabolgi, Pilkington, Scrope and Sandford.

The castle of Hornby stands on the site of a Roman villa, and is on a bold rock, having a noble appearance. The walls are strongly cemented, and of great thickness. Roger de Montbegon was in the early part of the twelfth century at Hornby Castle ; and in the grant of the possessions of Roger de Poictou, the lands of Roger de Montbegon are expressly excepted. The motto of sir Edward Stanley, lord Monteagle, is on the north side of the present castle, glaive (or sword) and glove "glav et gant, E. Stanley".[1] Stanley deceased A.D. 1529. A survey of Hornby demesne, copied from an old survey book, 1584, is preserved at Hornby, and the Inquisition contained in it gives a minute description of the state and appearance, together with the household resources of a baronial mansion in the reign of Elizabeth. Baines has copied this in his *History of Lancashire*.[2] James I rested at Hornby, August 11th, 1617, on his progress from Edinburgh to London; and in 1631 (August 31st), Oliver Cromwell wrote from Ripon to William Dawson, who was mayor of Doncaster in the Protector's time.[3] In 1643, during the civil wars, the parliament issued an ordinance for the spoliation of the castle, and it was effected to prevent the enemy making farther use of it. It remains only for me to record that it was on the 2nd of August, 1850, the Association had the gratification of visiting Mr. Pudsey Dawson, and inspecting the present building and grounds. No one present on that occasion can fail to remember in the most lively manner the frankness and hospitality with which we were then received.

COLONEL THOMAS WILDMAN was descended of a Lancashire family residing at Barking Goat, where they held a possession for many generations. The late colonel was born August 20, 1787, and dying September 20, 1859, was seventy-two years of age at the time of his decease. He was the eldest son of Thomas Wildman, esq., of Lincoln's Inn and Bacton Hall, Suffolk, who died in 1795. Colonel Wildman entered the lancers in 1808, and changed into the 7th hussars, with which regiment he served in Spain under sir John Moore, and was one in the memorable

---

[1] For particulars, see *Journal*, vol. vi, p. 343 et seq.
[2] Vol. iv, p. 605.
[3] This letter was shewn at the Lancashire Congress, and is printed in the *Journal*, vi, p. 344.

retreat to Corunna.   He was afterwards engaged in the Peninsula, and aide-de-camp to the marquis of Anglesea at the battle of Waterloo.   He returned to England at the peace of 1815, and in 1817 purchased Newstead abbey for the sum of £95,000.

I had, for many years, the happiness to enjoy great intimacy with colonel Wildman.   We were members of the same royal household, and I look back with great delight to the happy hours we passed together in the performance of our various duties, and in the discussion of subjects, literary and political.   Colonel Wildman was a good scholar, and received his education at Harrow.   Lord Byron and he were schoolfellows, and I have printed a letter[1] from the distinguished poet to the colonel, expressing his satisfaction that Newstead abbey had come into the colonel's possession, feeling assured that, by his ability and taste, the property would be recovered from its fallen condition, and that all that was remaining of interest in relation to it would be preserved.   Such, indeed, proved to be the case.   The colonel preserved with almost holy solicitude everything that was remarkable of the building and specially connected with its former possessor, and expended upon the mansion and grounds in alterations and improvements a very considerable sum.

In 1852, upon the holding of a Congress in Nottinghamshire, under the able and distinguished presidency of his grace the duke of Newcastle, I made known to my old friend our intention to view Newstead abbey, and I immediately received from him the most urgent entreaty that we should partake of his hospitality, and in furtherance of our views the abbey, its deeds, etc., were unreservedly placed at our disposal.   To Mr. Ashpitel I gave an introduction to the colonel, and the results derived from the examination of the abbey by the facilities thus afforded are given in the pages of our *Journal*, which is also enriched by a ground plan of the building.[2]   The colonel heartily joined our Association, and received us in a manner that must have been most gratifying to us all. The account of our visit is detailed in the ninth volume of our *Journal*,[3] and the particulars relating to the history of the abbey will there be found in a paper I had the honour to read in the drawing-room on that occasion, to which I must therefore refer our members.

The spot itself is so deeply interesting—its history, ecclesiastical in its early period, and so intimately connected with literature in its occupation by lord Byron in a later age, could not fail to render the visit to Newstead abbey one of the most powerfully interesting occurrences of our Congress.

The colonel leaves no family; but a widow, who deeply deplores his loss—who rendered his life happy by her virtues and endearing qualities, and with whom he was united in 1816.

---

[1] Journal, vol. ix, p. 28.   [2] Vol. ix, pp. 30–39, and plate 8.
                       [3] Ibid., viii, p. 253, and vol. ix, pp. 14–30.

ROBERT STEPHENSON, esq., M.P., D.C.L., F.R.S. This distinguished associate and celebrated engineer joined us in 1848, and died at the age of fifty-five, on the 12th October, 1859. The details connected with the life of this remarkable man have been so fully given in the public papers, and by the eulogies delivered at those societies to which he belonged, and with which he was from the nature of his pursuits especially connected, that little is left for me to say in regard to our particular objects and the interest he took in archæological matters. In the published biography of his renowned father, George Stephenson, we have the history of the son, born December 16th, 1803, under very humble circumstances. The want of education, so strongly felt by the father, was not to be experienced by the son. He was placed for education at an early period at Long Benton, and afterwards with Mr. Bruce at Newcastle, who presided over the most esteemed school of that district. There is, however, great reason to believe that the greatest advantage derived by young Stephenson proceeded from the example set him by his father, by whom he was cherished and cultivated with extraordinary solicitude. Influenced by the powerful example of his father, and established in industrial pursuits, he went to Edinburgh university, and attended lectures under Hope, Leslie, Jameson, and other distinguished teachers. Here, by his assiduity, he gained a prize in mathematics. From this time he was devoted to the great object of his life, being in 1822 apprenticed to his father, and engaged in those researches and operations connected with locomotive engines which have so justly rendered the names of father and son of enduring celebrity. His great works I need not enumerate, nor have I the necessary knowledge to descant upon their merits; they have received the seal of authority, and the decision has been adopted with unanimity and acknowledged by the most distinguished of rewards—a resting place for his remains in Westminster abbey.

MRS. ANN PERCIVAL died November 9th, 1859, at the age of seventy-three. She was the widow of an old and highly esteemed friend of mine, a banker in the city of London, and an associate of our body from its commencement. Although we derived no communications from the labours of Mr. Richard Percival, he was warmly attached to us, so much so as to induce his widow to desire to have her name placed as his successor, and subscribing to our funds from the time of her husband's decease, which occurred in 1854. Mr. Percival was a fellow of the Society of Antiquaries, a man of very general and useful information, possessed of many excellent qualities; and as one having had many opportunities through a series of years of witnessing his benevolent exertions in various institutions, I have great satisfaction in recording my testimony to his many virtues and kindly disposition.

The obituary of 1859 closes with one who was a member from the commencement of our Association, and one to whom for many years we are indebted for a variety of communications.

WILLIAM HENRY ROLFE, esq., was a native of Kent, having been born at Sandwich in 1778. He died on the 27th November last, being then in the eighty-first year of his age. He was a grandson of Boys, known as the historian of Sandwich, whose example may reasonably be supposed to have influenced his taste and inclination in antiquarian research; for first engaged in agricultural pursuits, he abandoned them, and having a sufficient competency, devoted himself to archæology, confining his labours, however, principally to the locality in which he resided. Mr. Rolfe's communications to our Association were made chiefly through the hands of Mr. C. Roach Smith, and date from the holding of our first Congress at Canterbury. The volumes of our *Journal* from i. to ix. contain numerous evidences of the interest he took in archæological research. From him we received an exhibition of two hundred Roman coins and a large quantity of fibulæ, rings, buckles, and bracelets in bronze, found near Margate;[1] and of Saxon coins, found in the Isle of Thanet, yielding an unpublished variety of the penny of Æthelheard, archbishop of Canterbury.[2] He also exhibited a leaden seal found at Canterbury;[3] a collection of antiquities obtained from a dealer, consisting of bronze celts, Roman fibulæ and keys, and various mediæval antiquities.[4] He submitted to us also the results of excavations on the site of a Saxon cemetery at Osengal in the Isle of Thanet;[5] an aureus of Carinus, found at Sandwich;[6] a bunch of early Saxon keys from Osengal;[7] two enamelled fibulæ, found at Richborough;[8] Saxon and Roman fibulæ, in the Isle of Thanet; and a silver Carausius, found near Richborough;[9] an ancient plated coin (brass, covered with a lamina of gold); a copy of an imperial coin, VERVS.IMP.;[10] Roman coins from Richborough, and a silver ring of the fifteenth century, with figures of saints, found at Minster;[11] and a communication in relation to the discovery of an amphitheatre at Richborough;[12] a silver cochlear found at Richborough castle;[13] a Norman spur, found in the Thames;[14] a satirical medal of the date of 1688;[15] a large silver medal of archbishop Sancroft and seven of his suffragans;[16] a pillow case, reported to have been that of Richard III, taken from Bosworth field;[17] a tile and bellarmine, found in Spitalfields, and tokens from Bonner hall;[18] a spur and keys, found at

[1] Vol. i, p. 146.
[2] Ib., p. 149.
[3] Vol. ii, p. 98.
[4] Ib., p. 186.
[5] Ibid., pp. 275, 352.
[6] Ib., p. 336.
[7] Vol. iii, p. 246.
[8] Vol. iv, p. 57.
[9] Ib., p. 144.
[10] Ib., p. 382.
[11] Vol. v, p. 337.
[12] Ib., p. 374.
[13] Vol. vi, p. 149.
[14] Ib., p. 452.
[15] Vol. vii, p. 169.
[16] Vol. viii, p. 64.
[17] Ib., p. 139.
[18] Ib., p. 142.

Sandwich;[1] an ivory drinking horn[2] (*temp.* Edw. IV); an embossed brick from Sandwich;[3] a bronze cup from Boughton hill, Kent; a bronze stirrup (*temp.* Henry VII), and a portion of painted glass from Canterbury, having the rebus of Robin Tree.[4]

In the course of many years assiduous attention to local antiquities, it will readily be conceived Mr. Rolfe collected together a large assemblage of antiquities, and it is satisfactory to know that a short time before his decease, they passed into the hands of our esteemed associate Mr. Joseph Mayer, F.S.A., a most zealous antiquary, and that they now occupy an appropriate position in his museum, being placed together with the Faussett collection, also purchased by Mr. Mayer, of which an account is given by Mr. C. R. Smith, in the "*Inventorium Sepulchrale.*"

[1] Vol. viii, p. 161.   [2] Ib., p. 367.   [3] P. 370.   [4] Vol. ix, p. 75.

Antiquarian Intelligence.

MR. THOS. BATEMAN, whose antiquarian researches have so frequently enriched the pages of our *Journal*, is about to publish[1] in a collected form, *Ten Years Diggings in Celtic and Saxon Grave Hills in the Counties of Derby, Stafford, and York, from* 1848 *to* 1858. To these reports will be added notices of some former discoveries hitherto unpublished, together with remarks on the crania and pottery from the mounds.

THE VERY REV. DR. HUSENBETH has just published a second and greatly enlarged edition of *Emblems of Saints, by which they are distinguished in Works of Art.*[2] A work indispensable to the mediæval antiquary.

COLLECTANEA ARCHÆOLOGICA.—Under this title, the Council of the British Archæological Association have determined upon publishing the more lengthened papers and communications, including Pedigrees and Original Documents, which from their number and extent it is impossible to put forth in the quarterly *Journal*. The work will be printed in 4to., to admit of extended illustration; and published as occasionally required, in parts, three of which are to constitute a volume of about five hundred pages. To members of the Association these will be obtainable by a subscription of ten shillings each part; to the public they will be sold at an advanced price; and such associates as desire to possess the COLLECTANEA are requested to signify their wish to T. J. PETTIGREW, ESQ., Treasurer, to whom also may be transmitted any donations in furtherance of this object, rendered essentially necessary by the abundance of materials contributed for publication.

[1] J. Russell Smith, Soho-square. The work will constitute one volume, 8vo., with fifty engravings on wood. The names of subscribers should be transmitted to Messrs. Bemrose & Sons, Derby.
[2] Longman & Co.

THE JOURNAL

OF THE

British Archaeological Association.

SEPTEMBER 1860.

ON READING AND ITS ANTIQUITIES.

BY T. J. PETTIGREW, F.R.S., F.S.A., V.P. AND TREASURER.

IF Reading was a town in the time of the Roman occupation in England, it was one of inconsiderable note; pertaining to Saxon times, it assumes a degree of importance. Towards the latter part of the fifth century it formed a part of the kingdom of Wessex; and the first notice we obtain of it is that Cerdic, accompanied by his son Kenric, made a descent at a place called Chardford, or Cerdic's ford, and obtained possession of the western coast. From its occupation by the Saxons in the sixth century, it may be presumed that the ancient inhabitants were either expelled or subdued. Peace seems to have been established, and civilization must have advanced, as, until the ninth century, when the Danes made their predatory excursion, we have no notices of its condition. Reading, A.D. 868, became the headquarters of Ivar, a Danish freebooter, a piratical king. The Saxons, however, succeeded in driving out the Danes after battles fought at Englefield, Reading, Aston, etc., in which sanguinary engagements Ethelwulph and Ethelred[1] lost their lives. The contests, at various times, between the Danes and Saxons continued; and although articles of peace were made, and sworn to be observed,—on the one part on the relics of the saints, and on the other by the bracelet,—they were yet evaded. In the eleventh century Sweyn carried devastation

[1] This is given upon the authority of Brompton, but the statement is doubtful.

into the towns and villages of Hampshire and Berkshire,
and reduced Reading, Wallingford, and Cholsey to ashes.
At this time a monastery for nuns, at Reading, to which I
shall presently more particularly allude, was destroyed.

In the twelfth century, under Henry I, Reading began to
acquire importance.   In the twentieth of this reign (1120),
the splendid abbey for Benedictine monks was erected; and
the period of building extended over five years.   The sovereign
endowed the abbey with large possessions, and presented to
it several relics.[1]   At his decease (occasioned, as has been
so often reported, by a surfeit of stewed lampreys), his body
was, agreeably to his expressed desire, conveyed from Normandy to Reading abbey for interment, and a monument of
much magnificence erected to his memory.   At the Reformation, in the reign of Edward VI, this was destroyed.
Sandford[2] is the authority for the destruction of the monument, the demolition of which was accompanied by aggra-
vating and disgraceful circumstances.   The bones of the
king, he says, "could not enjoy repose in his grave, but were
thrown out to make room for a stable for horses."   The
monument was in a sad condition *temp.* Ric. II, who gave
orders for its repair.   This was done satisfactorily, as a
prescript was directed to the treasurer and barons of the
Exchequer granting a patent of liberties to the abbot and
convent for repairing the tomb and statue of the founder.[3]
There is reason to believe that a portion of the stone sarcophagus which held the royal remains was discovered in
1815, upon digging to make a footway to the National
Schools, which must have been near the centre of the choir
of the abbey church.   My late friend archdeacon Nares gave
an account of this,[4] and we learn that the fragment discovered exhibited the bases and the bottoms of the shafts
of a complete row of small columns, or rather half columns,

---

[1] The principal relic appears to have been the reputed hand of St. James the
Apostle, which was enclosed in a case of gold ; but of which it was deprived by
Richard I.   John afterwards, as compensation, granted a mark of gold, to be
paid annually at the Exchequer, to the abbey.   Henry III reduced this to ten
marks of silver.   The charter of donation of the hand is given in Dugdale's
Monasticon, vol. iv, Appendix No. III, E Registro de Reading, M.S. Harl.
1708, fol. 155.   An inventory of the relics from a MS. in the Cottonian Collection, Cleop. E. iv, fol. 234, is also printed in Dugdale.
[2] Genealogical History, p. 28.
[3] This document is given in Dugdale, vol. iv, App., *Num.*, xxx.
[4] Archæologia, xviii, pp. 272-4.

which had evidently surrounded the whole coffin, the forms of which were fancifully varied, being alternately semi-circular and semi-hexagonal, and in the Norman style. The columns were fifty in number : eighteen on each side, eight at the broad and six at the narrow. The sarcophagus was seven feet long by two feet and a half broad at the head, gradually contracting to two feet at the smaller end. No bones were found near to it.

The revenues of the abbey were increased by other burials within its walls: Reginald, earl of Cornwall, the natural son of Henry I; William, son of Henry II; Adeliza, queen of Henry II ; John and Isabella, children of Richard Plantagenet, second son of John; Constantia, daughter of Edmund de Longley, duke of York. The viscera of Hugh Mortimer were also interred here.

The abbey church was completed in the reign of Henry II, and consecrated in 1164 by Thomas à Becket, in the presence of the monarch and ten bishops. Here the parliament met in 1171 and various statutes were enacted. Reading was a spot highly favoured by this king, and many events of historical importance here took place.

Little of importance happened during the reign of Richard I in relation to Reading, if we except an inquiry into the maladministration of affairs by the regent and chancellor Longchamp, who by sentence was excommunicated with lighted candles in a very solemn manner. A remarkable event occurred in 1209, arising out of the death of a woman, said to have been accidentally killed by a priest of the university of Oxford, who in consequence of the charge fled ; but was seized, and with three others committed to prison, and hanged by order of king John.[1] This mode of justice being in opposition to the privileges of his order, the clergy were exasperated, and masters and students, amounting in numbers to about three thousand, quitted the university in 1213, settled at Cambridge, Reading, and other places, and materially enriched and improved this town. During this reign several conventions were held in this place.[2]

[1] There is another version given of this event, and adopted by Coates in his *History of Reading*, namely that in 1209, in the reign of John, a *scholar* of Oxford killed a woman, and that three of his chamber fellows were seized and hanged. The scholar absconded.

[2] Two ecclesiastical councils are referred to by Coates (*Hist. of Reading*, p. 251), one in 1213, the other in 1279. It is probable they were held in the chapter house of the abbey.

Henry III selected Reading as a place of residence. The first charter granted by English sovereigns to the guild merchants of Reading was by this monarch in 1254 ;[1] it may be looked upon as the foundation of the corporate privileges, and in 1263 a parliament was held here instead of at London ; the conduct of the rebellious barons, however, with the earl of Essex at their head, prevented the business for which it had been summoned being entered upon. In 1273 a council was held here, at which it was decreed that the clergy of each diocese should elect two proctors to appear at the next convocation, " who, together with us, shall have authority to treat of these things, which are expedient for the common good of the Church of England, at our next meeting in the time of parliament."[2] From this period we may date the assembly of convocation at the commencement of every new parliament. Up to the reign of Anne they continued to actively operate, then sunk into a formality, and are now apparently approaching to a revival of active duty.

The abbey was loaded with debts in the time of Edward I, who, in 1275, took the management of its affairs into his own hands, and appointed commissioners to examine into them. In the reign of Edward II no matter of essential moment took place in reference to Reading; but in that of Edward III several circumstances occurred which, if time permitted, it would be interesting to dwell upon. I must not, however, even in this brief sketch, omit to mention that in 1346 Edward passed his Christmas here, held a great tournament, borrowed a large sum of money from the monks, for which he pledged his jewels, and thus obtained means to carry on his war with France. Here, in 1350, John of Gaunt espoused Blanche, daughter of Henry duke of Lancaster, an event duly celebrated by Chaucer in his *Dream*. The festivities upon this occasion were of no mean duration, as the poet records.[3] The marriage of Edward's son being honoured by the presence of the sovereign and his court,

---

[1] This charter is printed in Dugdale, but the early records of the guild are lost.

[2] "Qui auctoritatem habeant unâ nobiscum, tractare de his, quæ ecclesiæ communi utilitati expediant Anglicanæ in proxima congregatione nostra tempore parliamenti proximi."

[3] "And the feste holden was in tentes,
In a rome, in a large plaine,
Under a wode, in a champaine,

with the king of France at that time his prisoner, must have been one of the most imposing sights recorded in English history. Very different indeed was the scene in the subsequent reign of Richard II, when the rebels of Reading, uniting with those of Kent and Essex, marched under the guidance of Wat Tyler and Jack Straw into London, committing all manner of outrage by the way. The rebellion quashed, a reconciliation between the sovereign and his uncle the duke of Lancaster followed. The duke returned to England, was protected by bodies of archers and one thousand men at arms, who conducted him to Reading, where Richard awaited his arrival preparatory to their progress to London, where a parliament was summoned to assemble. By the medium of John of Gaunt, Richard in 1389 concluded a peace with the barons at Reading, and in 1390 another parliament was called at this place. The times were, however, troublous, and peace of very uncertain duration. Conspiracies were formed, and at length the monarch laid down his crown, whence issued the disastrous civil contentions between the houses of York and Lancaster.

Whether Henry IV ever visited Reading is uncertain, but Henry V issued a proclamation there in 1415, proposing to borrow money of his loving subjects to continue the war with France. He, dying at Vincennes in 1422, was succeeded by his son Henry VI, who in 1440 held a parliament at Reading, adjourned from Westminster, where a new order of nobility, that of viscount, was established, lord Beaumont being the first to bear that distinction. Other parliaments were holden here, and in the reign of Edward IV, upon the visitation of the plague in London, one in 1461. Others were held in 1467 and 1468.

The reformation abolished synods, councils, and ecclesiastical assemblies which had been frequently maintained at Reading, from the time of Henry II. In 1475, it is upon

> Betwixte a river, and a welle,
> Where never had abbay ne selle
> Yben, ne kirke, house, ne village;
> In time of any mane's age.
> And dured three monthes the fest,
> In one estate and never ceast,
> From early the rising of the sonne,
> Till the day spent was & yronne,
> In justing, dauncing, and lustinesse,
> And all that sowned to gentilnesse."

record in the "corporation diary," that the borough was assessed in the sum of 30s. 10d., by the parliament, as their proportion of the subsidy granted, and four persons were appointed by the corporation for its collection.   This is said to have been the first instance we have, of any taxes being levied upon the inhabitants in this manner.

We pass on to the reign of Henry VII, when we find that the king ordered the abbot Thorne, to convert St. John's house or hospital, a nunnery which had been suppressed, to pious uses.   This was in 1487, and in accordance with the abbot's suggestion, and the king's acquiescence, it gave rise to the foundation of the present free grammar school, the king endowing it with an annual stipend of £10, to be paid out of the crown rate of Reading.[1]

Henry VIII resided occasionally at the abbey, and his queen, Catherine of Arragon, was here in 1529.   The king was also here in 1541.   Edward VI was received in 1552, at Coley Cross with much ceremony by the mayor and corporation, and the same was observed towards Mary, who, with her husband Philip, visited Reading in 1553.   Queen Elizabeth in 1588, resided at the abbey, which had then been converted into a royal palace.   She, on one occasion in 1601, here knighted John Norris of Fyfield.   She conferred many benefits on the town, confirmed and enlarged the charter, and gave special encouragement to the woollen trade, the most substantial occupation of the inhabitants.

Among other matters of interest connected with this place of historical importance, not the least is, that it constitutes the birthplace of archbishop Laud, in 1573, in a house which is still standing on the north side of Broad-street.

Upon the breaking out of the plague in London and Westminster, in 1625, Charles adjourned a part of the Michaelmas term to be held at Reading, for the conduct of public business ; the disease, however, making its appearance, the market and staple of cloth were removed for safety and sanitary precaution.   Reading continued to be visited with the plague for nearly half a century, and it proved at times, particularly in 1626 and 1638, to be of great virulence. During the civil wars, the demands made upon the inhabitants were very great, and gave rise to strong remonstrances.

[1] See Dugdale, vol. iv, Appx., *Num.* xxxii.

The corporation petitioned the king, setting forth their inability to comply with the demands made, having already advanced such loans as extended even to the undoing of the town. Their petitions, however, produced little effect, for the king increased his demands, through the governor, sir Arthur Aston; and the corporation, unable to obtain the sums demanded of the inhabitants, were under the necessity of mortgaging their possessions to meet the exigency. These proceedings seemed to alienate the affections of his majesty's subjects, and to abate their zeal in the royal cause. The parliament determined to pursue the war with energy, and required of the earl of Essex, who had the command of the forces, to attempt the recovery of Reading, and thus open free communication with the west of England. Details of the proceedings connected with this portion of our history have been abundantly given, and do not need to be here further referred to, than to say that Aston, after having three times defeated the earl of Essex, received a severe wound which incapacitated him from retaining the command of the garrison, and that it was surrendered to the parliamentary forces in 1643. The town received no great damage during the siege, the chief injury falling upon the abbey and Saint Giles's church. In 1647, the king was brought to Reading and placed under a guard in the house of Lord Craven, at Caversham.

Charles II and his queen passed through Reading in 1663, and received from the corporation fifty pieces of gold for his own use, thirty for the queen, and £37 : 6 as fees to their servants. During this reign and that of James II, party and religious feuds were rife in Reading, as elsewhere. The revolution of 1688 gave repose to the inhabitants, and enabled them to promote the industrial occupations of the town. The manufacturing of sail cloth in lieu of woollen was now encouraged.

A curious practice prevailed at Reading in the time of George I :—All who could prove that they had been accustomed to boil a pot within the limits of the borough, were admitted to the privilege of voting for members to serve in parliament, and the election being ardently contested in 1714, the town of Reading is described as having had the appearance of a large encampment of gipsies, fires being lighted in every street and alley, lodgers being equally with

householders, admitted to the privilege.   They were called
pot-whabblers, a term, I presume, synonymous with that more
recently known as pot-whalloppers.   Let us now, however,
divert our attention from historical to more antiquarian
matters.

The origin of the name of Reading is uncertain, but from
its construction, one cannot but regard it as Saxon. Various
explanations have been attempted, and surmises put forth,
those, however, which appear to me most entitled to credit,
are derived from the compounding of two Saxon words : *ryð*,
a river, or *reod*, a reed, and *ing*, a pasture or meadow. These
answer to the situation and character of the place.   The
manor of Reading was in the possession of the abbots until the
dissolution of the abbey, when it came into the hands of the
crown.   It was subsequently settled by James I upon his
queen, and afterwards on prince Charles.   I am not aware
of the precise time in which it fell to the corporation.   The
mayor is now the lord of the manor.

Although the arms of Reading are inscribed with the
initials E. R., and one of the five maidens depicted upon them,
crowned, it is not to be inferred that the corporation hold
them from queen Elizabeth, a tablet being among the archives
of this body, which gives a representation of the same without the letters ; there is also a certificate relating to them,
signed by Henry, clarencieux-king-of-arms, of the date of
1566 ; under another representation, there is a certificate in
the College of Arms, and a further one among Ashmole's
MSS. at Oxford,—all confirmatory of this fact.   The origin
of the maiden's head is obscure ; it has been reasonably conjectured to bear reference to the convent of nuns established
by Elfrida in the tenth century, and the introduction of the
word *natalia* (native), in one of the certificates to which I
have alluded, may be regarded as a further proof of this
view.   But the heads are ornamented with flowers, not veils,
as might have been expected, and this throws some doubt
upon the matter.   The queen is the centre figure, and may
be considered as an addition probably made at the time of
the visit of her majesty.

A castle is said to have been at Reading ; Leland fixes its
erection in Saxon times.   In his day, however, he was unable
to obtain any precise information regarding it ; he could not
even determine its site, for no remains were to be found.

Castle-street probably bears some reference to it, but all is conjectural. The learned antiquary I have mentioned, says, " it is very likely that a peace of the abbey was builded of the ruins of it; peradventure it stood wher the abbey was." Hearne looked upon a part of the abbey as having been built with the castle remains. Camden following, and depending upon Leland, speaks of a *castrum vetustissimum*; but reference has been made to a manuscript in the Bodleian library, by Robert Beccensis, imperfectly published by Du Chesne, without the name of the author, in which the following passage occurs:—"Stephen, having raised the siege of Wallingford, destroyed Crowmarsh. For, in the preceding year, the followers of duke Henry, who resided at Wallingford, had not only destroyed the camp at Britwall, which had long infested their quarters, but also the *castle*, which king Stephen against all right had erected near the abbey of Reading."[1] This, I think, proves the existence of a castle, not indeed built by the Saxons, but in the time of Stephen, renowned as a castle builder. I am not aware whether any research has been made to determine the presence of any remains. Mr. Man[2] expresses his belief that they are to be found at the south-east corner of the Forbury, near Blake's Bridge, within the precincts of the abbey, but not connected with it, therefore forming no part of the original building. He goes further and states it, in his opinion, to have been a square building, with projecting towers at the four corners. The side next the river (he says,) was about sixty feet in length, and had a square tower at each end. That at the south-east has been removed, but the other has two sides almost perfect. The slope of the hill is faced with a strong perpendicular wall of flints, on which this tower is erected, and is about fifty feet high from the level of the water, the top seems to have been finished with battlements, but they are so covered with ivy, that this could not be satisfactorily determined. In the side walls are loop-holes, some of which front the river, whilst others command the space between the towers, in front of the building. These statements appear to me deserving of examination.

[1] " Soluta est itaque obsidio quæ circa Wallingford ordinata fuerat, rege Stephano Crauenense subvertente. Nam anno præterito familia ducis Henrici, quæ Wallingford incolebat non solum contra jus et fas erexerat apud abbatiam Radinges pessundederat."
[2] Hist. and Antiq. of Reading, p. 276.

The monastery at Reading constituted the chief religious establishment of the place.   It is regarded as having been founded by Elfrida, or Elfrith, the mother-in-law of Edward the martyr, and built as an atonement for having caused his death by a ruffian who stabbed him at the gate of Corfe castle in Dorsetshire, when in the act of drinking a cup of wine to her health.   The destruction of the monastery has caused the usual uncertainty as to its precise situation and arrangement.   Leland, who wrote in the time of Henry VIII, is our authority upon this, as on most occasions of subjects that came under his cognizance, and he writes thus: "for more certante, I know not, whither the old nunneries stood not yn the place whar th' abbaye of Reddinge stondeth, and whither St. Marie's be not a newer foundation."   This conjecture is, however, disputed, and indeed it appears to be little beyond assertion, and to have merely Leland's supposition for its authority.   It has been thought by some to have been where St. Mary's church now stands.

In the year of Edward's murder (A.D. 979), then, was founded the monastery, and it was destroyed by the Danes in 1006.   It never was rebuilt ; but it is referred to in the charter of the abbey founded by Henry I, in 1121, or rather according to Matthew Paris, 1120.   Of this abbey we have information given by Dugdale and other authorities.   Of the building we have still some, though but scanty remains, and the restoration or removal of these is still a matter *sub judice,* and upon which we may fairly be entitled to an opinion.   As archæologists, there can be little doubt as to what would be the nature of our decision.   In my introductory address to the present congress, I quoted authorities to show how sacred any historical land-mark deserves to be regarded,[1] and the remains in question may be fairly designated as belonging to that class of objects.   It is, however, worthy of discussion, now we are upon the spot, and have the advantage of making a personal inspection of the ruins, and it may not here be amiss to quote the expressed opinion of the late sir Henry Englefield, bart., in relation to their character.   He says, "the shattered and disjointed ruins of the building which now remain, bear a character of majesty very singular and almost peculiar to themselves.   Stript, by destroyers of more than ordinary patience and industry,

---

[1] See p. 26 *ante.*

of almost every stone which cased the walls, they still, though built only of small flints, defy the injuries of time and weather, and have more the appearance of rocks, than of the work of human hands."[1] No inconsiderable part of the materials of the abbey has been employed in the construction of St. Mary's and St. Lawrence's churches, and much was conveyed to Windsor for the erection of the hospital for the poor knights. Other purposes have also been effected by the aid of the abbey remains. The ceiling of the conventual church and twenty-one loads of other timber were, in 1550, purchased by the inhabitants of Reading for St. Mary's church. The corporation, under Elizabeth, had liberty to dig and carry away two hundred loads of freestone from the ruins. The wainscoting of the hall of Magdalene college, Oxford, is said to have been procured from this abbey. During the civil war, ruins of the north transept were blown up, and the abbey church further dilapidated. Masses of wall were, in more recent times, taken away by general Conway to build the bridge over the road leading from Henley to Wargrave. The ruins of the abbey were, in the time of Hearne, not inconsiderable. In one of his MS. diaries deposited in the Bodleian library (vol. 49, p. 24), there is the copy of a letter addressed by him to Browne Willis upon the extent of them. This epistle is dated in January, 1713. What is still exposed to view, unquestionably makes us acquainted with the solidity of the building, and only leads to regret, that by civil and other disturbances, the destruction of such walls should have been so materially promoted.[2]

We are not in possession of minute particulars in relation to the building. Sir H. Englefield made a ground plan, which perhaps gives more information regarding it than any other document, as from it we may form some idea as to its extent, arrangement and structure. Within the outward boundary, a space amounting to about thirty acres was enclosed. There were four arched gateways with battlements on their tops, which may be presumed to be of the same nature as on the walls. These gateways in the outer court are gone ; but that leading to the inner courts still

---

[1] Archæologia, vi, 61.

[2] The spoliation was continued up to a very recent date; but the remains have now been taken under the protection of the corporation. Since the holding of the Berkshire Congress, it has also been determined to preserve the gateway, and its restoration has been entrusted to the care and skill of Mr. Gilbert Scott.

remains, and is composed of bricks, chalk and stone.   Over
the archway is a flat timber floor supporting chambers,
which are surmounted by a modern parapet wall.   An
octangular tower presents itself at the corners of the building,
and near the spring of the arch on each side, there is a square
buttress.   The arch facing the north will be familiar to all,
and will be admired as Saxon work, with an obtuse point at
the top, rising from three stone clustered pillars, without
capitals, and rounded to the summit of the arch.   The arch
on the south varies from this, in being quite circular, and
has various ornamentations, a dolphin, dog, or fox, together
with the rose of the house of Lancaster, which go to form
spouts to discharge accumulated water.   Mr. Man gives
twenty feet square as the measurement of the space under
the building between the two outer arches, and this is
divided into two unequal departments, by an arch which
extends to the ceiling, and from which a gate was formerly
suspended by large hooks.   The character of this part of the
building and that of the ornaments, would lead us to place it
in the time of Henry VII, or beginning of that of Henry VIII.
Within the gateway was the inner court, leading, it may be
presumed, to the chief entrance of the abbey ; but it is not possible to speak with certainty.   A passage is marked in sir H.
Englefield's plan, forty-six feet long and fifteen wide, opening
into the south-east corner of the cloisters; it may have formed
a private way for the monks.   The cloisters occupied about
one hundred and forty-five feet square, and communicated
with the main building and the church.   The great hall or
consistory must have been a fine room, and of ample dimensions, not less than eighty feet by forty, having three entrance doors and five large windows.   From pilasters on the
side walls the arched ceiling sprung.   Upon digging within
the walls, Mr. Man acquaints us,[1] that the foundation of the
outer walls of this room (and probably of the rest of the
building) was found to be seven feet deep and twelve feet
thick to the set off ; above which the walls were six feet
thick, as in other parts of the building.   A national school
now occupies the spot where in former times assemblies and
parliaments were held, and whence the mandates of general
and provincial councils proceeded.[2]   But I must not detain

---

[1] P. 251.

[2] Parliaments were held at Reading in the reigns of Henry II, 1171;

you by conjectures as to passages and other portions belonging to the abbey. I have not a sufficient familiarity with the locality, and I shall therefore, proceeding upon the information to be derived from sir H. Englefield's plan, simply mention that the church was erected on the north side. The measurements given by Englefield are 102 feet by 52 feet within the walls. Choir, 98 feet by 34 feet. Side aisles, 19 feet in breadth. Transept, 196 feet by 56 feet. Nave is put down at 215 feet. The extreme length circa 420 feet. Breadth, exclusive of transept, 92 feet. It was not completed until 1164, in which year we learn that it was consecrated to the Virgin Mary and St. John the Evangelist (although it was generally called St. Mary's abbey) by Thomas à Becket, archbishop of Canterbury. It was for two hundred monks of the Benedictine order,[1] though it does not appear at any time to have been inhabited by so great a number. In 1305 there were only sixty-five inmates, and in 1377, one hundred. The charter recites that three abbeys, those of Radynge, Cholsey, and Leominster, having been destroyed, and their lands and possessions usurped and alienated by laymen, Henry, with the advice of his bishops and others, for his soul's health and for those of William his father, William his brother, William his son, Matilda his mother, Matilda his wife, etc., had built and endowed a new monastery at Radynge. He gives to the abbey various privileges, freeing them from all taxes, tributes, and customs, by land and water, with power to try all offences committed within and without the borough, in the same manner as belongs to royal authority. Upon the death of the abbot, all the possessions of the monastery are secured to the disposal of the prior and chapter of the monks, and seeing that the abbot has no revenues but what are in common with his brethren, it provides that whoever by divine consent, and canonical election, shall be made abbot, shall not bestow the alms of the monastery on his lay kindred, or any others, but for the entertainment of the poor and strangers. The charter is dated 1125, and was confirmed by subsequent charters and extended privileges.[2] Pope Innocent III, in

Richard II, 1191; John, 1213; Henry III, 1263; Richard II, 1384, 1389, 1390; Henry VI, 1439–40, 1451, 1452; Edward IV, 1461, 1467, 1468.

[1] See foundation charter of Henry I, Cotton MSS., Vespasian, E. v, fol. 17, printed in Dugdale's *Monasticon*, iv, p. 40.

[2] The following charters are given in the *Monasticon:*—Henry I, as already

·1207, gave letters confirmatory to the abbot and convent of Reading of the Cluniac order.

Among the privileges granted to the abbey by Henry I was that of coining money. Of this, however, they were afterwards deprived;[1] but it was restored to them by Edward III, who in the twelfth year of his reign, and by a writ to the treasurer and barons of the Exchequer, November 8th, 1338, gave to the abbots and monks the power of exercising one mint and one die at Radynge, to coin farthings (obolos), half farthings (forlingos), and pennies (sterlingos). Three dies are ordered to be prepared of hard, and competent metal for this purpose, with whatsoever impression and circumscription the abbot shall order; and they are directed to be sent to the Treasury at Westminster as soon as possible, that from them, within fifteen days next after the feast of St. Martin at the farthest, they may be delivered to the abbot.

Ruding[2] says that the profits arising from the mints were assigned to the archbishops, bishops, and abbots, although they were restrained from using their own dies, and were

referred to; also one giving relics (the hand of St. James the apostle), MS. Harl., 1708, fol. 15; charter of R. episcop. Sar. de Uno Monetario, Lond. Harl. MS., 1708, fol. 111; charter of Richard I (Num. xi); Richard II (Num. xxx). There is also a very curious "Inventorye off Relyques off the House off Redyng," MS. Cott., Cleopatra, E. iv, fol. 234 (Num. xxxiii). The rev. Mr. Coates gives, in his *History and Antiquities of Reading*, a parliamentary survey taken in 1650 (see also Dugdale, IV App., Num. xxxiv). The second charter of the abbey is of Stephen, who confirmed those of Henry I, and also the donations made by Adeliza, the empress Matilda, David king of Scotland, etc. Henry II confirmed them, and granted an annual payment of forty marks of silver at the Exchequer, until he could secure to them a revenue of a like amount. Richard I, John, Henry III, Edward II, III, Richard II, Henry V, VI, Edward IV, Henry VIII, all gave confirmatory charters. Leland (*Collect.* i, 69) gives a list of benefactors to the abbey. An enumeration of the contents of the several Registers of the abbey of Reading is given in the modern edition of Dugdale's *Monasticon* by Bandinel, Ellis, and Caley; also from a MS. belonging to Jesus College, Oxford, and from records in the office of the Lord Treasurer's Remembrancer, Exchequer, Reading; likewise from the King's Remembrancer's Office and the Chapter House, Westminster. Many MSS. which formerly were in the library of this monastery, are now in the British Museum, having passed, at the time of the dissolution, into the possession of Henry VIII. Mr. Coates has referred to these documents, the most important of which is that known as the Wollascot MS., which has a catalogue of the monastery library as it stood in the time of Henry III. The common seal of the abbey is given by Coates (p. 247).

[1] It was in the 8th of Edward II that the privilege of coining was taken away from the abbey, for in his charter of *Inspeximus* occurs the following passage: "Nos autem donationes, concessiones, et confirmationes prædictas, *dicta clausula de* MONETA et uno MONETARIO *excepta*." (Registr. Abb. MS. Harl., fol. 41*b*).

[2] Annals of the Coinage, iv, 163.

compelled to receive them from the chief Mint in the Tower
of London, and to pay an annual rent to the master of that
Mint. The dies which they were permitted to use were at
first for pennies only. It was Edward III who granted to
the abbot of Reading power to coin halfpence and farthings,
as well as pennies, which had been usual. In later times,
half-groats were struck by the archbishops of Canterbury
and York, and some groats by the latter prelate.

Of the coinage at Reading pennies have been met with,
and one of the reign of Edward I. On the *rev.*, VILLA
RADINGI, with an escallop shell in the second quarter of the
cross. The arms of the abbey are *azure*, three escallop shells,
or. Halfpennies of the time of Edward III have been
found : they read, on the *obv.*, EDWARDVS, and VILLA RA-
DINGY on the *rev.* No farthings have yet been discovered.
Mr. Hawkins[1] describes the halfpenny of Edward III struck
at Reading thus: " EDWARDVS REX. A scallop shell in one
angle instead of pellets."

The abbot of Reading was a mitred abbot, and had a seat
in Parliament. His order of precedence was after Glastonbury and St. Albans. Upon the reduction of the number of
abbots sitting in parliament in the reign of Edward III,
when from sixty-four (the number existing in the forty-ninth
year of Henry III), they were reduced to twenty-five, the
the abbot of Reading was retained, and he held his privilege
until the dissolution. Hugh Prior, of Lewes, was the first
abbot; and Hugh Cook, commonly called Faringdon, the
thirty-first and last. The abbey was dissolved in 1539, and
the revenues appropriated to the crown. Failing to acknowledge the king's supremacy in ecclesiastical affairs, the last
abbot was executed at Reading in the month of November
1539, he being there hanged and quartered as a traitor to
his king and country, on the same day that Whiting, abbot
of Glastonbury, also suffered.

Some idea of the importance of this monastery may be
formed by the knowledge that, at the dissolution, the gross
revenue was valued at £2,116 : 3 : 9. Dugdale gives a

[1] Silver Coins of England, p. 101, plate XXIV, No. 315. In the British
Museum. REX AN. Same type, a star after AN. and VILLA. Also in the British
Museum. Mr. Bartlett has treated of the monastic coins of Reading minted
in the reigns of Edward I, II, and III (*Archæologia*, v, 338). The penny is
engraved in *Tables of English Coins* by the Soc. of Antiq., plate III, No. 2;
Snelling's *View*, pl. i, No. 7. The halfpenny, Suppl., pl. I.

smaller sum, £1,938 : 14 : 3¾. As the estates, according to
the records in the Augmentation Office, amounted only to
£1,402 : 9 : 10, this may be more correct; but the site of
the monastery and demesne lands were not included in the
valuation. Henry VIII appointed Thomas Vachell to the
office of supervisor of the possessions of the monastery, the
king keeping the abbey in his own hands. In the 2nd Edward VI the king granted the manor of Reading to Edward
duke of Somerset ; but he being attainted of high treason
and beheaded in 1551, it reverted to the crown. Mary
appointed sir Francis Englefield keeper of the abbey, park,
etc., and in the same year granted the site of the abbey to
sir Henry Jerningham, the master of her household. Queen
Elizabeth kept it in her own hands; James I settled it upon
his queen, and upon the death of Anne of Denmark it was
given to prince Charles. He granted the site to sir Thomas
Clarges, under the yearly rent of forty shillings. Clarges
sold it to John Dalby and Anthony Blagrave, esq. Mr.
Dalby's share was purchased by Henry Vansittart, esq., and
it is now in the possession of that family. The other share
also is in that of the family of Blagrave.

Several bishops were consecrated at Reading abbey: I find
in 1206 Joceline de Welles, bishop of Bath and Wells ; in
1215, William de Cornhull, bishop of Lichfield and Coventry;
in 1235, Robert Grostete, bishop of Lincoln, and Howel ap
Ednevet, bishop of St. Asaph ; in 1244, Roger, bishop of Bath
and Wells ; and in 1245, Richard Blondy, bishop of Exeter.
The abbey mills are still entire, and distinguished by several small arches. Over the mill race is a large one with a
zig-zag moulding.

The FRANCISCANS, or FRIARS MINORS, came into England
in 1224, and about ten years posterior to this time (July
14th, 1233), the permission of the pope having been obtained, the grant of a piece of land was made by the abbot
and convent to them to build a friery at Reading. It was
on marshy ground adjoining the Caversham road, and the
locality was found so bad that in 1285 they were permitted
to build on another spot. In 33rd Edward I, 1306, a grant
was made for fifty-six oaks out of the wood of Ashbridge to
aid in this object. Agreeably to the regulations of their
order the Franciscans were forbidden to acquire property ;
but permitted to receive donations, and live on the bounty

of others. Although beggars and mendicants they exhibited extraordinary industry. The laziness of the monk had become proverbial, and the industry of the friar showed itself in strong contrast. The space of ground occupied by the friars at Reading was small; altogether it did not exceed seven acres, and the accommodations afforded were mean, but consistent with the principles professed and acted upon by the mendicants. The only portions of their buildings which offered anything like importance was their church. This was a substantial building, the ruins of which constitute the only part which has descended to us spared by the hand of time. It was composed principally of flints, put together and consolidated into one mass. It consisted of a nave, side aisles, and chancel; the latter has disappeared, but the other parts are still to be seen. They have been figured and described by Man.[1] The aisles are separated from the body of the church by lancet pointed arches, springing from six clustered stone columns with circular capitals, extending on each side of the nave from the two extremities. Between the pillars the space measures fourteen feet four inches, except the two at the east end, which are only eleven feet apart. Remains of paintings have been traced on the wall at this spot, which had been whitewashed over, but what had been represented could not be made out. The west end window is to be admired as a specimen of Gothic work; the windows on the north and south were small and devoid of ornamentation. An arched doorway, with circular mouldings, led into the building from the street, and on the opposite side was another, leading, it is presumed, to the cemetery and to the convent. The church measured, exclusive of the chancel, seventy-seven and a half feet; its breadth, including the side aisles, was fifty-one and a half feet; the aisles were ten and a half feet wide. A heavily tiled roof, reaching nearly to the ground, covered in the building, which has been converted into the Bridewell of the town. The friars appear with little or no reluctance to have given up their convent, and to have desired to conform themselves to ordinary customs. The surrender, which was made September 13th, of the 30th Henry VIII (1538), is a singular instrument in this respect, preserved at Lambeth (MSS. Wharton, fol. 129, No. 594), and given in

[1] P. 291 et seq., and plate 17.

Coates's *History*, p. 303.   After making admission that religion does not consist of the "wearing of a grey, black, white, or any other coloured garments, cloak, frock, or coat," or in "girding ourselves upon our outward garments, with girdles full of knots, or in like peculiar manner of papistical ceremonies, sequestering ourselves from the uniform, laudable, and conformable manner of living of all other Christian men, used many years from the beginning of Christ's religion;" it goes on to denounce the charges of hypocrisy and dissimulation, so constantly brought against them, and the consequences of those charges in the withdrawal of the benevolence by which they were sustained; and the guardian of the house and inmates submit themselves and all belonging to them to the king, and implore his majesty to grant to them letters under writing and his grace's seal to change their said habits, and to take to such manner of living as honest secular priests be preferred unto.   This document is signed by Peter Schefford, the guardian, and ten others.

The *Three Chapters of Letters Relating to the Suppression of Monasteries*, published by the Camden Society, and edited by Mr. T. Wright, contain many curious particulars relating to the friars of Reading.   Dr. John London, one of the commissioners employed to visit the monastic houses, writes to secretary Cromwell of the inmates of the Grey Friars, and describes them thus:

"The most partt of these be very agede men, & be nott of strength to go moch abrode for their lyvinges, wherfor ther desyer ys that yt myght please your lordeschippe to be a mediator unto the kinges grace for them, that they myght during their lyves enjoy ther chambres & orcharde,"[1] etc.

Another letter gives an insight into perhaps the principal source of their income:

"I have pullyd down the image of our ladye at Caversham, wherunto wasse great pilgremage.[2] The image ys platyd over with sylver, & I have putt yt in a cheste fast lockyd & naylyd uppe, & by the next bardge that comythe from Reding to London yt shall be browght to your lordeschippe. I have also pullyd down the place sche stode in, with all other ceremonyes, as lightes, schrowdes, crowchys, and imagies of wax, hangyng abowt the chapell, & have defacyd the same thorowly in exchuyng of any

---

[1] MS. Cotton., Cleop. E. iv, fol. 227.
[2] Caversham was about a mile and a half from Reading, and the convent stood on ground near Caversham bridge.

farther resortt thedyr. Thys chapell dydde belong to Notley abbey, &
ther always wasse a chanon of that monastery wiche wasse callyd the
warden of Caversham, & he songe in thys chapell, and hadde the offer-
inges for hys lyvyng. He was accostomyd to show many prety relykes,
among the wiche wer the holy dager that kylled kinge Henry (Henry VI),
& the holy knyfe that kylled seynt Edwarde (the Martyr). All thees,
with many other, with the cotes of thys image, her cappe & here, my
servant shall bring unto your lordeschippe thys wek, with the surrendre
of the freers under the covent seale, & ther seale also."[1]

He then goes on to beg the church for a town hall :

"I besek your gudde lordeschippe to admytt me a power sutar for
thees honest men of Redinge. They have a fayre towne & many gudde
occupiers in ytt, but they lacke that howse necessarye, of the wiche, for
the mynystracion of justice they have most nede of. Ther towne hall ys
a very small howse, & stondith upon the ryver, wher ys the commyn
wassching place of the most partt of the towne, & in the cession dayes
and other cowrt dayes ther ys such batyng with batildores as oon man
can nott here another, nor the quest here the chardg gevyng. The body
of the church of the Grey Fryers, wiche is solyd with lath and lyme,
wold be a very commodiose rowme for them. And now I have rydde all
the fasschen of that church in parcleses, ymages, & awlters, it wolde mak
a gudly towne hall."

Dr. London further communicates that he—

"Myssed no thing butt oonly a peece of the holy halter Judas wasse
hangyd withall";

and a relic taken away by the canon of Netley which he
succeeded in obtaining, as in another letter he says :

"I have sent uppe the principall relik of idolytrie within thys realme,
an aungell with oon wyng, that browʒt to Caversham the spere hedde
that percyd our Saviour is syde upon the crosse."[2]

From various records preserved in the Exchequer we
learn of some particulars relating to this body. Their library
was of the most insignificant character, consisting, according to Leland, of only four books, *Beda de Naturis Bestia-
rum, Alex. Necham super Marcianum Capellum, A. Necham Mythologicon,* and *Johannis Waley's Commentarii
super Mythologicon Fulgentii,* works neither of a very in-
structive nor theological character. Indeed they appear not
to have made any use of these, for they were unwillingly

[1] MS. Cott., Cleop. E. iv, fol. 225. [2] Ib., fol. 223.

shewn, and when seen were found to be covered with cob-
webs and insects.[1]

John Peckham, archbishop of Canterbury, addressed the
abbot of Reading in favour of the Franciscan friars. His
letter contains the following curious passage :

"We pray, earnestly, that amidst the increasing storms of the time,
no timid weakness may depress our mind ; for you know that powerful
waves are necessary to elevate the ark from the mire and dust; a flaming
furnace to purge the vessels of the Lord ; and repeated strokes of the
hammer to give metals their durability. And this we say to you on the
word of a priest, that if the authority of our superior would suffer it, and
the fear of giving offence did not prevent it, nothing is so firmly fixed in
our wishes as to walk with our brethren in the path which St. Francis
trod before us."[2]

The GREY FRIARS had a small convent in Castle street.
The chapel was only thirty feet and a half long and twelve
feet and a half wide, the chancel ten feet.   A dissenting
chapel now covers the spot which formerly was occupied
by the Grey Friars.

There are three churches in Reading : St. Mary, St. Lawrence, and St. Giles.

ST. MARY'S CHURCH.   Its antiquity is undisputed.   It is
the most ancient of the town, and is frequently called the
minster, a name it formerly enjoyed, and thus gave name
to the street adjoining it.   The original building was taken
down in 1547 with the exception of the spire, which was
allowed to remain till 1594, when a storm of wind removed
it. The small sum expended in the rebuilding of the church
(1550-53) will create surprise, for in the churchwarden's
accounts it is put down at £124 : 3 : 5, which includes the
old materials and those derived from the interior of the
abbey, which consisted of the entire roof of that building,
and for which £6 : 10 : 8 was paid. A door described as

---

[1] "Apud Franciscos sunt telæ aranearum in bibliotheca, præterea tineæ, et
blatæ, amplius, quicquid alii jactent, nihil, si spectes eruditos libros. Nam ego,
invitis fratribus omnibus, curiose bibliothecæ forrulos omnes excussi."

[2] "Rogamus insuper et obsecramus, ut inter crebrescentes seculi tempestates
nulla deprimat pusillanimitas mentem nostram. Scitis eciam, quod elevande
arche a luto et pulvere sunt necessarii fluctus fortes, et purgandis vasis domini
fornax urens, ac formandis tubis ductilibus multiplicata percussio malleorum,
et hoc nobis dicimus in eloquio sacerdotis, quod si pateretur Superioris aucto-
ritas et scandalum non obstaret, nichil sic pectoris nostri insidet desideriis, sicut
in camino beati Francisci cum fratribus expatiari."   (Regist. Peckham, fol.
118b.   De Fratribus.)

having stood in the cloisters cost eight shillings, and is probably the one at the west end of the church. It is certainly older than any other part of the building; the jambs and lintel are of freestone, and on each side is an escutcheon, but the arms are not to be distinguished. Over the door is a Norman window, with the letters T. R. three times repeated at the upper part of the arch. The church consists of a nave, south aisle, small north aisle, and a chancel. The south aisle is separated from the nave by a row of pillars of ancient date, supporting four circular arches. It is engraved in Coates' *History of Reading*, p. 74.

In the churchwarden's books there is what is interesting as being an early record of the election of a parish clerk, John Marshall being, in 1571, at the payment of 13s. 4d. *per ann.*, appointed to be clerk and sexton; in consideration for which it is specified that he is " from time to time to see the church clean kept, the seats swept and clean made, the mats beaten, the dogs driven out of the church, the windows made clean, and all other things done for the good and cleanly keeping of the church, and the quiet of divine service." He received also an addition of 3s. 4d. *per ann.* for ringing a bell, the curfew, as it was called, every evening at eight o'clock.

St. Lawrence's Church also presents materials derived from the abbey and employed in its erection at the close of the fifteenth century. Much of the stone work, thence derived, and the great western doorway was composed of a circular arch ornamented with mouldings, from which originally the arms of the abbey were suspended, nearly obliterated by time, but have been restored, is worthy of observation. A pillar adjoining the corporation pew is also conjectured to have been brought from the abbey, the carving of which is curious. It has two compartments—*dexter azure*, the Virgin Mary with the infant Jesus on her left arm, and a lighted torch in her right hand—*sinister*, on the top a lamb, and under it the figure of an ass rudely carved. The church is engraved in Coates' *History of Reading* (p. 158). It consists of a nave and a north aisle, separated from the body by a row of octagonal pillars, supporting five elliptical arches with ogee mouldings.

St. Lawrence Church was well stored with plate and vestments, as is shown by an inventory taken a few years prior to the reformation. It is too long to quote, but may be seen in Man's *History of Reading*, pp. 312-314. Many articles connected with superstitious uses were again introduced into the church upon the accession of Mary, and among others a new Judas was provided for the use of the paschal, the cost of which, however, only amounted to fourpence. Philip and Mary visited Reading in 1557, and attended the solemnities accompanying the restoration of the altars, and on this occasion made grants to the parish, and enlarged the churchyard by a part of Forbury. In 1558 Elizabeth reversed and abolished some of these things ; the altars were taken away, the two pair of organs were removed from St. John's chancel. They were sold, and the timber applied to the erection of elevated seats for the mayor and corporation. The clock in this church was put up as early as 1499, and entries for the payment for wire for it occur in the churchwarden's books. This is probably one of the earliest instances on record of the putting up of a clock in a country parish church. Queen Elizabeth frequently visited Reading and attended St. Lawrence. She had her seat in the chancel, furnished with a canopy having tapestry hung round it, and the aisles were then strewed with rushes and flowers, for which charges often occur in the churchwarden's accounts. Her seat was called " the state." She engaged for the repairs of the chancel, and the north door was made at her expense. Many entries occur of payments made by the crown in the auditor's book, the Office of Works' books, and the churchwardens' books, for the repairs of St. Lawrence. This church contains the monument of the celebrated mathematician, John Blagrave. It has been frequently described. He died in 1619.

ST. GILES. The records of this church and parish go no further back than 1518, long after the erection of the building, of the date of which we are in ignorance. It is a large structure, having nave and side aisles divided by arches, supported by massive pillars. The tower met with an unfortunate fate. It was a square one with four pinnacles until the reign of Charles I, when, at the siege of the town (1643), the king's soldiers placed upon it a piece of ordnance, thus rendering it a mark for the besiegers, who therefore attacked it by a battery and reduced it to a mass of rubbish. The materials were employed in its re-erection, but in the coarsest manner. It has since undergone many alterations and reparations. The clock of this church had a set of chimes in 1518.

To bring to a close this already, I fear, too long paper, I will briefly refer to a few particulars relating to the corporation. The earliest charter is of the date of 37th Henry III, A.D. 1253, which was confirmed by Edward III in 1345, by Richard II in 1379, by Henry IV in 1399, and by Henry V in 1418. In the reign of Henry VI the chief magistrate is for the first time made mention of as mayor. Elizabeth divided the burgesses into primary and secondary, forming together a council, nine being of the former class and sixteen of the latter. Charles I incorporated the body as mayor, aldermen, and burgesses in 1639, and his charter, called the " governing charter," has been printed at length.[1]

The condition of the corporation in the reign of Edward VI seems to have been of the poorest description; for it is on record that in the first year of this monarch's sovereignty, the corporation were under the necessity of borrowing the sum of £6 of the churchwardens of St. Lawrence's church, and that they required to be permitted to return the amount by payment in instalments of 10s. half yearly, and to be excused paying interest.

The documents in relation to the several companies belonging to the guild merchants of Reading, in the possession of the corporation, are curious and interesting, giving a variety of singular rules for their governance; whilst they present to our notice materials which exhibit the manners and customs and condition of society in which they were made. The strict manner in which the trades were kept apart, is apparent : the shoemakers could not intrude upon the occupation of the cobbler, nor the cobbler upon that of the shoemaker. The mercer or tailor was equally interdicted from interfering with the woollen draper and the haberdasher; the haberdasher from selling hats or caps, unless they were made of straw. No foreign barber was allowed to draw teeth, unless in a barber's shop. The barbers were forbid following their calling on Sundays, unless on the four fair days, when they might shave, trim, dress, or cut, any one who applied; and as the barber's shop has always been renowned as the place where news could be learnt, it appears

---

[1] In Man's *History*, Appendix A.

not unreasonably to have been suspected of constituting a place where treason might be concocted, or unlawful meetings held; and therefore, during the disputes between the houses of York and Lancaster, a prohibition was issued directing that no barber should shave any man after 10 P.M. between Easter and Michaelmas, nor after 9 P.M. from Michaelmas to Easter. Boots and shoes were to be made only in Shoemakers'-row. Clothiers were forbidden to employ more than two broad looms. One clothier was not to weave for another.

The powers given to the abbot of Reading by the charter of Henry I, occasioned frequent disputes between the convent and the town. Tenacity for prerogative gave rise to the usual amount of disputes. The peace of society was endangered, and the matter grew to such a height that reference was made to Fox, bishop of Winchester, lord privy seal, and others justices of the King's Bench; the result of which was a decree made at the close of the reign of Henry VII, to limit the powers of each in the election of various officers. Henry VIII, in 1510, had to reconsider the decision given; and he still more particularly defined their several powers and privileges.

GENEALOGICAL NOTICE OF THE FAMILY OF FETTIPLACE.

IN CONTINUATION OF REMARKS "ON THE MONUMENT OF A SUPPOSED PRINCESS OF PORTUGAL IN EAST SHEFFORD CHURCH, BERKSHIRE."
(PP. 145-157 ante.)

BY J. R. PLANCHÉ, ESQ., ROUGE CROIX, HON. SEC.

THE family of Fettiplace, which name is with the usual caprice of the middle ages spelt indifferently Feteplace, Fetyplace, and Phetiplace, is supposed to be of Norman origin ; but the earliest record of it I have hitherto met with occurs in a patent roll of the 41st of king Henry III (A.D. 1223), where I find the following entry. "Pro Ada Feteplace de Oxon de toto manerio de Wantinge in com. Berks." This, I presume, was the Adam Feteplace, who was mayor of Oxford in 1245, and again from 1253 to 1260 inclusive. In 1267, he was for the tenth time elected chief magistrate of that city, and somewhere about that period purchased of Ralph de Camoys the manor of Denchworth in Berkshire. (Ashmole and Dale's MSS., Coll. Arm.) That this Adam was a merchant or tradesman, appears from the curious fact of his "shop" being mentioned in a deed of gift by Jeffrey de Hinksey, a wealthy burgess of Oxford; of one shop or tenement "situated between the shop of Adam Fettiplace on the eastern side, and one belonging to Richard de Farendon on the western side." This grant is witnessed by Nicholas de Kingston, then mayor of Oxford. (Dunkin's *Hist. of the Hundred of Beckinston and Ploughley*, vol. i, p. 140.) About the same time, John Feteplace owned a mansion called Sampson's Hall, in the city of Oxford. (Peshall's *Oxford*, p. 125.)

In the Hundred Rolls of the reign of Edward I, Walter Fettiplace is found to hold lands in Abingdon as heir of his father Adam, and that Walter had a son Thomas, described in the same roll as the son of Walter the son of Adam. There is also mention in the same roll of another Thomas, who was the son of Walter the son of *Thomas*, and I therefore presume that Adam had a brother Thomas from whom that line descended : but after that period I have as yet discovered no trace of it. This latter branch of the early Oxfordshire Fettiplaces are not mentioned in any of the genealogical notices of the family that I have met with.

The next in point of date is an Almericus Fettiplace of Denchworth, stated by Dale in a MS. Ped. College of Arms as living 9th of Edward I, 1281. Sir Philip Pettiplace of North Denchworth was knight of the shire 29th of Edward I, 1301, and Henry Fettiplace was his son and heir. Another Almericus Fettiplace was witness to a charter of the 7th of Edward III, 1333. Richard Fettiplace, the son of an Almericus Fettiplace, according to Dale's Pedigree,[1] acquired lands in Lyford, co. Berks, 20th of Edward III, 1346 ; and a Richard Fettiplace of East Hanney, who was most probably the same person, had a son and heir named John, who was called John Southbury. His charter, in which he is described as " Johannes Fetiplace dictus Johannes Southbury filius et hæres. Rici. Feteplace de Esthanney," is dated anno 21 of Edward III (1347), and sealed with the arms of Fettiplace, two chevrons and a canton fretty for difference, and circumscribed, " Sigillum Jo. . . South. . ."[2] A (Emericus ?) Fettiplace, a third, I presume, of that name, owned one knight's fee in Denchworth and Papworth, 22nd of Richard II, 1399, at which time there were also living a John Fetiplace of South Denchworth and a Henry Fettiplace, who was witness to a charter of John Fettiplace of Buckland in that year, and died seized of Denchworth, 4th of Henry V, 1416, leaving a son and heir named John, aged twenty at that date. We have now arrived at the period when Thomas Fettiplace of East Shefford and Childrey was appointed steward of the manor and hundred of Bampton by Gilbert, lord Talbot, whose widow Beatrice he afterwards married. In no pedigree do we find an indication of the branch from which he descended ; but in one by Vincent, (MS., No. 143, Coll. Arm.) he is set down as having had a

---

[1] In Dale's *Pedigree* we find, on the same authority ("in eodem scripta pergam"), a Robert Fettiplace, "filius Richardi"; and a John Fettiplace, son of Robert, who is called of "Charney", and by charter leaves to his nephew or grandson ("nepoti et hæredi suo), Peter of North Denchworth, sundry lands and tenements. But John, son of Robert, son of Richard, if that descent be correct, was living 21st of Rich. (1399), and cannot be the same as John of Charney, who was living in 1464. I find also a "Thomas Fettiplace" of Buckland. in the *Inquisitiones Nonarum*, 14th of Edward III (1340).
[2] Clarke's Hundred of Wanting, p. 112. Ashm. MSS., 833.

brother described as John of Wolverley.[1] I know of no Wolverley except that in Worcestershire, and can find no trace of a Fettiplace in that locality ; but in the will of John Fettiplace, the son of Thomas by Beatrice, already quoted, there is, I think, a clue to the mystery. By that document, I find that he was seized of the manor of New Landport, or Langport, in the county of Kent, which he bequeathed to his eldest son Richard, with remainder to each of his other sons in regular succession. Now Hasted in his account of this manor (*Hist. of Kent*, vol. iii, p. 511) tells us that the mansion of it, usually called Seavan's Court, acquired that name from the eminent family of Septvans, the ancient possessors of it, and in which it continued till the beginning of the reign of Henry VI, when William Septvans passed the manor away to John Writtle, from which name, after it had remained some years, it was alienated to Henry Fettiplace, of the county of Oxford, esq., whose descendant, Edmund Fettiplace, had his lands disgavelled by the general act of the 31st year of king Henry VIII, and died the year after, John Fettiplace being his son and heir. (Rot. Esch. A. 33, Hen. VIII.) Now Edmund Fettiplace, who died April 1st, 32nd of Henry VIII, 1540, leaving a son John, afterwards sir John Fettiplace, was great grandson of the John who entailed the manor of New Langport, and it is clear therefore that the descent of that manor came in the direct male line from the Henry to whom it passed from Writtle. The will of Thomas, the husband of Beatrix, has not been discovered ; the earliest of that family, being that of his son John aforesaid, in the Prerogative office. The wills at Oxford and Salisbury, the other two most likely places for its registration, are not of a date earlier than the sixteenth century, and there is no mention of any escheat or inquisition at the time of his death : but there can be little question of his having possessed the manor of New Langport, which his son John held in 1464, and as Henry Fettiplace of the county of Oxford had only acquired it in the early part of the reign of Henry VI, Thomas would appear to have been the next possessor, and most probably the son as well as the heir of Henry. The description of this Henry as of " the county of Oxford" is

---

[1] The arms of Thomas are, in one example, differenced with a martlet, the mark of a fourth son.

too vague for us to be able to identify him with any of the family of Fettiplace of whom we find mention. If Hasted be correct in the date at which he says the manor passed from Writtle, he cannot be the same with Henry of Denchworth who died in 1416. The family of Writtle was of the county of Essex, and its connection with Kent, according to the pedigree in the visitation of the latter county, arose from the marriage of Eleanor, daughter of Walter Writtle, with Thomas, third son of Thomas Walsingham of Chislehurst. Walter Writtle died in 1473, leaving by a former wife, Johanna, daughter and coheir of sir John Hurd, a son John, the first of that name in the recorded pedigree, and who, therefore, it is clear, could not be the John Writtle who held the manor of New Langport in the beginning of the reign of Henry VI. The titledeeds of that manor, if in existence, would throw considerable light upon the question at issue.

In the meanwhile I can only repeat my conviction that the Henry Fettiplace, from whom the manor descended to Edmund Fettiplace, was either the father or uncle of Thomas, the husband of Beatrix, and of his brother John of Wolverley. That Thomas was of the Oxfordshire branch appears probable from the repetition of that Christian name in that line only, previous to the fifteenth century; and it may also be observed that Walter, an early name in that line, first appears in the pedigree of Writtle at the commencement of that century. In conclusion, two other circumstances are remarkable in the pedigree of Fettiplace. The first, that not a single match is recorded previous to that of Thomas with Beatrix, nor even the name of any female member of the family to be found; and the second, that the name of Beatrix has never been given to any of her descendants direct or collateral.

I subjoin a pedigree (see plate 17) of the Souzas descended from Alfonzo Denis and from Leonara Alfonza, the illegitimate issue of king Alphonso III, referred to at p. 147 *et seq.*

Pl. 17.

Sousa

 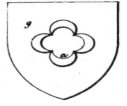

E. Laurencia
dadures
Sousa

Leonora Alfonsa
Married (ante 1271)
Don Stephan Aunez
de Sousa Dom de
Chaves
Son of John Garcia
de Sousa Senhor
D'Achuna e Pinto
2ndly
Gonzalvo Garcia de
Sousa (Uncle of her
1st Husband) Count
de Neyra 1273

Uracci
Married
Jo. Mendez
de Briteros

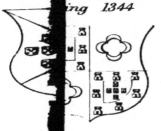

Ped— o Alfonso
Sousa
ing 1344

Yolande or Violante Lope
d of Lope Fernandez de Pacheco
Lord of Ferreira and Widow of
Martin Vasquez de Achuna

Bea—
de S—

Blanca de Sousa

- - - - - - - - - - - - - - -
Son   Daughter   Daughter

J.R.Jobbins.

Pl. 18.

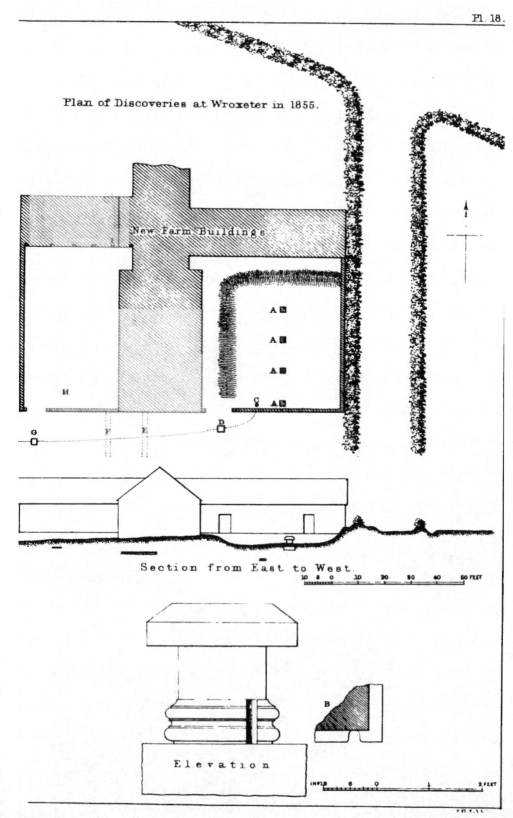

Plan of Discoveries at Wroxeter in 1855.

New Farm Buildings

A

A

A

C
A

H

G   F   E   D

Section from East to West.

10 5 0   10   20   30   40   50 FEET

B

Elevation

1 IN 1 2   6   0   1   2 FEET

URICONIUM.

BY THOS. WRIGHT, ESQ., M.A., F.S.A., ETC.

FOURTH ARTICLE.

EXCAVATIONS MADE ON FORMER OCCASIONS ON THE SITE OF THE ANCIENT CITY.

WE may form some notion of the extent and character of the ancient city of Uriconium by comparing with the present excavations what we know of former discoveries on different parts of the site ; and there is one of these discoveries which has a more particular relation to our present excavations.

Five years ago—in 1855—the tenant of the land, Mr. Stanier, raised the farm buildings which now stand on the opposite side of the road from the field in which the excavations are situated, and a little more to the northward. In clearing away the ground for the foundations, the men made some interesting discoveries, a plan and section of which, made at the time by sir Henry Dryden, bart., has been preserved by my friend Mr. Samuel Wood, of Shrewsbury, by whose kindness, and with sir Henry's permission, I am enabled to give an engraving of it on a reduced scale. (Plate 18.) In what is now the yard, were found a row of short square pillars, marked A, A, A, A, on the plan, and standing at equal distances from each, of about twelve feet. One of these pillars is given on a larger scale at the foot of the plate. It consists of a foundation stone about three feet square, upon which rested the base of the pillar, ornamented with mouldings, above which was a short square shaft, and at the top a square cap-stone, of which the engraving is an elevation. These cap-stones were roughly dressed, and not uniform in the colour of the stone, as two of them were red, one light red, and the other drab. The most singular characteristic of these pillars, which were taken up and are still preserved in Mr. Stanier's garden, is a vertical groove on the opposite sides of the base, a sectional plan of which is represented in the figure B. These grooves were on the sides of the pillars which faced each other when *in situ,* and had evidently received some connecting work of metal or wood, probably the latter, which extended from pillar to pillar. When we consider the position of these pillars in regard to the buildings which we have discovered in the field on the eastern side of the road, which I have given as nearly as I could ascertain it at B in the accompanying map of the site of the ancient city (plate 19), it seems not improbable that they formed part of the western side of the enclosure of the forum. A corresponding row of pillars may, perhaps, lie under the eastern side of the present Watling-street road. Another pillar was found at D in the plan, but quite out of the line of the four others.

No attempt, I believe, was made to carry out these excavations except as far as they were necessary for the construction of the modern buildings. In laying the modern drain, which is indicated by the dotted line, which led to the discovery of the pillar at D (plate 18), a concrete floor was found five feet below the surface of the ground at F, and there were scattered about a number of large stones, iron straps, bones, lead, and cramps, and other objects, among which one silver coin was picked up. A large squared stone was found at C, and a flagstone at G. At H a floor of flagstones was met with at a depth of six feet. In digging for the foundations at I a gold coin was found, which is said to have been carried away and sold privately by the man who found it.

In the accompanying map (plate 19) the dark line N, N, N, marks the course of the ancient town wall of Uriconium, which may be traced without difficulty in its whole circuit. Along a considerable portion of the western side, from the ford at the Watling-street road northward to the turn in the river, the ground rises from the bank of the Severn in a steep and in some parts almost precipitous bank, of considerable elevation. When the wall leaves the river to make a sweep round to Norton, the ground falls gradually to the stream called the Bell Brook, and then becomes uneven, though rising from the brook in banks to the northward. Through the fields to the south-east the mound which covers the remains of the wall is remarkably bold. Within these walls the ground which the ancient city occupied rises, though not rapidly, from the bank overlooking the river towards the north-east until it reaches its greatest

Pl. 19.

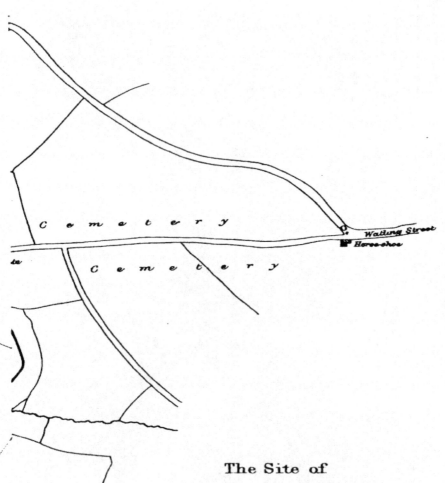

Watling Street

Horse-shoe

C e m e t e r y

C e m e t e r y

The Site of
URICONIUM
at
WROXETER
SALOP

Scale.

¼   ½   ¾   1 MILE

J.R.Jobbins

elevation in the field at D. It sinks gradually towards the village, and more abruptly towards the Bell Brook, from which it rises again towards the north, so that Uriconium stood upon two hills, with a stream running in the bottom between them.

The great Roman road from London, so well known as the Watling-street, approached the city from the east. At o, where there is an inn called the "Horse-shoe," the modern road onwards to Shrewsbury branches off from it, no doubt to avoid the ruins of the city, and the old road continues as a mere country lane. It entered the city by a gate at K, remains of which are said to exist, or to have existed, under the soil. On both sides of the road between this gate and the "Horse-shoe," lay the principal cemetery of Uriconium. The road is bordered to the south by a bank, upon which the inscribed sepulchral stones have been found, and burial urns are frequently met with in the lower ground on the northern side of the road. There has no doubt been another entrance to the city on the north-western side, probably somewhere near where the Bell Brook passed out of it, as the main road which went to Chester and to North Wales was evidently identical with the present road to Shrewsbury, passing by way of Tern-bridge and Atcham.[1]

The entrance to Uriconium from the river was at the south-eastern corner of the city. Opposite the entrance to the churchyard, the present Watling-street road makes an abrupt turn down to the side of the river, across which there is an ancient paved ford, leading to a continuation of

---

[1] Mr. H. M. Scarth has pointed out to me, in a manuscript in the British Museum (MS. Addit., No. 21,011), an account of a discovery of Roman sepulchral remains near Tern bridge on the line of this road : "Feb. 8th, 1798. Between Tern bridge and the Severn, at Attingham, in a ploughed field, at a little more than plough depth, an enclosure of large stones was come upon, within which were ranged three large glass urns of very elegant workmanship, one large earthen urn, and two small ones of fine red earth. Each of the urns had one handle, and the handles of the glass urns were elegantly ribbed. The glass urns were twelve inches high, by ten in diameter. The large earthen urn was so much broken, that the size could not be ascertained. On the handle were the letters SPAH. The small urns are about nine inches high. With the *glass urns* were *burnt bones* and fine mould, and in each a fine glass lachrymatory of the *same* material. These had a most beautiful light green tint. Near one of them was part of a jaw-bone, an earthen lamp, and a few Roman coins of the lower empire, of little value. The whole were covered with large flat stones covered with a quantity of coarse rock-stone. This was probably the burialplace of some family of Uriconium, or the remains of a villa might be found near." These remains are said to be preserved in the museum at Attingham.

the Watling-street road on the other side.   This in fact was
the Roman road leading to the south through the Stretton
valley and by way of Bravinium (the site of which is uncertain) and Magna (Kenchester, near Hereford) to South
Wales.   I am inclined to doubt if this were the principal
entrance to the town from the river, and it is very improbable that so large and important a place as Uriconium
should not have a bridge, especially when we consider that
the floods to which this district is subject would render the
ford totally unpassable during a part of the year.   Now, the
part of the Watling-street road which runs down to the
river passes along a break in the bank, which rises again to
the south in a small knoll at F.   The Ordnance Survey map
gives the town wall at this corner a curious form, marked
here by a single dotted line, I, which is not at all easy to
understand, and, in fact, in the Ordnance Survey map itself it
is marked by dotting the line as conjectural or doubtful.   In
an old map of this site, etched some seventy or eighty years
ago, and apparently made with very considerable care, the
form of the wall is given as marked in our plan by the
double dotted lines at H, indicating an entrance gateway of
a construction not uncommon in Roman fortifications.   The
gateway in the northern wall of Richborough in Kent
(*Rutupiæ*), presented somewhat the same character.   I think
it very probable that the line of streets represented by the
Watling-street-road was continued to this point, and that
here was the entrance to the city from the south.   I am
told that a little way further down the river the remains of
an ancient bridge, supposed to be Roman, have been found,
and it is curious that, although the lane opposite the ford
is called the Watling-street-road, yet the real line of the
Watling-street-road from Church-Stretton points more direct
to the site of these remains of a bridge than to the Wroxeter
ford.   I think it therefore not at all improbable that the
Roman road from Uriconium to the south left the city by a
gate at H, followed the left bank of the Severn to this
bridge, and there crossed the river. It may have been built
at this point as less exposed to the violence of the water in
great floods, than under the city, where the force of the stream
could be increased by the resistance of the hill on which it
was built. If the paved ford at M be Roman, it was probably
used as a convenient passage of the river when the season

allowed. In this case, perhaps, at the time of the ruin of the city the bridge also was destroyed, and afterwards in the middle ages people made for the ford to cross the river, and the old road was abandoned altogether.

Last year, during the period while the workmen were excluded from the field of our principal excavations, they were employed at the top of the knoll at F, above alluded to, which overlooks the ford. The earth was full of remains of building materials, and walls were found which had been so much broken away that it was difficult to say to what description of building they had belonged. They appeared to have formed a small square room attached to a more continuous wall. It might have been a tower, but it was of rough masonry, and might be either Roman or medieval. Now there appears to be documentary evidence of the existence of a medieval castle of Wroxeter, which is said to have been called Arundel castle (the earls of Arundel were feudal lords of this territory during the fourteenth century), and, as it was probably only a small fortress to command the ford, it has been conjectured that the walls uncovered last year on the knoll at F were remains of this castle. It must, however, be stated on the other hand, that all the objects found in digging at this spot were Roman. Among them was a head sculptured in stone, which is evidently of late Roman work, and appears to have belonged to a building which was rather highly ornamented. Coins and other articles were also found, and a coin mould, in which was the impress of a coin of Julia Domna, the wife of the emperor Severus.

It may be remarked that the village of Wroxeter must have been begun to be built ages after the destruction of the town, when the ruins were already covered with a considerable depth of earth, for the Roman buildings are found almost everywhere under the surface of the soil. The cottagers meet with the remains of walls in digging in their gardens, and Mr. Egremont has recently discovered that there are Roman buildings under the lawn of the vicarage. In the year 1827, a rather handsome tessellated pavement was found in what was then a stack-yard, at E in our map, but it was torn to pieces by people who came to see it from Shrewsbury and carried away the tessellæ, and was thus destroyed before any drawing could be made of it. It pro-

bably belonged to a room of a house which abutted on one
of the line of streets which ran from the forum to the town
gate at H.   Trenches have been dug in various parts of the
fields on the other side of the Watling-street-road, immediately opposite the church, and on the top of the hill, but
no traces of buildings were discovered, though the ground
was full of Roman materials.   In one field a Roman well
was found and cleared out, and I believe that it is now in
use for drawing water.   It was at the spot marked by the
letter G that the human remains were found which produced the deformed skulls, which have been the subject of
so much discussion.

A glance at our map will show that the excavations now
in progress (A) are nearly in the centre of the ancient city,
and the buildings they have brought to light occupied a
high position, though not quite the highest ground within
the walls.   The field to the east of it, in which the remains
marked D were found, is a little more elevated, and I am
told that water can be procured there, so that it was probably conveyed thence to the reservoir in the baths.   In
digging in the field A, to the eastward of the excavations,
portions of leaden pipes were found, coming from that direction.   The drain discovered in the baths ran in a northerly
direction, and perhaps emptied itself into the Bell Brook.
The discoveries made on the occasion of the erection of
Mr. Stanier's farm buildings are inserted in their position at
B, and their relation to the supposed forum is evident.

We should naturally expect that the principal public
buildings and mansions of the town would be scattered over
the higher ground, and I anticipate that the remains of
temples will be found in the field C and in that to the north
of it, where we may everywhere trace indications of buildings under ground.   At C, in the first of these fields, partial
excavations were made in the year 1788, and are described in
a communication made in the following year to the Society
of Antiquaries by the rev. Francis Leighton, and printed in
the *Archæologia*, vol. ix.   We are there informed that in
the month of June of the year 1788, the tenant of this
farm, then a farmer named Clayton, "having occasion for
some stone to rebuild a smith's shop lately burnt down,
and knowing by the dryness of the ground that there were
ruins at no great depth beneath the surface of a field near

his house, began to dig, and soon came to a floor and a small bath. Application was made to William Pulteney, esq., the proprietor of the soil, for leave to open the ground farther, which was readily granted. Coins both of the upper and lower empire, bones of animals (some of which were burnt), fragments of earthen vessels of various sizes, shapes, and manufactures, some of them black, and resembling Mr. Wedgewood's imitation of the Etruscan vase, and (as Mr. Telford the architect informed me) pieces of glass, were found in various places; and the whole ground was full of charred substances." The floor alluded to was at a small depth under the ground, and was paved with tiles sixteen inches long, twelve inches wide, and half an inch thick, lying on a bed of mortar one foot thick, under which were rubble stones to a considerable depth. Adjoining this pavement, to the north, was what Mr. Leighton appears to have rightly denominated a bath. It was seven feet four inches long, ' by three feet seven inches broad at one end, and three feet eleven at the other, so that it was not quite square. It had two steps or seats running along the southern side, and, as Mr. Leighton calculated, it was "capable of holding four persons, supposing them to sit on the steps or seats." He adds, "through the north side is a hole through the bottom, at the distance of two feet six inches from the west end. The bottom is paved with tiles, and the sides and seats plastered with mortar, consisting of three layers or coats; the first, or that next the stones, is formed of lime and bruised or pounded brick without sand; the third of the same, but a greater proportion of lime, and a little sand; this is very smooth on the surface and very hard." On the eastern side of the boundary wall of the floor, which was the limit of the excavations in this direction, was found what Mr. Leighton calls "a place four feet deep below the level of the floor. It has a paved bottom; and is formed by large granite stones on the southern and eastern sides, on the north by a large thin red stone set on edge." This "place" was about four feet square. On the west of the floor and pavement, separated from them only by a wall, was an apartment with hypocaust, twelve feet wide by twenty long, its length running north and south. This hypocaust was formed of round pillars of stone, instead of the ordinary columns of bricks, and of different sizes, as though they had been taken from former buildings which had been demolished. " The pillars," as Mr. Leighton describes them, " are not uniform in their shape, size, or disposition ; some rows consisted of six, some of seven pillars ; some pillars were much shorter than others, and the deficiency was made up by tiles or stones laid upon them ; some were apparently the fragments of large columns of a kind of granite, one foot six inches, and one foot two inches, in diameter ; others were of a red free-stone, ten inches in diameter." At the south-west corner were four square pillars formed of tiles in the ordinary way, and there were two passages through the western wall, both clogged with ashes. In the south-eastern corner of this apartment, similar pillars of tiles supported " a small bath, with one seat or step on two of its sides, the whole of the inside well plastered with mortar. From this bath, in a direction southward, there was found a piece of leaden pipe, not soldered, but hammered together, and the seam, or puncture, secured by a kind of mortar ; and there appears a kind of channel or groove cut in large stones, which falls three inches in twelve feet." To the north of these buildings, were small apartments, some with hypocausts and others without ; and beyond these, again, a larger enclosure, which, like two of the small apartments just mentioned, had " tessellated floors made of pieces of brick one inch and a quarter square, not disposed in any fancied form, but in a simple chequer ; the tessellæ are all red."

Such were the remains of buildings uncovered in the year 1788. They were contained within a rectangle of between fifty and sixty feet by somewhat less than thirty, and appeared to be part of some more extensive buildings, but the baths are of rather small dimensions, and might possibly have belonged to some large mansion; though this question can only be decided by further excavations.

The large field marked D, to the north of the present excavations, and inclosing the highest part of the ground, has certainly buildings under it in every part, and excavations in any part of it would doubtless be attended with very interesting results. I am informed that tessellated pavements are known to exist at no great depth under the surface. It was in this field, at the spot indicated by the letter D, that the discovery was made in the year 1701, which was communicated to the Royal Society by Dr. Harwood, and printed in the *Philosophical Transactions*, vol. xxv, where the following account is given of the discovery. " About forty perches distant north from a ruinous wall called the Old Work of Wroxeter, once Uriconium, a famous city in Shropshire, in a piece of arable land in the tenure of Mr. Bennet, he observed, that although these fields had formerly been fertilized and made very rich by the flames and destruction of the city, yet a small square parcel thereof to be fruitless, and not to be improved by the best manure. He then guessing the cause of sterility to be underneath, sent his men to dig and search into it; but the soil being then unsown, caused them to mistake, and search in a wrong place; where they happened upon bottoms of old walls, buried in their own rubbish (being such as are often found in those fields); and the inhabitants digging one of them up, for the benefit of the building stone, were thereby guided to the western corner of the said unprofitable spot of land; where they found (near the foundation) a little door place, which, when cleansed, gave entrance into the vacancy of a square room, walled about, and floored under and over, with some ashes and earth therein." The discovery on this occasion only extended to the opening of a hypocaust, with its floor above, of which a model was made, and the latter is still preserved, with some other objects found at Wroxeter, in the library of Shrewsbury school.

The smith's shop or forge, alluded to in the account of the discoveries at c, stands on the road-side, at the corner of this field (at P), and I have heard it reported that buildings were found under it, and that a large capital of a Roman column forms the foundation for the smith's anvil.

It is not improbable that the commoner orders of the inhabitants of Uriconium inhabited the lower parts of the town bordering on the stream now called the Bell Brook and the northern banks, and their houses may have been constructed chiefly of wood. The earth is everywhere black from the mixture of burnt materials, as in all other parts within the limits of the ancient city. Last year, with the ready and friendly permission of the tenant, Mr. Bailey, trenches were dug in several directions, but no walls were met with, though the pavement of a street was found, as indicated in our map. Roman coins, and other small objects, were turned up by the spade, and among them a bronze fibula.

A curious document, at present in the possession of
C. L. Prince, esq., has been communicated to me by a friend
(M. A. Lower, esq., of Lewes in Sussex); it is a rent-roll of
the manor of Wroxeter in the twenty-fourth year of the
reign of Edward III (A.D. 1350). As it appears to me in
many respects worthy of being printed, I have appended it
to this paper. It will appear at once that a very small
portion of the acreage of the parish, which is now estimated
at 4774 acres, two roods, and thirty perches, was then
under cultivation; for, reckoning the virgate at sixty
acres (I believe the ordinary estimate in this part of the
country), and the *noca*, or quarter of a virgate, at fifteen,
we can hardly account for more than six or seven hundred
acres, including a considerable quantity of waste. I am informed, moreover, that some of the land mentioned in this
document is not now included in the parish. It is evident
that a great part of the land was then waste,—the ground
at Norton was a heath, which must have been extensive.
Probably a part at least of the site of Uriconium was so
covered on the surface with the ruins of buildings as to be
left wild. One of the residents bears the very significant
name of *Johannes atte Walle*, or John at the Wall, which
was in all probability given to him because his *messuage*
was adjacent to a part of the ancient town wall. The whole
parish at this time appears to have contained twenty-two
messuagia, or houses of men holding generally about thirty
acres of land, and eleven cottages. By the census of 1821,
the latest to which I can at present refer, there were a hundred and twelve houses in the present parish. The *dominus*,
or feudal lord, was the earl of Arundel.

There is one local name in this record which is interesting. Hugh Maunseil held a piece of pasture "called le
Rowemelne," *melne* being of course the usual old English
word for a mill. It may perhaps be allowable to conjecture
that the first part of the word is some corruption of Rome
or Roman, and that the pasture received its name from the
ruins of a Roman mill, or the tradition that there had been
one there. There is, I am informed, a field through which
the Bell Brook runs, on the right hand of the Watling-street
road as we go to the *Horse-shoe* inn, which is still called
Rue-mill, and which is no doubt the pasture in question.
Perhaps the Romans had a mill on the Bell Brook, within
the town.

It is also worthy of remark that, of four pieces of pasture held by the tenants in common, two have names compounded of the word ȝete, or gate. Chesterȝete may mean the gate of the *chester*, or ancient city, from which the place received its modern name; and its position is thus not defined. Boweȝete may possibly mean the southern gate, from the curve which, according to the plan, its walls seem to have made. Pole may have been named from a pool of water, and Wyggestan, from some remarkable monument of stone.

RENTAL OF WROXETER, A.D. 1350.

Rentale de Wroxcestre, factum super compotum ibidem ad festum sancti Michaelis anno regni regis Edwardi tertii post con. xxiiij°.

Abbas de Haghmoun tenet per cartam unam placeam vasti juxta Tyrne fossato inclusam . . reddit vj. s. ad terminum Michaelis.
Abbas de Lilleshulle pro attachiamento stagni molendini de Tyrne.
r. vj. d. ad eundem terminum.
Dominus Rogerus Corbet tenet Hadeley pro dimidio feodo militis. r. j. spervarium sorum ad dictum festum sancti Michaelis.
Johannes de Westoun Coyne tenet Westoun Coyne pro dimidio feodo.
r. vj.s. viij.d. ad festum Annunciationis pro omni servitio.
Johannes le Poynour tenet j. messuagium et dimidiam virgatam terræ, et debet sumonere omnes liberos tenentes curiæ de Upton et districtiones et attachiamenta facere super eosdem.
Idem tenet per cartam domini unam placeam brusseti vocatam le Lee, et xxv. acras dimidiam regales vasti super brueram de Nortoun. r. inde per annum ad festa sancti Michaelis et Annunciationis per æquales portiones xxviij. s. xj. d.
Thomas de Smethecote tenet xxx. acras regales vasti super brueram de Nortoun. r. per annum ad ij. terminos prædictos xxx. s. et sectam curiæ de Wroxcestre.
Rogerus de Golynghale tenet super eandem brueram xij. acras. r. per annum ad ij. terminos prædictos xij. s. et ij. apparenc' ad magnam curiam ibidem.
Idem tenet iij. acras regales ibidem. r. per annum iij. s.
Hugo Maunseil tenet j. messuagium et dimidiam virgatam terræ ibidem.
r. per annum ad ij. terminos prædictos v. s. et sectam ad curiam.
Idem tenet j. placeam pasturæ ex tradicione seneschalli vocatam le Rowemelne. r. ad ij. terminos prædictos xiiij d.
Johannes de Donyntoun capellanus tenet ij. cotagia cum uno crofto, et iiij. acras terræ regales super eandem brueram. r. ad ij. terminos viij.s. vj. d.
Sibilla de Bromptoun tenet j. messuagium et dimidiam virgatam terræ libere ad terminum vitæ. r. ad ij. terminos prædictos x. s.

Idem tenet j. acram vasti sine scripto.   r. ad ij. terminos prædictos xij. d.

Johannes Selke tenet j. messuagium et dimidiam virgatam terræ, et j.
    acram super brueram.   r.   .   .   . xj. s. ad ij. terminos.

†¹Ricardus Ady tenet j. messuagium, dimi-
    diam virgatam et j. acram terræ super
    brueram. r.   .   .   .   .   . xj. s. ad eosdem terminos.

Thomas le Poynour tenet tantum, et r.   . xj. s. ad eosdem terminos.

Rogerus de Wythintoun tenet tantum. r.   . xj. s. ad eosdem terminos.

Margareta le Hare tenet tantum. r.   .   . xj. s. ad eosdem terminos.

Johannes Wyteacre tenet tantum. r.   .   . xj. s. ad eosdem terminos.

Petronilla Baker tenet tantum. r.   .   . xj. s. ad eosdem terminos.

Margeria Hare tenet tantum. r.   .   . xj. s. ad eosdem terminos.

Eadem tenet j. placeam pasturæ juxta gardi-
    num suum. r.   .   .   .   . ij. gallinas ad Nat' Domini.

Rogerus le Hare tenet j. messuagium, dimi-
    diam virgatam terræ, et j. acram super
    brueram. r.   .   .   .   . xj. s. ad ij. terminos.

†Johannes Selk tenet j. messuagium, et j. no-
    cam terræ, et j. acram super brueram. r.   vj. s. iiij. d. ad terminos præ-
                dictos.   Int' ad festum annunciationis a° x x vjᵗᵒ

Johannes de la Grene tenet tantum. r.   . vj. s. ad terminos prædictos.

Johannes Traventer tenet tantum. r.   . vj. s. ad terminos prædictos.

Idem tenet j. parvam placeam in augmento
    gardini sui. r.   .   .   .   . j. d. ad eosdem terminos.

Johannes atte Walle tenet j. messuagium et
    j. nocam terræ. r   .   .   . vj. s. ad eosdem terminos.

Idem tenet j. nocam cum gardino juxta
    grangiam domini. r.   .   .   . ij. s. ad eosdem terminos.

*²Johannes Knotte tenet j. messuagium et j.
    nocam terræ. r.   .   .   . vj. s. ad eosdem terminos.

Idem dat ad eosdem terminos pro j. placea
    in augmento terræ suæ   .   . iij. d. et j. gall' ad Nat' Domini.

Ricardus filius Reginaldi tenet j. messuagium,
    et j. nocam terræ, j. acram vasti, et j.
    acram campestrem. r.   .   vj. s. vj. d. ad eosdem terminos prædictos.

Alicia relicta Hugonis filii Reginaldi tenet j.
    messuagium, j. nocam terræ, et j.
    acram super brueram. r.   .   . vj. s. ad eosdem terminos.

¹ † In each of the cases indicated by this mark the name of one tenant is
crossed out to make way for another, the latter being the one given in the text.
Thus, in the first instance, the name of the tenant was Adam Gurry, which is
crossed out, and Ricardus Ady written above ; so, in the second case, Adam de
Harnegge occupied the place of Johannes Selk, and, in the third, Stephanus de
Lee de Prestoun that of Thomas de Berewik. Stephen de Lee had given up the
fishing after the rental had been written, and it was let out to Thomas de Berwick.
² * Each of the sentences to which a star is prefixed, is marked *vac'* (*vacat*)
in the margin, as being unoccupied, the tenant having quitted.

* Isabella Hare tenet j. messuagium, et j.
    acram super brueram, et j. placeam. r. vj. s. viij. d.

Sibilla Jonkneros tenet j. messuagium et
    dimidiam nocam terræ. r. . . . iij. s. ad ij. terminos.

Ricardus de Sywaldesdoun tenet j. cotagium
    et iij. acras terræ. r. . . . . iij. s. ij. d. ad ij. terminos.

Thomas Wychart tenet j. messuagium et vj.
    acras terræ. r. . . . . v. s. iij. d.

Amicia le Traventer tenet j. cotagium et iij.
    acras terræ. r. . . . . iiij. s. ix d.

Matilda Wychart tenet j. cotagium et iij.
    acras terræ. r. . . . . iiij. s.

Idem (sic) tenet unam forgiam. r. . . xij. d.

* Johannes le Longe tenet j. cotagium cum vj.
    acris terræ. r. . . . . vj. s. iiij. d.

* Thomas le Chaloner tenet j. cotagium. r. ij. s.

* Willelmus Fishare tenet j. cotagium. r. ij. s.

Willelmus Wychart tenet j. cotagium et iij.
    acras terræ. r. . . . . ij. s. x. d.

Isolda Raynald tenet j. cotagium et iij. acras
    terræ. r. . . . . . ij. s. x. d.

Jonkin le Baker tenet vj. acras terræ domi-
    nicæ et j. acram vasti sine messuagio. r. iij. s. ij. d. ad dictos terminos

* Petronilla Swetedoughter tenet j. cotagium
    cum gardino. r. . . . xviij. d. ad ij. terminos.

Et prædicti tenentes tenent quatuor placeas pasturæ, videlicet
    pastur' de Chestreȝete, Pole, Boweȝete, et de Wyggestan.
    r. per annum ad ij. terminos . . vj. s.

† Thomas de Berewik dat pro licentia pis-
    candi super Tyrne . . . . iij. s. iiij. d. ad ij. terminos.

Et villata de Atyncham dat pro aisiamento
    habendo ad riveram de Tyrne . . vj. d. ad festum sancti Mi-
                                  chaelis tantum.

    Summa totalis redditus . xvj. li. ij. s. x. d.

        Unde { Ad festum sancti Michaelis . viij. li. xiiij. d.
                { Ad festum Annunciationis . viij. li. xvj. d.
                 Item, ad Nativitatem Domini. iij. gallinas.
                 Item, ad Gulam Augusti . j. spervarium, vel ij. s.

    (In dorso.)

Item, de firma gurgitis ibidem.

Item, de abbate de Buldewas vj. plaustratas claustruræ singulis annis
    pro dicta gurgite reparanda ante Pascham quandocunque domino
    quærere placuerit.

ON THE DATE OF THE BATTLE OF KALTRAETH, OTHERWISE THE BATTLE OF GODODIN OR COR-EIDDIN.

BY THE REV. BEALE POSTE.

THE success of the Saxons in this battle, it is universally admitted, broke the power of the ancient Britons in Scotland; and though it did not ultimately establish the Saxons in those regions, who had a much richer prey further south, yet it gradually led to the formation of the Scottish kingdom, such as we find it in the middle ages, which was composed of somewhat new elements. This event, therefore, makes a turning point equally in ancient British, Scotch and Anglo-Saxon history; and as such the date of the battle requires, if possible, to be correctly ascertained.

I submit the above by way of an introductory remark; and as I am permitted to make some comments on a paper of G. Vere Irving, esq., on the same subject, in our *Journal* for Sept. 1859 (vol. xv, pp. 237, 245), I will proceed to do so, though feeling somewhat diffident at varying in opinion from so learned a researcher and so powerful a writer.

Some terms and names are likewise requiring explanation. The word Gododin for instance, which is written short or colloquially for the Otodini, is a generic name, and formed the appellation of the inhabitants of the eastern part of the southern portion of Scotland. They comprised several states or kingdoms; as Rheged, Argoed, Eiddin, etc., though there was no particular state named Gododin. The battle of Gododin, therefore, means the battle of the Otodini. Kaltraeth is interpreted Gwal-traeth, or "the sea shore at the extremity of the wall." Coreddin, that is, the environs of the church so called, is the present name of the locality in which the fortress once stood. I judge its ancient name was very similar, in the form of Cor-Eiddin, for the fortress is positively called Eidin in stanza 17, the present name is Coreddin, so the ancient form "Cor"-Eiddin is very probable; the prefix cor being accustomed to be attached to the names of places where festivals were held; as in the instance of Cor-Ambri, or Stonehenge. The battle of Kaltraeth was not fought in any plain or field, but, according to the poem, consisted in numerous sallies from the fortress, where the Britons were pent up, who were assembled for the purpose of a festival, till the ultimate storming, when the British force was overpowered and slaughtered in the streets, and in and among the public buildings; the fortress being extensively on fire at the same time. The attack, defence, and capture, lasted seven days. The Britons, likewise, held during the battle an entrenchment called Adoen, or Odren, within a mile, or a mile and a half, the rampart of which had been dug down, or breached in some of the attacks. (See stanza 91, Williams' edition).

To begin with Ida, king of Northumberland. This person we find, from Taliesin's *Moranad*, on the death of Owen, bore the formidable name of the FLAMEBEARER, which we may interpret was given him from its being his usual custom to commit every town, village, or private house of the enemy's, to the flames immediately it came into his possession. He is said, according to Matthew of Westminster's *Chronicle*, to have arrived in the year 547 with a fleet of forty ships and a large body of troops; after which we find that the Northumbrian kingdom came more particularly into note. This was so, but as the Saxons had already been located in Northumberland for nearly a century, since the times of Ochta and Elissa, who had been sent to settle there by Hengist. The requirement of history, which speaks of his marriage, and of the wars of his sons and successors, evidently is, that he was born in Britain, and continued to live there, and that towards his middle time of life, and long after the birth of his warlike sons, he went over to Saxony on the enterprise of raising a large body of troops among his countrymen, to bring them over to Britain to make conquests in this island. This appears to be the best comment on the history of the times; and if so, he seems to have succeeded perfectly in this design.

It is pretty evident, from the various engagements between the northern Britons and the Northumbrians, mentioned by Taliesin, as the battles of Menao, Argoed-Zwyfain, and Gwen-Istrad, that the battle of Kaltraeth, which was so great a feature in the contest between the two nations, took place after a war of several years duration, and was the termination of it. Difficult it is to assign the precise years of the battles respectively, but we have two leading events given us, the deaths of Ida and Urien, the first of which, apparently, belongs to the former part of the war, and the second to the latter part of it. Ida, on his arrival with his forces, as far as we can comprehend the events of the times, did not at first employ them against the northern Britons, but overran the northern parts of the territories of the Brigantes, that is of Yorkshire, which the Saxons thoroughly brought into subjection, so that they almost immediately raised an auxiliary force among them, which they employed in their own wars against their countrymen, and had them in the field at, or rather soon after, the battle of Argoed-Zwyfain. It was when Ida commanded a body of these auxiliaries that, according to Taliesin's *Moranad*, on the death of Owen, he was cut off by that leader, and his force dispersed. This death of Ida is placed by the *Saxon Chronicle*, and Matthew of Westminster, in 560.

As to the death of Urien. He commanded at the battle of Menao in an inroad on the Northumbrian territories. He commanded also at the battle of Gwen-Ystrad, when a Saxon inroad was repulsed; both of which events are narrated with great animation by Taliesin. It was after this that in a confederacy with three other British chiefs, or kings of those days, Riderc-hen, Guallauc, and Mordcant, that he was pressing the Northumbrian kingdom hard, and apparently near overturning it, as the two sons of the late king Hussa and Deodoric were closely besieged in the island of Medcaut or Lindisfarne, when he was suddenly assassinated, as related by Nennius in his *Genealogies*, c. 66, by Mordcant, or as he is called in *Triad* 47, Llovan-lau-dino; which deep tragedy appears to have broken up the confederacy, and to have turned the tables on the Britons. The death of Urien seems best placed in the year 567; and I have inferred, in the *Analysis* of Aneurin's poem of Gododin, in my *Britannia Antiqua*, pp. 236-7, to which Mr. G. V. Irving has made reference, that the battle of Kaltraeth took place three years after it, or in or about the year 570. We have now then to reconcile the annals of Caledonia with those of Britain as to the date of this event.

I am strengthened by the authority of the rev. John Williams ap Ithel, the eminent Welsh scholar, and translator of the Gododin, in having assigned this date, as he adopts it himself in his *Introduction* to the poem (p. 8). The rev. Thomas Price, historian of Wales, assigns it from 520 to 570. The viscount Villemarqué to 578. Mr. G. V. Irving from 640 to 650. The late Sharon Turner from 547 to 568; and M. A. Thierry, subsequent to the year 560. It is pretty evident, from the average of the above dates, that the majority of researchers have thought it necessary to assign the battle of Kaltraeth to a period which would be not irreconcileable to ancient British history. Having mentioned Mr. Williams, I must here take occasion to say that Mr. Irving much misrepresents a passage which he quotes from him. As the passage is given, he is cited as expressing himself, "This was in the reign of Rhum, a descendant in the fourth degree of Cunedda, Welsh king of Gododin." *Introduction*, p. 8; whereas what he really does say is, "This was in the reign of Rhum, descendant in the fourth degree of Cunedda Wledig (*i. e.* Cunedda the Illustrious) king of Gododin:" taking this last word in the sense of the race or section of the Northern Britons, of whom mention has been before made.

Mr. Irving doubts about the prevalence of the custom of pendragon-ship, or generalissimoship, among the Britons. As he adduces no argument on this head, it may be sufficient to meet assertion with counter assertion, and to observe that all that is said as to the existence of this practice, before Roman times in Britain and after Roman times, from the reign of Vortigern in the reign 449 to the retirement of the Britons into Wales in 586, and indeed in later times than that, is perfectly true and authentic. As well as this, the custom usually extended to Caledonia, of having one pendragon for both.

Mr. Irving refers to the ancient Greek states as not having the pendragonship. It is true they had not: and what was the consequence? They yielded to the Macedonians, who were their Saxons, in a few years, whilst the Britons maintained a struggle with the Anglo-Saxons, backed as they were by the whole of the north of Germany from 449 to 586; or for the space of one hundred and thirty-seven years; and mostly on equal terms.

As to the epoch to which the poem of the Gododin refers, I am free to confess that the periods at which various of the actors in it, or those referred to in it, are known to have lived, enable the historical student to apply a very closely approximating date to it. I allude to the names of Cenau, Caradoc Vreichvras, Taliesin, Owen, Bearnoch or Bun, widow of Ida, Mab Cian Gwyngwyn, the Druidic pagan poet mentioned in the *History* of Nennius, c. 66, as contemporary with Taliesin; some fragments of whose compositions are still extant, Geraint king of Dumnonia and others, which appear to be full proof on this head: and so I conclude Mr. Williams thinks, whose account as well as my own is commented on by Mr. Irving. In this view I would not be over solicitous as to what conflicting dates may be discovered in the *Annals* of Tigernach, or in those of Ulster, or in other like sources; for ancient British history does not admit that the persons above referred to could possibly have lived three quarters of a century later than the year 570, so that the battle of Kaltraeth could have taken place in the year 642 instead of the period above assigned. I do not credit that Taliesin, the court bard of Maelgwyn Gwynedd, the Welsh sovereign who died in 560, could have survived to the year 642; still less to 677, or 685, as some copies of the Ulster Chronicle would imply that the conflict took place: nor can the reign of Geraint, king of Dumnonia, who arrives though too late to the succour of the Britons, be postponed with the slightest show of probability so as to correspond with any of those dates. These are considerations which appear deserving of attention; and archbishop Usher and other writers may be consulted as to the real date at which this Geraint, or Gerennius, lived.

I view the marriage of Bun or Bearnoch, a British princess, sister to Owen's wife, as asserted in *Triad* 105, with Ida the FLAMEBEARER, king of Northumberland, as a real fact: and if so, it may be regarded as a political marriage intended to reconcile opposite interests and to preserve peace: which, for all we know, it might have effected for some space of time.

This may be the place to notice another point, incidentally arising in treating of the circumstances connected with the battle of Kaltraeth, namely, that Mr. Irving asserts that I am in error in supposing the word Brec means Pict, whereas according to his views it is merely personal, applying to freckles or discolourations of the skin, and used as a species of nickname, or soubriquet.

The death of Domnal, or otherwise Donald Brec, a Scottish king, is one of the events commemorated in the poem of the Gododin. He is represented in stanzas 22, 40, and 59, as left lying a corpse on the ground in the same state as he was slain; no smile on his features, and without his royal bandeau or coronet, and abandoned to the birds of the air. This Donald, though a Scottish king, as we know from the annals of Caledonia, seems on this occasion to have commanded a warlike array of the Picts, as no doubt the kings of the Scots frequently did when they held portions of that race under subjection; as we read in Buchanan's *History*, p. 159, of Scotch governors about the year 761 of Galloway, which is considered to have formed part of the Pictish territories of Scotland. Indeed, the two nations seem to have been much intermixed.

His style in the poem is not king of Scotland, but Dyvynaul Vrych for Bomnal Brec, that is, " Domnal the Pict :" this term in its various forms having the signification of " Pict " in Celtic literature: as in " Breagh Magh," a Pictish district in Ireland; " Coeman Brec," *i. e.*, Colman the Pict; and in the designation of Nectan the First in Pictish history, who was surnamed " Nectan Morbreac," as in the Gaelic translation of the Pictish Chronicle (*Irish Nennius*, p. 161), the addition implying the same as " Pictus Magnus," or the " Great Pict." There are also other instances. The same thing may be suspected in the name of Mervyn Vrych in the ninth century, who was king of the Isle of Man; Vrych, as noted just above, has a parallel signification with Brec, and there were numerous Picts in the Isle of Man, as appears in the *Annals* of Tigernach, who has in the year 711 this insertion: " Strages Pictorum in campo Manaud," *i. e.*, the slaughter of the Picts in the war of the Isle of Man; and it is also recorded by the *Chronicle of Ulster*, that Drus the Eighth was king of the Picts in the year 751, except of those of the Isle of Man.

The narrative in the poem leads us to the same conclusion. For in the *Epilogue*, stanza 63, when Geraint, king of Dumnonia, comes to Dunbarton, like the Fortinbras in *Hamlet*, to wind up this tragedy of Gododin, he leads the Britons at once, strengthened by his succours, against the " white figured skins," that is, the Picts, who now appear to stand in the position of their chief enemies, the Saxons not yet having advanced to this western extremity of the Wall from the neighbourhood of Cor-Eiddin at the other end, where they had been so long engaged. Besides this, the manuscript of the *Chronicle of Ulster* in the Bodleian Library, styles Eochy, surnamed Flavus or the Yellow, in Celtic Buidhe, the father of Donald Brec, as a king of the Picts. Another manuscript Chronicle does the same. (See Ritson's *Annals*, 12mo., 1828, vol. ii, p. 41.)

To revert to the Irish Chronicles, I am apprehensive that Mr. Irving

will find nothing very satisfactory to his purpose in them as to establishing the later date he supposes; for if he compares their account with
Bede's *History* (book iii, c. 9), he will find that in the year 642 the
kingdom of Northumberland was at war with the province of Mercia,
and that Oswald the Northumbrian king was killed in that war, so that
it would be less likely that the Saxons' grand expedition to the North,
that is, the campaign of Gododin, would have taken place at that junc-
ture. It likewise occasions some little distrust of Tigernach, in that he
says that Domnal Brec fell in a battle at Strath-Cawn against Hoian
(Owen) king of the Britons, whereas it appears difficult, if not impossible, to connect the name of Strath-cawn with Gododin : however, as
there was actually a conflict of great importance that year with the Mercians, called by Bede (*loco citato*) the battle of Maserfield, and by
Nennius and the *Annales Cambriæ* the battle of Cocboy or Chochui, in
which the Northumbrian monarch fell, Tigernach may have inserted
the date of that year 642 by way of conjecture, supposing that Donald
Brec fell also at the same time. Respecting the Chronicle of Ulster :
the date 685 is found in some copies, but that is the year of the great
battle of Drumnechtan among the mountains in Forfarshire, between the
Northumbrians and the Picts, in which Birdei king of the latter race was
killed. Thus again, this particular year may have been preferred by
some other scribe to the former one of 642, who possibly might have
thought that Birdei was Donald himself, and apparently in reality did
think so.

Mr. Irving likewise quotes the *Duan Albanic*, the *Register* of St. An-
drew's Priory, and the *Chronicles of Wintown* and *Fordun*, as tending to
support a date for the battle of Kaltraeth later than 570 : but from the
point of view which I have submitted, that the said important conflict if
it took place at all must have occurred in that year or not long before or
after, I judge that they have fallen into a not unusual error in ancient
chronologies, namely, that of placing concurrent reigns of monarchs, not
together, but in a sequence; by which in the result the order of time
becomes not observed.

In this way the ancient chronicles which treat of Scottish affairs about
this time, are for two or three centuries or more the most deceiving
guides that can be met with; for it is very often extremely difficult, if
not impossible, for us now to know the real order in which particular
monarchs reigned. I will give instances in point from Buchanan, historian of Scotland, relating to the times in question.

He supplies us with a series of kings, the first of them being stated as
a contemporary with Aurelius Ambrosius, a south British king, who is
known to have died in 504. His list is thus—Congallus (Guallauc),
Goran, Kinat, Eugenius (or Ewen), another Guallauc, Aidan, Kenneth,
Ferquard, another Eugenius or Ewen, or otherwise Eochy the yellow,

and at last the said Domnal Brec, whom he advances in chronology about seventy years, and makes contemporary with Oswald, king of Northumberland, before spoken of, and not with Ida, in the time of north British kings Urien and Owen. (See his *Rerum Scoticarum Historia*, 8vo, 1643, pp. 143-56.) Well he might, for he places the reigns of these ten kings, which were of various lengths, from thirty-four years to four months, all as I have observed in sequence; whereas ancient Caledonia having been, as is well known, divided into various minor states, it is beyond all question that the reigns of some of the kings were concurrent with each other. Thus he gains the seventy years on the ten reigns. Nor can I easily trace in how many reigns afterwards he comes into correct chronology again. Ritson, in his *Annals* (vol. ii, p. 42), pronounces Ferquard and Domnal Brec to have reigned at the same time; which correction alone would make fourteen years difference in the Scottish chronology of this period.

However, we have one faithful old guide among all this *embarras*, who will supply us with due direction. This is Nennius, with his *Genealogies*; in which we find recorded that Urien carried on war with Hussa and Deodoric, sons of the deceased king Ida. This informs us, as plain as words can do, that those two kings had possessed themselves of portions of their late father's dominions, and that their reigns were concurrent. At least so I understand it. This corresponds with the usual date assigned to the war of Urien with the Northumbrian kingdom, and his death in 567. Then a short interval of peace ensues, as the poem of Gododin itself informs us in stanza 6, which period being accounted for, and three years being allowed from the death of Urien to the conclusion of it, you will appear to arrive, by a very natural process, to the date of 570, as that of the battle of Kaltraeth, at which I have ventured to fix it.

However, further, Mr. Irving cites an extract from Adomnan's *Life of St. Columba* in support of a later date for Domnal Brec; but this being a passage referring to an alleged prophecy of St. Columba and its completion, would be one, as must be allowed, peculiarly open to interpolations, additions, and comments, by later copyists, so that I may be excused for not treating of it more particularly.

In regard to the nature of the locality of Cor-Eiddin, assumed by me as the *arena* and battle place of Kaltraeth, I can only say that I have followed Roy, the most accurate of all military surveyors, and I advance it as incontestable that the wall of Antoninus terminated with a fortress, the site of which is at present called Coreddin, and I judge had also the same name in old times, or one closely resembling it. The site of the ancient fortress is immediately contiguous to the sea, a circumstance which is evidently required by several passages of the Gododin.

I have thus given every explanation in my power on the subject of this historical event, and the fine epic poem recording it. These explanations are due to the importance of the event, which accelerated the decline of the ancient British power in the island and confirmed the supremacy of the Teutonic domination instead. These explanations are also due to Mr. G. Vere Irving, who has the merit of having first brought the subject forward, and whose observations I read with extreme interest and pleasure when they appeared. I found them of the greatest utility to me when going over the same ground myself, and it is far from my intention to say anything in disparagement of those dissertations, which will ever be considered as important illustrations of the events treated of, though I have ventured to differ on points of chronology, and also, indeed, on some of geography, from the learned writer of them. I have also to thank Mr. Irving for the very courteous manner in which he is kind enough to mention my name.

Corrections and additions to sir J. Gardner Wilkinson's paper, "On the Rock-Basins of Dartmoor, and some British Remains in England," printed in the preceding number of the *Journal* for June:

Plate 7. For "circular cists of slabs, 2 ft. high by 9 broad," read "by 0.9 broad, or "by 9 inches broad."

Page 108, line 9, add as note to the word remains, "I have since learnt from Mr. Rhind, that on the tallest stone among the ortholithic remains at Crendi, in Malta,—which is about 20 feet high,—he found a carefully cut trough, 3 feet long by 1 broad, and 10 inches deep; which is very analogous to our rock-basins. Again, in the *Revue Africaine*, an enormous cromlech in the interior of Algeria is described as having two or three basins and connecting channels cut in the surface of the capstone; and Merimée (*Voyage en Corse*) describes other cromlechs in Corsica with similar artificial hollows."

Page 117, line 29, add as note to "Hecatæus," "I find from Ælian (*Hist. An.*, xi, 1), that this was Hecatæus, not of Miletus, but of Abdera. He lived in the time of Alexander."

Proceedings of the Congress.

(Continued from p. 100.)

THURSDAY, SEPTEMBER 15.

AT nine A.M. the Association assembled to proceed first to Grimsbury Camp, now almost entirely covered by thick plantations, rendering its examination difficult. By the aid of Mr. Vere Irving, however, its arrangement became sufficiently perspicuous. Upon this spot, and other earthworks and ancient fortifications, Mr. Vere Irving has, since the holding of the Congress, submitted the following report, which will place the subject more satisfactorily before the reader :—

"In order to render more easily intelligible the following remarks on the earthworks and other ancient fortifications visited by the Association during their Congress at Newbury, especially to those who joined us for the first time on that occasion, I take this opportunity of shortly recapitulating the ideas which I first broached at our Norwich meeting as to the necessity of dividing into separate periods the Roman occupation of this island, and assigning to each of these its distinctive remains. Formerly it was the custom of antiquaries to consider the Roman dominion in this country as an undivided and homogeneous whole, to which all the vestiges of that people were at once referred without any attempt to discriminate between those which belonged to the earlier and those which appertained to the later portion of their sojourn. This, I believe, has often led to great errors and confusion. The position of the Romans altered most materially during the time which elapsed between their first appearance in the island and the withdrawal of the legions. These alterations appear to be referable to four distinct epochs, each of which is marked by distinctive characters in the fortifications and buildings erected.

"1. The Romans first appeared as an invading and expeditionary army; fortifying, as was their custom, their camps from night to night.

The entrenchments of this period are generally large. They consist invariably of earthworks of more or less strength ; and their position was determined according to the exigencies of the campaign, and without any reference to roads or the best lines of permanent communication.

" 2. In the second period, the natives had been subdued but were still prone to revolt. The legions had assumed the character of an army of occupation. Military roads were formed, which were at certain distances defended by castella or præsidia. These are generally of smaller sizes, but more strongly fortified than the camps of the preceding epoch.

" 3. When the native tribes had fully adopted the Roman civilization, and had been taught by the policy of Agricola and his successors to build houses, towns sprung up, containing a mixed civil and military population. These, however, were still surrounded by ramparts. On the sea coast, where these towns were exposed to piratical attacks, they appear to have been early defended by stone walls ; while in the interior, their inhabitants were contented with earthwork defences until a very late period; in fact, until the removal of the Roman forces led to the revival of violence and turbulence, when they also adopted the more formidable protection afforded by fortified walls of masonry.

" The 4th, and last, period arrived when tranquillity was so perfectly established as to permit the erection of open hamlets and detached villas, the latter often of great size, adorned with fountains, tessellated pavements, pictures, and, in fact, all the luxuries so much prized by the patricians and high officers of the empire.

" The importance of these distinctions is at once apparent when we come to consider the first camp on our list, namely, that at

" Speen. It is very rarely indeed that we meet with an instance where the modern name of a place in any way resembles that which it bore in the times of Roman occupation. To this Speen forms a remarkable exception, as its present name is unequivocally the same as the Spinæ of the Antonine *Iters ;* a fact which becomes more apparent if we give to the latter the Scotch and continental pronunciations, which was that most probably used by the Romans. Where, then, was this station situated ? As far as the name is concerned it might be anywhere in the parish of Speen, including the hamlet of Speenhamland. What was its type and character? Looking to the date at which the Antonine *Iters* were compiled, it must have belonged either to the second or third of the above-mentioned periods of the Roman dominion, and most probably to the last of these. Now, there is above Speen church the mutilated remains of a camp, which Mr. Adams (see page 70 *ante*) conjectures may have been the station in question. From this, however, I am inclined to dissent. The camp above Speen church is of large size. Its defences, so far as they are preserved, consist of a simple escarpment ; while on the sides where they have been destroyed, they most probably

were formed by a rampart and ditch, which, however, could only have
been very slight, otherwise more vestiges of them would have remained.
These characteristics mark decisively that this camp, although undoubtedly Roman, belongs to the type of entrenchments of the first or
expeditionary class. The situation, moreover, is not that which this
nation ever selected either for their towns or their permanent præsidia.
Looking to the whole of the country, I am inclined to believe that the
permanent station was situated at the bottom of the hill, on the bank of
the river, not far from the junction of the Kennet and the Lambourn.
In this idea I am confirmed by the discovery of the Roman cemetery at
the Newbury railway station. That people very frequently placed their
towns or forts on the banks of a river or stream, and had their place of
interment on the opposite side; a practice not only recommended on
sanitary grounds, but consonant with their religious ideas, the river to
be crossed becoming emblematical of the mythological Styx.

"At SILCHESTER we encountered a splendid specimen of the towns
of the third period, reminding us of Caerwent and Caistor. The amphitheatre, however, presented us with an interesting feature of Roman
times, which is not found in the other two examples. The walls are,
however, most probably of a late date. As our visit was necessarily
short, without any opportunity for making excavations, and as the place
has been frequently described in archæological publications, I pass on to

"PERBOROUGH CASTLE, an extensive and magnificent villa belonging
to the fourth period of the Roman occupation. It occupies the summit
of a hill, commanding a most extensive view. It is, as is usual with
these buildings, of large extent, providing accommodation not only for
the immediate family of its opulent proprietors, but also for the numerous
slaves who cultivated his lands, and in the case of a high military
officer, for the soldiers who formed his escort or body guard. On
examining it we met with a number of those pits or hollows so often
found in connection with buildings of this class, some of which were
used as receptacles for ashes and other refuse, and others as enclosures
or pounds for the safe custody of sheep, swine, and even larger cattle.
It had evidently been destroyed by fire, many of the walls being most
strongly calcined. We were informed that a pot, containing a large
number of Roman coins, had been found in the hollow at the bottom of
the hill on which the villa stands.

"BEACON HILL is, from the steepness of its ascent, a formidable
military position. The view from the top is most extensive on all sides,
and especially on the south, where it reaches across the whole breadth
of Hampshire to the Southampton water. The camp which occupies the
plateau on the summit, both by its position and the character of the
earthworks by which it is defended, recalls forcibly to recollection the
entrenchments at Cissbury, and other places on the South Downs, and

must be referred to the same period. The resemblance is further increased by the existence within its ramparts of some of those remarkable artificial hollows which form so characteristic a feature in the camps referred to, and which the excavations at Cissbury and Highdown have proved to have been constructed for the purpose of enclosing cattle and other animals.

"At GRIMSBURY we encountered a camp of a type which is by no means uncommon. It occupies the top of a considerable eminence, which is comparatively inaccessible on three sides owing to the abruptness of the ascent and the morasses which must formerly have filled the surrounding valleys on these sides; it is defended by a ditch with scarp and counterscarp. On the fourth, where the approach is easy, along a projecting ridge, the defences are more formidable, consisting of two lines of fortifications, each composed of a deep ditch and a strong earthen rampart. The construction of the whole evinces considerable military skill. At the bottom of the ditch, at one of the points where it would be most difficult to approach, there is a strong spring, which has been collected; its position reminds us of that of the well at Caistor, near Norwich. Within the *enceinte* of the camp are several small barrows. This, although an unusual occurrence, is by no means singular. Roy (plate xviii) gives an example at Inch Stuthill, on the Tay. Similar barrows are found in the camp at Hollinsbury, which overlooks Brighton; and I met with another instance within a small Roman fortification in the vicinity of Moffat. These barrows have, however, no connection with the camp, and must have been thrown up long previous to its construction.

"Near HAMPSTEAD NORRIS we were shown another earthwork enclosure. Being situated in a wood it was by no means easy to trace its lines or obtain an idea of its form. As far as I could judge, it is an irregular parallelogram of considerable size, defended on two sides by a ditch with scarp and counterscarp, and on the others by a ditch and rampart of a slight character. Regarded from a military point of view, this earthwork is open to very grave objections, especially in that portion which consists of a ditch and scarps. These are not, as at Grimsbury, carried along the face of a steep ascent, but are placed at the bottom of the rise, and abut on a piece of perfectly level and sound land. From this circumstance I am inclined to believe that this earthwork was not constructed as a military post, and to agree with Mr. Thomas Wright, that it is one of those enclosures which in lawless and troubled times were raised round a house, and into which the cattle were gathered at night to diminish the risk of their being stolen; in fact, something analogous to the fence called the "tun," which in the present day surrounds every farm house in Iceland.[1] At one corner of the enclosure

---

[1] See lord's Dufferin's *Cruise in High Latitudes.*

there is a considerable tumulus; this, however, like the above-mentioned barrows, must have existed long previous to the rest of the earthwork, the makers of which have merely availed themselves of it as a convenience and a saving of labour."

At Grimsbury, referred to in the preceding report, are six or seven mounds, conceived to be barrows, and Mr. Brown, the proprietor of the estate, kindly engaged his men to make excavations in regard to them. Unfortunately the diggers had cut crossways instead of longitudinally, time was lost and nothing found; the mode was altered, but no satisfactory results were obtained. The mounds are about twenty feet long by twelve in breadth, and deserving of attention; but time pressing to accomplish the many objects assigned for the day, the party were obliged to abandon the research for the present, and thence proceeded to Hampstead Norris, where they were hospitably received at the Manor House by Mr. Luke Lousley, who had zealously attended the Congress, and by whom many Roman tiles, pottery, together with mediæval objects found in the neighbourhood, were exhibited. Here also the Association met with a large and valuable library containing an immense collection of curious tracts and works relating to the history and antiquities of the county, which had been collected together by his late father; the knowledge of which may be important to those who are engaged in researches relating to the county. A visit was paid to the church, dedicated to St. Mary. It has a stone tower, on which are eight faces of grotesque character. The roof of the church presents a peculiar appearance, being in the interior of a circular form, without any straight beams, but having large pieces of wood framed together. There is a date of 1635, probably the period of its erection. The bottom of the pulpit is of stone, and on each side, in the wall, there is a niche, intended formerly to hold the image of some saint. Another niche, with a circular top, just within the north door, probably contained a figure of the Virgin. The windows in the chancel are four in number, and lancet-shaped, and on the south side there is a stone seat. At the entrance are two other windows, at the top of one of which, cut out in the stonework, is the figure of a monk's head and neck, with ornamental glass.

Thence the Association proceeded by Compton Downs, taking the remains of Perborough castle (see Mr. Vere Irving's Report, p. 228, *ante*) on the way to Aldworth church, where they were met by the rev. Mr. Lloyd. In the churchyard is a remarkable yew tree, measuring 27 feet 5 inches in girth, about 5 feet from the ground. It rises about 25 feet in height, and branches out between seven and eight yards on each side from the trunk.[1] The church was commented on by Mr. C. E. Davis,

[1] A view of the churchyard and tree may be found in the *Gent.'s Mag.*, vol. 68; also in a *History of Newbury and its Environs*, published by Hall and Marsh. Speenhamland 1839. 8vo., p. 232.

who remarked that, from its general aspect, although all important vestiges of this first building have been obliterated, with the exception of the low western tower and arch, that it was originally built in the Early English period, and that shortly after the building was almost entirely remodelled, in order that it might be made a mausoleum of the De La Beche family rather than that of their parish church. It now consists of a western tower, nave and chancel (from which latter there is no separation, except that of a late perpendicular wooden screen), and a south aisle, communicating with the nave by three very bold and effective arches. All this building, with the exception previously mentioned, is of the best period of the Decorated style. The entrance is by a doorway in the western bay of the south aisle, immediately contiguous to which was formerly a recess and tabernacle, enclosing a monument, which has entirely perished. The doorway is as large as the western entrance to many larger churches, and quite unfitted as a means of egress and ingress for the congregation of so small a building, and was evidently built so capacious, in order that it might the more readily admit the funeral procession of the members of that family, who have left us such splendid monuments of their magnificence and power. The southern wall of the aisle is occupied, with the exception of the entrance, by three beautifully decorated canopies, one of which is in a great measure destroyed; they span three of the effigies, and are most admirably designed in geometric tracery with the ball-flower, and enriched studding to the hollows of the mouldings. The tracery, although strictly geometrical, is as elegant as that where more flaming lines were used, and this fact must be attributed to the very clever balancing of its parts, which unfortunately has been carried out so lightly, as to require the assistance of iron work, and it is to this latter circumstance that we have to regret its partial ruin. On the northern wall of the nave are three very similar canopies, but they have been in part repaired, when the true aspiring principles of Gothic were on the decline. The pinnacles, which on the south side are most perfect, are here restored, when the continuity of the vertical line was not thought, as it should be, the aim of ·Gothic. Mr. C. E. Davis, although at first of opinion that the canopies, with these exceptions, were all of the same time, upon examination, expressed his belief that those of the nave were erected subsequently to the others, with the wish that they should be precise copies, but almost involuntarily adopting a contour of moulding, a newer fashion, less voluptuous and harsher in its form.

Mr. Planché then discoursed on the interesting monuments.

The party were elegantly regaled in the grounds of the rectory by the rev. F. Le Lloyd and Mrs. Lloyd, and the thanks of the Association warmly expressed for their kind entertainment.

At Ilsley church the Association was received by the rev. Mr. Loveday. Mr. Roberts remarked that the nave piers on the south side have been apparently reworked in the age subsequent to their erection, causing them to be much lessened in size, so as to have the effect of an excessive overhanging of the wall above. The mouldings on the caps and bases being early English, and the stonework semi-Norman.

Returning to Newbury, a *table d'hôte* was held at the *Pelican*, George Godwin, F.R.S., F.S.A., V.P., in the chair, after which a meeting was held in the Mansion House,

THE HON. P. P. BOUVERIE, M.P., V.P., IN THE CHAIR.

Mr. Henry Godwin, F.S.A., read a paper on the worthies and celebrities connected with Newbury and its neighbourhood.

"Commencing with the Saxon abbot Bethune, who in A.D. 821 obtained a charter to the monastery of Abingdon from king Kenwulf, he proceeded upon the authority of Domesday Book to name one of the Conqueror's followers, Ernulph de Hesding, ancestor of the Earls of Perche, as the possessor of a town the site of which he conceived to be identical with that of Newbiri. The earls of Perche here built a castle,[1] which was taken by siege and force of assault by king Stephen in 1152.[2] King John seized the estates of the earl of Perche at Newbury.[3] He had a palace at Kingsclere, and often visited the town of Newbury; and agreeably to legendary history,[4] took refuge with an old woman when pursued by his insurgent barons. Here in disguise he was sheltered, and in requital of this service he is generally reported to have founded the almshouses situate in King John's-court. He also granted to the master and brethren of St. Bartholomew's hospital the profits of a fair held on the eve of that saint's day.[5] Passing to the reign of Henry III, Mr. Godwin introduced to our notice Wm. Marshall, earl of Pembroke, to whom in 1217 the Berkshire estates of the earl of Perche (who fell in the battle of Lincoln) were given. Mr. Godwin briefly sketched the history of the Pembrokes, who held Hampstead Marshall by tenure of the Marshall's gold enamelled staff, and gave the name of their office to their domain. Roger de Mortimer was lord of the manor of Newbury in the reign of Edward I, and in 1297 from an *Inquis. post-mortem anno regni* 25°, Mr. Godwin produced a Wm. de Mortimer holding sundry rents in Newbury, Speenhamland, and Woodspeen. Passing to the next century, he detailed particulars relating to Roger Mortimer, earl of March, the protector and paramour of Isabella, the queen and widow of Edward II. He died A.D. 1355, possessed of the manor of Newbury and the moiety of the lordship of the town.

Mr. Godwin entered minutely into particulars connected with the pos-

[1] Lysons, *Magn. Brit.*, i, 317.　[3] Norman Roll, No. 35.
[2] Holinshed, ii, 103.　[4] King John and the abbot of Canterbury.
[5] Rot. Claus. John., 17, p. 1, m. 28.

sessors of Donnington castle, and satisfactorily disputed its occupation by Geoffrey Chaucer the poet. It was neither purchased by him, for in the decline of his life he was not possessed of means sufficient to obtain it, nor was it presented to him by John of Gaunt, as often asserted. The duke of Lancaster was never the owner of Donnington castle in Berkshire, but Castle Donnington in Leicestershire belonged to him. Dismissing Chaucer, therefore, as entitled to be a worthy of Berkshire by ownership of Donnington castle, Mr. Godwin retained a hold on his granddaughter Alice, espoused to Sir John Phelipp, who, by an *Inquisition* 3° *Hen. V, No.* 42, appears to have held the castle and manor of Donnington. The conveyance of this property, Mr. Godwin shows, could not have been made until after 1404, because that was the year of Alice Chaucer's birth, and as the conveyance was made to her, as well as her husband, and she was only eleven years old at her husband's death, it could not have been conveyed long previously. Chaucer died in 1400, and the inevitable conclusion is that the poet was never the owner of Donnington castle. Thomas Chaucer, the father of Alice and the son of the poet, is likely from the early widowhood of his daughter to have visited the estate at Donnington, and there he may have planted the oaks so frequently associated with the poet's name. Alice contracted a second marriage with Thomas de Montague, earl of Salisbury, who falling at the blockade of Orleans in 1428, left his brother in arms Wm. de la Pole, earl, afterwards marquis, and finally duke of Suffolk, his successor in the siege, and also in that of the heart of his widow, whom he married in 1430, and resided with her in Donnington castle.

Jack of Newbury formed a conspicuous celebrity in Mr. Godwin's memorials; his history was traced, and upon the conclusion of the paper, in the course of discussion, a conjecture was ingeniously thrown out by the rev. Charles Kingsley, that his real name was John Smallwode, and that he was a native of Winchcomb, in Gloucestershire. The rev. Mr. Milton making inquiry upon the subject, produced at a future meeting extracts from the parish register of Winchcomb, in which are the following entries relating to his family:—

"Anno Dni. 1539. Junii 28. Robertus filius Johannes Smallwode sepult.

"Anno Dni. 1541. Novembris 27. Margareta Smawlwode purific."

In his will, Jack of Newbury designates himself "John Smalwoode the elder als. John Wynchcombe." It is, therefore, pretty evident that he was a native of Gloucestershire, not Berkshire. His family was traced by Mr. Godwin, and carried down to the present possessor of the estate, — Hartley, esq. Another celebrated clothier demanded Mr. Godwin's attention, Thomas Dolman, whose connexion with Shaw-place was duly noticed.[1]

[1] See *ante*, p. 43.

The battles of Newbury gave to Mr. Godwin associations with the most important persons of the period, names recorded in history for their devotion to their king and country. Sunderland, Carnarvon, Falkland, Essex, Manchester, Cromwell, Boys, Rudyerd, Twiss, Woodbridge, Ferrar, the Castillons, Craven, Evelyn, Pepys, Foster, Ashmole, Congreve, Bolingbroke, etc., together with many of a later date, were all most interestingly introduced.[1]

Mr. W. H. Black, F.S.A., then proceeded to examine the deeds belonging to the corporation of Newbury, which were brought for examination under the custody of R. F. Graham, esq., the town clerk.

Mr. Black gave a general sketch of the corporation records of Newbury. It appeared that the earlier and more important records had been either lost or destroyed, but many ancient ones were still in the possession of the municipality, some of which were dated as far back as the reign of Edward I, and were peculiarly interesting to the locality. By reference to some of the parish records Mr. Black set at rest the doubts which had been raised as to whether Charles I, at the time of the first battle of Newbury, really stayed in the house of one Gabriell Cox, then mayor of the town. It appeared that Cox was the owner of it at that time, and that the person in whose house other authorities said Charles lodged subsequently became the owner, thus perhaps accounting for the mistake which had been made.

Among the corporation records was a duplicate of a petition from and signed by two hundred inhabitants of Newbury, to Charles II, on his restoration, praying that the corporation might be accepted as purchasers of the manorial rights so as to become lords of the manor; and other documents examined, showed that on the celebrated Jack of Newbury retiring from business, the corporation had employed his workmen; thus it probably was that the two hundred petitioners were so perfectly satisfied with the conduct of the corporate body of that day, that they were willing and desired that they should possess the manorial rights. Lord Craven, however, had at the time agreed to purchase them, but in consequence of the petition referred to, the contract was actually set aside, and the rights were transferred to the corporation of Newbury. Another document, dated 5th June, 1627, directed the payment to lord Craven of the amount which he had actually paid into the exchequer for the purchase of the manorial rights, since sold to the corporation of Newbury.

[1] We abstain from entering into particulars, being enabled to refer our readers to Mr. Godwin's paper printed *in extenso*, and published, by Blacket of Newbury, and Simpkin & Co., London.

FRIDAY, SEPTEMBER 16TH.

A very large attendance of members and visitors assembled at the *Pelican* to proceed, in the first instance, to Beacon-hill, and afterwards to visit the President at Highclere castle.

Beacon-hill constitutes one of the highest points in the county, and the day being fine, a view could be obtained as distant as the Solent. Here Mr. Geo. Vere Irving made a few observations in relation to the spot (see p. 228, *ante*), after which the party moved towards Highclere, where they were received and cordially welcomed by the earl of Carnarvon, the hon. A. J. Herbert, the countess of Portsmouth, and other members of this noble family. The attendance was large and distinguished, embracing in addition to those who had been present at the several meetings and investigations during the Congress, lord Bolton, sir Richard Bethell, M.P., Attorney-General, sir Robt. and Miss Throckmorton, sir Joshua Walmsley, hon. and rev. S. Best, hon. Mr. Bouverie, M.P., J. R. Mowbray, M.P., W. W. B. Beach, M.P., John Walter, M.P., colonel and the hon. Mrs. Lindsay, Mr. alderman Cubitt, M.P., archdeacon Randall, W. S. Portal, esq., J. A. Winterbotham, esq., baroness Weld, F. A. Carrington, esq., W. Mount, esq., capt. Slocock, E. B. Bunny, esq., Miss Locke King, etc., etc.

Highclere Castle is almost entirely a modern erection, not yet completed, under the superintendence of sir Charles Barry, by Mr. Thomas Allom. The rooms of this superb mansion were all thrown open, and the magnificent pictures which adorn its walls inspected. Many fine examples of the skill of Vandyke, sir Joshua Reynolds, and other celebrated artists, are here to be seen. Various refreshments of the most elegant description were laid out, and having been heartily partaken of by the visitors, Mr. Pettigrew summoned their attendance on the lawn, and then, in the name and on the part of the Association, tendered to the noble President their warmest thanks for the kindness he had displayed to them, and the attention he had devoted to the business of the Congress.

MR. PETTIGREW said, he was sure all would be exceedingly loth to depart from that beautiful spot, without embracing an opportunity of evincing the pleasure which they had experienced from the very elegant entertainment provided, and returning their thanks for the kindness they had received from lord Carnarvon. He was confident that every member who had taken part in or attended the Congress, must have been delighted with the manner in which the business had been conducted by his lordship; and no one could have heard his introductory address without being satisfied that it was the result of profound study and classical taste, such as they would desire should be the characteristics of the nobility of their land. It was not for him to occupy their time by giving utterance to opinions as to the utility of archæological researches; that had been established, and now the holding of Archæological Congresses in special localities had been satisfactorily proved to be attended by the best results—to disprove or corroborate theories which had been received for ages in regard to the historical institutions of their country, and to aid them to appreciate and revere those monuments which were landmarks in history, however insignificant was the appearance they might present in these days. No county in England needed, or was deserving of, more attention than the county of Berks. He begged publicly to acknowledge the kindness the members of the Association had received from the gentry of the county, and the readiness displayed on the part of all in promoting their researches during the week. And he would especially allude to the bishop of the diocese and clergy of the county, to whom they must refer in these matters, and who, from the education they had received and the information they possessed, were the best calculated to afford them what they needed. He was justified in hoping that the best results would attend their Congress. They had on these occasions simply, in fact, to look about them, and that was all they had been enabled to do; for they had not time to go far into their researches, but only to lay a foundation of remarks and facts which required explanation, and would afterwards be looked into by the society, and appear printed in the *Journal* of the Association. He would now return to the performance of a duty most grateful to his heart, most grateful to the officers of the Association, and to all who had in any way taken part in this Congress, or participated in the studies either as members or officers, namely, that of expressing, in the name of the Association, their great gratitude for the noble earl's kind assistance— the value of which would be indelibly impressed upon them. They had now to part, as they had duties to perform at Reading, and the train would not wait for them. Delightful as it was to refresh the body, and to charm the eye by beholding those beautiful works of art (which could be only viewed with the greatest admiration), they must take their departure; but he could not conclude his hurried observations, without returning the warmest thanks of all to the noble earl for his unbounded hospitality to the large numbers who had attended on this occasion. He most heartily wished their distinguished host, in the name of every one present, long life, health, and happiness.

The EARL CARNARVON said, he had had such a perfect experience during the past week of the activity and rapidity of motion of his friend Mr. Pettigrew, that even this last move which he had stolen upon him, and the unexpected honour which he had done him, could hardly surprise him. He, perhaps, felt some difficulty in expressing to them his sincere acknowledgments for the kindness with which the honour had been proposed and the compliment had been rendered by them, and in his extremity he might almost say, if he rightly remembered the words of queen Katherine in *Henry VIII* :—" But how to make ye suddenly an answer, with my weak wit, and to such men of gravity and learning, in truth I know not." He felt very grateful for the honour just paid ; and he should be very cold, and dull of apprehension, if he did not hail the opportunity which Mr. Pettigrew's kindness had afforded him of expressing his high sense of the deep pleasure he felt in being able to welcome there so many old friends, kind neighbours, and famed and distinguished archæologists, and still more, in the words of the old Spaniard, in placing himself and his poor house at the disposal of all present, and laying his heart at the feet of so many fair ladies. The last discussion he heard at Newbury was connected with legends and fables. He did wish it were possible to realise one legend and one fable in his person. He wished much for the moment, that he could be one of those fabled giants of old, with one hundred heads, one hundred hands, one hundred eyes, to bid welcome to all his friends, and to interchange with them a cordial and a hearty greeting. He trusted that the Association, when they left, would carry away a favourable opinion of them. Ignorant, perhaps, they might be, but that was for the want of teaching—unskilful they might be, but that again was from want of experience. That teaching and that experience must come, as it had in the present instance, from the Archæological Association. Though, perhaps, the Association had not succeeded in accomplishing quite all the work they cut out for themselves, they they had still done a great deal, and he hoped that in future the inhabitants would profit by the lessons given to them by that learned body, and reap a golden harvest from the seeds which they had set amongst them.

Having bid adieu to Highclere, the Association made for the Newbury railway, to proceed to Reading, where, upon their arrival, they were received at the Town Hall by C. J. Andrews, esq., the mayor, J. J. Blandy, esq., the town clerk, and many members of the corporation. Under the guidance of the mayor an immediate inspection of parts of Reading was proceeded with, visiting the remains of the abbey, the abbey gateway, the churches of St. Lawrence and St. Mary, the abbey mill, and the friary. The description and peculiarities of these were ably given by Geo. Godwin, esq., F.R.S., F.S.A., one of the Vice-Presidents.

The abbey, Mr. Godwin remarked, was founded by Henry I. in the year 1120 or 1121 ; the abbey church completed about 1164. The walls, of flint concrete, were cased with freestone ; but, after the dissolution, the abbey was destroyed, and parts were used in the construction of St. Mary's and St. Lawrence's, while some of the materials were taken to Windsor. The ruins, in fact, served as a quarry, as the Coliseum did at Rome. The remains of the abbey are considerable, and serve to show that the pile must have been one of great dignity. The chapter-house, which looks about eighty-four feet long and forty-two feet wide, has walls of considerable height, and a plan, which had been prepared, showed how the various portions remaining formed part of the great church, the cloisters, the kitchen, and so forth.   Some large bases (in the church) have been recently exposed.   Great credit is due to the local board, and their surveyor, Mr. Marshall, for the pains taken to preserve the ruins.   The land around them has been purchased, and formed into a public pleasure ground.   Additional purchases, with the same end in view, are contemplated.

The abbey gateway, a later erection, and close to the assize courts, now in course of erection under the superintendence of Mr. Clacy, is in a miserably dilapidated state, so much so indeed, that a part of it positively may fall at any moment.   It was urged by Mr. Godwin that the authorities should forthwith take steps, under proper advice, to restore it to its proper shape.

In excavating for the assize courts, contiguous to the abbey gateway, and on the site (according to local history and tradition) of 'an hospital for poor pilgrims,' some foundations and walls were discovered, of which Mr. Clacy supplied a plan.   The surface of the ground had been raised about nine feet by the *débris* of the fallen buildings.   The old walls above the original surface were mostly faced with squared freestone, and filled in with concrete of chalk, flint, lime, and sand.   In the centre of the wall, about two feet above the original ground surface, the remains of three human skeletons were found embedded in the concrete, the bodies having apparently been laid in the wall, and the concrete or rubble thrown around them.   The bodies, it was thought, had been placed in the wall whilst building.   There was no appearance of decayed wood or covering, and the remains were mostly in dry powder; but with a sufficient portion of bones to identify them as human, and to indicate the position of the bodies—one had apparently been placed with the knees bent.

The church of St. Lawrence, the well proportioned tower of which is seen from the railway, is described as having been "rebuilt or considerably repaired in 1434."   Notwithstanding this statement, the chancel is of the thirteenth century.   This church is viewed as a sort of rival to St. Mary's, and the tradition is that it was built by an apprentice of the builder of that church, and that the master, annoyed by its superiority, threw himself off the steeple and was killed!   Every one will remember the same story in connection with Roslyn chapel, Edinburgh, and some of the French cathedrals.   There are interesting old church books remaining.   The inventory of the plate, taken a few years prior to the Reformation, includes,—

"Itm.   A gredyron of silver and gilt, with a bone of Saynt lawrence therein, weighing iii qrs. of an ounce."

The various altars were restored at the accession of queen Mary, and the queen and king Philip came to Reading to see this done. The tower arch is blocked up with a pile of ugly galleries and an organ. The tower, externally, has been messed with restorations in ' compo.' A charge for wire for the clock, 1499, shows that here was an early instance of a clock in a parish church. The quaint-looking covered way, on the south side of the tower, having a range of gablets, was built at the cost of John Blagrave, esq. in 1619. The church, coming to our own time, is intimately connected with the late estimable justice Talfourd, who, as a scholar of the late Dr. Valpy, cut his name in the pew where he sat, and as a man put up a stained-glass window in the chancel in memory of a friend.

Away now to St. Mary's church, which was called the Minster. The statement is that it was taken down, except the spire, in 1547, and rebuilt in 1551; that the spire was left till 1594, when, being blown down, it was rebuilt. Over a door on the south side, too, a tablet says this church was rebuilt in 1551. It is quite evident, however, that the chancel and north transept are of the thirteenth century. The former contains, too, an Easter sepulchre, with two canopies, and Purbeck marble columns, disguised by an ugly support erected in the centre. Some main columns in the nave, whether brought from the abbey or not, are apparently of the twelfth century. The churchwardens' books show amongst the entries :—

"1555. Payde the man for watching the sepulcher . . 0s. 8d.
1557. Payde to the mynstrells and the hobby-horse upon
     May-day 3 0
1570. Paid for two paxe of cardes 0 4
. 1626. P^d for carving Mr. John Kenricke's arms over the
     south arch of the tower . . . . . 2 6."

In 1670, it was ordered that a boy should be carried to London to be touched for the king's evil at the charge of the parish!

Amongst the entries as to charges for getting the spoils of the abbey are found :—

"Payde for takyng downe of the quyer of the abbeye,
     and the carriage home of the same, 21 lodes . . £0 10s. 6d.
Payde for the rowfe in the abbeye 6 18 8
Payde for the door that stood in the cloyster . . 0 0 8."

Some maintain that the roof of the nave here came from the church of the Friary. Whether this were so or not, that edifice is unroofed; and, when the Association proceeded thither, and found parts of it occupied as a gaol, and steps in contemplation for further destroying it, lamentations were strongly expressed. It belongs to the thirteenth and fourteenth centuries, and displays a fine imbricated window. Mr. Godwin urged the duty devolving on the authorities of a rising town like

Reading of preserving those ancient buildings which remained within it, and, deploring the fact that there was no museum in the town, suggested that the Friary should be restored, and so appropriated, if a church were not needed.

Messrs. Poulton and Woodman showed, by a plan they had prepared, the existence of various foundations around indicating the extent of the establishment originally.

Returning to the Mansion House, under the presidency of the mayor, Mr. Pettigrew read a portion of his paper on the History and Antiquities of Reading (see pp. 177-200, *ante*), after which Mr. Black inspected and commented upon the charters of the corporation.

The earliest document possessed by the corporation is an *indenture* bearing the date of 1345, eighteenth year of Edward III. This indenture confirms the charter of 1253, granted by Henry III, allowing the guild-merchants of " Radynge" " to buy and sell wheresoever they will throughout all England without paying toll." This privilege, a not uncommon one in the early history of chartered boroughs, is still claimed by the inhabitants of Clent (so intimately associated with the poetry of Shenstone), who generally, however, prefer paying the allotted toll to proving their legal exemption from it. This charter is a very short one, and is in good preservation, having the great seal very nearly entire. Edward the third's charter is confirmed (except the exemption from paying toll, which is withheld), by a subsequent one granted in the second year of Richard II; the only reason apparently for having it renewed being the fine of five marks paid to " Yᵉ King's Majestie." These privileges were afterwards renewed, by charters granted in the 4th year of Henry IV, and the 5th of Henry VI, in the latter of which the master of the guild is first styled mayor. A charter granted in the reign of Henry VIII is the first of a series of beautifully-executed skins of parchment, showing the high state of perfection attained by the calligraphists of the middle ages. The first membrane of this charter has a very finely-executed pen and ink portrait of Henry VIII, recalling forcibly to mind the famous portraits of that monarch painted by Hans Holbein. The ornamentation at the head of the charter is very delicately worked, and is in excellent preservation. The charter granted in the 1st of Edward VI is also well worthy of inspection. Although in an unfinished state, it has a good portrait of the youthful king, enthroned. The capital letters in its early part are entirely omitted, owing perhaps to the immediate want of the charter for civic purposes by the corporation, or, more probably, from its poverty not enabling it to pay the requisite fines for its proper ornamentation; for we find from the diary of the corporation, that in the first year of Edward VI (the same year in which the charter is issued), having borrowed £6 from the churchwardens of Saint Lawrence, the mayor and burgesses begged to be allowed to repay the loan by instal-

ments of ten shillings, half-yearly, and to be forgiven the interest altogether. This charter is also interesting, as showing the oath required
from persons in authority:—"So help you God; *all Saints, and the
Holy Evangelists.*" The next charter possesses a very fine scroll-worked
heading, together with a neat though somewhat exaggerated portrait of
"Our Virgin Queen," with ruff of lawn, long stiff boddice, and fardingale to match. It is a well worn and soiled document, having entirely
lost its great seal from constant reference. It is the great working
charter of the borough, and that by which it holds the greater part of its
property, and possesses civic jurisdiction. It is a very long one, consisting of seven skins, and is a plain and evenly-executed piece of penman-
ship. The charter of James the First, however, is the best of the whole
collection, and is one of the finest and most highly-finished specimens of
law writing in existence. It consists of six membranes or skins, and is
merely an exemplification of that issued in the preceding reign. In the
illumination of this charter, the calligraphist seems to have exhausted
all the resources of his art. The entire borders of the whole six membranes are highly ornamented with numberless cuts of the flowers, fruits,
shrubs, and trees most common in England; iron beacons filled with
flaming fire; heraldic devices; prince of Wales' feathers; and numerous
emblematic figures, whose meaning was known only to the artist. On
the first membrane the greatest labour seems to have been bestowed.
The illuminations in gold and blue are of the richest kind; while within
the head-letter is a large portrait of James I, in royal costume, with the
handsome but melancholy face of the Stuart sovereigns. So carefully
was it written, that only two or three erasures can be detected, and these
only after the most searching scrutiny. The charter of Charles I has a
heading impressed by a plate, and is interesting as having a portrait of
that monarch in mezzo-tinto, an invention just given to the world by the
"Fiery Rupert," the soldier and sailor nephew of the Martyr King.
This charter is not illuminated, nor is that granted by his son Charles II,
though both have the mezzo-tinto portraits, as well as numerous pieces
of scroll-work, in addition to the impression left by the plate. By a
careful examination these may be distinguished apart, the black ink
used in the etching having faded to a dull brown, while that used by the
ornamentalist still retains its original freshness of colour. The great
seal of Charles I is quite entire, and its features in relief are as sharply
defined as though just impressed.

The charter granted by "The Lords Keepers of the Liberties of
England" during the Commonwealth is one of the most interesting
documents possessed by the corporation. Documents issued during this
period are very rare indeed, owing to the extraordinary means taken after
the Restoration to destroy all the records of the Protectorate. These
skins of parchment seem to have been cast aside in some damp place.

In many places the whole of the membranes have been eaten away by the mice.   The seal attached, although much mutilated, is very interesting, as showing the manner in which the House of Commons sat, while the reverse has a mounted figure of St. George of England.   The last of the charters is that granted by James II.   This is illuminated, but in its execution is much inferior to most of the others.   It is a very showy document, and is completely wanting in the delicate embellishments to be found in the previous ones.   Like most of the others it possesses a portrait of the grantor, having the first capital letter as an illuminated border to it.   These are the whole of the public charters in the possession of the corporation, but one or two others are not without local interest.   A singular document may be seen of an award between "the abbott and corporation of Radynge," respecting the tolls to be levied on some new shambles.   This instrument has three pendant seals, one of them being the *present* seal used by the corporation.   The existence of this seal completely sets aside the impression so prevalent, that queen Elizabeth figures in the corporate arms.   When it is remembered that this document bears date of 1526, the bare impossibility of the thing will at once be seen.   From a careful examination of the corporation seal, it has been thought to be not later than the fourteenth century, some going so far as to say, however, that it is the *original* seal granted to the guild merchants of Radynge by the first charter of Henry III—the figures upon it being probably that of St. Mary the Virgin, supported by the patron saint of the abbey and borough.   There is also a patent incorporating the weavers of Reading, giving directions as to the number and quality of the threads used in making " Radynge cloth," and allowing the guild to stamp it with their seal, as a security for the buyer that the article he is purchasing is genuine.   Fines can also be recovered in the king's courts from any persons counterfeiting these trade marks. Two patents, called committees of association, issued in the 16th Charles I, are also in the possession of the corporation.   By these patents, the mayor is commanded to associate other gentlemen with himself in his magisterial capacity, so as to form a bench of magistrates.   At first, these documents were thought to be connected with the famous Committee of Association for Counties, for the defence of the kingdom during the troublous times of the civil war.   Had this been the case, they would have been very valuable indeed, as not one has yet been discovered.   A small box of documents respecting the *rectories* of St. Mary and St. Giles is also in the possession of the corporation for safe custody. It is accompanied by a letter from lord chancellor Ellesmere, ordering the corporation to keep them safely, and allow the *rectors* to examine them when they list.

Amongst the by-laws of the corporation, one passed in 1443 is somewhat curious.   It is this :—The mayor and burgesses " grant and ordain that no barber in Reading open any shop nor shave any man after ten at night between Easter and Michaelmas, nor after nine from Michaelmas to Easter; but if [except] it be any stranger or any worthy man of the town, he shall pay three hundred tiles [*tegulas*] to the guildhall of Reading, as oftentimes as he is found faulty, to be received by the cofferers for the time being." An instance of the payment of the fine is given, and it is suggested that the motive for levying the penalty in tiles was a desire to introduce these into general use, and to discourage thatching, which increased the danger of fires.

The larger portion of the Association returned to Newbury to be present at the *soirée* given at the Mansion House by the Mayor and Local Committee, which was numerously attended. In the course of the evening Mr. B. Blundell delivered, in the unavoidable absence of Mr. Thos. Hughes, a paper " On the Two Battles of Newbury." [1]

The meeting was prolonged to a late hour.

SATURDAY, SEPTEMBER 17.

The Association quitted Newbury to visit Walford church, where they were received by the rev. W. Nicholson the rector, who acquainted the Association that the church had undergone entire rebuilding under his auspices, and that the tower was an exact restoration of the old one, with the exception of the arch into the church, which was taken from an example at Durham. Had sufficient professional supervision been obtained, Mr. Roberts thought we should not have had to regret the obliteration of one of the most interesting towers in this country—a round tower of the earliest Norman period, and few examples of which remain. The chancel is exactly the same size as to ground plan as the old one, but higher. Five of the windows are original. There are three sedilia; the fourth was found built in as rubble into the wall as pieces. The sedilia are of excellent early English workmanship, but the mouldings have been much interfered with in the refitting them in the new walls. There are a few fragments (early English) of painted glass in the chancel windows.

In one of the recesses on the south side is a lid of an early English stone coffin. It had been taken by the Perpendicular builders, broken across, and used to construct a flat arch over the principal doorway, and Perpendicular moulding was observable upon it. At the side lies the cap of a Norman column, converted in Perpendicular times into the bowl of a piscina; it was a bad piscina placed in the south-east corner of the chancel, but entirely in the south wall. Mr. Nicholson suggested the

---

[1] This paper has been published by Mr. Blundell, and may be obtained of Messrs. Simpkin, Marshall, & Co. We therefore abstain from giving any abstract of it in this place.

probability of the coffin being that of the early English restorer of the church. In the drain of the piscina some silver coins were found of Edward III; ancient broken glass; bits of charcoal; and some small bones, perhaps those of a bat.

Under the foundations of the Norman wall taken down (north side of the church), but in ground undisturbed by them, were found in the clay forms where coffins had decayed, showing burials to have taken place there before that wall was built. Close by were found deep in the ground foundations of an old building. It seems probable there was a church here before the Norman church. A bit of evidence in support of this supposition was produced by Mr. Nicholson, who exhibited a small silver coin dug up in the course of the works. It was entrusted to Mr. Pettigrew for examination, and has proved (for the characters were rather illegible) to be a coin of Edward the Confessor, the type of which is given in *Ruding*, Plate 25, No. 26. It appears to have been struck at Bristol.

On the large bell of this church is *Missi de cœlis habeo nomen Gabrielis*. The reredos is taken from St. Albans; the east window, north aisle, Sleaford; chancel triplet, Polehampton; east window, south aisle, Irthlingborough; porch, Heckington. In the jamb of the chancel doorway, west side, is an ancient cross of consecration scratched on the stone. This cross is inverted, because the jamb stone was carelessly set in the wrong place; it belonged to the east side.

The church was altogether very peculiar, and excited much interest in the architects. Mr. C. E. Davis thought the tower had originally been capped with a conical roof; but if so, it had been removed in the thirteenth century to allow of the erection of a spire, which is cleverly incorporated into the circular form. It springs from an octagon which is formed on the circle by a series at each angle of small columns which support a trefoil tableing, from which springs the spire, enriched at the base by some very good windows. Mr. Davis remarked that much had been written upon the difficulty of designing the springing of a spire from the tower, and many examples had been cited of the successful way in which this had been accomplished; few of them, however, could be compared in this respect with that of Walford, which he believed had not been noticed in any architectural work until the publication of *Towers and Spires of England*, in which there is a small illustration given. There are monuments in the church of the Fortescue, Johnes, Archer, Pigott, Mundy, Shirley, Houblon, and other families; and an ancient brass, with the figure of a priest in his vestments and with shaven crown, now somewhat defaced, but containing the following lines:—

Quisquis eris, qui transieris, sta, perlege, plora.
Sum quod eris, fueramque quod es, pro me precor ora.
Rex Christe Westlake anime miserere Johannis.

This is a form employed at a very early date, and Mr. Pettigrew[1] has given an example so early as the tenth century on Eadulph, bishop of Devon, who died in A.D. 932.

The Association, having completed their survey of the church, accepted the kind invitation of Charles Eyre, esq. of Welford-park, who attended the examination, to take refreshment at his mansion. Here they were most elegantly received by Mrs. Eyre, and hospitably entertained. It was interesting to be under the roof of one lineally descended from sir Isaac Newton, and the present possessor of some of his property.

East or Little Shefford church formed the subject of the next visitation. The melancholy appearance of this small church is very striking. Originally built at a low level, it now is, as it were, submerged; the churchyard has risen around it, and the river, which is near, is much above the level of the floor, and the result is, a slimy oozing through the walls, which vegetates, and is of that peculiar green, and altogether has, as Mr. Roberts observed, the character of the mortuary chapels in Ravenna and its neighbourhood. It is matter of regret that in the present day, in this wealthy and advancing country, such desolation should be allowed. The church is very small, and a trifling sum would save it and its contents from destruction.

The principal object in visiting this church was to examine a fine alabaster monument, connected with which Mr. Planché was desirous of correcting some long received errors. Here he read his paper on the subject, for which see pp. 145-157 *ante*.

Returning from East Shefford, the Association proceeded to view the encampment at Speen, the remains of Speen church and its monuments, and Donnington hospital, of which the inclemency of the day assigned to it prevented a survey.

The encampment of Speen (see pp. 70-71, *ante*) was viewed under the guidance of the rev. Mr. Adams and Mr. Vere Irving. In its neighbourhood there is a well of exquisitely pure water, and the spot is celebrated, also, for a very fine and distinct echo, with which the visitors were much amused. A short distance from this spot are to be seen the remains of Speen church, together with its monuments.

Speen church. Like to many of the churches visited by the Congress, this was undergoing extensive alterations, all being destroyed but two walls of the north aisle and a range of pillars and arches between that and the nave. Care had, however, been taken of some ancient tombs and broken pieces of monumental crosses and slabs, of which there are several, one being a cross fleury, on a coffin lid, of the early English period, and very early in the style. The pillars of the nave are of Purbeck marble, but coated very thickly with paint and whitewash. The

[1] Chronicles of the Tombs, p. 65.

old walling is probably of the same age as the Purbeck pillars, which appear, with the arches, to be of the end of the twelfth century.

There are two tombs here, one to John Battist Castillion, 1597, and the other to Theodosia Craven, which have been frequently described, and are interesting objects of examination. The monuments, and all else here, were seen to great disadvantage, from the confusion attendant upon the rebuilding in progress, but the Association could not fail to be gratified in viewing monuments exhibiting the sculpture of Bacon, Canova, and Chantrey. Bacon's work is dedicated to the memory of Thos. Wyld and his son, both of whom died in 1789. It presents a female figure kneeling, holding an urn, on which is inscribed T. W., aged 29, and underneath, "UNTO THEE O GOD." Below is a head in basso relievo, entwined by a wreath formed of fruit. An urn also surmounts this, with the initials T. W., aged 78. Canova's monument was brought from Italy by the late margravine of Anspach, and presents a female weeping over an urn. The expression of intense grief, the form of the limbs, and the arrangement of the drapery, alike bespeak the hand of the master. The figure is of the margravine, and the tomb is that of her husband. The inscription reads—

Sacred to the Memory of
The Best of Sovereigns and of Men,
THE MARGRAVE OF ANSPACH,
Who died at Benham Valence
On the 5th of January, 1806,
Aged Sixty-nine years
and Eleven Months.

Chantrey's work is a monument to Wm. Brinton, esq. It is of beautiful white marble, with a head of the deceased carved in basso relievo. Mr. Brinton was of Speen-hill, and resided for fifty years at the island of Antigua. He died Oct. 31, 1823, aged seventy-four years.

Quitting Speen, the Association proceeded to Donnington hospital, one of the most celebrated charitable foundations of the neighbourhood. It dates from the time of Richard II, A.D. 1394, and owes its establishment to sir Richard Abberbury. At the reformation the hospital was dissolved and its property vested in the crown. Elizabeth, by a grant, Nov. 25, 1602, at the instance of the earl of Nottingham, at that time owner of the estate, refounded it, and over the doorway of the entrance the royal arms are affixed. The grant of refoundation was exhibited to the Association, and read by Mr. Black; also the rules made by the earl of Nottingham, and sanctioned by the archbishop of Canterbury, for the government of the hospital in the 16th of James I (1619).

A table d'hôte was held at the *Pelican*, under the presidency of John Walter, esq., M.P., one of the Vice-Presidents of the Congress, who had only just returned from Switzerland, and most kindly put himself to some inconvenience to be present before the conclusion of the proceedings. A meeting was afterwards held at the Mansion House to close the business of the week,

JOHN WALTER, ESQ., M.P., V.P., in the Chair.

Votes of thanks to the marquis of Winchester, marquis of Downshire, the earl of Abingdon, the earl of Craven, and the lord bishop of Oxford, the patrons; the earl of Carnarvon, president; the vice-presidents and officers; the mayor and corporation; the clergy of the county; the local committee; the authors of papers and exhibitors of antiquities; those who had so hospitably received and entertained the Association during the Congress; and to the chairman, were unanimously passed and responded to, which terminated a Congress highly satisfactory to all who had taken part in its proceedings, and which may be regarded as one not the least interesting in its results among the many held by the Association.

The local committee, in preparing for the congress, very assiduously laboured to collect together, in the Mansion House, and at the Museum of the Literary Institute in Newbury, portraits and antiquities to illustrate the history of the county. The possessors of these in the neighbourhood were very liberal in placing their treasures before the Association on the occasion, and among others we may specify the following:—

By the earl Craven, four full length portraits, of prince Rupert, prince Maurice, an earl Craven (all by Vandyck), and Elizabeth, queen of Bohemia, by Honthorst.

By captain Leicester Vernon, M.P., portraits of Charles I, Henrietta Maria, his queen, by Vandyck, and another smaller portrait of Charles by the same great master. The representation of Charles is one of the finest specimens ever seen, and descended to its present owner from the late Robt. Vernon, esq. General sir John Lambert, the son-in-law of Cromwell, and general Monk, from the pencil of sir Peter Lely, also Henry, the second son of Cromwell, and the famous Villiers, duke of Buckingham, assassinated at Portsmouth, by Felton.

By Winchcombe H. H. Hartley, esq., the lineal descendant of Jack of Newbury, a fine view of Donnington castle, from Snelsmore common; the portrait (original) of the son of Winchcomb, Jack of Newbury, a fine production by Holbein, of lady Arabella Stuart, lord Bolingbroke, Robert Packer, once the lord of Donnington castle, the earl of Effingham, and Pope's celebrated beauty, Belinda, by sir Peter Lely; the original portrait of England's great bard, Geoffrey Chaucer, a relic of antiquity, in a state of fine preservation; and Hugh Peters.

By the royal borough of Windsor three portraits; one of Charles I, one of prince Rupert, and another of Charles, earl of Nottingham, lord high admiral of England A.D. 1588.

By the hon. P. Pleydell Bouverie, M.P., portraits of John Pym, member for Tavistock in 1641, and of Elizabeth, queen of Bohemia.

By R. Martin, esq., a view of Windsor castle, *temp.* Henry VIII.

By H. R. Eyre, esq., some large and good specimens of ancient tapestry, which formerly constituted the hangings in the bed room in which queen Anne slept during her stay at Shaw house. Portrait of sir Joseph Andrews of Shaw house; archbishop Laud's palace at Reading; the old Litton, Newbury; the old market house, Newbury.

Among the antiquities, a very elaborately worked shield, some swords and halberds, and two complete suits of polished steel armour, from Henry Hippisley, esq.; from the town of Hungerford, the hunting horn of John o'Gaunt; a silver flagon used at the marriage of Henry Ireton with Bridget, daughter of Oliver Cromwell, in the year 1646; a wassail bowl, once the property of the earl of Huntingdon, found in the old manor house at Stanton Harcourt. W. Gray, esq., exhibited a very beautifully carved cabinet, a splendid specimen of workmanship, the subject representing various passages in scripture. Many other contributions were sent by various individuals, and by the directors of the Newbury museum, an iron casket, dug up on the battlefield of Naseby June 14th, 1645. It is twelve inches long, six in breadth, and six and a quarter in height. A bureau, of the date of 1314, from Donnington priory, belonging to Mr. alderman Gray; cavaliers' helmets in steel and of leather; a sword, with a rifle pistol attached, which loaded in the middle; a sword-like cutlass, with lock of pistol on the back of the blade, and trigger within the guard, found in a field at Speen; a large Roman bottle of red ware, measuring twenty inches in circumference, and twelve and a half in height; a pair of holsters used in the civil wars; a rapier, with a heavy pommel. It measured thirty-six inches and half in length; the handle was of oak, much wormeaten. It was found in the Great Meadow, at Speen; a wassail bowl, ten inches and a quarter in height, twenty-six and a quarter in circumference, with a circular stem five inches and three-quarters round, and a foot with a circumference of twenty-four inches and a half. This was formerly the property of the earl of Huntingdon, and was found in the old manor house at Stanton Harcourt, Oxon; a silver seal of the borough of Hungerford, a crescent surmounted by a star; iron arrow head found in the peat; horn cores and portion of the skull of the *Bos Primigenius*, from Speen moor, measuring in extent forty inches, the breadth of the forehead between the horns being ten inches; a specimen also of the *Bos Longifrons* from the valley of Kennet, measuring sixteen inches; another of the *Cervus Elephas*, and a portion of a flint arrow head found in the skull of the *Bos Primigenius*. A very extraordinary specimen of this extinct species was exhibited to the Association by Mr. Padbury, of Speenhamland, who kindly furnished the treasurer with letters relating to it by the late rev. Dr. Buckland, dean of Westminster. It was dug out of the peat in Ham marsh, six feet below the surface, and gives in measurement, from the top of the head to the lower part of the upper jaw, two feet five inches and a half. Between the horns, three feet; and across the skull, twelve inches and a half.

In the museum many interesting specimens of antiquities, independently of what belongs to the literary and scientific institution, were exhibited. The rev. Dr. John Wilson, of Trinity College, Oxford, sent a collection obtained, in 1848, from some barrows in the neighbourhood of Ilsley downs. The tumuli here are numerous, and some were of large dimensions; the plough has, however, levelled many, and the insignia by which they are to be detected have disappeared. Churn Knob, how-ever, having been planted with fir trees about thirty years since, has been preserved, and forms an interesting landmark for many miles round. A smaller and lower one formed the subject of Dr. Wilson's research.[1] It seemed to present the novelty of a supplemental tumulus to the larger one, and was composed of the ordinary soil around it. In the middle was a conical heap of loose stones without any deposit, whereas on the north, south, and east sides, the west not being examined, there was a blackness of soil, produced by decayed animal matter, presumed by Dr. Wilson to have been produced by the decomposed bodies of small horses, as amongst it were discovered several bones and teeth of those animals, also teeth of swine, small bones of other animals, and lumps of iron, con-jectured to have belonged to horse furniture. Few portions of charcoal were found, and no evidences of the practice of cremation were apparent.

Another was examined, situated upon the down, in the bottom, between Churn and Chance farms. It is of a size which caused it to be described on the ordnance map; of a bell shape, one hundred and nine feet across the top to the middle of the fosse, and about ten or twelve feet high. At a spot near to the centre, and eight feet below the surface, the place of cremation was found abundantly strewed with wood ashes of oak, and then a deposit of calcined human bones. These were not inclosed within an urn, but in the moist clay soil, and if ever they had been enveloped by any covering, time had so completely destroyed it that no vestige could be discovered. A bronze instrument, now deposited in the Ashmolean museum, Oxford, was here found. Its purpose is unknown; it was of a somewhat elliptical shape, had two openings, and the rivets by which it had been affixed to a handle are quite perfect. It seems to have been a kind of chisel. Dr. Wilson has likened it to a plumber's knife, rather blunt at the end, and designed to cut at the sides. There is a similar specimen in the Blandford museum, Dorset. We are not at all inclined to adopt Dr. Wilson's suggestion, that it may have been a sacrificial instrument employed in flaying the victim. It would form no

[1] For particulars attending the excavation, see *Brit. Arch. Journ.*, v, p. 279.

bad instrument to remove the skin of an animal; but it is vain to conjecture where so little is known of the practices adopted by the people
to whom it belonged. No trinkets or coins were discovered.

Mr. Bunny exhibited two bronze spear heads of the Celtic period, one
of which measured ten inches and a half in length, and two and three-
quarters in breadth. The other, leaf-shaped, was nine inches long in
the blade, and had two holes at the base of the leaf above the ferrule.
They were obtained from a meadow at Speen.

Mr. Lousley exhibited a collection of Roman brass coins of various
emperors; some in good condition, and amounting altogether to between
six and seven hundred specimens. Many portions of pottery, from a
barrow at Hampstead Norris, opened in April 1845. He also sent a
curious crossbow, furnished with a moveable sight, like to the modern
rifle.

Spear heads in bronze and iron, of Roman and Saxon periods, were
exhibited, discovered in Newbury, at Pangbourne, at Wallingford, and
on Ardington downs.

The rev. Mr. Nicholson sent a bronze sacring bell from Welford church,
it measured two inches, and the loop half an inch. The width of metal
at the mouth was one-sixteenth of an inch, and it measured two inches
in width at this part.

Several spurs were exhibited, mostly of the time of the Commonwealth,
and discovered in various parts of the county. One from Mr. Valpy
measured five inches and three-quarters by five, and the rowel, which
was two inches in diameter, was furnished with fifteen points.

A variety of cannon and musket balls, obtained from Donnington
castle, Estbury, Wash common, the battlefields, etc.

Mr. Mount sent a fine bronze representing a Roman sacrificer crowned
with laurel. In his right hand is a *patera*, from which he is pouring out
as a sacrifice to the cornucopia, which he held in his left hand, but
which is now wanting. He is habited like a cup bearer, having a tunic
fastened with a girdle, and falling only to the knee. This was found at
Silchester, and has been figured in *Montfaucon, Antiq. Expl.*

Dr. Bunny sent two ornamented balls, one of which, one inch and
seven-eighths in diameter, was found at Ladlehill, near the Roman
encampment; the other in a field north of the Hampshire hills and to
the west of Buckhanger.[1] Dr. Bunny also exhibited several paalstabs,
but of well known shape and character.

Mr. R. H. Valpy exhibited the remains found in a barrow at Lough-
borough camp; they consisted of Roman coins and ashes.

The rev. Mr. Adams sent a good example of Roman pottery, a vase of
a black colour, indented at the sides, found in the New Forest. A great

---

[1] These have been since exhibited to the Association in London, are still
under examination, and will be treated of in a future *Journal.*

variety of coins in gold, silver, and copper, found in various parts of the county, discovered in sewers, were exhibited by their different possessors; among which may be particularly specified Mr. Godwin's extensive collection of silver pennies from the conquest downwards. Many Newbury tokens were also presented, principally of the dates of 1657 and 1658. In the churchwardens' books for the latter year is :— " Pd. Jas. Foster for 300 tokens for Mr. Woodbridge the rector 3s. 6d." The succeeding rector issued tokens of his own.

Several carvings in ivory, wood, and composition, were displayed. Two portions of an ivory triptych, exhibited by Dr. Palmer, were worthy of notice. Also some fine specimens in walnut wood from old Basing house, and a wooden cabinet, inlaid with ivory, left during the civil wars at the house of Mr. Richard Webb, of East Ilsley. It measured in length sixteen inches and a quarter, eleven in breadth, and seven in depth. Mr. Bodman sent a carved cradle, having the date of 1602. Mr. Wheble exhibited some good specimens of the Kimmeridge coal money, as it is usually called, from Dorset. One example measured four inches in diameter, and had a hole in the centre; another was three inches and a quarter.

A piece of lead, bearing the date of 1581, from an old cistern at Shaw house, the figures of which were chased out two-eighths of an inch deep, and three inches and a half in length.

Some of the most interesting of the objects above enumerated, have, since the Congress, been exhibited at the public meetings of the Association; the transmission of others is promised, and more particular accounts of them, together with illustrations, will appear in successive numbers of the *Journal*.

Pl. 20

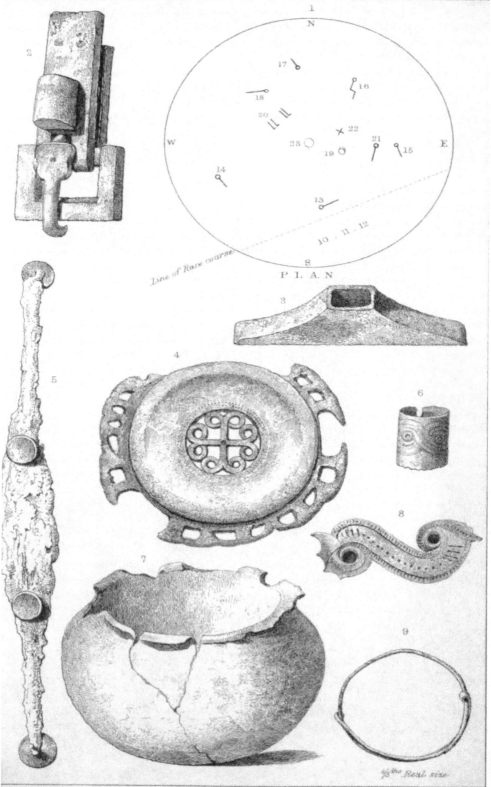

Line of Race course

PLAN

⅕the Real size

J.R.Jobbins

THE JOURNAL

OF THE

British Archaeological Association.

DECEMBER 1860.

ACCOUNT OF THE

EXAMINATION OF THE LARGEST BARROW IN THE ANGLO-SAXON CEMETERY ON BOW-COMBE DOWN, ISLE OF WIGHT.

BY B. P. WILKINS, M.D., F.G.S.; REV. E. KELL, M.A., F.S.A.; AND MR. JOHN LOCKE.

THE barrow, an account of the examination of which is now submitted to the British Archæological Association, was opened on the 25th May, 1859. It forms the largest of a considerable group (see plan on pl. 20, fig. 1) in its immediate vicinity, nine of which were opened by the Isle of Wight Museum Society of Newport, in 1854; the description of which will be found in the *Journal* for March 1855 (vol. xi, pp. 34-40). On the latter occasion this barrow was not examined, from its exhibiting the appearance of previous disruption; which, from the present exploration, appears to be accounted for by the removal of a portion of its western side,—when, or for what purpose, we are unable to determine.

In preparing the ground for the Isle of Wight races, in August 1858, its south-eastern side was levelled; and in the course of this process, the remains of three or more skeletons were turned up, with various relics, some of which were preserved,—a sword, spear-heads, knife, etc. From this discovery, Dr. Wilkins concluded that the whole mound deserved examination; and having obtained the permission of the lord of the soil, sir John Simeon, bart., together with the assent of his tenant, Mr. John Hillier, invited the cooperation of two other gentlemen in the proposed exploration.

The barrow measured sixty-two feet in diameter, and had a central elevation of five or six feet.

The situation of the cemetery, like many other Anglo-Saxon cemeteries, appears to have been selected from its commanding height and picturesque views. It would seem as if the generations of those days were animated by the same feelings which determine the locality of many of our modern burial-places,—the desire to deposit the remains of their loved ones in spots which should invite resort by their agreeable aspect, and thus soften the pang of separation by pensive and pleasing associations. It is obvious, from the beautiful, or even rich ornaments deposited in these graves, with what warm affection they regarded the departed, and the importance they attached to the rites of sepulture. To the north of this cemetery, the eye glances over the Solent to the varied scenery of the New Forest. Towards the east and south it takes in Sandown with its distant sea view and the range of downs which skirt the southern coast of the Isle of Wight. Close by, the picturesque castle of Carisbrooke, in that early period existing as the "caer by the brook," arrests one's observation; whilst towards the west an expanse as far as Christchurch opens to the sight. Like many other Anglo-Saxon cemeteries, this is situated near to the line of a Roman road which passes over the downs from Carisbrooke to Brightstone.

To simplify the account of the contents of this barrow, it should be premised that the relics found with the skeletons in the south-east portion, during the alteration of the race-course, will first be described; and we shall designate these interments as Nos. 10, 11, and 12, regarding our account as a continuation of the examination made in 1854. (See *Journal*, vol. xi, p. 34.) These interments will be described together, because no distinction was made in the appropriation of the relics by those who removed this portion of the barrow. The following articles have been deposited in the museum at Newport, as the produce of Nos. 10, 11, and 12: an iron sword, thirty-five inches in length, the blade near the handle being two inches and a quarter wide; portions of the wooden scabbard adhered to the sword; a great part of the bronze mounting of the open end of the scabbard is preserved, although much oxidized, and one of the bronze rivets by which the scabbard was affixed to the girdle;—two iron spear-heads, their sockets still retaining portions of their wooden handles; one measures eleven inches in length; the other measures ten inches and a quarter;[1]—the bronze girdle-buckle is worthy of observation (pl. 20, fig. 2); it is massive, well preserved, and resembles a buckle found in the Chessell cemetery;—an iron knife, five inches and a half in length;—a bronze clasp with small bronze perforated plates attached to it by its rivets;—fig. 3 represents a piece of bronze with a square perforation, which evidently formed the pommel of a sword-hilt. Some of the workmen say they met with an urn, but no remains of it have been rescued.

We found the substance of the barrow to consist of picked flints, which had been heaped to a height of three feet in the centre, immediately over the original Celtic interment. These flints sloped towards the circumference; and upon them a mass of chalk rubble and mould was accumulated. In the latter the Anglo-Saxons were interred at a distance of three yards or less, one from the other.

From the following description of the articles found with the bodies, it will be evident that they had been interred in accordance with the Anglo-Saxon customs.

No. 13 in the plan marks the position of the first skeleton discovered. It measured five feet two inches in length, and was of the male sex ; the skull, which is preserved, was to the south-west, the feet to the north-east. The following articles were also met with:—on the chest, a bronze circular ornament (fig. 4), its nature is doubtful; that it was not a brooch is evident from the absence of any provision for fastening it to the dress : an iron knife, four inches and three-quarters long, grasped by the left hand, lay on the corresponding hip-bone: at the centre of the waist were a bronze buckle (similar to two in the *Nenia Britannica*, pl. 1, fig. 4; pl. xx, fig. 3), its tongue, of bronze, being connected by an iron hinge: a bronze circular brooch or button, and a bead of lead, whitened by oxidation, which may be

---

[1] The form of these is well known; and the reader is referred to the thirteenth volume of the *Journal*, in which Mr. Syer Cuming has described the several kinds and peculiarities of these instruments, which are figured in pl. 31 of that volume, inserted at p. 203. Reference may also be made to Akerman's *Pagan Saxondom*, plate ix.

compared with an example given in the *Nenia Britannica* (pl. 15, fig. 12): on the right side of the waist were pieces of bronze with rivet-holes, apparently belonging to the sheath of the knife, and three bronze kite-formed rivets, which served to attach the knife-sheath to the girdle. In this grave pieces of pottery and glass were found; also, two iron rings.

No. 14 marks the position of a skeleton, with the head to the north-west and feet to the south-east. No remains were discovered with it beyond fragments of pottery scattered about, and an abundance of black wood-ashes.

No. 15 marks the position of a male skeleton, five feet nine inches in length; the head was to the north-west, the feet to the south-east; the hands had been placed under the thigh. On the right side of the skull we found a fine iron spear-head, of common form, with a portion of the wooden handle in its socket. On the left of the skull was an urn, broken into small fragments. The spear-head measures eighteen inches and a half in length: the urn was apparently a drinking vessel, and deposited without contents, or if it contained anything, it must have been of a perishable nature, for no traces of it could be found. It appears to have collapsed soon after the interment, and was still further broken in extracting: all idea of restoring it was regarded as hopeless; but Dr. Wilkins has succeeded in joining fragments so as to exhibit its original shape, two-thirds of the rim, one side of the whole of its bottom having been re-united; it measures seven inches in height, and eight inches in its greatest diameter. On the chest was deposited a circular shield, the umbo and handle alone being preserved. The umbo (which bears considerable resemblance to one engraved in this *Journal*, ii, 53, fig. 4) was broken by the workmen, but being subsequently mended, is now quite perfect. It is twenty-three inches in circumference, its material is iron, the rivets being of bronze, with silver-plated heads: the handle (fig. 5) is of iron, with silver-plaited rivets; it measures twenty-one inches and a half in length; that part of this relic grasped by the hand is surrounded by thick string or cord, the fibres of which appear to have been preserved by its infiltration with the oxide of the metal. At the waist were a bead of agate, a bronze buckle, and a bronze hasp. Under the left hip-bone we found an iron dagger, seven inches long, together with appurtenances of its sheath, viz., a piece of bronze plate, and three rivets, the latter being similar to those given in the *Nenia Britannica* (xv, fig. 9). In this grave were scattered fragments of pottery and iron.

No. 16 marks the position of a female skeleton, which we found reclining on the left side, with the knees drawn up; the skull, which is preserved, was towards the north, the feet being to the south; around the neck was a string of beads, chiefly of amber. Dr. Wilkins arranged them, with a green glass bead in the centre, having a figured terra-cotta bead on each side; these are followed by amber beads, and the latter by very small hollow glass beads, so fragile as scarcely to bear handling. On the chest were found, close below the necklace, a richly gilt brooch, with a projecting rim surrounding a full face, and which bears a strong resemblance to one given in this *Journal* (xi, 187, fig. 2), and also to an example in the *Nenia Britannica* (pl. ii, fig. 7). The left hand, which grasped an iron knife five inches and a quarter long, was placed under the left hip-bone, while the right hand lay extended over the pelvis. We found a silver ferrule (fig. 6) near this skeleton, ornamented by a beautifully engraved pattern. Scattered about the grass were fragments of pottery, and small pieces of oxidised iron.

No. 17 marks the position of a male skeleton, with its left hand lying over the pelvis; the skull, which is preserved, was to the south-east, the feet to the north-west. A bronze clasp, fastened by its rivets to a piece of wood, was found at the left side of the skull.

No. 18 marks the position of a male skeleton, six feet in length, the skull lying to the south-west, the feet to the north-east. On the chest were the remains of a shield, *i.e.* its umbo and handle; both were much oxidised and broken into fragments; they have subsequently been carefully put together by Dr. Wilkins, and the result is tolerably complete specimens. The workmanship and material of this shield are much inferior to that of No. 15; the umbo is also more conical, although of the same circumference. We found an iron knife, eight inches and a half long, under the left blade-bone. Scattered in the grave were fragments of pottery, with teeth of the ox and dog.

No. 19 marks the position of an Anglo-Saxon urn, measuring four inches high and six inches in its greatest diameter (fig. 7).   On the evening of May 28th, after we had ceased our labour, the pupils of Mr. Evans, attracted to the spot by the fame of the discoveries, commenced to indulge their curiosity by removing the material of the barrow near the apex, and came upon what they fancied was a "cannon-ball."   This attracted the attention of their preceptor (who fortunately was present).   He ordered the young gentlemen aside, and rescued this urn, although their ardour had already broken the vessel.   Mr. Evans very properly collected the fragments, and subsequently handed them over to Dr. Wilkins, who on joining them found the urn perfect.

No. 20 marks the position of interments which had been disturbed when that portion of the barrow before alluded to was removed.   We found, close beneath the turf, the legs of two skeletons : these legs evidently had not been moved since their original burial.   The whole of these two skele-tons, as low as the middle of the thigh-bones, had been removed, together with any ornaments which might have been deposited with them.   Near these remains were blocks of sandstone, which must have been obtained from a con-siderable distance; and on further search at the western side of the barrow, we met with numerous bones of disturbed skeletons, together with an iron arrow-head, *half an iron horse-shoe*,[1] and fragments of iron too much oxidized to per-mit of explanation ; also fragments of a Celtic urn, a bronze clasp, a large iron ring, a bead, etc.

No. 21 marks the position of a male skeleton lying due north and south (the head being to the north), and, although the last skeleton met with, was the most interesting, from the variety and richness of its ornaments, etc.   The skull is preserved.   Under the right chest was a bronze gilt brooch (fig. 8); at the right side of the waist were three bronze gilt brooches, two of which were alike, and of the same general character with that given in this *Journal*, xi, 187, fig. 4 ; the other had the shape of a hare, and was composed of bronze, inlaid with red and blue enamel.   It much resembles that taken from No. 2 interment in 1854, which is figured in this *Journal* for 1855, pl. 4, fig. 1.   All these brooches had iron pins, and had been bound round with string, frag-ments of which still adhere to the oxidized pins.   This fact

[1] For remarks on Teutonic horse-shoes, see *Journal*, vi, 411 ; xiv, 274.

would prove that these fibulæ had been laid in the grave with the body, and were not, as is usually supposed, fixed in the dress to keep it together as during life. Near these fibulæ was a small bronze buckle, probably belonging to the girdle; its iron tongue fell to pieces from oxidation. Near the left knee were six large beads—three of amber, two of terra cotta, and one of glass; a bronze sliding ring (fig. 9) (resembling an armilla), with a bronze pendant; the latter, apparently, had hung from the ring. An iron knife, four inches and a half long, was under the left hip-bone. Birds' bones, white snail-shells, and fragments of pottery, were scattered about this interment.

It is obvious, from these discoveries, that beads were worn for ornamental purposes, by both sexes, among the Anglo-Saxons. It may also be observed, in the plan of this barrow, that the bodies were deposited in various directions. In no instance were the head and feet due east and west; hence it may be inferred that this race had not been converted to Christianity.

No. 22 marks the position of an incineration which we found near the apex, over the east of the centre of the tumulus, about fourteen inches under the turf. This body had been burnt elsewhere, the fragments of the bones having been collected and deposited at this spot, for we did not find a particle of ashes, and the bones were bleached quite white. Six inches above this incineration we found a bronze dagger-blade deposited; it is three inches long, and at its base one inch and two-thirds wide, and is of similar character to that discovered at Ashey Down, engraved in this *Journal*, x, 164, fig. 2. This interment was apparently prior to those of the skeletons, but secondary to that of No. 23, although evidently referable to the Celtic period.

No. 23 marks the position of the primary interment exactly in the centre of the barrow. It consisted of the burnt remains of a body and a very great quantity of wood-ashes, which had been fired on the spot. After removing the mass of flints which had been heaped over this incineration, we found a hole, which had been dug in the chalk stratum, measuring ten inches in depth and sixteen inches in diameter. This hole was filled with ashes, and surrounded by the same to a distance of two or three feet. On searching for fragments of the body, we found the bones had been so thoroughly burnt that but few could be collected. No other relics could be discovered excepting a burnt bead.

An excavation of this kind made into the solid chalk, indicates the interment to be of a very remote period, and no doubt it was of Celtic origin, such being the funereal usage of that race.

The relics of the neighbouring ancient British villages of Gallibury, Rowborough, Newbarn, etc., and the British barrows found in various parts of the Isle of Wight, as on Ashey, Wroxhall, and Shalcombe Downs, accounts of which have been given in the pages of this *Journal*, are in unison with the Celtic origin of this barrow. When the barrow was so formed, the Anglo-Saxons employed its ample dimensions for their funereal purposes, while round it clustered other of their graves, forming from their numbers a complete cemetery. Many of the ornaments, weapons, etc., discovered, have a striking similarity to those exhumed at Chessell, while in its elevated position and beauty of site we perceive an additional resemblance.

The Bowcombe Down cemetery may be numbered as the eighty-second Anglo-Saxon cemetery in England, according to Mr. Thomas Wright's enumeration, in the Introduction of C. Roach Smith's *Inventorium Sepulchrale,* p. 54. Other graves will probably be found in the same spot, although the mounds originally raised over them have disappeared during the ages which have elapsed since their formation.

A careful examination of the Anglo-Saxon cemeteries of the Isle of Wight confirms the opinion, now generally adopted, that the branch of the Teutonic race which settled in this island was the same as that which first occupied Kent, viz., the Jutes ; the contents of the graves in the two localities being precisely similar, and thus identifying the common origin of the occupants of both. It is generally believed that the Jutes were the first who settled in England, establishing themselves in Kent about the middle of the fifth century. The reasons which induced the Jutes to fix upon the Isle of Wight for a first settlement, it is difficult to determine, unless we attribute it to be some attraction of superior wealth or fertility, which, like Kent, this island exhibited. From what source the wealth which the inhabitants obviously possessed, who were interred in these graves, arose, whether from the lingering affluence produced by the ancient British tin trade, as may be thought by those who consider the Isle of Wight the mart of that lucrative commerce, or from the results of a continued Roman residence (which is now fully established), we do not offer any decided opinion, but there can be no doubt, that at the period of the settlement of the Jutes in this island, it was in a state of great prosperity. Nor would the conquest of the Isle of Wight from the Jutes by the Saxons under Cerdic, who established the kingdom of Wessex in 519, make any material difference in the manners and customs of the inhabitants, who were of a kindred race, and would soon be amalgamated into one people.

Roman remains have been discovered at various times within a few yards of this cemetery, some of which are preserved in the museum at Newport, viz., a Roman tile, fragments of pottery, a coin (large brass) of Marcus Aurelius, etc.

In concluding, we desire to record our thanks to Mrs. Daly, the lady of lieutenant-colonel H. Daly, C.B., for her kindness in furnishing us with excellent drawings of the objects, which have enabled us to illustrate this paper.

Lastly, we congratulate the inhabitants of the Isle of Wight in having resident so enlightened and excellent a landed proprietor as sir John Simeon, bart., who aids *in every way* the labours of local antiquarian explorers on his estates, laudably reserving his rights by insisting on the LOCAL exhibition and depository of all historical and antiquarian discoveries.

ON OLD ENGLISH ARROW-HEADS.

BY HENRY SYER CUMING, ESQ., HON. SEC.

SIR JOHN FORTESCUE declared, that "the might of this realme of Englande standyth ypon her archers." This was no idle boast; for history records how the trusty bows of English yew, bent by the stalwart arms of England's yeomen, triumphed over the vaunted chivalry of France upon the fields of Crecy, Poitiers, and Agincourt. The victory at Flodden was won by the might of England's archers, whose unerring aim became proverbial, it being said that each one bore beneath his belt twenty-four Scots, in allusion to the number of arrows with which each was provided. With these and numerous other like facts familiar to us, we might well expect to find upon the old battle-ground and amid the ruined castle, many of those countless arrows that darkened heaven in their flight, and fell in death-showers upon the assailed : but the iron piles, in common with the wooden shafts, seem all to have well-nigh perished, so that an old English arrow-head is now among the rarest items of old English warcraft that can be produced. I am, however, able to bring before the Association some few examples of these scarce objects, these little spicules upon which the might of England once rested. Before proceeding to describe them, it may not be out of place to observe, that the practice of archery is of remote antiquity in the Britannic islands, a fact proven by the abundance of flint arrow-blades exhumed with undoubted remains of the stone period. We gather from the poems of Ossian, and other sources, that the British bows were formed of the wood of the *Pren Yw*, or yew-tree; and the ancient adage, "*Nid hyder ond Bwa*"—"there is no reliance but on the bow", points to the high estimation in which the weapon was held by our Celtic forefathers, who celebrated in their triads Gwrneth, as a sharpshooter whose shafts were of reed. They termed the arrow *saeth*, and seem to have sometimes envenomed its blade; for it is related of the Irish Druid Trosdan, that he "found an antidote against the poyson'd arrows of certain British invaders."[1] They also made use of the quiver, which they called *cawell saethau, i.e.*, arrow-basket. There is, therefore, no lack of evidence that archery was as well known to the Celtæ as to the earlier tribes of Britain; and yet, strange to say, few traces of Celtic archery have been noticed in this country, though in Ireland both brazen piles and the moulds in which they were cast have been discovered.[2]

In the death-song of Regnar Lodbroc, king of Denmark, it is said of one of the warriors, "*Amidst the gust of swords ne'er did the string of his unerring bow dismiss his bolts in vain,*"—"*the flexile yew sent forth the barbed reed,*"—"*clouds of arrows pierced the close-ring'd harness.*" Tradition speaks of the Danes having shot St. Edmund of East Anglia to death with arrows.[3] "*To shoot well with the bow,*" was looked upon as a necessary accomplishment by the men of Lochlyn. Were it needful, other lays and records might be cited in proof that archery was well known to the Danes, and that they employed it in battle. Such being the case, it becomes a matter of surprise that their *consanguinei*, the Angles, Jutes, and Saxons, seem to have paid little attention to the science, using the *boga* and *ariwe* principally, if not solely, in hunting.[4] In Douglas's *Nenia Britannica* (pl. xix) are delineated five examples of what are there considered as arrow-piles, but which are thought by some to be the heads of small javelins. Four of them were found in barrows on Chatham Lines; two having somewhat fusiformed blades, the others being long spiculi. The fifth example is of a short, stout, and more spear-formed contour; and was discovered at St. Margaret's cliff, between Dover and Deal. All these heads differ entirely in character from the arrows depicted in Anglo-Saxon MSS., which have long sharp barbs similar to the one held by the archer on the ivory reliquary of the twelfth century, engraved in our *Journal* (x, 185); and which form continued a favourite with painter and sculptor throughout the middle ages, even down to the eighteenth century : so that those sources which generally

---

[1] Toland's *History of the Druids*, p. 90.

[2] A bronze arrow-head was discovered, some years since, in a cist-vaen at Whitfield, about seven miles south-west of Hereford.

[3] For a notice of what was said to be one of these arrows, see *Journal*, vol. v, p. 3.

[4] It must be admitted that Asser, in his Life of Alfred the Great, says, the "king, sitting at the hearth, made ready his bow and arrows and *other warlike instruments.*"

shed light on the civil and military fashions of our ancestors, do not, in this special point, furnish any reliable information. We do occasionally, though rarely, meet with other than barbed arrows on mediæval productions, as, for example, on the curious font of the close of the twelfth century, in Darenth church, Kent;[1] and in the mural painting of the latter part of the fourteenth century, representing the martyrdom of St. Christopher, in Shorwell church, Isle of Wight;[2] in both of which arrows with triangular blades are introduced. The arrow held by the Cupid on the ivory casket of the fourteenth century, engraved in our *Journal* (v, 272), has a lozenge-formed blade resembling the spears of the period, one of which may be seen in the hand of an earl of Gloucester in the painted window of Tewkesbury, also engraved in our *Journal* (v, 373).

If we could obtain arrow-heads from ancient battlefields, they would aid greatly in determining the dates of specimens met with in other localities; but I have failed in tracing a single well-authenticated arrow from such a site. The arrows shewn in the library of Trinity college, Cambridge, as relics of the fight of Bosworth, are nothing more nor less than common Indian reed-arrows, having as just a claim to antiquity as the arrow formerly in the Leverian museum, which was said to have been found, about the year 1776, near the ruins of Harwood castle, W. R. of York. The latter was twenty-nine inches long; the barbed pile, shaft, and feathers, being all wrought out of one piece of iron, for the purpose, according to the late sir Samuel Meyrick, of being placed in the hand of a statue of Diana. And, no doubt, equally authentic were the "two ancient broad arrows of Robin Hood," which once figured among the "rarities" at Don Saltero's Coffee House in Chelsea. Though these have vanished, we are not left without a reputed memorial of the bold outlaw; for one of his arrows still stands erect on the end of the gable roof of the Fletcher's chancel of St. Lawrence's church, Ludlow, Shropshire; and which, if tradition says true, Robin shot into its present position whilst standing in the Old Field, some few miles distant.

One of the earliest English arrow-heads, of which the date is well defined, is figured in our *Journal* (xi, 142) from the original, exhumed in 1848, with remains palpably of the

---

[1] See *Gent. Mag.*, Sept. 1837, p. 217.   [2] See *Journal*, iii, p. 85.

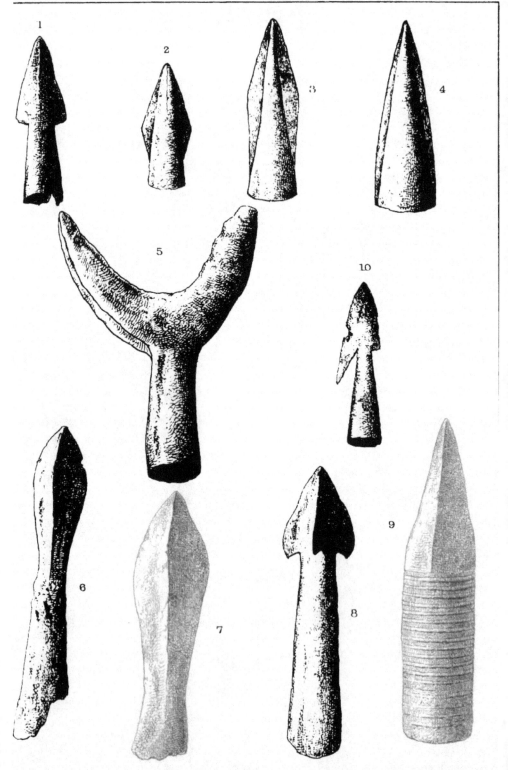

thirteenth century, in Angel-court, Throgmorton-street, and which is here reproduced for the sake of comparison.

Mr. Wills exhibits an arrow-head (see plate 21, fig. 1) which we are perhaps justified in referring to a somewhat prior epoch : indeed, it so much resembles the one held by the Centaur on the Darenth font, that we might well believe it to be as early as the twelfth century. The blade is of an oblong-triangular form, seven-eighths long and four-eighths across the cusps; thick in the centre, and gradually thinning off to the edges. The socket is little longer than the blade; and there is no indication of a collar round the mouth, which was at times added for the purpose of giving timely warning to the archer when to let fly, so that he did not overdraw the arrow. It was found in 1840, near the hospital of St. Cross, Hants. This specimen, with those from Throgmorton-street and Clifford's Tower (the latter in the Meyrick collection), are examples of what were termed *sheaf-* or *war-arrows*, differing from *flight-* or *roving-arrows* in having flat, or nearly flat, sided blades; the piles of the latter being more pyramidal or conical in form.[1] Both kinds were, however, at times employed in warfare, as is evident from Hall's account of the battle of Towton, fought in 1461, where he says : " The lord Fawconbridge, which led the forward of kyng Edwarde's battail, being a man of great polyce and of muche experience in marciall feates, caused every archer under his standard to shot one *flight* (which before he caused them to provyde), and then made them to stand still. The northern men felying the shoot, but by reason of the snow not wel vewyng the distance betwene them and their enemies, like hardy men shot their *schefe arrowes* as fast as they might; but al their shot was lost, and their labor vayn, for thei came not nere the southern men by xl tailor's yerdes."

The flight- or roving-arrow is mentioned, among other kinds, by Drayton in his *Poly-Olbion* (song 26th), where, speaking of Robin Hood and his merry men, he says :

[1] The old arrows shewn at Cothele, in Cornwall, have pyramidal piles much like the one held by the bowman on the seal of West Looe, of the time of James I, engraved in Gilbert's *History of Cornwall*, vol. iv, p. 21.

"All made of Spanish yew, their bows were wondrous strong,
They not an arrow drew, but was a clothyard long :
Of archery they had the very perfect craft,
With broad arrow, or but, or prick, or roving shaft." [1]

I now exhibit five arrow-piles found together in the
Thames, close to old London bridge; and which present some
curious varieties in form from those we have previously
seen.   The smallest (see pl. 21, fig. 2) is one inch and five-
sixteenths in length.   It has a somewhat lozenge-shaped
cusp, the socket extending up the blade.   Another (fig. 3)
is little short of one inch and seven-eighths in length.   It
is almost leaf-shaped; the socket, like the last, extending up
the centre of the blade.   The remaining three specimens
measure respectively one inch and nine-sixteenths, one inch
and eleven-sixteenths, and one inch and seven-eighths in
length.   They are hollow cones, with a sharp ridge extending from point to base on each side; and had there
been three instead of two ridges, they would have been
almost identical in form with the brazen piles exhumed
from the plains of Marathon.   As these five specimens were
found together, it is perhaps no undue strain on probability
to regard them as having been all employed on the same
occasion; and the annals of London bridge record two
events in the fifteenth century, in which they may have
been used.   The first was in July 1430, when Jack Cade, at
the head of the Kentish rebels, endeavoured to enter the
city.   The second in May 1471, when the Bastard of Faul-
conbridge, making a last effort in favour of king Henry VI,
assaulted London bridge "with a riotous company of ship-
men and others of Essex and Kent."   In these encounters,
arrows no doubt formed a fearful ingredient; and the piles
now under consideration were, in all probability, some of
the instruments of death employed on one of these occasions.
    Mr. Wills favours us with another pile of a roving- or
flight-arrow, of the same form as three of the above, but of
larger size, perfect condition, and evidently of later date
(fig. 4).   It measures about two inches in length; and from
the dimensions of the base, the stele or shaft must have
been little less than half an inch in diameter.   It was recovered from the Thames, off Paul's wharf, about the middle of

[1] In the library of Cannon Hall, W. R. of York, is preserved the "bow of
Little John," one of Robin Hood's companions.

September, 1857; and in close proximity with it were two crampets of sword-scabbards, and other remains, referrible to the early part of the sixteenth century; to which period this pile also probably belongs. The majority of the old English arrow-piles we meet with, are of the fashion of this specimen, and is, perhaps, the best adapted for rapid flight. If it would not inflict so terrible a stab as the barbed blade, it would surely penetrate deeper into the body, and be equally fatal in its effects. It is a form which has maintained its ground among civilized races, from the æra of Hellenic greatness down to the extinction of military archery in the seventeenth century; and even now, with some slight modifications, survives in the piles of the butt-shafts, or practice-arrows of our toxophilite societies.

Mr. Durden brings to our notice several curious arrow-heads discovered in a field at Langton, about one mile south-east of Blandford, Dorset; but unaccompanied by any facts elucidating their age. Two of them are what are called *broad-arrows;* the most perfect closely resembling the *vire* or *verou* in the Meyrick collection, the other having longer barbs. Of more singular contour are the two bifurcate blades, reminding us of the lunate arrows of the Persians. One of these (fig. 5) may be compared with a specimen engraved in Skelton's *Meyrick* (xciv, 10), but has a longer and more cylindrical socket. Bolts of this description were employed in field-sports, and are represented with the cross-bow in a painting of a stag-hunt given by the elector of Saxony to Charles V.[1] Mr. Durden's other Langton specimens seem to be bolts discharged from the *latch,* or cross-bow; a piece of artillery which continued to be employed in the chase until the days of James I, soon after which it was superseded by the gun.

Since writing the above, Mr. Ambrose Boyson has placed in my hands for exhibition some highly curious arrow-heads of iron, he obtained during a sojourn in Germany in 1857, and which offer important materials for comparison with examples discovered in our own country. The first (fig. 6) appears, from its eroded condition, to be the earliest, and may possibly be the pile of a flight- or roving-arrow. It is nearly three inches and a quarter in length; the socket extending to the base of the quadrifacial blade, which is

[1] See *Journal of the Archæological Institute,* v, 303.

somewhat obtusely pointed. It was exhumed, together with a war-axe, wooden coffin, etc., from a depth of about ten feet, in the old castle of Trifelds,—a spot renowned as the prison of Richard Cœur de Lion. The next two specimens (figs. 7, 8) were found with the caltrap already engraved in this *Journal* (xiv, pl. 15, fig. 4), in the ruins of the ancient castle of Oberstein. One of these is much like the pile from Trifelds, but more heavy and robust in fabric; and I have little hesitation in affirming it to be the head of a *viraton* or *vireton,* a kind of bolt discharged from the arbalest or cross-bow; and so called from its revolving in its flight, the feathers being placed diagonally, for the purpose of giving it a rotary motion. It is two inches and three-quarters in length, but has suffered somewhat at the base of the socket. The second of the Oberstein specimens (fig. 8) is of an extraordinary character, and may be compared with an arrow-head from the Thames, given in this *Journal* (iv, pl. 17, fig. 5), and with one in Mr. Gunston's possession, found at Bankside in 1850. The trifacial, pyramidal blade is slightly barbed at the cusps, and surmounts a long, stout socket; the entire length of the object being three inches. The form, size, and weight of this pile would lead to the belief that it was discharged from the cross-bow.

The last of Mr. Boyson's specimens (fig. 9) is a quadrangular, pyramidal spike, three inches and three-eighths long; the cylindrical socket, five-eighths in diameter, one inch and three-eighths deep, and annulated on the outside. Though this object looks somewhat like the butt of a pike, still it is more probably the pile of a large bolt thrown from one of those destructive machines known in the middle ages as bricolles, catapults, espringals, mate-griffons, robinets, scorpions, etc., which shot forth missiles called carreaux, or quarrels, muchettæ, and viretons. Amid all these names, it is no easy matter to decide to which to refer the specimen before us : it is, however, most probably the head of a carreaux-shot from a bricolle. It was discovered with the first described arrow-pile at Trifelds, and is an object of much rarity.

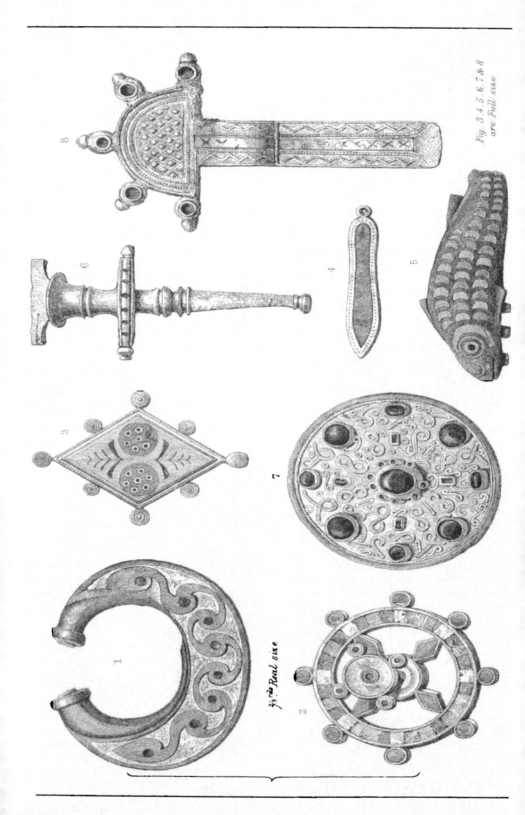

Fig. 3. 4. 5. 6. 7. & 8
are Full size.

⅔ᵈˢ Real size.

ANCIENT ORNAMENTS.

BY H. SYER CUMING, ESQ., HON. SEC.

DURING the past and present session, various examples of ancient ornaments have been brought before the notice of the Association; and it has been thought best to reserve their exhibition until such time as the whole could be offered at one view for comparison and description. The specimens consist of Celtic, Roman, and Teutonic ornaments, and may serve as well-marked types of style and manufacture adopted by these several races.

The earliest object (see pl. 22, fig. 1) is the property of Mr. T. Wills, and was exhumed, some time since, at Bapchild, about two miles from Sittingbourne, Kent. It is a portion of horse-gear, cognate in character and date with examples discovered at Westhall, Suffolk; Polden hill, Somersetshire; Stanwick, Yorkshire; and Middleby, Annandale, Scotland; and may safely be assigned to the close of the Bronze or Celtic period, when native taste began to feel the influence of transmontine art. It is of bronze, covered with a beautiful apple-green patina; the sunk portions on either side exhibiting traces of red enamel, whilst the broader parts of the meander still retain little discs of the same material, of a deep sapphire-blue colour. A fine line is engraved throughout the length of the meander; and the crescent has a sort of milling along its edge. The flat suspending-bar which crossed from boss to boss, is broken away; but in other respects the object is in a fair state of preservation. It is almost identical with seven out of the eight crescents from Westhall, now in the British Museum; and we probably have in these curious objects, examples of the enameled ornaments of horse-trappings described by Flavius Philostratus in his *Icones*, as being made by the barbarians dwelling on the ocean, who, he says, pour colours upon heated brass, which become hard and durable. This is the first distinct notice of enameling that has yet been pointed out; and as Philostratus flourished about the middle of the third century of the Christian æra, his words would seem to imply that it was after this period that the Greeks and Romans began to practise the art; and certain it is that all the Roman enameled fibulæ exhumed in this country and on the continent, appear to belong to a late epoch. But against the inference drawn from the passage in the *Icones,* we have the fact of the discovery in the Bartlow hills, at Ashdon in Essex,[1] of a splendid vessel covered with designs in blue, red, and green enamel; which there is reason to believe cannot be referred to a later period than the first half of the second century, nor to any other people than the Romans; to whom must also be assigned the curious enameled bronze cup found at Harwood, near Cambo, Northumberland, preserved in the British Museum. But whether the Romans were, or were not, acquainted with the process of enameling in the days of Philostratus, we have no reason to question the high antiquity of the art in Britain, nor the national origin of the bridle-bits and other horse-trappings of the Celtæ here exhumed; and of which the brazen crescent from Bapchild is a beautiful example.

The enameled fibulæ of the Romans are well illustrated by three examples now presented. The two largest are in the collection of Mr. W. H. Forman. The first (fig. 2) is similar to an example in the British Museum; and also resembles, in some degree, the one of bronze discovered at Ixworth in Suffolk, engraved in the *Journal* (viii, 364), and here reproduced. The frame of Mr. Forman's specimen is of yellow bronze or brass, decorated with enamel of three colours : that in the eight encircling discs is red ; red and white alternately in the ring ; the cross, formed of four lozenges, is blue, the centre being white and blue ; and the projecting disc, with its four accompanying satellites, appear to have been filled with red enamel. The acus moved between two staples, and its point was received in a broad catch with a perforation through its side. This extraordinary example measures no less than two inches and three-quarters diameter, and is in a fair state of preservation.[2]

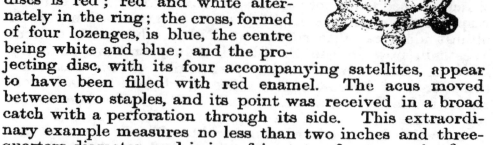

[1] See *Archæologia*, vols. xxvi, xxviii, and xxix.
[2] Besides the Ixworth fibula already referred to, two other circular enamelled fibulæ with convex centres, are given in the *Journal* (i, 147 ; v, 334)

Mr. Forman's second fibula (fig. 3) is of a lozenge form, and may therefore be classed with one discovered in the Lac d'Antre (Jura), described in the *Journal* (1858, p. 280). It is of yellow bronze, rather above one inch and seven-eighths high. The eight discs along its edges are stamped with circlets. The central field is filled with white, and the two large discs with blue enamel; the dots and dendritic figures being plain metal. The hinge of the acus resembles that of the first mentioned fibula.

The third fibula (fig. 4), in the possession of Mr. Pettigrew, is in the form of a sandal, and may be cited as one of the many fanciful devices in vogue among the Roman colonists of Gaul and Britain. The centre is of rich blue enamel; the verge, etc., apparently composed of impure silver; the acus having been of bronze. From the heel of the *solea* projects a little annular loop, in like way to the excrescence at the end of the sandal-shaped fibula discovered in July 1846, in Botolph-lane, now deposited in the British Museum. The two beautiful pelta-formed fibulæ found in Northamptonshire, and engraved in the *Journal* (i, 327; iii, 251), have also rings at their bases, to which fine chains were probably attached to secure the ornaments to the dress of the wearer. The locality of Mr. Pettigrew's specimen is unknown; but from its peculiarly neat contour and finish, has been conjectured to be of continental fabric.[1]

As a further illustration of Roman enamel work, we have from Mr. Forman an exquisite bronze relic in form of a fish somewhat resembling the mullet; the eye and treble row of scales being of red and turquois-blue enamel. (Fig. 5.) This, like the Celtic and other early enamels, is produced by the process termed by the French *champ-levé; i.e.,* the subject is tooled out of the metal, the enamel placed in the cavities in a powdered state, and then fused by the action of fire. What the original purpose of this beautiful object was, is not at once apparent. We know that the Romans had brooches in form of animals, as is shewn in the hare-shaped specimen from the Isle of Wight, engraved in the *Journal* (1855, p. 36); and among the "*fibulæ Iconicæ*" in Beger's *Thesaur. Brandenburg.* (tom. i, p. 434) occurs one like a fish; and a dolphin-shaped fibula of silver is in the British Museum. I am, however, inclined to regard this specimen

---

[1] Enamelled fibulæ of other forms will be seen in *Journal*, ii, 42, and v, 231.

as the lid of a sort of locket, the three projections below the jowl being remains of the hinge. A *capsella* of this form would serve at once as an amulet and *theca* for a relic, which might be worn suspended from a *catella* round the neck. The locality of this bijou is involved in uncertainty. It is said to have been brought from Egypt; but there is no evidence to support the statement.

I also regret my inability to state the exact locality of the cruciformed fibula (fig. 6); but it is believed to have been exhumed in the north of Kent. It is of bronze, or rather brass, above two inches and five-eighths in length, covered with a thin plating of silver, the horizontal beam being decorated with seven or eight small pieces of *nigellum*. Though the art of nielloing did not arrive at its greatest perfection until the thirteenth or fourteenth century, it was still practised with considerable success by the Romans, as is proved in the adornments of the *lorica* of the bronze statuette found about 1799, near Barking Hall, Suffolk; presented to the British Museum by the earl of Ashburnham. The mode pursued in the production of nigellum decorations, was near akin to one species of enameling. The device was sculptured in the metal; then filled in with small grains of an alloy composed of silver and lead, to which copper was occasionally added; the whole being blackened by the aid of sulphur, which, after fusion, was polished. Few examples of Roman nielli have yet been pointed out; but they are probably of more frequent occurrence than generally supposed.

From these Roman fibulæ, we pass to some fine Teutonic brooches in the possession of Mr. Forman. We have had examples of enamel and nigellum; and the specimen now engraved (fig. 7) introduces us to another species of decoration, namely that of setting. This fibula is one inch seven-eighths diameter; the verge and back being of silver inlaid with a disc of pure gold profusely decorated with small objects resembling a figure of eight, wrought of funicular threads of gold. To this disc are also attached nine cells, or bezels, arranged as a cross, with a bezel between each limb. These four cells, the central one, and those terminating the limbs of the cross, are set with convex paste of a rich sapphire-blue colour. The intermediate bezels are smaller than the others, and of an oblong square

Pl. 23

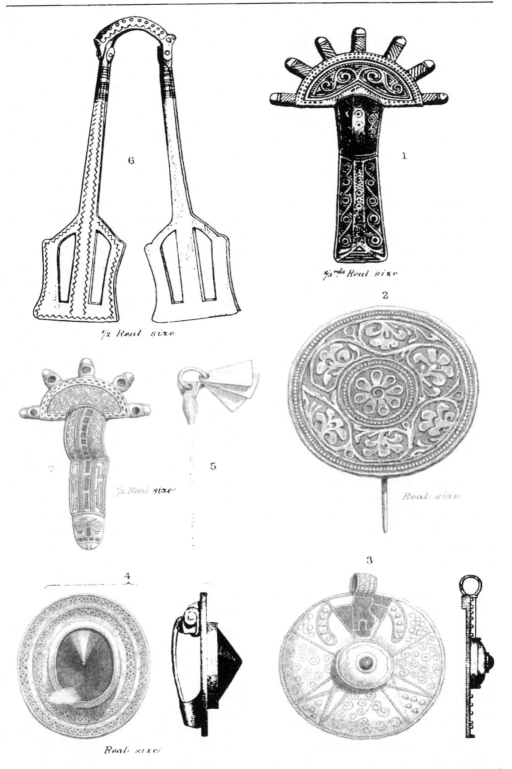

6

1

½ Real size

⅔rds Real size

2

7

5

½ Real size

Real size

4

3

Real size

form, set with crystals of jacinth. The central paste is sur-rounded by nine (originally ten) tubular cells, which were probably once set, but are now *sine gemmis*. The silver rim of the fibula is unadorned; but the back of the brooch is stamped with a kind of stellar device, the points being filled with lines; and outside this is a circle of twenty little double rings known as eyelet-holes. The acus, which moved upon a transverse pin held by two staples, is lost; but suffi-cient trace remains to shew that it was of iron. The place in which this jewel was found, is unrecorded; but it bears a close resemblance in ornamentation and style of workman-ship to Saxon brooches exhumed in Kent and the Isle of Wight; *i.e.*, in the districts occupied by the Jute tribes on their settlement in Britain in the fifth century.[1]

The brooch represented in fig. 8 resembles examples ex-humed in Kent; in proof of which we may refer to one dis-covered at Folkstone hill, engraved in the *Journal* (iv, 159), here re-produced. The present specimen is composed of silver, apparently cast and sculptured. The five discs which spring from the semicircular member, are set with flat garnets, heightened by stamped gold-foil at back. The setting of the gold cross found at Lakenheath, Suffolk (en-graved in vol. viii, 139) was height-ened in a similar way; and, indeed, it seems to have been a common practice with the Anglo-Saxon jew-ellers to heighten the brilliancy of their gems with gold-foil. 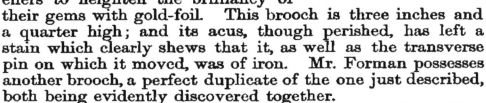 This brooch is three inches and a quarter high; and its acus, though perished, has left a stain which clearly shews that it, as well as the transverse pin on which it moved, was of iron. Mr. Forman possesses another brooch, a perfect duplicate of the one just described, both being evidently discovered together.

Mr. Forman brings to our notice another brooch of allied design to the above, and which assimilates in character to

---

[1] The above brooch is also much like one engraved in Tafel viii, fig. 7, of Lindenschmit's *Die Alterthümer unserer heidnischen Vorzeit.* Mainz, Verlag von Victor von Zabern, 1858. 4to.

that engraved in the *Journal* (iii, 120), which is also again introduced into our pages. The latter has its seven rays and central band set with flat garnets, and the incised portions of the guilloche ornament filled with nigellum. Mr. Forman's specimen has never been set; but a considerable portion of its incised configurations exhibit remains of niello work. It is about three inches and five-eighths high, and like to the one previously engraved, is of silver-gilt, and has had an iron acus moving on a transverse pin. (Plate 23, fig. 1.)

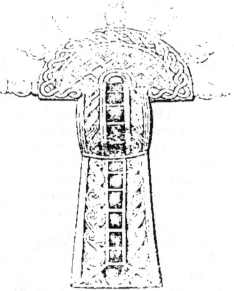

The last of the series of Teutonic brooches exhibited by Mr. Forman, is stated to have been discovered near Oxford in 1856, and is clearly of Danish origin, assignable to the eleventh century. (Fig. 2.) It is a silver disc, one inch and three-quarters diameter, sculptured in low relief, with a rich foliated meander surrounding an octopetalous flower. The acus, or tongue, is also of silver, nearly two inches and a quarter in length. This Danish brooch offers an interesting contrast, in the style of its decoration, to the other specimens adduced; well exemplifying the power of the graver when in skilful hands, and proving that neither enamel, niello, nor jewel, is absolutely needed for the production of a graceful ornament.

... before the king & queene his ...
... of our Lord 1638

1792
1591

155

At the Corpit the 26ᵗʰ of march
At the Corpit the 27ᵗʰ of march
At the Corpit the 3 of Aprile
At the Blackfryers the 23 of Aprill ...
At the Corpit the 24 of may ...
At Richmond the 7 of January
... our day ...

THE ENGLISH STAGE IN THE YEAR 1638.

BY GEORGE R. WRIGHT, ESQ., F.S.A.

THE extreme rarity and literary importance of all documents connected with the history of the English stage previously to the suppression of the theatres during the Commonwealth, must be my apology, if any be necessary, for introducing before the notice of the Association a subject which is somewhat out of the ordinary range of their transactions. There seems to have been a fatality attending the records of the ancient English theatre. It is only by the merest chance that any fragments are now found. They were not considered of importance in their own day by the public, who did not set value on anything of the kind that came into their hands; while, during the civil wars, the Puritans, from conscientious motives, destroyed, as far as they could, all play-books and papers connected with them. The consequence is, that it is now extremely difficult to ascertain any facts connected with the theatrical history of the early period; and hence arises the value of a document like that now submitted to the Association.

This paper, the authenticity of which is undoubted, contains a list of the plays acted "before the king and queene this year of our Lord, 1638." As a fac-simile of the document is here given (see plate 24), and is easy to be deciphered, it is unnecessary to copy it into these pages. The list appears to have been drawn up by the manager of that theatrical company who were then known as "the lady Elizabeth's servants," or, as they are sometimes denominated, "the queen of Bohemia's players," who performed at the Cockpit in Drury-lane. It will be observed from the list, that, with the exception of performances at the court itself, all the plays named, were represented at the Cockpit, save only one day's representation of the *Unfortunate Lovers,* which took place at the Blackfriars' Theatre. There can be but little doubt that the last-named theatre was lent for the occasion to the Cockpit company, it being extremely improbable that the present list refers to the plays of more than one body of actors. The Blackfriars' Theatre was situated near the place where now stands Apothecaries' Hall, and

not far from *The Times'* printing office.   The Cockpit, as
has just been stated, was in Drury-lane.   The latter theatre
was built, or rebuilt, not very long before the year 1617;
in which year, according to a statement in Camden's *Annals,*
it was pulled down by the mob : " 1617, Martii 4.   Thea-
trum ludionum *nuper erectum in Drury-lane* a furente
multitudine diruitur, et apparatus dilaceratur."   According
to Malone, the Cockpit " was situated opposite the Castle
Tavern in Drury-lane, and was standing some time after the
Restoration."   It was also called " The Phœnix," a representation of that fabulous bird having been its external sign.
     This list of plays includes two entries of great interest.
I of course allude to the notice of the performance of Shakespeare's *Julius Cæsar*——here called simply *Cæsar*——at the
Cockpit on November the 13th ; and that of *The Merry
Wives of Windsor,* at the same place, two days afterwards.
It is pleasing to find that the works of our great dramatist
had not been displaced by the novelties of the day.   There
is also the notice of another play, *Sir John Oldcastle,* which
will always be connected with the name of Shakespeare,
having so often been attributed to his pen; but it is now
well known to have been written by Munday, assisted by
Drayton and two others.
     The other plays named are equally well known, and call
for little remark.   The note of *The Passionate Lover* being
represented at Somerset House in July, is perhaps the most
curious of these.   It confirms a statement in the title-page
to the original edition of that play, which appeared in the
year 1655 as " *The Passionate Lover,* a tragi-comedy by
Lodowick Carlell, in two parts, *twice acted before the king
and queen at Somerset House,* and very often afterwards at
Black Friars, with great applause."
     It will be observed that the writer of this list is careful
to note more than once, that, owing to the performance at
court, " the day was lost at our house"; in other words, the
Cockpit was necessarily closed on such occasions.   The
object of this memorandum was to call attention to the
pecuniary loss thus incurred.   There can, I think, be little,
if any doubt that the list was drawn up with the view of
obtaining payment for the performances alluded to in it.
Such a list would pass with the account through the proper
office, previously to payment being ordered.

ON THE BATTLE OF KALTRAETH.

BY GEORGE VERE IRVING, ESQ.

In making the following remarks on Mr. Beale Poste's paper in the last number of our *Journal* (p. 218), I feel that some apology is due to the members of the Association for the length to which the controversy has extended; but this is found in the fact that on the date of the battle or campaign of Kaltraeth, hinges the whole history of the northern portion of this island for a period of several centuries. I am the more emboldened to continue the discussion, from the tone in which it has been conducted. No one who has read the various papers connected with it, but must be convinced that both Mr. Beale Poste and myself are only striving to ascertain the *truth;* and that there has been no attempt on either part to contend for victory, as partizans of one or another theory. I may add that it has always given me most sincere pleasure to peruse the arguments of my learned opponent; for although they do not always carry conviction to my mind, they are always of that weight and force which compel me to reexamine most carefully my former conclusions; and these examinations invariably elucidate some new information on the subject in dispute. On the present occasion I have to thank Mr. Poste for leading me to discover a most inexcusable blunder in my geography, to which I shall afterwards advert. As, however, in this case, geography holds a second place to chronology, I shall in the first place direct your attention to the latter. Before, however, entering on the main question, I may refer shortly to two points on which I wish to set myself right with Mr. Poste.

1st. He has entirely misconceived my meaning in the remarks I made in a former paper, upon the pendragonship. I never intended to convey any doubt of the prevalence of this office; on the contrary, I believe it to have been not only usual, but universal, among the Celtic tribes of Britain. What I combated was a common, but in my opinion a mistaken, idea of its character and importance.

2nd. Mr. Poste accuses me of misrepresenting a passage in John Williams ap Ithel's preface to the *Gododin;* and I must at once admit that, through inadvertence, I interpolated the word "Welsh" in the quotation; but I cannot see how this materially affects the sense. The passage is now correctly given by Mr. Poste, p. 220; and I contend that my criticism applies as much to it now as it did when read with my interpolated word. It must mean one or other of two

things : either that this Rhum was the actual chief of Gododin at the
time the battle of Kaltraeth was fought,—if so, how does it happen that
the name never occurs in the poem of Aneurin? where did the craven
hide his head when his tribe played their last stake for liberty and independence?—or that, although his forefathers had long left the district,
he had some vague rights of suzerainty over it.   Of this, however, we
have not only no proof; but it is inconsistent with a passage in Nennius,
which declares that in the time of Ida, Maelgyn represented Cuneda;
while Matthew of Westminster places his death in 586, after the supposed date of the battle of Kaltraeth; thus rendering it impossible
that Rhum could have been the ruling descendant of Cuneda at that
time.

Returning to the main question of chronology, the first observation of
Mr. Poste to which I would refer, is the following : " I would not be
over-solicitous as to what conflicting dates may be discovered in the
Annals of Tigernach, or in those of Ulster, or in other like sources; for
ancient British history does not admit that the persons referred to (I
shall immediately enumerate them) could possibly have lived three-
quarters of a century later than the year 570; so that the battle of Kaltraez could not have taken place in the year 642."   On this I would
remark that, among all the materials which we possess for the construction of this period of our history, none are more liable to suspicion than
the ancient British traditions and the poems of the Celtic bards.   The
very form in which the latter are composed, with their rhyming triplets,
as Mr. Wright mentioned in his recent paper on Uriconium, is sufficient
to raise most serious doubts as to their authenticity.   Again, many of
these poems, especially those assigned to Taliesin, are full of the magic
mysteries of a later age, and palpably spurious.   So great, indeed, are
these difficulties, that I should hesitate to found on these poems at all,
were it not that after an attentive study of their contents, I have become
convinced that if we shake off the influence of more modern fables, and
candidly read them by the light of their own text *alone*, we shall find a
most marked and striking accordance between them and the records
derived from other sources, in which they illustrate and clear up many
obscure passages.   Under these circumstances it is impossible to consider them, as Mr. Poste appears inclined to do, the paramount authority, and reject the evidence of the other records as comparatively insignificant.

Before adverting in detail to the persons whose æras Mr. Poste
considers so definitely fixed, I would remark that the modern Welsh are
remarkable for the small number of their surnames, which necessitates
such additions as " Ap Ithel"; and we have reason to suspect that the
same was the case among the ancient Celts.   Under these circumstances
it becomes more than usually necessary to guard against an error to

which the early history of all nations is subject,—as witness the myth of the Grecian Hercules,—viz. that of confounding persons of the same name, and relating the deeds of two distinct individuals as those of a single hero. Now the question between Mr. Poste and myself resolves itself into this, whether we have evidence that the names he cites were borne by a single individual, or whether they were common to several. In the former case, the mention of the name would certainly fix the æra of an event with which the person who bore it is represented to have been connected; in the latter case we have still to inquire to which of the individuals the reference is intended to be made. In the present instance I shall endeavour to shew that most of the names cited by Mr. Poste belonged to more than one person, and therefore do not fix the period of Aneurin's poem.

1. *Owen.* I have in my former paper given my reasons for holding that the Owen of the *Gododin* was a separate person from Owen the son of Urien; and it is unnecessary to repeat them.

2. *Cenau* or *Keneu.* In this case there can be no doubt of the duality. The Keneu of Taliesin's *Lay of Argoed* is the son of Koel; while the warrior of the same name mentioned in the *Gododin*, is described as the son of Liwarch.

3. *Caradoc.* The existence of more than one hero of this name is undeniable: in fact it appears to have been a popular cognomen. I may also observe that the word "*Vreichvras*," quoted by Mr. Poste, does not occur in any passage where Karadoc is referred to by Aneurin.

4. *Cian Gwyngwyn,*—or, as Villemarqué has it, the Kian-Maen-Gwenn of the *Gododin*,—Mr. Poste identifies with the Cian-Guenith Guant of Nennius. In this case the affixes are so various that the identity may be reasonably doubted; but even if we admit it, this will not support my learned opponent's conclusion, for the simple reason that it is Cian *himself* who, according to Nennius, flourished *intra* 547-60; while Aneurin is speaking of his son, Maban e Kian (*Gododin*, st. 9.)

5. *Geraint, king of Dumnonia.* A lay of Liwarch celebrates the death of this prince at the battle of Longport. From the whole tenor of the other poems of this bard, it is clear that this occurred previous to the fall of Urien of Reghed; and consequently before the battle of Kaltraez. Again, the name Geraint does not occur in the *Gododin* poem itself, but in an addition to it called an "Epilogue." This is confessedly composed at a later period than the bulk of the poem; and it may be by another hand. As we know that many of the inhabitants of the Scottish lowlands, after the defeat of Kaltraeth, left their country, and joined the kindred tribes who still maintained their independence in the west and south of England; and as we have no means of estimating the interval which occurred between the composition of the poem and the Epilogue, I think it highly probable that the latter refers to a Geraint who shed a

faint gleam of success over the cause of Celtic liberty some half century afterwards, as recorded in the *Saxon Chronicle* (710) : "Ina also, and his relatives, fought with *Gerainte, king of the Welsh*."

Taliesin is the last of the Celtic names referred to ; but there is no reason to suppose that he was present at Kaltraez, or was even alive at the time. The only passage in which the name occurs, is the following : " I, Aneurin, know the things which are shown to Taliesin, whose spirit is in unison with mine." Which amounts to nothing more than the statement that the former knew the poems of the latter : indeed, it forcibly reminds us of the manner in which more than one of the authors of the mediæval romances assert their knowledge of Thomas, or "good" Thomas, when it is evident that they could have had no personal acquaintance with Learmont of Ercildonne.

The whole gist of the matter, therefore, is confined to the two names, Ida and Bun ; and to the questions—

1. Was Ida the Flamebearer of Taliesin and the other Celtic bards ? and—

2. Was Bun, who fell at Kaltraez, his widow ?

1. The identification of Ida with the Flamebearer appears to me to be simply an assumption supported by no evidence whatever. It necessitates the further assumption that it was "his usual custom to commit every town, village, or private house, of the enemy's to the flames immediately it came into his possession." But this seems totally inconsistent with what we know of his proceedings. *Alone*, perhaps, of all the Saxon invaders of England, he seems to have had the tact of reconciling to his rule the British tribes with which he came in contact. So much so that he incorporated their forces completely with his own ; and the armies of the Saxons of Northumberland are continually described by the Celtic bards as the Logriens. How is this compatible with this supposed system of severity and devastation? Look also at the character given of him by William of Malmesbury : "*Satis constat magna et vetere prosapia oriundum* PURIS ET DEFÆCATIS MORIBUS *splendoris generosis, contulisse natalibus, Adea* BELLO INVICTUS *domi severitatem regiam mansuetudine animi temperabat*." Contrast this with the description given by the same author of his grandson, who, I contend, was really the Flamebearer : "*Ethefridus igitur ut dicere cæperam regnum nactus primo acriter sua defendere post etiam* IMPROBE *aliena invadere gloriæ occasionis, undecunque* CONFLARE"; or with that of Bede : "*His temporibus regno Nordanhymbrorum præfuit rex fortissimus, et gloria cupidissimus, Eadfrid, qui plus omnibus Anglorum primatibus gentem vastavit Britonum. . . . Nemo enim in tribunis nemo in regibus plures eorum terras exterminatas vel subjugabis, indegenis aut tributarias gente Anglorum aut habitabiles fecit*."

We have no record of any soubriquet having been applied to Ida ; but

Nennius informs us that Ethelfrid was called " Flesaurs," or the De-
stroyer; which seems synonymous with the Celtic " Flamzonen." Again,
the Celtic bards state that the Flamebearer was surprised and slain
by Owen, son of Urien of Reghed. How are we to reconcile this with
the statement of William of Malmesbury, who wrote long afterwards,
that Ida died *"bello invictus"?* These very circumstances, however,
attend the defeat and death of Ethelfrid; in consequence of which his
family had to take refuge in the north. Again, how can we reconcile
Ida being *"bello invictus,"* with the repulse of the Flamebearer at Argoed,
as related by Taliesin? Lastly, Urien was, according to the bards, the
chief opponent of the Flamebearer; but Nennius states that Dutigim
was the British chief who encountered Ida, and refers the contests with
Urien to the reign of the successors of the latter.

2. Mr. Poste, admitting the force of my argument, that, as we know
Bun to have been a British princess, she could not have been the wife of
Ida, if he first landed in Northumberland in 547, has endeavoured to
obviate the objection by the conjecture that this was a second visit of
his, after having returned to Germany for fresh recruits. In doing so,
I, however, think that he overlooks the full force of the passage in
Matthew of Westminster, to which he refers: " Genuit autem Ida ex
regna sua, sex filios. Praeterea ex concubinis alios sex filios. *Isti omnes
venerunt in Britanniam* cum navibus xl." This surely points to the
arrival of a new immigration, and not to the return of a recruiting party.
But admit Mr. Poste's conjecture to be true, and we still find insuperable
difficulties in the identification of the widow of Ida with the lady who
took so prominent a part in the battle of Kaltraez, even under the supposition that it occurred in 570. William of Malmesbury informs us,
in the strongest terms, that when Athelric, the fourth or fifth son of Ida,
ascended the Northumberland throne, in 588, he was in *extreme old age.*
If so, that statement must have applied still more forcibly to his mother
in 570. Can we conceive that a woman at this age played the Amazo-
nian *rôle* attributed by Aneurin to his heroine? Still less can we conceive it possible that, at this age, she should have retained so much of
her pristine charms as to force a poet of a hostile sept once and again to
refer pointedly to her *beauty.* No difficulty of the kind occurs if Bun
was the second wife of Ethelfrid, and Kaltraez was fought in 642.

The manner in which Ida has become confounded with the Flamebearer and with Bun, is easily traced. The *Saxon Chronicle* states, Ida
" construxit Bebbanburgh et circumdedit eam prius sepe postea muro";
and Bede informs us that the town acquired its name from a former
queen. But this is fully explained by Nennius, who tells us that Ida
joined Dynguayth to Berneich : that is, joined this town, which, lying
to the north of the Aln, belonged to the Ottodani, to his previous conquests in the territories of the Brigantes : that the town kept its pre-

vious name until the time of his grandson, Ethefrid, who presented it to his wife, Bebba, from whom it is now called Bebbanburgh.

Mr. Poste objects to the date of 642 as that of Kaltraez, because the battle of Maserfield occurred in the same year. If he refers to Bede, A.D. 603, he will find the Scots contending within the twelvemonth in localities more widely separate. Independent of which, he must surely be aware that there is continually a discrepancy of a single year between the dates in which the Saxon and Irish *Annals* record the same event, which completely invalidates the objection.

As to Domnal Brec, so long as it is admitted that he was a *Scottish* king, which Mr. Poste has candidly done on p. 222, and identical with the *Dovenaldus Varius* of the Scotch and Irish *Annals* and *Chronicles*, the reason of his surname is of little consequence. I, however, still adhere to my former opinion. The Latin *varius* refers evidently, not to a national but a personal peculiarity. He could not, moreover, receive the name from being a Pict who had ascended the Scottish throne; because his father Eochus, his grandfather Aidan, and his grandfather Gauran, had all possessed the chieftainship of that tribe; and we cannot conceive that a name derived from origin, should never have been applied to these, but should be revived in the person of their descendant when the fact must have been almost forgotten. At the same time I at once admit that the word "*Vrych*" or "*Brec*" is often used to designate the nation of the Picts, who, I have always maintained, were present as allies of the Saxons in the campaign of Kaltraeth. Indeed, I am inclined to believe that the words "*pra Brech*," in stanza 43 of Villemarqué's edition, should be translated as the Picts, and not the followers of Domnal. Had Mr. Poste produced any passage in the *Ulster Annals*, which assigned the death of the latter to the sixth century, I should have given much greater weight to his remarks; but all he has done, is to refer to certain discordant statements in the seventh, which, as I have already shewn, may be easily explained. I may also remind him that the date of the death of Domnal does not exclusively rest on any reference these records contain, as to himself, but is founded on a *catena* of circumstances only remotely connected with him; to ignore the whole of which, is simply to deny all faith to these chronicles because they do not agree with *one interpretation* of the Celtic bards. This, for the reasons I have given, it is impossible to accede to. No theory is admissible *which does not reconcile into one consistent whole, every one of these ancient testimonies.*

Mr. Poste will excuse me stating that I have never mentioned Buchannan's *History*, nor founded on it in any way; and that I must decline entering into any discussion of the writings of a hireling scribe who was employed by a political party to falsify the history of his country, and put forth mendacious statements in support of their opinions.

I have no hesitation in admitting that there do happen, in the annals of the Scottish and Pictish kings, instances in which we must reckon their reigns, not as successive, but contemporary. This, however, clearly does not occur in the case of Domnal Brec, as the æra of his grandfather, Aidan, is clearly fixed; and the years assigned to the reigns of his successors completely fill up, in consecutive order, the interval between this and the entry in the *Ulster Annals* which records Domnal's death in 642. Mr. Poste objects to my reference to Adonnanus on account of the prophecy contained in it; but whatever opinion we may hold of the credulity of Bede and Adamnanus in relating such predictions, we can never suppose that in describing their fulfilment "*nostris temporibus,*" they would have the hardihood to assert that a chieftain was alive in their own day, who had died half a century before the writer was born. Mr. Poste further objects that, according to the *Ulster Annals,* Domnal was killed in Strath Cairvinn, and not at Kaltraez; but this is just one of the difficulties we have to solve in fixing the place of this battle. Where Kaltraez is, there you must find a Strath Cairvinn; otherwise your locality will not agree with the premises.

In the same way, there is no ground for any supposition of contemporaneous reigns among the Saxons of Northumberland. The æra of Ida is fixed; so is that of his grandson, Ethelfrid; and to fill up the interval it is necessary to count the years of the various kings consecutively. How then was it that Urien, who, according to Mr. Poste, was killed in 567, fought against Fridolguald, 577-583, and Hussu, 583-588?

In conclusion, I may now offer some remarks on the geographical aspect of the subject; and here I will at once candidly confess that, until I read Mr. Poste's paper, I was under the impression that the city of Godeu lay on the west instead of the east coast of Scotland. Into this (which now appears to me a most stupid blunder) I was undoubtedly betrayed by local associations, which led me to overlook the clear and definite testimony of Bede on the subject. I cannot, however, agree with Mr. Poste, that there was no "particular state named Gododin." The manner in which it is again and again referred to by Aneurin, is totally inconsistent with any idea but that of a particular locality. In stanzas 6 and 7 the warriors depart for Gododin; and in the 29th an event is related as occurring "between the two armies before Gododin." But the matter is entirely set at rest by Bede, who tells us that the north part of Britain is intersected by two firths (*sinibus*), the one from the east, the other from the west; and that the eastern firth has in its middle the city of Giudi; and the western on it (*i.e.*, on its right side), the city of Alcluith. (*Hist. Soc. Edit.*, p. 28.) The latter is admittedly Dunbarton; and it is clear that Giudi was equally an individual place. It is not easy to determine its precise situation; but from its description as on the middle of the Firth of Forth, it must have been to the east of the Queen's Ferry; while the Cariden referred to by Mr. Poste is to the west of that point. In regard to this last locality, Mr. Poste has most naturally trusted to a plate of general Roy's, whose extreme accuracy no one will contest. But there are spots even in the sun; and unfortunately my learned opponent has fallen into one of these, the plate to which he refers being the only inaccurate one in the work of that eminent topographer. I must, however, add that nothing but local knowledge could have detected this; which, nevertheless, is sufficiently evident from other blunders, as, for instance, "Reneel" for "Kiniel." These mistakes are, however, corrected on p. 162 of the letter-press. Beyond this misspelt map there is no authority for the name *Cor Eïddin*. In our ancient records the place appears Caer-ridden, Carredyne, Caredyn, Carriden, Caridden, Carridene, Carridine, Caribden, —the last evidently a mistake. In these, as well as in the modern pronunciation of the name, the penultimate syllable is short; while in the places derived from Eiddin it is long, as in Dunedin.

My objection to Mr. Poste's theory of this place being the locality of Kaltraez, in no way, however, hinges upon its name, or the question whether the wall here ended in a *castrum* or not; but on much broader grounds:

1. On the remote corner on which it is situated, why should such a place so far east have been selected for a meeting of the intramural tribes, including the warriors of Strathclyde and the Selgovæ of Dumfries and Galloway? Surely a more central point would have been natural; and for what reason should they choose a locality which has never been of any importance in the subsequent history of the county?

2. In the second place, how did the Saxons get there? It is impossible to suppose that both they and their allies, the Picts and Scots, could assemble their forces for a combined movement in a day; or that this could have been done without the British tribes having some intimation of their preparations. Can we then conceive the latter to have been so insane as not to have taken some precautions for the defence of their frontiers? Or if this were not the case, that the Saxons should have pushed forward to a doubtful struggle, leaving behind them such a tempting prey as the strong fortress of Dunedin, the modern Edinburgh, and thus jeopardizing the line of their retreat in case of failure?

3. Look, again, at the strategical position; or, I should rather say, the most transparent trap into which the leader of the northern tribes must have led his forces. He must have passed the narrow defile of Kiniel, and placed them in a locality where a repulse (and the *Gododin* relates several such events) must have led to their certain annihilation.

The more I study the poem of Aneurin, the more am I convinced that it does not record the events of a single battle, but the incidents of a lengthened campaign; including different engagements which occurred at Kaltraeth, in front of the city of Godein and elsewhere; and that its seven days do not refer to literal periods of twenty-four hours, but represent a week of years, commencing with the "Bella Ossa (Oswi) apud Britones, A.D. 642," and closing with the "Bellum Ossa per Pante (Penda), in 649" of the *Ulster Annals*. This interpretation does away with the insuperable difficulties which the locality of the battle of Kaltraez otherwise presents; and affords an explanation not only of passages in the poem of *Gododin* otherwise unintelligible, but of some still more obscure in the other records; as, for example, the connexion which Nennius mentions between Penda and the city of Godeu.

Proceedings of the Association.

JANUARY 11, 1860.

T. J. PETTIGREW, ESQ., F.R.S., F.S.A., V.P., IN THE CHAIR.

THE following were elected associates:

Rev. John M'Caul, LL.D., president of the University of Toronto.
Lieut. Samuel Unwin, Militia Barracks, Turnham Green.
Thomas Greenhalgh, esq., Astley House, Bolton-le-Moors.
John Millard, esq., 12, Charing Cross.

Thanks were voted for the following presents:

To the Society. Transactions of the Society of Antiquaries of Edinburgh. Vol. II. Part 3. Edinb., 1859; 4to.

„ „ Journal of the Royal Dublin Society. Nos. I to XIV. Dublin, 1856-59; 8vo.

To the Publisher. Gentleman's Magazine for January 1860. Lond.; 8vo.

Mr. Briggs, of King's Newton, Derbyshire, forwarded a drawing of a mural painting discovered during the reparation of Melbourne church, upon the removal of the whitewash on the north pillar which supports the central tower, the most ancient part of the building. It represents, in a very rude manner, the temptation of our Lord; is in outline, in red paint or ochre; four feet in height, and two feet and a half in breadth. Upon it is an abbreviated Latin inscription, apparently reading, ICEST RELIADEABOL. ("Hic, est relictus a Diabolo." Here he is left by the Devil.—Matth. iv, 11.) The Devil is figured with horns, large ears, wings, claws, etc., and attended by two imps; altogether extremely grotesque.

The rev. Joseph Deans, the vicar of Melbourne, has recently printed some account of the wall-paintings.[1] At the Derby Congress, in 1851,

[1] In *The Reliquary* (No. I, p. 31), a new archæological publication, edited by Ll. Jewitt, esq.; to whom the Association are indebted for the use of the accompanying woodcut.

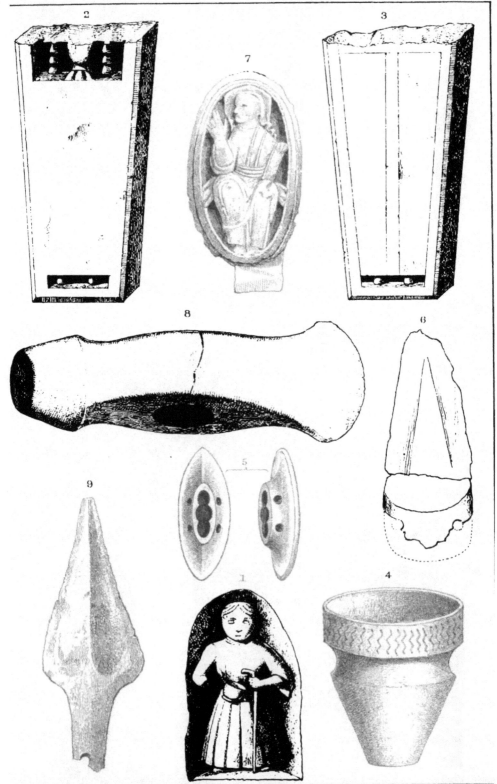

Pl. 25.

J.R.Jobbins

the church was visited by the Association; when Mr. Deans obligingly
conducted the visitors over the building, and read an interesting paper
on its structure.[1] Mr. Ll. Jewitt conjectures the picture engraved in the
annexed cut to be a representation of one of a series of the Vices, which

probably at one time decorated the walls of the church; and is disposed
to read the legend, IC EST CELLA(M) DEABOL(I),—*this is the cell, secret
place, or storehouse of the Devil.* He regards the painting as of the fourteenth century; and the dresses of the female figures support his
opinion.   The painting was in bold, black outline, filled in with red,
blue, and yellow.

Mr. T. N. Brushfield forwarded a drawing of a sculptured figure seen
by the Association on occasion of their visit at the Derbyshire Congress.
(See plate 25, fig. 1.)   It is only eighteen inches in height, sculptured in
sandstone, and placed in an irregular niche in the north wall of the nave
of Yolgrave church.   The execution is very rough, but perfect, with the
exception of the right hand, which has been broken off. The diminutive
figure is that of a man in a loose gown with open sleeve.   In the left
hand he holds a crutch or stick, and the right appears to have been
employed in carrying a cup or basin.   It has been considered as the
figure of a pilgrim or of a leper. It is unquestionably of an early date.

In Yolgrave churchyard there are also two diminutive sepulchral slabs

[1] See *Journal*, vii, p. 348 et seq.; and plates xxxvi and xxxvii.

found in Bakewell church in 1851. (Figs. 2, 3.) They are remarkable on account of their small size, being about two feet only in length, eleven inches wide at the head, and nine and a half at the feet. In the more perfect one (fig. 2) is a rectangular recess at the upper part, displaying a representation of the head, neck, and two hands approximated together, and holding what appears to be a heart between them. The arrangement of the hair is very peculiar, and shews that the effigy represented is a female. At the lower part of each is a small square recess displaying the feet. Fig. 3 is peculiar, owing to the incised cross on its surface : whether it contained a similar effigy to fig. 2, it is impossible now to ascertain. As to their date, they appear to belong to the thirteenth century ; the rectangular form of the recess being of much earlier date than the quatrefoil. They were found in some blocked up clerestory windows at the west end of the church, and are now preserved with other slabs, etc., in the porch.

Mr. Allom called the attention of the meeting to an iron mount of the butt of a large pistol, probably of French manufacture. It is richly chisseled, and has a hinged lid in its centre, which covered a little magazine in the stock, wherein the picker was deposited. It appears to be of the time of William III, and was exhumed from the battlefield of Culloden.[1]

Mr. H. Syer Cuming exhibited five brass medals relating to Culloden, representing the Chevalier, duke of Cumberland, etc.; and Mr. A. Thompson produced a cast-iron cannon ball found, in 1859, on Culloden Moor, weighing two pounds and three-quarters.

Mr. George Patrick exhibited three rubbings from brasses in Bexley church, one of which was to the memory of Thomas Sparrow, a merchant (ob. 1557).

Mr. Bateman forwarded for exhibition some Celtic antiquities lately presented to his museum by the rev. John Colston of Wilmslow, in the county of Chester, where they were found. (See plate 25.) They consist of :—A cinerary urn (fig. 4) found in 1859 ; fig. 5, a small bone stud, with perforations for attaching it to something by no means obvious, found amongst the burnt bones in the urn. Two similar studs have occurred in the course of Mr. Bateman's excavations, and both were found with deposits of calcined bones. Fig. 6 is a small knife or dagger, of bronze, which has been attached to its handle by two pegs or rivets, the holes for which are broken away : found, about the year 1839, with burnt bones, in another urn, about twenty yards from that discovered in the present year. The account of their discovery is detailed in

---

[1] In the collection of the Scottish Antiquaries at Edinburgh, are preserved some interesting relics from Culloden, viz., a lead bullet, pistol-lock and barrel, pair of steel pistols of Cameron of Lochiel, marked with his initials ; elegant basket-hilt of a sword, *skein dhu*, brass spur, and the marble *quech* or drinking-cup carried by Breck, one of prince Charles's guard at Culloden.

the following extract from a letter addressed by the rev. Mr. Colston to Mr. Bateman :

"The spot where the urn was found, is about one hundred yards distant from the Wilmslow railway station, in a ridge of gravel between the new and the old roads leading to the village of Prestbury. The circumstance which first attracted the notice of the labourers employed in cutting down the said ridge of gravel, was the appearance of a quantity of dark soil in the gravel; a portion of which falling down, led to the exposure of the urn. Curiosity on the part of the workmen to ascertain the contents thereof, unfortunately led to a too free use of the spade ; by means of which the urn was considerably injured. When found, the urn was placed with the mouth downwards; and on raising it up, a quantity of dark earthy matter, mixed with bones, fell out of it. The bones, with several pieces of charcoal mixed with them, were collected and deposited in the urn ; the other matter was passed through a riddle, and then thrown aside. I send you a sketch of the urn, which is sixteen inches deep, and thirteen broad at the mouth. At the top of the urn is a broad rim, four inches and a half deep, covered with a number of irregular zigzag lines. The materials of which the urn is composed, are of a very coarse and friable kind, and seem to have been baked in the sun rather than in an oven or fire. The bones are much charred, and shew evident traces of the action of fire. The teeth are nearly perfect, and appear to be those of a young person about fourteen years of age.

"On making further inquiry into the matter, I was told that a similar urn was found near the same spot, in the cutting of the line of rail which passes through Wilmslow ; and that a small bronze dagger was found in the urn, mixed with the bones. This dagger or knife is now in my possession ; and as it is desirable that such objects should be deposited in the museum of some individual by whom they will be carefully treasured, I shall have much pleasure in giving both the stud and the bronze knife or dagger to you."

Mr. Bateman also exhibited a fine gold bulla, or pendant, of Anglo-Saxon workmanship, found with a skeleton. It is represented on plate 23, fig. 3, of the actual size. The pattern is cruciform, and the centre is of ivory, with an interior setting of garnet. The irregular shape of the garnet slabs worked into the upper limb of the cross, is very remarkable. The back is of gold, and quite plain.

Mrs. White laid before the meeting a highly curious carving in bone, representing the nimbed figure of the Saviour seated on a rainbow, and looking towards the right. (See plate 25, fig. 7.) The Sacred Person is clothed in a long garment wound round the waist, and raises the right hand in the act of benediction, whilst the left rests upon the gospel; the whole subject being surrounded by an ovoidal aureole nearly two inches high and one inch wide. It is undoubtedly a work of the twelfth century, and was exhumed in 1831, in the garden of the rectory at Leck-hamstead, Bucks, which was formerly a convent.

Mr. Curle exhibited a Mauro-Spanish spur of iron, dredged up from the Thames off Fulham, October 1859. The broad, flat shanks are straight, and decorated with a zigzag band; the ring-shaped ends are divided by a horizontal bar across their centres; and at the back is a flat disc with short neck, within which turns a rowel of seven points. Apparent date, second half of the sixteenth century.

Mr. Pettigrew read a paper, "On Monumental Crosses, Coffin Slabs, and Effigies," forming the first portion of a series of essays on these subjects; being explanatory of a collection of drawings communicated to the Association by Edward Falkener, esq.; which will appear in the *Journal* or *Collectanea Archæologica*, as opportunity presents itself for their publication.

JANUARY 25.

NATHANIEL GOULD, ESQ., F.S.A., V.P., IN THE CHAIR.

The following were elected associates:

William Burr, esq., the mayor of Shrewsbury.
William Harley Bayley, esq., Claremont Buildings, Shrewsbury.
George Maw, esq., Benthall Hall, Broseley, Salop.
Rev. John Adams, M.A., Stockcross, Newbury.
James Corbould, esq., St. Mary Place, Newbury.
William Mount, esq., Wasing, Berks.
Charles White, esq., Warrington.
William Freudenthal, M.D., 4, Newington Place.
Reginald Scaife, esq., Inverness Terrace, Bayswater.

Thanks were voted for the following presents:

To the Society. Journal of the Archæological Institute. No. 63. 1859; 8vo.
To the Author. Address by Lord Neaves at the Conversazione of the Society of Antiquaries of Scotland. Edinb., 1860; 8vo.
„   „   Analysis of Ancient Domestic Architecture, by F. T. Dollman and J. R. Jobbins. No. II. 1860; 4to.

Mr. Halliwell presented to the Association three sheets of fac-similes, taken from the originals at Dulwich College, of notice-bills used at the Rose Theatre, to direct the attention of the performers to their several parts in the acting of the plays.

Dr. Palmer of Newbury communicated that some archæological discoveries had recently been made on the estate of Mr. Bunbury at Maelstone. In a wood at Birch Farm he found, on making slight excavations, some portions of pottery, Roman flue and pavement tiles, tesseræ, etc., together with many bones of animals; but at present no human remains. The buildings cover an extent of nearly an acre. The portion now uncovered is circular, measuring between fifteen and sixteen feet in diameter; and among the *débris* were the usual stone roofing-tiles, whilst the interior appears to have been lined with flints carefully faced. Further particulars and photographs will be transmitted to the Association. Mr. Bunbury intends shortly to recommence operations, which have been suspended on account of the recent heavy rains. He promises also to re-exhume a villa which was uncovered thirty years since; and afterwards filled in by Mr. Goddard, at that time possessor of the ground, because it occasioned him annoyance by the intrusion of persons on his estate. It is probable, therefore, something may remain to reward Mr. Bunbury's assiduity; and the particulars, if deserving of notice, will be forwarded to the Association.

Mr. H. Syer Cuming exhibited various memorials of Charles I, and gave particulars respecting them. He remarked that—

In 1857, sir W. C. Trevelyan placed before the Society of Antiquaries a portrait of Charles I, wrought in the monarch's hair. A beautiful profile likeness of the king, worked in coloured silks by the princess Mary, was shewn by lady Fellows at the Isle of Wight Congress of the Association in 1855;[1] and Mr. G. R. Corner now laid before the Association an interesting family piece, consisting of Charles and his queen, with six of their children. This picture, thirteen inches and a half high, by sixteen inches wide, is wrought in coloured silks on fine canvas, and sewed upon a frame. In the centre stand Charles and Henrietta Maria, hand in hand, with *amorini* in the clouds, holding crowns above their heads. The monarch and his consort are each about nine inches high. The coat and trunk-hose of the king are of a brownish hue. He has a falling collar, and cuffs with deep lace-edgings; a ribband and jewel on the breast; large topped boots spurred; and his right hand rests upon his hip, just above the sword-hilt. The dress of the queen now appears of a dingy white shaded with brown; but it has evidently faded. She has a cord and jewel on her neck;[2] a collar edged with lace covers her shoulders; and the rich, full sleeves descend a little below the elbows, and have ruffled ends; and in her left hand is placed a blue flower. To the right of the king stand his three sons, viz., Charles, prince of Wales; James, duke of York; and Henry of Oatlands, duke of Gloucester. The eldest holds a baton in his right hand; the second has a hawk perched on his left fist, and his garters with great bows and depending ends, and red soled shoes with large rosettes, are worthy of remark; the youngest prince is dressed in a cap crossed by a yellow feather, pink frock, long

---

[1] See *Journal*, xi, 234.
[2] Mr. A. Thompson has a miniature of the queen, in which she wears a narrow ribband and pendant ring. See *Journal*, xii, 251.

white apron with *bavette*, and a coral and bells are hung round his neck by a ribband. On the left of the queen is the princess Mary. She wears a blue dress, open in front so as to expose a yellow stomacher and petticoat. On her shoulders is a lace-edged falling collar, and in her left hand a fan. Behind her stands the princess Elizabeth in a pink or salmon-coloured frock, holding a rose in her right hand. The third daughter, Anne, stands between her parents, and grasps the right side of her mother's dress. She wears a yellow frock, with white fall, cuffs, and apron.

In the centre of the upper part of the picture is the English rose; on the extreme right and left, a dove; beneath, on the right of the king, is a unicorn *passant* gorged; and on the left of the queen, a stag lodged. The lion and lamb occupy places in the foreground, together with red flowers, and a squirrel seated on a nut-branch.

This memorial, Mr. Cuming regarded as a work in progress rather than a finished production, as upon examination some small patches of the canvas are still visible, other parts being only covered with tent-stitch, whilst a portion of the picture exhibits the bold and final cross-stitch in all its entirety. No tradition has been preserved regarding the worker of this family picture; but assuming that all the individuals represented were living when the subject was begun, Mr. Cuming felt disposed to fix the period of its execution between July 20 and December 8, 1640; *i.e.*, between the birth of the duke of Gloucester and the death of the princess Anne. The latter event may have been the cause of the piece being left in an unfinished state; or, like the king's profile in lady Fellows' possession, it may have been wrought by the princess Mary, whose marriage with William of Orange on May 2, 1641, would afford an additional excuse for the abandonment of the design.

The next memorial exhibited by Mr. Cuming consisted of a bust of the king, in white marble, about eleven inches in height. It is not a work of high art, and was probably executed as an architectural embellishment, or placed above the monument of some devoted cavalier.

Among the portraits of Charles I, whether painted or glyptic, none have created so much interest, and regarding the fate of which so much doubt and obscurity exist, as the bust executed in marble by Giovanni Lorenzo Bernini; for which the king sent him a ring valued at six thousand crowns. The bust was placed over the door of the king's closet at Whitehall, and continued there till the building was destroyed by fire in 1697. Whether it perished in, or was lost during, the conflagration, is matter of great uncertainty. As late as 1790 there was a bust of Charles I in the passage to Westminster Hall, ascribed to Bernini, but thought by Vertue to be of an earlier date. It was moved from its old situation; and a writer in the *Gent. Mag.* (October, 1791, p. 904) says it was then "under the care of Mr. Woolfe, in Scotland Yard, clerk of his majesty's works there." An engraving of this bust, by P. Mazell, is given in the *Additions and Corrections to Pennant's London.*

It is stated in the *Gent. Mag.* (February 1791, p. 115), that casts of Bernini's bust of Charles were then common; but Mr. Cuming had not met with them. Mr. T. J. Mackinlay has in his possession a terra-cotta bust of the king, which is asserted to be the original model sent by the artist to England for approval. In this, Charles appears with an abundance of flowing hair, the gorget partly covered by a plain falling band, lion-head pauldrons, and the breast crossed by a full and richly folded scarf. Mr. Mackinlay states that this bust has been in his possession upwards of twenty years, and was previously the property of Mr. Fairs; and according to the latter gentleman's account, the treasure had been carefully preserved by a royalist family, from whom it was purchased for George IV, with the intent of placing it in the corridor at Windsor Castle; but the king dying before it was delivered, his successor declined completing the transaction.

A fac-simile of Mr. Macinlay's bust has lately emerged from obscurity, and become the property of Mr. S. Pratt; by whose permission it is now exhibited to the Association. It is not, however, of terra-cotta, but of lead, thickly painted, of a light stone colour; and until within a month or two it occupied a niche in Hurlingham House, Fulham, where it was put up about twenty years since. Its pedigree is as yet incomplete; but those interested in the matter are not without hope of tracing the bust to its first restingplace, and proving that the leaden cast, like the original model, is of the time of the king.

Busts of Charles I are now rarely seen; but to those already enumerated, Mr. Cuming cited examples in Barbers' Hall, Monkwell-street, spoken of by Hatton in his *New View of London* (1708, p. 597). Another at Windsor Castle. And in the *Gent. Mag.* (June 1788, p. 669) mention is made of "a very fine bust of king Charles I, in the possession of George Augustus Selwyn, esq., of Matson, near Gloucester. On one side the pedestal is inscribed, "King Charles came to Matson, with his two sons, 10 August, 1643"; and on the other side, "L. F. Roubilliac fec. 1759."

If tradition is to be credited, one of the most precious and authentic portraits of the king is still preserved in Northampton. In the *Standard* newspaper of September 9, 1859, is a report of an archæological meeting at Apethorpe Hall, the seat of the earl of Westmorland; in which it is stated: "The beautiful head of Charles I, in plaster of Paris, which was presented to the friends of that monarch after his death, was exhibited in the case in which it had been originally placed."

Many efforts were made, prior and subsequent to the king's death, to supply every grade of society with his resemblance.

Mr. Cuming had, on previous occasions, described the seven mourning rings and other mortuary trinkets,[1] and now produced the only instance of the kind he had met with, a necklace-snap of gilt brass, of an oblong square form, the front enameled with a full-faced bust of the monarch in a black habit and white falling band, on a blue field; the reverse engraved with a record of his death, "January 30, 1648." In the possession of Mr. W. H. Forman.

In addition to several heart-shaped lockets worn in memory of king Charles, Mrs. Fitch of Norwich now exhibited one of these trinkets, which differs in some respects from the other examples described. On most of these lockets there is some word or device indicative of their purpose as royal mementos; but in the present instance the bauble might be taken as an ordinary gift, and exposed in any company without raising a suspicion of the loyalty of the wearer. On its front, and within a border, is engraved a heart transfixed by two arrows, saltire; from which flow five gouts of blood; and above is a crown, or rather coronet. Within, on a black field, is placed a gold or silver-gilt profile, in relief, of the king; on whose shoulder is W, the initial, probably, of the name of the artist.[2]

In connexion with these mementos, it may be mentioned that six churches in England are dedicated to the honour of "CHARLES, KING AND MARTYR," viz. one at Falmouth, one at Tonbridge Wells, two at Plymouth; the church of Peak Forest, Derbyshire; and the church of Newtown, in Wem, Salop.

Mr. Planché exhibited some portions of armour belonging to Mr. S. Pratt. They formed part of a suit elaborately engraved and gilt, which, from the great resemblance of its peculiar ornamentation to that of the armour represented on an original bust of Charles I (a copy of which is in the Crystal Palace), he believed to have belonged to that monarch. Of its being of that period there could be no doubt; and he trusted to obtain the rest of the suit, which had long been preserved at Worcester, when further evidence might be produced in support of its identification.

The remainder of the evening was occupied in the inspection of an extensive collection of drawings and details of the most remarkable buildings in Scotland, embracing the old Tolbooth at Edinburgh; Haggs Castle, Glasgow; ancient house at Elgin, Borthwick Castle, Newark Castle on the Clyde, Maybole Castle, Dirleton Castle, Roslin Castle, Dumfermline Castle, Stirling Castle, Crichton Castle, Clackmannan Tower, etc.; exhibiting peculiarities not to be met with in English architecture, and presenting details of great beauty and interest. This collection of drawings is from the pencil of F. T. Dollman, esq., and intended

---

[1] See *Journal*, xi, 234, 236, 361; xii, 254.
[2] In the *Gent. Mag.* for May 1791, p. 401, is an engraving of a locket containing a bust apparently from the same mould, but the initial on which is read as VI.

for publication in the work now in progress by that gentleman and Mr. J. R. Jobbins. Mr. Dollman accompanied the exhibition by remarks upon the peculiarities the different structures displayed; and kindly promised, at some future time, some remarks upon them. The thanks of the meeting were given to Mr. Dollman and Mr. Jobbins for their kind attention on this occasion.

FEBRUARY 8.

T. J. PETTIGREW, ESQ., F.R.S., F.S.A., V.P., IN THE CHAIR.

The following were elected associates:

Sir C. H. Rouse Boughton, bart., Downton Hall, Ludlow.
Samuel Wood, esq., F.S.A., the Abbey, Shrewsbury.
John Dunkin Lee, esq., Welwyn, Herts.
David Tweedie, esq., Crawford Castle, Abington, Lanarkshire.

Thanks were voted to—
The Royal Society for Proceedings of the Society. No. 37. 1860; 8vo.

Dr. Kendrick transmitted for inspection a stone axe-hammer, bronze javelin-blade, calcined bones, and fragments of a sepulchral urn, discovered a few weeks since; and accompanied the exhibition with the following memoranda:

"These remains were taken from a barrow at Winwick, about three miles from Warrington; a locality which has perhaps furnished more interesting archæological treasures than any other in this neighbourhood. They were laid bare in the act of leveling a barrow to fill up a large ditch near to it. In the Ordnance Map of Lancashire, this tumulus and another within twenty or thirty yards to the westward of it, have been considered and laid down as parts of one large, elongated tumulus, through which a lane or bye-road has been cut in later times. There is, however, reason to believe that they have always formed two distinct tumuli; the more so as a third, of an equal size, formerly existed about a quarter of a mile to the east. From the account given by the farm labourers, who were at work alone at the time of the discovery, the bones, which are human, were contained in a large jar, of which I send four fragments. The part above the shoulder bears the chevron pattern, whilst that below it is quite plain. This urn is said to have been found two feet below the surface of the mound; and immediately above it was found a layer of burnt wood. The stone celt (plate 25, fig. 8) and bronze spear-head (fig. 9) were found in the urn along with the bones. A few weeks previously, the tumulus alluded to as being to the westward of the present, was very carefully explored by a party of gentlemen from Warrington and the neighbourhood; at which examination, unfortunately, I was prevented being present. Fragments of funereal urns and of human bones were also found here; but they appeared to have been much broken and disturbed by husbandry operations. Of these remains I also send a few specimens."

To Dr. Kendrick's communication, Mr. Syer Cuming appended the subjoined remarks:

"The above remains must be referred to that transition period when the stone implements had arrived at their greatest perfection, but were still gradually giving way before the introduction of arms and instruments of bronze. Nothing can exceed in neatness and precision the little axe-hammer, which is of light-coloured claystone porphyry, and measures four inches and three-quarters in length, and about one inch and a quarter across its cutting edge, having a perforation seven-eighths of an inch in diameter worked through its centre to admit the haft. It is a perfect gem in its way; and brings to mind the beautiful double-axe found at Llanmadoc in Gower, preserved in the museum of the Royal Institution at Swansea. The thin bronze blade is probably that of a *colp* or *picell*, a light dart or javelin. It is of a primitive type; and has a flat tang, which was placed in the divided end of the staff, and secured by a peg or rivet, the hole for which has been drilled from the opposite sides of the metal. The entire length of this object is nearly four inches and a quarter; but the point is broken off. Its greatest width is one inch and seven-sixteenths; and it weighs about one ounce and three-quarters.

"The human remains have evidently undergone the process of cremation, and are much cracked, broken, and contorted. The urn in which these relics were contained, must have been of considerable size, a fragment of the base enabling us to decide that that part was four inches in diameter. The vessel is hand-moulded, the decorations dotted on with a wooden point; and the embellishments on the upper edge are particularly worthy of observation. The paste consists of clay with a slight admixture of angular pieces of stone; and is imperfectly baked, or rather burnt, on the exterior surface.

"The human bones from the second barrow have also suffered cremation; and the unornamented fragment of the sepulchral urn presents the same general features as the first mentioned vessel.

"These recent discoveries in Lancashire are valuable additions to those detailed in vol. xv, pp. 231-236, of our *Journal;* supplying, as they do, a connecting link between the stone and bronze periods, and displaying implements and fictile adornments of a highly interesting character."

Dr. Kendrick also exhibited the hilt of a page's sword, recently dug up in a field at Winwick. The pommel and shell-guard are of cast brass, displaying hunting subjects, etc. A small fragment of the triangular blade is still attached to the tang. The date of this may be assumed to be of the commencement of the eighteenth century. In the second half of the eighteenth century, page's swords were at times provided with grips of Dresden porcelain.

Mr. W. Calder Marshall, R.A., exhibited a bronze circular matrix of a seal, one inch and one-sixteenth diameter. Device, a bearded androgynous bull attended by two sucking calves: legend, + S'MIKIEL DE RIVIRE LE ROVCI. Apparent date, close of the thirteenth century; but some doubts have been expressed as to the authenticity of the matrix.

Mr. W. H. Forman exhibited a knife and fork in a sheath, to be worn at the girdle, as described in Mr. Syer Cuming's paper read before the Association, December 8, 1858. The sides of the silver hilts are elegantly sculptured with floral designs, the cavities being filled with translucid enamel of different hues. The upper portions are cruciform, terminating in little gilded vases. On the edge of both hilts are graven the initials M.V.K. The iron blade of the knife is about three inches long, with a broad obtuse point, and stamped with the manufacturer's mark, a low crown. The silver fork is of peculiar contour, the double prong resembling the bowl of a spoon with the centre cut away. The case in which these choice objects are contained, is about eight inches long, and consists of two receptacles of cuir-bouilli covered with stout shagreen. The date may be assigned to the middle of the sixteenth century.

Mr. Forman also laid before the meeting a silver-hilted knife and fork in sheath of polished shagreen accoutred with silver rim and chape. The knife-hilt represents Mercury, or more probably his son Hermaphroditus, in Roman costume, with a spear in his right, and a hunting horn in his left hand; a sword by his side, and attended by a dog. This haft may be compared with one of ivory, described in vol. xiv, p. 358. The iron blade measures four inches and three-eighths in length, and bears the mark of a bill and crescent. The haft of the fork consists of a most elegant figure of Diana with bow and quiver depending at her back. The sheath is adapted for the reception of three articles, viz., a knife, fork, and bodkin (now lost); the apparatus of a hunter of about the middle of the seventeenth century. These curious objects are said to be of Augsburg manufacture; and were purchased, a short time since, at Frankfort.

A further contribution from Mr. Forman was a rare and beautiful little knife and sheath, doubtlessly wrought as a present for some Hungarian noble. The sheath is a rich example of *repoussé-work* in silver; the embellishments consisting of medallion profiles of a German emperor (? Leopold I), arms of Hungary surrounded by the collar of the order of the Golden Fleece, surmounted by the imperial crown; figure of the blessed Virgin, the patron of Hungary, and of another saint; and flowers, leaves, and tendrils; the field being covered with deep blue enamel. The silver rim is engraved with hearts, the chape with flowers. The iron blade is full three inches in length, and stamped with three crosses like those on sir Francis Drake's knife, given in vol. xv, p. 349; and the pistol-shaped hilt is silver repoussé and blue enamel; the devices being flowers of the forget-me-not, Cupids, and three-quarter busts of a lady. This *bijou* is stated to have formerly belonged to Horace Walpole, and was afterwards in the Bernal collection, at the sale of which, in March 1855, it formed lot 3377.

Mr. C. H. Luxmoore, F.S.A., produced a pair of wedding-knives in their embossed sheath of black cuir-bouilli. The hilts of both knives are of silver, with cruciform and vase-shaped terminations, richly engraved with arabesques, together with scriptural and allegorical subjects. On one is the angelic salutation, LVCAS I CAP; and the wise men's offering, MATEVS 2 C, with figures of IVSTICIA and SPES. On the other, the meeting of Mary and Elizabeth, LVCAS I CAP, and the adoration of the shepherds, LVCAS 2 CA, with figures of FIDES and CHARITAS. Both hilts are graven with the name and date of ANNE BARNARDE, 1629; but they cannot be assigned to a later period than the close of the sixteenth century. The iron blades are about five inches long. One is stamped with a pair of shears (?) and a dagger; the other (which appears to be more modern than its fellow) with an arched crown and star of six points. The sheath is a double receptacle, measuring about nine inches and three-quarters in length, and is intended for suspension to the girdle.

Mr. Pettigrew communicated the following paper

ON THE ARCHÆOLOGY OF AMERICA.

Nine volumes,[1] on various branches of knowledge, have emanated from the Smithsonian Institution since the year 1848. JAMES SMITHSON, an Englishman, and a reputed natural son of a duke of Northumberland, bequeathed his property in trust to the United States of America, to found, at Washington, an institute to bear his name, and to have for its objects 'the increase and diffusion of knowledge among men.' The trust was cheerfully accepted by the government of the United States; and in 1846, an act of Congress passed, establishing the Institution. Its organization is too well known to require any detail on my part; and the liberality evinced by the dispersion of its books to various societies in all parts of the civilized world, will ultimately, by the established interchange of publications, lead to the formation of a library of immense extent and importance in the country where the plan has originated and been carried out. Among other literary and scientific societies, the

---

[1] *Smithsonian Contributions to Knowledge.* Washington: vol. i, 1848; vol. ii, 1851; vols. iii, iv, 1852; vol. v, 1853; vol. vi, 1854; vol. vii, 1855; vol. viii, 1856; vol. ix, 1857. 4to.

British Archæological Association has been one of the first to be selected and to respond to the proposals of the regents of the Smithsonian Institution; and I have therefore thought it due to the members of our body to communicate to them some account of the contents (as far as they relate to antiquities and archæology) which have been received and placed for our use and disposal. In addition to these communications, the British Archæological Association has also had the gratification of receiving at some of its meetings, and associating with its body, one of the most eminent contributors to the Smithsonian Institution in the department of antiquities, E. G. Squier, esq., A.M.; whose researches, combined with those of Dr. E. H. Davis, on the *Ancient Monuments of the Mississippi Valley*, constitute the first, and not the least important, paper of the *Smithsonian Contributions to Knowledge*. These observations embrace a variety of topics, arranged under the several heads of, ‘ General Observations,’ ‘ Earthwork,’ ‘ Enclosures,’ ‘ Works of Defence,’ ‘ Sacred Enclosures,’ ‘ Monuments of the Southern States,’ ‘ Monuments of the North-West,’ ‘ Mounds of Sacrifice, of Sepulture, Temple Mounds, Anomalous Mounds,’ Mounds of Observation,’ ‘ Stone Heaps,’ ‘ Remains of Art in the Mounds, of Pottery, Metal, Stone, Bone,’ etc.; ‘ Sculptures from the Mounds,’ ‘ Metals, Fossils, Minerals, Crania,’ ‘ Sculptured or Inscribed Rocks.’

No general attempt towards an account of the ancient monuments of the West had been made, until undertaken by Mr. Caleb Atwater, who, in 1819, published a memoir on the subject in the first volume of the *Archæologia Americana*. Able as is this work, it yet abounds with many errors, inseparable, it may be, from a first essay on a subject of much difficulty. It has, however, led to the recent researches of Mr. Squier and Dr. Davis, and has therefore been productive of much information to the archæologist. The middle of southern Ohio was selected for the commencement of operations; it being apparently one of the centres of ancient population, and likely to yield a rich and interesting field to the antiquary. The surveys of ancient works were for the most part made by the authors in person; and the excavations of mounds, etc., were conducted under their own personal direction and supervision. Care was exercised to note down every fact which might be considered of value; and especial attention was bestowed in observing the dependencies of the position, structure, and contents, of the various works in respect to each other; and the general features of the country. No exertion, indeed, appears to have been spared to ensure entire accuracy; and the compass, line, and rule, were alone relied upon in all matters where an approximate estimate might lead to erroneous conclusions.[1] One hundred enclosures and groups of works were examined or surveyed; and about two hundred mounds of all forms and sizes, and occupying every variety of position,

[1] Preface, p. xxxiv.

were excavated.   Several thousand remains of ancient art have been thereby collected together, and are justly described as forming 'a cabinet as valuable in its extent, as it is interesting in the great variety and singular character of the illustrations which it furnishes of the condition of the minor arts, and the connexions and communications of the people by whom these monuments were erected.'

The ancient monuments of the western United States, consisting of elevations and embankments of earth and stone, erected evidently with great labour and manifest design, are spread over a vast extent of country.   Mr. Squier states them to be found on the sources of the Alleghany, in the western part of the state of New York on the east; and to extend thence westwardly along the southern shore of Lake Erie, and through Michigan and Wisconsin, to Iowa and the Nebraska territory, on the west.   There exists no record of their occurrence above the great lakes.   Carver mentions some on the shores of Lake Pepin; and some are said to occur near Lake Travers, under the forty-sixth parallel of latitude.   Lewis and Clarke saw them on the Missouri river, a thousand miles above its junction with the Mississippi; and they have been observed on the Kansas and Platte, and on other remote western rivers. They are found all over the intermediate country, and spread over the valley of the Mississippi to the Gulf of Mexico.   They line the shores of the Gulf from Texas to Florida; and extend, in diminished numbers, into South Carolina.   They occur in great numbers in Ohio, Indiana, Illinois, Wisconsin, Missouri, Arkansas, Kentucky, Tennessee, Louisiana, Mississippi, Alabama, Georgia, Florida, and Texas.   They are found in less numbers in the western portions of New York, Pennsylvania, Virginia, and North and South Carolina; as also in Michigan, Iowa, and in the Mexican territory beyond the Rio Grande del Norte. In short, they occupy the entire basin of the Mississippi and its tributaries, as also the fertile plains along the Gulf.[1]

In the region bordering the upper lakes is found a succession of remains entirely singular in their form, and presenting but slight analogy to any others of which we have an account in any portion of the globe. The larger portion of these are described as structures of earth, bearing the forms of beasts, birds, reptiles, and even of men.   They are frequently of gigantic dimensions, constituting, as it were, 'huge *bassi-relievi* upon the face of the country.'   They are numerous, and mostly occur in long and apparently dependent ranges.   In connexion with them are conical mounds, and occasional short lines of embankment, in some rare instances forming enclosures.   These animal effigies are chiefly confined to Wisconsin, and extend across that territory from Fond du Lac in a south-west direction, ascending the Fox River, and following the general course of Rock and Wisconsin rivers to the Mississippi.   To the south-

[1] Page 2.

ward, in the region watered by the Ohio and its tributaries, ancient works of greater magnitude and more manifest design are observed. Here, we are informed, are to be found numberless mounds, mostly of a conical, but occasionally of a pyramidal form, and of considerable dimensions. The latter are always truncated, sometimes terraced, and generally with graded ascents to their summits. Accompanying these, and in some instances sustaining an intimate relation to them, are numerous enclosures of earth and stone. These constitute the most imposing class of aboriginal remains, and demonstrate the numbers and power of the people who built them. Bordering on the Gulf of Mexico, they increase in size, and in regularity, and also in numbers. Traces of bricks are now found in the mounds, and in the walls of enclosures. Not far from a hundred enclosures of various sizes, and five hundred mounds, are found in Ross county, Ohio. The number of tumuli in the State may be estimated at ten thousand, and the number of enclosures at a thousand or fifteen hundred.[1] Occasional works are found enclosing as many as four hundred acres. The magnitude of the area enclosed, is not, however, always a correct index of the amount of labour expended in the erection of these works. Thoughout the West, the enclosures are called 'Forts.' Some are possessed of features implying a military origin; whilst others appear to be connected with the superstitions of their builders, and other objects now not very apparent. The square and the circle, separate or in combination, were the favourite forms among the mound builders.[2]

The earthworks forming sacred enclosures are distinguished in general by the small dimensions of their circles. Their character is thus described : 'They are mostly regular in their structure, and occupy the broad and level river bottoms, seldom occurring upon the table lands, or where the surface of the ground is undulating or broken. They are usually square or circular in form : sometimes they are slightly elliptical. Occasionally we find them isolated, but more frequently in groups. The greater number of the circles are of small size, with a nearly uniform diameter of two hundred and fifty or three hundred feet, and invariably have the ditch interior to the wall. These have always a single gateway, opening oftenest to the east, though by no means observing a fixed rule in that respect.'[3]

The most extraordinary earthwork discovered at the West, is what

---

[1] Page 4.
[2] The peculiarities connected with these forms would seem to point out, in an especial manner, the several uses for which they were designed; and the reader will find these well carried out in chap. ii. of this memoir. Without the assistance of plans, it would be very difficult to display the ingenuity that has been exercised in building them for purposes of defence, to which they appear unquestionably to have been assigned.
[3] Page 48.

is called 'The Great Serpent.' It is situated upon a high crescent-form hill or spur of land, rising a hundred and fifty feet above the level of Brush Creek, which waters its base. According to the form of the hill, and occupying its very summit, it is said, is the serpent; its head resting near the point, and its body winding back for seven hundred feet in gradual undulations, terminating in a triple coil at the tail. The entire length, if extended, would be not less than a thousand feet.[1] In Pick-away county, Ohio, is an earthwork exhibiting the form of a cross; and in Licking county another, giving the form of an alligator or large lizard. These constitute the only earthworks yielding the forms of animals, etc., observed in Ohio. In Wisconsin they are numerous; but the purposes to which they are attributed are different in their nature, according to the views of Mr. Squier and Dr. Davis. In Wisconsin they occur usually in considerable numbers, in ranges, upon the level prairies; whilst those of Ohio occupy elevated and commanding positions,—'high places,' as if designed to be set apart for sacred purposes. An 'altar,' it is remarked, if we may so term it, is distinctly to be observed in the oval enclosure connected with the 'Great Serpent,' one also in 'The Cross,' and another in 'The Alligator.'[2] The conclusions drawn from a consideration of the foregoing monuments are that, as by the magnitude of their size they cannot be regarded as temples in the general acceptation of the term, they were probably, like the great circles of England, and the squares of India, Peru, and Mexico, the sacred enclosures within which were erected the shrines of the gods of the ancient worship, and the altars of the ancient religion. They may have embraced consecrated groves, and also, as in Mexico, the residences of the priesthood. They may also have been secondarily designed for protection in time of danger.

The monuments of the southern states have not yet been adequately explored; but labourers are engaged in the field, from whom a rich harvest may be anticipated. Mounds abound from Florida to the Texas. They are usually of great dimensions, and occur with extraordinary regularity. Enclosures, on the other hand, are comparatively few, especially such as would be assigned to a military origin. At Seltzertown, near Washington, is a mound of singular construction. It forms a truncated pyramid, six hundred feet long by four hundred feet at the base, and covers nearly six acres of ground. It is forty feet in height, and is surrounded by a ditch averaging in depth about ten feet. It is ascended by graded avenues. The area on the top is about four acres. Near each of the ends is a large conical mound. Eight others are regularly placed at various points, measuring from eight to ten feet in height. Human bones were discovered by the washing away of the sides of this structure. Since the examination made by Mr. Squier and Dr. Davis, this mound

---

[1] Page 97.   [2] Page 101.

has been more particularly examined; and Dr. Dickeson states that in it were found vast quantities of human skeletons, numerous specimens of pottery, vases filled with pigments, ashes, ornaments, etc.   On the north side the mound was found to be supported by a wall of *sun-dried bricks*, two feet thick, filled with grass, rushes, and leaves.

The monuments of the north-west vary in their character from those of the southern United States, the mounds partaking of 'the shape of animals, presenting a thousand singular forms and combinations.'   The effigies are situated upon the undulating prairies and level plains, and are accompanied by conical mounds and occasional lines of embankment.[1]   The country in which these remarkable works appear, is to the extent of about a hundred and fifty miles in length by fifty in width, embraced within the lower counties of Wisconsin; and extends from Prairie du Chien on the Mississippi, by the way of the Wisconsin and Rock rivers, eastwards towards Fond du Lac on Lake Winnebago, and Milwaukie on Lake Michigan.   This forms the route of communication between the Great Lakes and the Great River.   Birds, beasts, reptiles, and the human species, constitute the forms of the effigies upon mounds circular, square, and oblong.   The circular rarely exceed fifteen feet in height; the parallelogram are sometimes upwards of five hundred feet, and seldom less than a hundred in length.   They are, however, of small height, and occur in groups or ranges.[2]   Some of these mounds have been opened, and found to contain human remains.   The position of the skeletons indicated that the bodies had been placed upon the original surface previous to being heaped over.   There was no appearance of excavation beneath the surface in any of the interments; and it has been suggested that the human remains found were deposited by the existing tribes of Indians, for it is known that the Indians to this day bury in these structures, conceiving that they were originally designed for that purpose, although they possess no tradition respecting their origin.   On the other hand, a belief has been expressed that the mounds in the form of animals were made by the '*Great Manitou*,' and are indicative of a plentiful supply of game in the world of spirits.   They are regarded with reverence by all the Indians, and are never disturbed by them but for the purpose of sepulture.[3]   The most reasonable conjecture in regard to them appears to be, that their forms were intended to designate the cemeteries of the respective tribes or families to which they belonged. The plough is now breaking in upon the outlines and symmetry of these mounds, and they will soon be obliterated for ever.

The mounds of the west are arranged under four principal divisions:

[1] Chap. v, p. 124.
[2] Several plates are given representing these curious monuments, and the diversities of form which they present.
[3] Page 134.

1, altar mounds ; 2, mounds of sepulture ; 3, temple mounds ; 4, anomalous mounds. Of the relative proportion of these, some idea may be
arrived at by stating that, of one hundred examined, sixty were either
altar or temple mounds, twenty sepulchral, and the remainder anomalous.[1] The altar or sacrificial mounds were the most productive in
relics. ALTAR MOUNDS are met with principally within, or, as in more
rare cases, in the immediate neighbourhood of enclosures or sacred
places. These are all found to be stratified, and they contain symmetrical altars of burned clay or stone, upon which the remains were to be
found deposited,—all giving evidence of having been subjected to the
operation of fire. The fact of *stratification* is one which has not been
sufficiently dwelt upon ; but it is one of much interest and importance,
and deservedly recognized as such by Mr. Squier and Dr. Davis. In
their examination of the altar or sacrificial mounds of the west, they
state the stratification to be, as far as was observed, not horizontal, but
always in conformity to the convex outline of the mound. They remark
that it does not resemble the stratification produced by the action of
water, where the layers run one into another; but that it is defined with
the utmost distinctness, and always terminates upon reaching the level
of the surrounding earth.[2] The altars found were of different shapes
and sizes, but always symmetrical. The majority were of clay; but
there were a few composed of stone, and they uniformly rested upon the
original surface of the earth, though in a few instances a small elevation
of sand was made for the plan of their erection. In their formation,
these mounds were of layers of coarse gravel and pebbles, of earth, loam,
or clay, of fine sand, etc. The altar was invariably of burnt material;
and in its basin dry ashes, pottery, copper discs resembling the bosses
upon harness, were found. Above the aforesaid deposit of ashes in the
basin of the altar, a layer of silvery or opaque mica, in sheets overlapping each other, was laid ; and upon these, immediately over the centre
of the basin, a heap of burnt human bones, amounting in quantity to
what might be expected to be derived from a single skeleton. In a
section given to illustrate this examination, a skeleton was found at
about the distance of two feet from the surface of the mound. With this
no relics were met, and it was doubtless a recent deposit. Marks indicative of disturbance of the superincumbent earth and stones were also
observed, confirmatory of this opinion. Subsequent examination of
other mounds tended satisfactorily to shew that the Indians were accustomed to view the mounds with veneration, and frequently to select
them as burial-places for their deceased. Bodies have consequently been

---

[1] This comparative statement is not to be received as one that would be constantly maintained, inasmuch as the mounds were not indiscriminately selected,
but rather with a view of obtaining particular results, seeking for relics, objects
of ancient art, etc.
[2] Page 143.

found in various positions, but in no instance at any great depth. Lest any doubt should remain in regard to these interments, it may be noticed that rude implements made of bone or stone, and coarse vessels of pottery, familiarly known as common in the intercourse between the Indians and Europeans at an early period, in some, and more modern implements and ornaments, in some cases of European origin, in others, have been found in the more recent burials. These are circumstances necessary to be borne in mind, to prevent any confusion of dates in the consideration of this subject. No remains found in these mounds can be considered as decidedly belonging to the period of their formation, unless obtained from immediately beneath the apex of the mound, and on a level with the original surface of the earth. All deposits in other parts of the mound must be regarded as of more recent occurrence. The stratification of the mound, whether disturbed or otherwise, will serve also essentially to demonstrate whether the original erection has been at any time disturbed.

SEPULCHRAL MOUNDS, in their dimensions, are liable to the greatest variety: some are of considerable magnitude, whilst others are diminutive. They vary from six to eighty feet in height, but average from fifteen to twenty or twenty-five feet. They are not found within enclosures, but are more or less remote from them. Some are distinct or isolated; others are grouped or connected together. Altars are never found within them; nor are they stratified, as in the altar mounds, but homogeneous in their nature. In shape they may be considered as subject to less varieties than the altar-mounds, being mostly conical, though at times elliptical or pear-shaped. They rarely contain more than one skeleton; but instances have been found of their holding two. These are variously disposed, being sometimes contained in a sort of coffin made from the mere arrangement of unhewn logs of timber, or on sheets of bark, or in coarse matting, or in a chamber of stone; but in these cases always without cement of any kind. Examination of several of these mounds has shewn the practice of burning to have been frequent; for layers of charcoal and traces of ashes are commonly met with, and occasionally, particularly in the Southern States, urn-burial seems to have prevailed. Accompanying the skeletons, various remains of art have been discovered; thus exhibiting the ornaments, implements, and other articles used by the original builders of these mounds.

One mound, excavated in 1838, known by the designation of 'Grave Creek Mound,' deserves to be specially mentioned, as it is the only one in which more than one body was found belonging to the original deposit. It is in the state of Virginia, and forms one of the largest dimensions in the Ohio valley, being about seventy feet high, and a thousand feet in circumference at the base. There were two distinct funeral chambers: one at the base, and the other about thirty feet above. They were

formed of large logs of timber, and were covered with stones. The
lower chamber contained two skeletons ; the upper chamber, one. There
were between three and four thousand shell-beads, several ornaments of
mica, bracelets of copper, and other articles carved in stone. The
mound is conjectured to have been that of a chieftain, or distinguished
individual among the mound-builders ; and it has been suggested that
when these mounds, as is frequently the case, are found in groups, they
may be looked upon as family tombs, the larger one of which (for there
is always a principal one in size among the group) might contain the
head of the family. To find one burial over another, as is the case of
Grave Creek Mound, is similar to what we find in England in the so
denominated ' Bell Barrows,' supposed to have been produced by a modification of the Bowl Barrow, by having had an additional one placed on
the top of the other for a fresh interment. This mound has been
adverted to as an instance offering evidence of the practice of sacrifice ;
and Mr. Squier and Dr. Davis esteem the remains of a smaller or female
skeleton, in the vault of the tumulus, as of one having, along with others
surrounding it, been, in accordance with the barbarian practice, offered
up as attendants in the world of spirits upon the chieftain in honour of
whom the mound was erected. The practice was common among the
Natchez, Mexicans, Peruvians, and other aboriginal nations. That the
mounds formed the burial-places only of chieftains is apparent from the
occurrence of extensive cemeteries in various places where remains almost
innumerable are now constantly being thrown up by the plough, or
washed away by rivers ; and their extent may be inferred by the names
these places bear, as Big Bone Bank, Little Bone Bank, etc. In the
states north of the Ohio, thousands of graves occur, placed in ranges
parallel to each other. The cemeteries of Tennessee and Missouri, and
the caves of Kentucky and Ohio, are esteemed the great depositories of
the dead of the ancient people. This, however, is only to be received
as conjectural, for there exists no positive evidence upon the subject ;
and it is not unlikely, as has been suggested by Mr. Squier, that many
of the dead were burned, their ashes heaped together, and thus mounds
were constituted of their remains. Where inhumation has been simply
practised by the North American Indians, the body has generally been
found to have been placed in a sitting posture. Such was likewise the
case with the Mexicans ; and the same practice was adopted by the
Central Americans and Peruvians ; but the mode was not universal.

   The TEMPLE MOUNDS in America present to us great regularity in
their form and in their general dimensions. They are generally found
within, very rarely without, the walls of enclosures. They are pyramidal
and truncated, and have graded avenues to their tops. In the larger
ones they have successive stages, and are what are called terraced.
They cover no remains, and appear to have been solely for the performance of religious rites or ceremonies.

The ANOMALOUS MOUNDS admit of no classification. They differ individually from each other; and, not exhibiting any specific design, description is here unnecessary.[1]

The STONE HEAPS of America offer, certainly, a very rude and primæval kind of grave. They vary in size, being altogether of a very irregular character. Sometimes they consist of not more than a couple of cartloads of stones, and cover a skeleton with which, perhaps, some rude implements have been buried. They are common in Ohio and Kentucky. In the Atlantic States the Indians were accustomed to raise heaps of this description over the bodies of those who had met their death by accidents. Their formation, however, is to be attributed to accumulation, it being the practice for passers-by to add a stone to the pile; and it is worthy of remark that they are generally found near some frequented trail or pathway.

Of ARTICLES FOUND IN THE MOUNDS, it cannot be supposed that any list now drawn up of the different ornaments, implements, etc., can be regarded as perfect; for many objects of a destructible nature may have been deposited, and gone to decay. The remains offered to our notice at the present day must necessarily consist of such as are composed of substances offering resistance to the destructive hand of time: house articles in clay, bone, ivory, shell, stone, and metal, most commonly present themselves. Wooden instruments are not uncommon; but exposed to the air, they mostly are reduced to powder. Articles of dress are subject also to decomposition, and not easily preserved.

Of all the remains found within the tumuli, *pottery* offers to us the most general and the most durable examples. The making of pottery is traceable to the earliest times, and its several processes of manufacture are shewn even in the Egyptian tombs. It is worthy of remark that the pottery found in the American mounds exceeds in elegance of form, in delicacy of execution, and in fineness of composition, that which is produced by any known existing Indian tribes of the present day. They were made of fine clay mixed with siliceous matter, giving to it a durability; and by an admixture also of mica, in small flakes, conferring a rather brilliant appearance. Some specimens have a vitrified appearance, though none have been glazed. It is, therefore, attributable to the degree of heat to which they have been subjected.

In *metal* implements in the mounds of America, copper formed the principal material. Several celts or axes have been obtained, similar to those found in Britain. One of the former weighed two pounds five ounces, and was seven inches in length and four inches in breadth. At the cutting edge it was about four-tenths of an inch thick. Adzes, drills or gravers, chisels, spear and lance heads, and knives, have been found.

---

[1] I must refer my readers to the specific instances detailed in chapter ix, p. 178.

The execution of all these is rude ; and no iron or European instruments were found with them ; and the metal was found by analysis to correspond exactly with the native copper obtained from Lake Superior. Among ornaments of the same material, there were bracelets, pendants, beads, gorgets, discs, tubes, bosses, etc. Some of the bracelets were fitted to encircle the entire arm, were smooth, uniformly hammered, but had no fastening points. Some of the beads were found covered with a very thin plate of silver, which metal appears to have been of much scarcity.

In *stone*, the implements were the axe, the arrow-head, spear-head, the chisel or gouge, rings, etc. They were composed of quartz, syenite, and greenstone.

Bone furnished examples of pins, awls, chisels, bodkins, needles, rings, &c., and were derived from the deer and elk. Beads from bone were very numerous, also from shell, and oftentimes, enveloped in metal. Perforated tusks of the wolf, the wild cat, and the shark, and the claws of different animals, together with the bones of birds, were strung together, and arranged as beads and other ornaments, and it may be presumed that they also served for amulets. These, with pearls in considerable numbers, were met with in the altar tombs. Gorgets or ornaments for suspension of beautiful stones, and of various shapes, were found in the mounds. Of these, seventeen different varieties have been distinguished and figured. Scrolls and discs formed of mica have been met with, and are conjectured to have been attached to articles of dress.

SCULPTURED ARTICLES from the tombs were found to belong principally to pipes, and in these the mound builders appear to have exerted no inconsiderable degree of cunning and art. They represent the human head, and are of interest in an ethnological point of view ; the heads and figures of various animals, most of which are indigenous —the lamantin, beaver, otter, elk, bear, wolf, panther, wild cat, racoon, opossum, and squirrel. The representations of birds are very numerous, and consist of the eagle, hawk, heron, owl, buzzard, toucan, raven, swallow, parroquet, duck, grouse, and other land and water birds. Amphibious animals are found, among which frogs and toads are remarkable ; there are also serpents and turtles ; also an union of the head of a man with the body of an animal. The sculptured pipes in the altar mounds are chiefly in porphyry, and are reported to be works of art immeasurably beyond anything which the American Indians are known to produce, even at this day, with all the suggestions of European art and other advantages afforded by steel instruments. They are declared to combine taste in arrangement with skill in workmanship, and to be faithful copies, not distorted caricatures from nature. They are esteemed as displaying not only the figures and characteristic attitudes, but, in some cases, the very habits of the objects represented; and, as far as fidelity is concerned, many of them would seem to deserve to rank by the side of the best efforts of the artist naturalists of our own day.[1]

SCULPTURED TABLETS have been found in the mounds, and although some of the characters depicted upon them have been, by some, looked upon as hieroglyphics, there does not appear to be reason to regard them as approaching to anything like a system or alphabetical arrangement.

The decay of HUMAN REMAINS, and their inability to withstand the effects of superincumbent pressure, have almost entirely precluded the possibility of arriving at anything like the definite character of the people living at the time of the erection of the mounds. In all the researches made, one skull only was obtained not too much crushed to give us any real information, and this head has been figured and described.[2] It was obtained from a mound in the valley of the Scioto, about four miles below the city of Chillicothe. Its most striking feature is ‘its extraordinary compactness or roundness.’ Dr. Morton examined it, and considered its features characteristic of the American race, but more particularly of the family which he denominates the *Toltecan*, and of which the Peruvian head may be taken as the type. He has given its measurements, and in his collection there are several other crania said to have been derived from the mounds, accounts of which will be found in his ‘Crania Americana.’ Some of these, however, may be suspected of belonging to a more recent period than that of the original mound builders.

From the preceding summary, principally derived from the first volume of the ‘Smithsonian Contributions,’ Mr. Squier and Dr. Davis arrive at the following conclusions as to the probable character and condition of the ancient population of the Mississippi valley : ‘ That it was numerous and widely spread, is evident from the number and magnitude of the ancient monuments, and the extensive range of their occurrence. That it was essentially homogeneous in customs, habits, religion, and government, seems well sustained by the great uniformity which the ancient remains display, not only as regards position and form, but in respect also to those minor particulars, which, not less than more obvious and imposing features, assist us in arriving at correct conclusions. This opinion can in no way be affected, whether we assume that the ancient race was at one time diffused over the entire valley, or that it migrated slowly from one portion of it to the other, under the pressure of hostile neighbours, or the attractions of a more genial climate. The differences which have already been pointed out between the monuments of the several portions of the valley, of the northern, central, and southern divisions, are not

Page 272.   [2] Plates XLVII and XLVIII, pp. 288-290.
1860   41

sufficiently marked to authorize the belief that they were the works of separate nations. The features common to all are elementary, and identify them as appertaining to a single grand system, owing its origin to a family of men, moving in the same general direction, acting under common impulses, and influenced by similar causes.' "[1]

FEBRUARY 22.

T. J. PETTIGREW, ESQ., F.R.S., F.S.A., V.P., IN THE CHAIR.

Thanks were voted for the following presents:—

To the Canadian Institute. For their Journal, January 1860. 8vo.

To the Publisher. Gentleman's Magazine for February. 8vo.

Mr. Wentworth forwarded the following order, issued during the plague, in 1665—

"West Ridd. ⎱ To the Constables of Barneslay, Darton, Wooley & Bretton.
Comit. Ebor. ⎰   To be sent to each other with speed.

"By vertue of an order from severall of his ma[ties] justices of y[e] peace for this ridd. By meanes of the continuance of the plague, which by the immediate hand of God is still continued at London & several places in this rydeing, to the danger of the countrey, It is thought fit & accordingly ordered, that not only y[e] ward, but also the watch, be still continued within this division of the sayde rydeing untill upon good cause it be ordered to the contrary; & that the same be p'formed by every householder in p'son, or by a sufficient man for that purpose; & if any p'son refuse or neglect the same, then the constable of each towne is hereby ordered to convort (*sic*) such p'son before the next justice of y[e] peace, to be bound over to the next sessions. And it is further ordered y[t] if any householder shall receive any p'son or p'sons y[t] comes (*sic*) from any infected or suspected place for the same, then the constable of each towne is not only to secure such p'son as comes from any infected or suspected place, but also such p'son as shall receive him, her, or them; & cause y[e] house where they are, to be shut up untill such time as they shall receive order from the next justice of the peace for theire reliefe.

"You are likewise to give notice to all p'sons charged with foot and armes within your constabularies, belonging to s[r] Thomas Osborne, that theire souldiers appeare at Ringstone Hill upon the twenty-sixth day of October, by nine of the clocke in the forenoone, before maior John Beverley, muster-master for this county, to be mustered; or otherwise sende sixpence for each foot soldier, to be payde to the sayde muster-master according to act of parliament. And by so doing theire appear-

[1] Page 301.

ance at this time may be excused. And you are to informe all principall bearers within your constabularies, that they are desired to lay up and keepe the caps and coats provided for theire souldiers, y^t they may not be used at any other times then they are summoned to appeare with theire armes. Hereof you are not to faile, as you will answer the contrary. Dated the 17th of October, 1665, by me,

"JOHN ADAMS."

Mr. J. J. Briggs made the following communication:

DISCOVERY OF REMAINS AT SYSONBY, NEAR MELTON MOWBRAY, LEICESTERSHIRE.—It appears that in June 1859, some men were digging for gravel, in a field upon the farm of Mr. Wright, of Sysonby, near Melton Mowbray, when they came upon some antiquarian remains of interest. The field lay sloping towards the west. In pursuing their labours the men found several human bones and spear-heads, a ring, part of a buckle, and boss of a shield. The buckle is made of brass, the spear heads and boss of iron. There was no barrow or tumulus over the remains. No coins were found. There is no tradition connected with the place. It appears from a communication from Mr. Latham, of Melton Mowbray, that about thirty years ago, some men in digging for gravel in the parish of Saxby, about four miles from Melton Mowbray, discovered several very interesting articles apparently Saxon; spear-heads, bosses, beads, buckles, etc., an account of which was written and published by the rev. Mr. Gresley, Overseal, near Ashby-de-la-Zouch, with illustrative etchings.

Mr. Sim sent for exhibition an extensive collection of antiquities derived from researches made in Lanarkshire—Ancient British, Roman and Mediæval. They were arranged and explained by Mr. George Vere Irving, and illustrations of them will appear in future numbers of the Journal.

Mr. Bateman's Anglo-Saxon antiquities found near Caistor, Lincolnshire, noticed at a former meeting of the Association, were produced, and some have been figured on Plate 23.

Fig. 5 represents a bronze pin for the hair, with three small triangular shreds of the same metal, attached by a ring for the purpose of making a tinkling sound. The ornaments exhumed from the Livonian graves by Dr. Bahr, and now in the British Museum, abound with these tinkling plates, but as far as Mr. Bateman knows, no example found in England has yet been published; and only one pin of a similar character found in Denmark is figured in Worsaae's Afbildninger af Danske old Sager, Fig. 182.

Fig. 6. Plate 23, represents a pair of the so called girdle hangers of bronze with traces of gilding. They are both ornamented alike, and the transverse striæ at the top are quite as confused as appears in the drawing.

Fig 7 is a fibula of silver-gilt, ornamented with niello and settings of garnet or red glass. The fretted pattern is confused as represented, and conveys the idea of an unartistic but careful workman attempting to follow an intricate geometrical pattern, the principle of which he was unacquainted with; the effect is, however, good.

There were, besides these specimens herewith illustrated, a small bronze buckle; a bronze beaded ring; a bronze fibula, the surface silvered, a small boss in the centre and fastenings for the pin behind; a bronze ring fibula of rather coarse work, the iron pin wanting; an iron spear with an unusually contracted socket, part of which is broken away, and it may have been a little larger; an iron key, which may be compared with one in Mr. Neville's *Saxon Obsequies*, plate 39; and another in the *Inventorium Sepulchrale*, p. 171; two plain iron rings, two and a quarter and three inches diameter, and a necklace consisting of forty-six beads of amber, and twenty-one of variegated glass or porcelain.

Subsequently to these exhibitions to the Association, Mr. C. Roach Smith has figured many of the articles, and they are to be seen in the *Collectanea Antiqua*, vol. v, part iii, plates xii and xiii. Of the radiated fibula (fig. 7), Mr. S. says, " they are common in the Frankish graves of France and Germany, but comparatively rare in the Anglo-Saxon cemeteries. No example, in the burial places of Kent in which excavations had been made by Bryan Faussett occurring, and only one in Cambridgeshire, at Little Wilbraham, explored by the hon. R. C. Neville." One was found in a grave near Folkestone (*Collectanea Antiqua*, vol. ii, plate 50, fig. 3), another at Osengal (*Collectanea Antiqua*, iii, plate 6, fig. 2); and a third lately at Harietsham, deposited in the Charles Museum at Maidstone. A portion of another is referred to by Mr. Smith, as found at Chessell Down, Isle of Wight (Hillier, *Hist. and Antiq.*, p. 32). Mr. Smith entertains an opinion that the radiated form of fibula is of an earlier date than the cruciform.

The following paper, by the rev. Edmund Kell, giving an account of a recent discovery at the Roman villa at Carisbrooke, Isle of Wight, revised from descriptive notes submitted to the Association at the Newbury Congress, was laid before the meeting.

" Until within a few years it had been the opinion of antiquaries generally, that the Romans resided very little in the Isle of Wight. Sir R. Worsley, sir H. Engelfield, the rev. R. Warner, and others, historians of the Isle, either ignored any traces of their residence, or limited those simply to half a dozen Roman coins found at Carisbrooke. The successive discoveries of Roman coins since the date of their publications amounting at Shanklin to six hundred in an ampulla; in Barton Wood, near Osborne, to a gallon measure of them; to one hundred and fifty others from various parts of the Isle, now deposited in the Museum at Newport; with others in private collections, have tended to shew, that probably few parts of England of equal extent are more prolific of Roman coins than the Isle of Wight. Independently of these coins and of various Roman relics found in the Isle of Wight, the discovery of a Romano-British pottery at Brixton, and of the sites of the scattered relics of two Roman villas at Clatterford and Brixton, recorded in the *Journal* of this Association, 1856, vol. xii, p. 141, have led to the conviction of a much larger Roman occupation than had previously prevailed. Newport, itself, the ancient Medina, was probably of Roman origin. Several Roman roads have been pointed out, and it is certain from the sculptured Roman stones in the ancient Roman station of Clausentum near Southampton, that the Romans quarried both on the north and south of the Isle of Wight. But though these evidences of Roman occupation have crowded upon us of late years, there was still wanting more of that decidedly ocular proof which should satisfy the still doubting antiquary. That proof has been lately afforded by the discovery of a Roman villa, in good preservation at Carisbrooke, and it is to a brief sketch of this discovery that I now call the attention of the Members of the Association.

"This Roman Villa was discovered by William Spickernell, esq., on the 28th of April, 1859, at the bottom of the vicarage field, about a quarter of a mile east of the scattered relics of the Roman villa at Clatterford. Whilst observing the operations of some workmen excavating the ground for the foundation of the vicarage stables, he perceived some Roman tiles among the upturned earth, and having obtained the permission of the vicar, the rev. E. B. James, to make any investigation he desired, he cut trenches in various directions, until he had arrived at the outer walls of the villa, and ascertained its dimensions. On the day following the discovery, Mr. Spickernell, knowing the interest I had taken in the Roman antiquities of the Isle of Wight, kindly acquainted me with the discovery, and I have had frequent opportunities since that period by personal inspection of verifying the information which I now offer of the villa, for the particulars of which I am mainly indebted to William Spickernell, esq.,[1] and to Dr. Wilkins, a well known and able antiquary in the Isle of Wight.[2]

"The villa is from one hundred and ten to a hundred and twenty feet long, its northern side being forty-eight feet broad, and its southern side sixty-four feet broad. Its floors at the north were six feet below the level of the turf, gradually diminishing with the slope of the ground to three

---

[1] Vide letter to the *Hants Advertiser*, on the Roman villa at Carisbrooke, August 27, 1859.

[2] As Dr. Wilkins and Mr. Brion are about to publish *An Exposition of the Geology, Antiquities, and Topogrgphy of the Isle of Wight*, to be illustrated by plates of the tessellated pavement and other antiquities discovered at Carisbrooke, it has not been thought necessary to illustrate Mr. Kell's paper; but in justice to Dr. Wilkins and Mr. Brion, to refer our readers to their publication.

feet at the south. The walls were about two feet thick and were built of chalk, the outer ones being faced with flint. Painted plaster on their first discovery was found on many of the walls, and cement moulding may still be seen skirting several rooms.

"The villa fronted the south, and was opposite Carisbrooke castle, which no doubt then existed, as it is of ancient British origin, and Roman bricks have been found in the interior; there appears to have been about twelve rooms, arranged with considerable regard to convenience; three on the south, the atrium — two on each side, one on the north of the atrium, and three at the northern side of the villa. The three on the south side of the villa cannot now be made out, in consequence of the vicarage stables being built on them. They had a kind of cement floor. The westward one appears to have been the sudatorium, having a hypocaust under it, and contiguous; outside the stabling and at the south-western extremity of the atrium was the bath, having also a hypocaust beneath it, visible through a small hole made accidentally by the workmen. The bath is in good preservation; it is semicircular; its height is about sixteen inches, and its greatest length seven and a half feet. Three stone steps near it descend to a part which has various indications of having been the site of the furnace. Beyond the three rooms on which the stable stands is the atrium, the floor of which was formed of roughly formed red brick tesseræ, without any plan. It is not quite clear what the exact dimensions of the atrium were, but Dr. Wilkins, who enjoyed the best means of examination during the excavation, considers that it occupied two rectangular shaped spaces, which were nearly of the same width from north to south. The upper rectangular space was only about twenty-four feet from east to west, whilst the lower rectangular space was forty-six feet from east to west, occupying very nearly the whole breadth of the villa. The length of the atrium in its greatest extent was thirty-eight feet. Supposing, then, the whole of this space to have been the atrium, at the upper end of its western side was an entrance into a small room, paved with eight inch red tiles, which conducted to long narrow apartments north and south of it, which were probably dormitories. The atrium opened on its north side into a large square apartment twenty-two feet by twenty-one feet, paved with one inch tessellæ, which may have been the dining room. There is some appearance of accommodation for a stove at the west of its entrance. On its north side is an opening into a smaller room with a cement floor, probably another dormitory. The dormitories varying in length from fourteen to thirty-one feet, were from nine to ten feet wide. The entrance from the atrium to the eastern side of the villa was into an apartment twenty-four feet long and nine feet in width, which had a room of similar width on its south, and an apartment of fourteen feet square on its northern side; in this apartment there is a projection four feet square from what I have considered as the dining room. That apartment formed the gem of the villa, having in it a beautiful tessellated pavement. The fine tesseræ of which this pavement is composed are of white, black, blue, and red colours, and are worked into parallelograms and other figures with scrolled or chain-like borders, enclosing the lotus flower and leaves. In the centre of the pavement are a beautiful vase and flowers. The borders are wide, and are composed of coarse white and red tesseræ. On one side of the room portions of the plastering, which was painted in panels, remain; among the fragments on the ground, pieces were found, having flowers, leaves, and other figures in various colours of a bright hue. I have not seen any tessellated pavement of this pattern, but the chain-like bordering resembles a part of the pavement at Bramdean in Hants, and portions of the pavements found at Aldborough.[1] From the hollow sound proceeding from the floor of this apartment, it is not improbable that flues are extended beneath it.

"There are no marks of doors on the north side of the villa. A long wall of about sixty feet extends on the western side from the vicinity of the bath, which probably inclosed outer offices of some kind. The villa was covered with stone roofing tiles, many of which were found with the nails sticking in them. They were cut in angular ornamental shapes, and, composed of a similar stone to Portland, and must have formed a handsome roof. There were six large square stones found in the villa, four of them connected with the atrium, which have been supposed to have formed the foundation of the pillars which supported a roof.

"The articles discovered in the villa have not proved of great value. Among them were three Roman coins, a Constantinus, a Claudius, a Posthumus, and a few of later times, as a silver penny of Edward. So many Roman coins have been found at Carisbrooke, that it was expected more would have been turned up. Besides the coins were found iron and bronze rings, hinges, knife-blade, ladies' bone hair pins, some nails eight or nine inches long, portions of querns and mortaria, window and other glass, many pieces of pottery, consisting of fragments of urns, pateræ, etc. Wood ashes in various parts. There were besides, as is usual in Roman villas, abundance of oyster shells, with deer horns and the bones of other animals, as sheep, etc.

"The tessellated pavement at the principal room and the bath have fortunately been protected from the weather by sheds, and it is hoped that the intention originally entertained of roofing over the Villa, may still be effected."

[1] See Woodward's *Hampshire*, p. 128. Smith's *Reliquiæ Isaurianæ*, plates 12 and 14.

MARCH 14.

T. J. PETTIGREW, F.R.S., F.S.A., V.P., IN THE CHAIR.

The following were elected associates :

A. Bingham Trevenen, esq., 8, Danes Inn, Strand.

Rev. Jno. James Moss, M.A., Upton Parsonage, Birkenhead.

Henry Gray, esq., 37, Gloucester Street, Warwick Square.

Thomas Page, esq., C.E., Tower Cressy, Campden Hill.

Thanks were voted for the following presents :

To the Treasurer, for Emblems of Saints, by which they are distinguished in Works of Art. By the Very Rev. Dr. Husenbeth. 2nd edition. London, 1860 ; 8vo.

To the Editor. Lettre de l'Abbé Haimon sur la Construction de l'Eglise de St. Pierre-sur-Dive en 1145. Par Leopold Delisle. Paris, 1860 ; 8vo.

To the Society. Transactions of the Historic Society of Lancashire and Cheshire. Vol. XI. Liverpool, 1859 ; 8vo.

To the Authors. An Analysis of Ancient Domestic Architecture in Great Britain. By F. T. Dollman, and J. R. Jobbins. Part IV. London, 1860 ; 4to.

To the Publisher. Gentleman's Magazine for March, 1860 ; 8vo.

Dr. Kendrick sent for exhibition, an Egyptian papyrus which had been presented to the Warrington Museum by the late Colonel Thomas Legh. It was obtained from a mummy cave at the Memnonium at Thebes, and was contained within a wooden case representing an Osirian figure, measuring seventeen inches in height, and resting upon a block as a pedestal.

Mr. Pettigrew described the papyrus, which was in the hieratic character, and consisted of some portions of the Great Funereal Ritual, usually denominated, *The Book of Gates concerning the Manifestation to Light*. The name Mr. Pettigrew read *Onkhf-n-Khons*. The MS. measured 3 feet 4¼ inches in length and 9½ inches in breadth, and the writing was arranged in four columns, the heads of the divisions in the ritual being distinguished by a red colour. The deceased was in one compartment represented making offerings of incense, food, etc., and a libation of wine to Osiris, who, with his accustomed emblems, was seated before him.

Mr. Pettigrew exhibited two wooden cases which had contained papyri and offered the Osirian character, and also three papyri from his own collection. One measuring twenty-six inches by six, gave a coloured representation of the judgment scene, and related to an individual whose name reads Patshopefbai. This papyrus was in linear hieroglyphics.

Another, very small, taken from the neck of a mummy, he had unrolled consisting of a very small extract from the ritual, and expressed in the hieratic character, measured only four inches square. The third papyrus was an unopened one in the Coptic character.

Mr. Thomas Wright produced an iron box, found at Wroxeter, exhibited by him on a former occasion, which he had had sawn through, and it was found to be filled with wood, in four several compartments. This object will be further examined and figured with other antiquities from Uriconium.

Mr. W. H. Forman exhibited a steel plaque, eight inches and three quarters high, by eleven inches and three quarters wide, which has apparently formed part of a German coffer of about the middle of the sixteenth century. It is engraved with rich and elegant designs upon a field pounced with dots. In the centre is a forest scene with two bears attacked by four collared dogs, and two huntsmen wearing salades, tunics, high boots, etc., armed with spears, with cross-guards just below the blades. The broad arabesque border has at each corner a circle, and at each side an oval containing a stork or other bird. Above is an oval with a fool's head, in profile, the long tongue thrust out towards a little bird, and the cap accoutred with cascabels. Below is another oval with a wolf *courant*. It may be remarked, that whilst representations of boar hunts are abundant, those of bear hunts are rarely met with, a fact which adds greatly to the value and interest of this beautiful plaque.

Mr. H. Syer Cuming exhibited a curious and well executed piece of French embroidery on white silk, representing a three-quarter bust of the Virgin. A red mantle covers the head and falls about the person, but is open in front so as to expose a blue dress edged with point lace. Above the mantle is placed a rich crown, around the throat is a necklace, and the left hand presses the breast. In the distance is a city and landscape with male and female figures; the whole surrounded by a projecting oval wreath of narrow leaves formed of green silk *filigrane;* and beyond, in each corner, is a cherub's head in relief with expanded wings. The Virgin is probably copied from a picture of the fourteenth or fifteenth century, but the actual date of execution cannot be earlier than the first half of the seventeenth century. This piece is about thirteen inches high by ten wide, and is preserved in a carved wooden frame, of equal, if not superior, antiquity to itself. It forms an interesting addition to the examples of needlework already produced, and noticed in this journal, i, 54, 175; vi, 85; vii, 164; viii, 143, 154; ix, 85; xi, 234, 337. Tapestry is described in vols. vi, 347; xii, 130; xiii, 113, 329.

Mr. Gunston exhibited a small bronze object—a human head with slender ram's horns, surmounting an annulated shaft or pillar, which formed the haft of some iron implement, conjectured to have been a corkscrew. It is of the seventeenth century, and was discovered in

boring for a well at Carshalton, Surrey.   In the *Journal* (i, 245) is engraved an ivory apple-scoop, surmounted by a cornuted bust of a jester,
and cornuted heads are also seen on the wooden nut-crackers of the
seventeenth century.

Mr. Mark Philips sent the impression of a massive gold ring in the
possession of sir W. Clay, bart., which had been found in the Thames
at Richmond, from ten to fifteen feet below the bed of the river, during
some excavations on the part of the Grand Junction Waterworks Company.   The impression gives a merchant's monogram and mark, having
at the upper part the letters H.N.R.; in the centre, I.S.M.; and, at the
base, V and A reversed.   It is not earlier than the later part of the
sixteenth, or beginning of the seventeenth century.

Mr. Geo. Vere Irving produced some additional antiquities obtained
by Mr. A. Sim in Lanarkshire.   They will be arranged with those exhibited at the previous meeting.

The following document was communicated by Mr. Halliwell, from
Thos. Serel, esq., of Wells, co. Somerset, relating to shews arranged
for the entertainment of Queen Anne in 1613, and derived from the
Wells Corporation Records.

"Welles civitas sive ⎱ Convocacō ibm. tent. xix diē Julij anno RR's
burg. in com. Som'st. ⎰   Jacobi xi.

　　　　　"Presentibus :

Mᵣₒ Will'o Bull, mᵣₑ	Mᵣₒ Marco Tabor	Henrico Foster
Thoma Southworth, arᵒ	Hugone Mead	Valen. Appowell
Mᵣₒ Thoma Coward	Robto Maise	Henrico Baron
Mᵣₒ Alex. Towse	Anthō Atwell	Rob'to Lane
Mᵣₒ Edrē Smyth	Humfrō Palmer	Will'o Atwell
Mᵣₒ Thoma Baron	Petro Cooke	Robto Brodbeard.

"Order conc'nynge a bole to bee given to the queene's maᵗⁱᵉ.——
Forasmuche as by a l're sent from the lord buishoppe, it appeareth
that the queene's maᵗⁱᵉ doth intend to come to Wells; and therefore it
is desired by his loᵖᵖ that there should bee a silver bole given to her
maᵗⁱᵉ of the price of xx*l*.; that streets should bee made handsome, and
the towne to be ridd of beggers and rogues.

"It is therefore nowe ordered that there shalbee a bole p'vided of
silver and guilt, of the price of xx*l*., to bee given to her maᵗⁱᵉ.

"Order for amending the streets of the towne.——It is alsoe ordered
that the streets within the towne shalbee pitched where need is, and
especiallie in Sadler streete.   And for the more better effecting hereof,
it is likewise ordered that the pitchers shall wⁱᵗʰ the sūpvisors of the
highe waies take vpp a stone before eu'y man's doore where it is need
to bee pitched.

"It is alsoe orderred that the conduit shalbee colored, and laid wᵗʰ
oyle, wᶜʰ is refered to the consideracōn of Mr. mayor.

"Welles civitas sive ⎱ Convocacō ibm. tent. xxii° die Julij anno xi sūp'-
burg. in com. Som'st. ⎰ dcō.

"Presentibus :

M˚ Will'o Bull, m˚	Hugone Mead	Petro Cooke
Thoma Southworth, ar°	Robto Maise	Henrico Baron
M˚ Thoma Coward	Petro Lane	Robto Lane
M˚ Jacobo Godwyn	Anthō Atwell	Will'o Attwell
M˚ Alexō Towse	Humfrō Palm.	Robto Brodbeard
M˚ Edrō Smyth	Valentin Appowell	Virtue Hunt
M˚ Thoma Baron	Henrico Foster	Will'o Tav'ner.
M˚ Marco Tabor		

"It is ordered for thentertainment of the queene's ma^tie that the
mayor and his brethren shall attend in their scarlett gownes neere aboute
Browne's gate, and the residue of the xxiiij^tie to attend likewise in p'son
in blacke gownes. And the residue of the burgesses to attend likewise
in their gownes and best apparrell. And this is to bee done by the ou'sight
of Mr. mayor, Mr. Baron, and Mr. Smyth.

"For the ou'seeinge of the armed men, Mr. Coward, Mr. Tabor,
Henrie Foster, and Will'm Atwell.

"For the overseeinge of the shewes to be made before her ma^tie, and
to bee directors, Mr. Southworth, Mr. Godwyn, and Mr. Coward; and
they to give allowance for the matter of the shewes, whether they bee fitt
or not; and eu'y companie to be contributorie as they have benne in
tymes past, to the shewes aforesaid.

"*The Order and Mann' of the Shewes by the Master and Wardens of eu'y
trade and occupac'on w^thin the Cittie or Boroughe of Welles, as it was
presented before the Queenes Matie in Welles, uppon Fridaie the xx^th
daie of Auguste anno D'ni 1613.*

"The first companie.—The hammermen wch were the carpenters,
joyners, cowpers, masons, tylers, and blacksmeths. And they presented
a streamer wth their armes, and Noath buildinge the arke, Vulcan worck-
inge at the forge, Venus carried in a charriott, and Cupid sittinge in her
lapp wth his bowe bent; a morrice daunce; the dragon which devoured
the virgines.

"The second companie.—The shermen and tuckers. And they presented a streamer wth their armes.

"The third companie.—The tanners, chaundlers, and butchers. And
they presented a carte of old virgines; the carte cou'ed wth hides and
harnes, and the virgines wth their attires made of cowtayles, and brace-
letts for their necks of harnes sawed and banged about their necks for
rich jewells. Their charriott was drawne by men and boyes in oxeskines,
calue skines, and other skines.

"St. Clement, their st., rode allsoe wth his booke; and his frier rode allsoe, who dealt his almes out of his m^{rs} bagge, wch hee carried verie full of graynes, verie plentifullie.   Acteon wth his huntsmen.

"The fowerth companie.—The cordyners, who presented St. Crispian &   (*sic*); both of them sonnes to a kinge, and the youngest a shoe-maker, who married his master's daughter.   They allsoe presented a morris daunce and a streamer wth their armes.

" The fifth companie.—The taylors, who presented a streamer, Herod and Herodias, and the daughter of Herodias, who daunced for St. John Baptiste hedd.   St John Baptiste beheaded.

" The sixth companie.—The mercers, who presented a streamer, a morrice daunce of younge children, the giant and the giantesse, kinge Ptolomeus wth his queene & doughters wch was to bee devoured of the dragon ; St. George with his knights, who slew the dragon and rescued the virgin ; Diana and her nympes carried in a charriott, who turned Acteon to a harte.

" Memorand allsoe that the same day there were invited to dynn wth Mr. William Bull, then mayor of Welles, the right hon. the earle of Worr., the earle of Tumoth, the lord busshoppe of Bath & Wells, s^r Thomas Som'st, the countess of Darbie, the lady Cary, the lady Gray, the lady Winzor, the lady Hatton, the lady Walsingh'm, the fower maydes of honor, wth other p'sons wch came accordinglie, except the earle of Worcester.

" Welles civitas ⎰ Convocãco ib'm tent. xvj^{to} die Augusti anno R. Rs.
  sive burg. ⎱
  in com. S't.   Jacobi xj°.

" Presentibus :

M^{ro} Will'o Bull, m^{re}	M^{ro} Marco Tabor	Robto Lane
Thoma Sowthworth, a^{ro}	Petro Cooke	Robto Brodbeard
M^{ro} Thoma Coward	Valen. Appowell	Will'o Atwell
M^{ro} Alexõ Towse	Henrico Foster	Will'o Taverner.
M^{ro} Edrõ Smyth		

" It is this day ordered and agreed that eu'y companie wthin this towne shall make themselues readie accordinge to the auncient orders and cus-tomes, to shewe themselues before the queenes ma^{tie}; and that eu'y companie and eu'y seu'all man wthin the companie shall contribute such som'e and sommes of money towards the said shewes as shalbee agreed vppon amongst themselues ; or in defalt of such agreem^t by them, then by the great^e p'te of the xxiiij^{tie}, vppon paine of imprisonment, and there to lie till such seu'all rates be payd and satisfied."

Order made at a meeting held 4 *March*, 1614.

" It is ordered that whereas there haue diu'se charges laid out by diu'se companyes of this towne conc'ninge the shewes presented before the queene's ma^{tie} at her late beinge there, whereof there ar diu'se somes yet remayneinge vnpaid. First, that there shalbee a gen'all callinge of eu'y companye, to geve notice what theire charges haue been, and how it have been taxed. And if vppon consideracōn had, it shall then seem fitt that the companies haue ou'charged, and cannot well noe more, that there shalbee a contribucōn made out of the com'on live hode, as it shall then seem fitt in the discretion of the mayor, masters, and burgesses, or companies; and that such thinges wch the co'valtie shall pay is to broughte into this house, and laid vp vntill such tyme as farther occasion shalbee vsed for the same."

Order made at a meeting of the corporation, 7 April, 1614.

"It is ordered that the gen'all receivor shall pay vnto Mr. Will'm Bull the some of £ix ixs., by him laid out as it appeareth by his bill now redd and shewed at this convocacōn. That Mr. Coward and the said receivor will take the paines to collecte into theire hands such things as the company of the mercers have not yett spent in their late shew before the queene's ma^tie; to be safely kept vnto the vse of the towne, if they have any further occasion to vse them."

Further notes from the corporation books, 7 Dec., 8 Jac. I.

"Liveries for the musicke."—It is likewise agreed that the musicions shall hove coates of broadcloth this yeare, which shall serue them for their liveries these 2 years; for which they shall have allowance of £iii xs. in money."

9 Jan., x Jac. I.

"Order for the musicians to have xls. p^r annum.—It is agreed and condiscinded by all the p'sons above written, that the towne musitions that nowe ar within this citie, shalbee yearlie allowed vnto them out of the com'on rents, xls. per annum, provyded that yf they doe not geve theire intendance vnto the mayor and his brethren at Christmas, Easter, Whitsondaie, and other especiall tymes of ye metynges, or shall goe forth of the towne at any of the saide tymes, then this acte to be voyd. The money to be paid yearlie at Christmas, and the receyvor to pay xls. for this Christmas last."

8 June, xvi Jac. I.

"In regard the towne hath div'se occasions to vse money, it is ordered by the consent of the mayor, Mr. Meade, Mr. Edwards, Mr. Williams, Mr. Smyth, Mr. Tho. Baron, Mr. Henry Baron, Ralph Gorway, Jos. Hill, Humphrey Palmer, Valentine Appowell, Willm. Tav'ner, Thos. Norris, & Willm Alford, that the musitions shall not hereafter have the allowance of xls. p' ann., but onely theyre coates, vntill further order be ther vppon had; and that it shalbe lawful for theym to take theyre profitt at Xmas."

MARCH 28.

T. J. PETTIGREW, F.R.S., F.S.A., V.P., IN THE CHAIR.

The following were elected associates:

Samuel Leigh Sotheby, esq., F.S.A., Forest Hill, Norwood.
George Atkinson, esq., 2, Highbury Park.
Thomas Walcot, esq., 20, St. James's Square.
William Charles Hood, M.D., F.S.A., Royal Bethlem Hospital.
Rev. John James, M.A., Avington Rectory.
Rev. Archibald Robt. Hamilton, M.A., Greenham, Berks.
Edward Greenall, esq., Grappen Hall, near Warrington.

Mr. H. Syer Cuming exhibited drawings of two Celtic swords of bronze in the Norwich Museum, one found at Woolpit in Suffolk, the other at Windsor. They each measure about twenty-one inches and a half in length, and are similar to an example in Mr. Sim's Lanark Collection, shewing the same type of cleddyr, to be found far and wide in the Britannic Islands.

Dr. Palmer forwarded a bronze blade, apparently of a bidogan or dagger, seven inches and one-eighth in length, two inches and a half of which consists of a flat tang perforated towards the end to admit a fixing rivet. (See plate 26, fig. 1.) It was found at the upper side of Newbury, whilst excavating for the railway. Bones of the Caledonian ox were discovered with it.[1]

Mr. Marr (through Dr. Palmer) exhibited a very fine bronze head of a war-spear, recovered from the Thames between Runnymede and old Windsor. (Plate 26, fig. 2). About three inches of the point is broken off, but in its mutilated state it measures sixteen inches and a quarter in length; the socket, which extends up the centre of the blade, being one inch in diameter at the base. It is exactly similar to a spear head found in the Thames off Battersea, and engraved in this *Journal* (xiv. p. 329, fig. 4). A third example, from the Thames near Datchet Bridge is described in v, 89, and xv, 229: it is twenty-two inches in length, now in the British Museum.

Mr. E. B. Bunny, of Newbury, sent for exhibition two bronze heads of Celtic weapons, discovered in the peat at Speen. One is a looped spear-head, seven inches long, of ordinary type, and demanding no special notice (plate 26, fig. 3). The other is of great interest and rarity, being only the second example of its kind that has been brought to light. In form it may be likened to a huge, lancet-shaped, barbed arrow-head, measuring ten inches and seven-twelfths in length, by two

---

[1] Examples of bronze daggers are engraved in this *Journal*, xiv, plate 13, fig. 4 ; xv, pp. 228, 329.

Pl. 26.

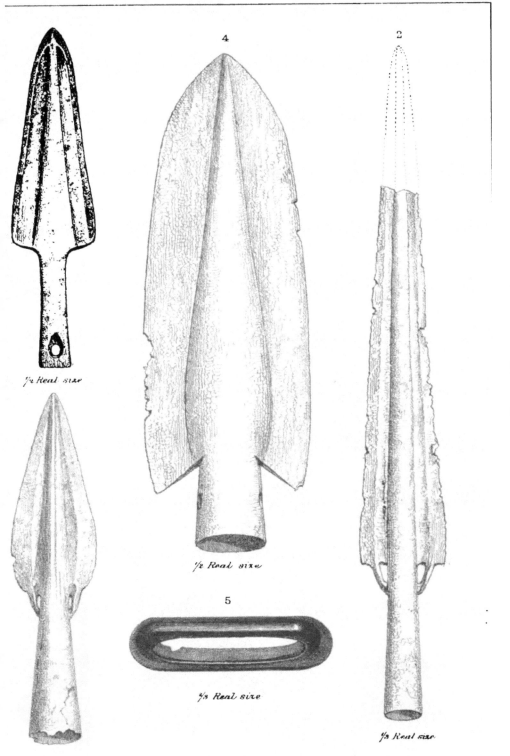

4

2

½ Real size

½ Real size

5

⅔ Real size

½ Real size

⅔ Real size

J.R.Jobbins

inches and ten-twelfths in its greatest breadth. The socket extends up the centre of the blade, and will admit a staff ten-twelfths of an inch in diameter, the holes for the fixing rivets being three-tenths of an inch in diameter. (See fig. 4.) The only other known example of this curious weapon was, in 1844, dredged from the bed of the Severn, about a mile and a half below Worcester, and is engraved in the *Journal* of the Archæological Institute (ii, 187). Its size (ten inches and a half by two inches and three-quarters) is so nearly that of the Speen relic, that it would lead to the inference they were both cast in the same mould; but the Severn blade weighs only eight ounces whilst that from Speen is eleven ounces and three-quarters troy. Mr. Syer Cuming suggested that these rare blades are not the heads of hand weapons but of heavy darts to be cast from a war engine, cognate to the classic catapulta, the title of which may be lost in the night of antiquity. Jones in his *Geiriadur Saesoney a Chymraeg* does indeed give *Tafl-beiriant* (*i.e.*, the throwing engine) as the Welsh for catapulta, but Mr. Wakeman considers this rather as an explicative than an equivalent of the Roman name. Regarding the example from Speen, Mr. Bateman says, in a letter to Mr. C. :—"I am quite at a loss to offer an opinion as to its original use. Had it not been so large, the barbs would suggest harpoon or fish-spear. I was not aware that military engines were used by the Britons so early as the age of bronze, but of course, if the Celtic name is of equal antiquity, it testifies to the fact, and, in that case, your theory will be satisfactory."

From the Newbury Museum, to which it had been presented by Mr. Bunny, was sent an interesting specimen of barbed iron head of a sheaf or war arrow, found in the peat at Newbury. It measures only one inch and eleven-sixteenths in length. (See plate 21, fig. 10.)

Dr. Palmer exhibited a singular object, wrought of highly polished jet, two inches and five-eighths in length, with a broad aperture down the centre, apparently for the purpose of its employment as a slider for securing some portion of dress. (See plate 26, fig. 5.) It was discovered eight feet below the surface in the peat at Newbury, with remains of the red-deer, roebuck, and cavern bear *(ursus spelæus)*.

Mr. Syer Cuming exhibited two oval medalets of brass, of the seventeenth century, bearing profile busts of the Virgin, coronated with the regal crown of the period. The royal diadem never ought to be placed on the Virgin's brow until her assumption, but this point has been overlooked by the mediæval artists, who have represented her as coronated at all periods of her career, as for instance, in the painting on the walls of St. John's Church, Winchester, executed in the later part of the thirteenth century, where she appears with the queenly crown, although suckling the infant Saviour (see *Journal*, ix, 10). An elegant figure of the Virgin, royally crowned as Queen of Heaven, is given in the *Journal* (i, 60) from a painting of the early part of the fourteenth century, in Lenham Church, Kent.

Mr. Adnam sent a photogragh of a Roman urn, of black earth, for containing ashes, found in Box Meadow near Aldermaston.

Mr. Thomas Wright exhibited some specimens of mineral coal recently obtained from one of the hypocausts excavated at Wroxeter, thus placing the employment of this material for heating the flues of the Romans beyond further question.

Mr. Cecil Brent exhibited a fibula (see plate 23, fig. 4), found about three weeks since, in the Martyr's Field, adjoining the Dane John, Canterbury, in cutting for the Mid-Kent Railway.   It is of an oval form, one inch and a half high, by nearly one inch and a quarter wide, made of bronze, the face plated with gold, and decorated with an outer and inner band of cross lines, and the centre set with an oval conic deep blue, or rather, black stone, supposed to be amethyst, three-quarters of an inch high by half an inch wide.   The bronze acus has a spiral hinge, moving on a thin staple, the catch for the point consisting of a thin plate with curved edge.   Mr. Syer Cuming stated that he believed only two other fibulæ of this type had yet been noticed in England, both having been discovered in East Anglia; the one at Wickham Brook, in Suffolk, in 1788 (engraved in the *Gent. Mag.*, lviii, 702), the other at Swaffham in Norfolk, in 1855, and now in the Museum of Mr. R. Fitch (engraved in the *Transactions* of the Norfolk Archæological Society).   The Suffolk fibula was accompanied by Roman coins, the latest being some of Constantine's, and from the rude sketch given of it in the *Gent. Mag.*, seems to have borne similar bands of ornaments to those on the Canterbury trinket.

Mr. C. A. Elliott produced a gold ring set with three antique intaglios, viz., a calcedony with a profile bust of Ceres, a cornelian with draped figure holding a *volumen* with both hands, and a cornelian with a dolphin.

Mr. S. Wood exhibited a third brass coin, of Tetricus the Elder, a French jetton of the fourteenth, and a Nuremberg counter of the fifteenth century, found near the site of the Winchester Palace, Bankside.   He called attention to a fictitious find of Greek, Roman, and Romano-Egyptian coins in Lawrence Lane, Cheapside, and produced examples of the pretended *trouvaille*.   Mr. Syer Cuming stated that a similar lot of coins professed to have come from the same locality had lately been brought to him; and that he had frequently been in the house of a dealer in antiquities (now deceased) when the excavators had called for "a shilling's or sixpennies' worth of Romans," meaning thereby a certain number of Roman coins, which they carried to the sewers or other works in hand, and sold as *just found*, at an enormous profit.

The rev. T. J. Williams made the following communication through Mr. Syer Cuming, relative to discoveries made in the parish church of

Penmynydd, Anglesey.—"Credival was the patron saint of Penmynydd Church, where he settled and built a church A.D. 630. With respect to himself and his brother, Rowland, in the *Mona Antiqua*, p. 154, says— "Credifael and Fflewin were the sons of Ithel Hoel, a nobleman of Armorica or Little Britain: they had their cells or churches at Penmynydd and Llanfflewin."[1] In the year 1847, whilst restoring St. Credival's Church I had occasion to carry out the floor (all of earth), to the depth of about fifteen inches, both chancel and nave. The earth close to the surface was found to be literally impregnated with human bones, without the least vestige of flesh or hair—nothing but the bare bones mixed up with the earth, with here and there a thin coating of lime just above each body, but I should say most certainly there had been *no coffin* used whatsoever. The skulls shewed that each body had been buried with the feet towards the east. Near each body there was found a *white stone*, round, and about the size of a moderate potatoe. Very many of them were found (that is, one I should say, where ever there was a body). They might have been originally in either hand, but there was no hand to hold them, so entire was the decomposition, and so promiscuously did the bones appear to be mixed up with the earth. About the same depth on the south side of the chancel arch I discovered a "put" of the same kind of stones heaped together with nothing save the earth above them. They were all much alike in size, and all *white* evidently throughout. I am not aware that I have seen stones like them, though a stray one might possibly be found among the myriads on a sea-beach, but I doubt if there are any on this coast. These white stones seem to bear reference not only to the passage in *Revelations* (ii, 17), I "will give him a white stone, and in the stone a new name written, which no man knoweth saving he that receiveth it," but also to a custom amongst the Romans (if not also the Grecians), at their judicial trials, to put a "white stone" into the hand of an acquitted criminal, and a black one into that of one condemned. So the Ancient Britons, following such custom, seem to have acquitted their deceased brethren as far as they were able, by giving them each a white stone.

"Underneath the middle of the chancel I found a small vault. Nothing was discovered there but the remains of two coffins; no part of the bodies was left (not even the bones), but only as it were a layer of fatness on a few pieces of wood. They were, I believe, a part of the old Tudor family of Plas Penmynydd, in that parish; a mansion belonging to sir Owen Tudor and his family. Right above the vault was placed a very large oblong alabaster monument; the sides finished with tracery and shields, with two recumbent figures on the top—a warrior in complete armour, helmet, coat of mail, etc., and his lady on his left side, with

[1] A paper on the early communication between Brittany and Wales, is printed in the *Journal*, iv, 229.

angels supporting the heads, and a lion (I believe) at his feet, and two dogs or some such animal at her's. This monument I removed to a small chapel on the north side of the nave and open by a fine arch to the rest of the church. This arch proves that the chapel was built at the same time with the rest of the nave, and most probably of the chancel as well. By excavating, I found a mural tomb of stone, under the north wall of the chapel, in beautiful preservation, with an exquisite arch built into the wall above it. All this must have been of the age of the church itself. I did not open the stone tomb, but lowered the floor with steps to descend right in front of it, so as to bring it altogether to light. The top of the tomb is only about level with the floor of the church. In clearing a stone bench, rudely put together around the inside of the said chapel, I discovered a stone pillar about two and a half or three feet long, round and tapering towards the top, in which was a hollow like a round bowl. I could not divine what the use of it could possibly have been, unless it was in some age to burn incense in.

" I should not forget to mention that the Tudor arms are built into the walls of this church both inside and out. On the outside, on either side the east window there appears a shield with their arms, and also inside, above a "sedile" on the south side of the chancel, showing the "*three bloody heads*" very clearly. This sedile is a cavity in the wall, and of course made when the church was first built. The present building I conclude to be of the Tudor age. Here and there on the outer wall appear stones of an older building, the zigzag of the Norman style; and farther, apparently of a very rude and still older date, a peculiar make of coarse fluting: all which proves to my mind the existence of two churches successively, prior to the present one, on the same spot."

Mr. Cuming remarked, that "the discoveries detailed in Mr. Williams's communication, presented some singular features for consideration. What was the creed of those whose bones have now been brought to light? Did they come fairly to their end, or were they the victims of some savage slaughter? are questions which force themselves upon the mind, but are difficult to answer. It is evident that a considerable number of uncoffined bodies have been inhumed at Penmynydd, each body laid east and west, and *accompanied by a round white stone.* The heap of unemployed boulders would lead to the inference that more had been brought to the spot than were required for the occasion, and that the burials did not therefore extend over a lengthened period, but were almost simultaneous, and that the people, whoever they may have been, died out together. These interments may have taken place long anterior to the erection of the church of St. Credival, or may possibly have been the immediate cause of its erection, though, in fairness to Mr. Williams it must be stated, that he believes the remains were deposited *within the*

walls of a church. Mr. Williams's explanation of the presence of the
"*white stones*" is novel and ingenious. Mr. Bateman has occasionally
observed "a sand stone ball for slinging," in the archaic tumuli of
Derbyshire (see *Journal*, iii, 351), and a "small flint sphere" has been
met with in a Scarborough barrow (see *Journal*, iv, 103), but the Penmynydd boulders, like the *salagrama* of the Brahmins, may be connected
with the passage of the soul from earth to heaven, and regarded as relics
of some ancient druidic custom, for be it remembered, that *Ynys Mon* was
the great and last stronghold of the druids, and where traces of their
faith lingered for ages after its avowed votaries had vanished from the
earth.

"The stone pillar with hollowed out top, found in the small chapel on
the north side of the nave of the church is somewhat of a puzzle. It
may have served as a *thuribulum*, but more probably, as a *stoup* or *holy
water font*, which, though generally placed in a niche, was occasionally
supported on a plinth or pillar like a *piscina*, but distinguished from it by
its imperforated bottom.

"Penmynydd (*i.e.* the head mountain), was the seat of the Tudor
family from a very early period. Tudor ap Gronow, was lord of Penmynydd in the thirteenth century, and here was born Owen Tudor, who
married Katharine, widow of Henry V, who falling into the hands of the
Yorkists at Mortimer's Cross in 1461, was beheaded, and his corpse
interred in the Grey Friars at Hereford. The remains discovered in the
vault of St. Credival's church may have been those of some ancestors of
the grandsire of king Henry VII."

Dr. Bunny placed in the Newbury Museum, at the Congress, two remarkable balls to which Mr. Pettigrew was desirous of calling the attention of the Association, and they had been kindly forwarded for exhibition. Mr. Pettigrew remarked that his late friend, Dr. Gideon Mantell,
exhibited at the York meeting of the Archæological Institute in 1846, a
ball, which is thus described : "A singular ball, composed of a nodule
of flint, coated over with a hard composition, the ground white, with
seven circular ornaments formed of incrustations of a reddish brown
colour, each circle enclosing a star of eight points. The diameter of the
ball is about two inches and a half. This unique object was found in a
sepulchral urn of coarse fabrication, in a tumulus, near the Race-course
at Brighton. It has been supposed to have been used as a charm,
possibly of the same description as the *ovum anguinum* of the Druids.[1]

This ball was again exhibited at the Bristol Institute meeting in 1851 ;
and in the catalogue, on that occasion, it is reported to have been contained in an urn of coarse, half-burnt pottery ; and the urn is stated to
have also "held ashes." One side of the ball being fractured, a stony
nucleus became visible, described as apparently a kind of chert (silicious

[1] Catalogue of Antiquities, York Volume, p. 2.

sandstone), upon which the layers of coloured paste had been attached, and the surface rubbed down to a truly spherical figure. The ball and portion of urn are now deposited in the British Museum. At the Bristol meeting another ball, of a larger size, was exhibited. It was in the possession of the rev. R. M. White, D.D., rector of Slymbridge, and is described as "a remarkable ball ornamented with stars formed of clays (?) of various colours." It was found in 1847, in cleansing the drain of the ancient moat surrounding the rectory garden of Slymbridge, Gloucestershire, adjoining the churchyard. It lay embedded in gravel, beneath the mud; and its weight was two pounds twelve ounces and a quarter. This is now also in the British Museum. The specimens are figured in the Bristol volume (p. lxv), by which they will be seen to be of precisely the same nature as those possessed by Dr. Bunny. Dr. Bunny's balls, now exhibited to the Association, are each two inches in diameter. One weighs four ounces and a half; the other, five ounces. One presents three circles enclosing stars; the other, seven circles with stars. These have all eight points; but are of diverse forms, and present ingenuity in their arrangement. One of the specimens was found at the base of Ladle Hill, Berks, and was ploughed up about thirty-five years ago. The other was found ten years later, between Inkpen Beacon and the hill behind West Woodhaye House, and was also discovered during tillage of the ground.

Various opinions were conjectured as to the period to which these balls belonged, and the purposes to which they may have been applied. They might be ancient British, Roman, or Saxon; and have been either used in a game, or in divination, or placed in an interment as an emblem of dignity or office. Their use is worthy of attention.

Sir Wm. Clay, bart., kindly sent for exhibition the ring, for inspection of which an impression was exhibited at a former meeting. It is of massive gold, weighing one ounce; and from the character of the letters engraved, and the mounting of the ring, was assigned to the commencement of the seventeenth century. The letters under arrangement, may be made to read, W. HARISV HIS MARK. It may, therefore, be regarded as a monogram, or rather polygram; and the mark of a merchant of the name of William Harrison, living in the time of James I or Charles I.

APRIL 11.

ANNUAL GENERAL MEETING.

The Proceedings, Report of Auditors, List of Associates Elected, Deceased, Withdrawn, and Erased, together with Obituary Notices for 1859, are printed pp. 163-175, *ante*.

APRIL 25.

T. J. PETTIGREW, F.R.S., F.S.A., V.P., IN THE CHAIR.

Henry Hensman, esq., 3, Garway Road, Bayswater.
George Lewine, esq., Jagerstrasse, Berlin.
were elected Associates.

Thanks were voted for the following presents-:
To the Archæological Institute for their *Journal* for December, 1859;
8vo.
To the Architectural Museum, for the Report for 1860 ; 8vo.
To the Canadian Institute, for the *Canadian Journal* for March, 1860 :
8vo.
To the Author. Supplement to the Coinage of Scotland. By John
Lindsay, esq. Cork, 1859 ; 4to.
    „   „   Ancient and Domestic Architecture. By F. T. Doll-
man, and J. R. Jobbins. No. V. 4to.
To the Publisher. *Gentleman's Magazine* for April, 1860 ; 8vo.

Mr. S. Wood exhibited the following Greek coins : 1, Tetradrachm
of Alexander Magnus (B.C. 336-324); 2, Chalcos of Philip Aridacus
(B.C. 324-317); 3, Didrachm ? of Dyrrachium (Durazzo) in Illyricum.

Mr. Oliver exhibited an arched-topped casket of wood, covered with
deep blue or black leather, impressed in gold, with richly bordered panels,
containing different subjects. On the cover is a landscape, with a distant
view of a city, on either side of which is a combat between an equestrian,
armed with a sword and shield, and a pedestrian with a spear. At each
end of the box is a tree, on one side of which stands the soldier with
his spear, and on the other is seated a man playing on a pipe, before
whom kneels a figure on whose back is perched a bird. The panel on
the back is filled with a diaper pattern, and that on the front contains
standing figures of a lady and gentleman, with birds, bees, and gnats,
dispersed about the trees and flowers. The casket is supported on four
knobs, which, with the handles and escutcheon, are of brass. One
end of the box slides up so as to permit the removal of a drawer, concealed beneath the interior bottom of the casket, which measures six
inches and three-quarters in height, nine inches and a half in length,
and six inches wide, and was probably produced in the south of Germany about the close of the sixteenth century.

Mr. Wills, Captain Tupper and Mr. Forman exhibited various specimens of large keys, keys used as signs, etc., which were referred for
arrangement and illustration in a future *Journal*.

Mr. G. R. Corner, F.S.A., exhibited the following objects lately received from Gibraltar : 1, small Egyptian pendant, of green porcelain,

representing a bunch of grapes ; 2, bronze otis, or ear of a vessel, consisting of a mask of Dionysius, surmounted by a stout ring.   It is of
rude archaic work, and may have been brought hither from Sicily by the
Carthaginians ; 3, bihamus, or double hook of bronze wire, upon which
the chains of a lancula or scale of a statera had been suspended ; 4,
blade of a bronze stilus, with its edge bevelled like a chisel ; 5, bronze
stilus with narrow lingula or spoon at one end, six inches long ; 6,
bronze implement about four inches and three-quarters long, one end being
eyed, the other spade-shaped.   It bears resemblance to a small cau-
terium discovered in a surgeon's house at Pompeii ; 7, slender bronze
pipe, of a conic form, terminating in a minute screw, five inches and a
half long ; 8, double stud, of bronze, shaped like a dumb-bell ; 9, pa-
pilla-shaped bulla, or stud of bronze, the thin shank perforated for a
rivet ; 10, bronze key, the bit adapted for a single warded lock, and the
piped stem terminating in a transverse bar ; 11, bronze ornament in the
shape of a dolphin ; 12, apparently, an inauris, or ear-ring of bronze,
one inch and a quarter in diameter, the flat sides adorned with a cable
pattern ; 13, front plate of a bronze fibula, representing a rabbit, an
animal for which Spain was once famous.   Along the side is a chevron
band, bordered with dots, and on the thigh a quatrefoil.   It is of very
late Roman, or, perhaps, early gothic workmanship ; 14, gutturnium, or
ewer, of lead, seven-eighths of an inch high.   A child's plaything ;
15, cylindrical piece of lead, five-eighths of an inch thick, one inch in
diameter at one end, and eight-tenths at the other.   It weighs two
ounces and twelve grains, and appears to be an ancient pondus ; 16,
bronze spur rowel, of six points, about one inch and six-tenths in
diameter, of the fashion of the fifteenth century, but the character of
the patina would indicate it to be of a greater age ; 17, pectoral cross
of copper, its front plated with gold, and graven with a diaper pattern.
It measures two inches and a quarter high by two inches and one-eighth
wide, with a loop at top for suspension.   Date, thirteenth century ;
18, brass matrix of a seal, in shape of the buckler of the first half of
the fourteenth century.   It is charged with five fleurs-de-lys, the verge
inscribed + : s : roi : lovrenco : davale.   This matrix appears to
belong to the class described in the *Journal*, xiv, 348 ; 19, snuff-box,
of a round form, turned out of one of the brass guns employed at the
siege of Gibraltar, July 1779, to February 1783.

Dr. Kendrick sent for exhibition a fragment of a little cross and
portions of a beam in which it had been concealed ; accompanied by a
letter addressed to Mr. Syer Cuming, in which he says :—" A friend of
mine has a large piece of the oaken lintel of the fire-place in Shakespeare's house at Stratford, one side of which is still blackened by the
smoke.   The way in which it came into his possession is so clear, that I
have myself no doubt of its genuineness.   But my principal reason for

mentioning it is, that my friend gave me permission to cut off a small piece for myself, as it had already been greatly shortened to make goblets, etc. On the carpenter sawing off the piece I chose, he laid open a rather large auger-hole, running almost through the beam, but closed and nearly filled by a plug of deal well fitted to the hole in the timber, and made fast by another plug of a smaller size being driven into it. In the space left between the end of the plug and the bottom of the auger-hole was part of a small wooden cross, apparently carved with a knife. It was carefully bedded in coarse tow, and a number of grains of barley were also taken from the cavity. In consulting the memoir of Shakespeare, by Knight, in his "*Old England's Worthies*," I find mention made, that in 1770, whilst some repairs were going on in the roof of the house of the Shakespeares, in Henley street, one of the workmen named Mosely, discovered between the joists and tiles, a MS. purporting to be the "*Spirituall Will*," of John Shakespeare, in which he professes himself a Roman Catholic, and leaves instruction for masses for his soul after death. The MS. occupied six leaves stitched together, and is printed *in extenso* in Reed's and Drake's lives of Shakespeare. Malone accepted it at first as genuine, but subsequently reversed his opinion, though I cannot clearly make out upon what grounds. It appears to me, that the question is opened anew by the discovery of the cross.

Mr. Syer Cuming observed, that "trifling as this discovery might at first sight appear, it was well worthy of record, for in it is involved much that is singular and curious. We have to consider the date of the cross, its material, the reason of its concealment within the old lintel of the fire-place, and by whose hands or orders was it so concealed? these queries are all more or less beset with difficulties, but some explanation may perhaps be found for them. The object itself resembles the simple way-side crosses of the thirteenth and fourteenth centuries, and consists of a plain quadrangular shaft supported on a flat plinth, reached by four steps encompassing it on either side. In its present fractured condition it measures but one inch and a quarter in height, and eight-tenths in diameter at the base, which retains traces of the cement wherewith it was probably once attached to some woodwork. Professor Quekett, after a careful examination of the cross, has pronounced its material to be willow, and the branch from which it was carved to be of eight years growth,—a fact which at once establishes the origin, purpose, and possibly the date of the little relic, which will be well illustrated by a short extract from a rare tract, entitled — *A Dialogue or Familiar Talke betweene two Neighbours, from Roane, by Michael Wodde, the* 20 *February*, 1554. 12mo. After mentioning the various ceremonies practised in the church on Palm Sunday, it goes on to say—" the prest at the alter al this while, because it was tedious to be unoccupied, made crosses of palme to set upon your doors, and to beare in your purses, to chase away the divel—But tell me, Nicholas, hath not thy wyfe a crosse of palme aboute her? (*Nich*). Yes, in her purse, (*Oliver*) And agoon felowshippe tel me, thinckest thou not sometyme the devil is in her tongue? Syghe not, man.' (*Nich.*) I wold she heard you, you might fortune to finde him in her tong and fist both. (*Oliver*) Then I se wel he cometh not in her purse, because the holi palme crosse is ther; but if thou couldest entreate her to beare a crosse in her mouth, then he would not come there neither." His satanic majesty could therefore no more invade a house guarded by a holy palm cross, than a witch could pass a threshold protected by a horseshoe, or the fiend *Mara* ride the steeds in a stable in which a holy stone is suspended. The little cross now before us was no doubt deposited in the auger-hole, by some devout person who received it from the hands of the officiating priest, in the old church of Stratford-upon-Avon on some Palm Sunday in the first half of the sixteenth century."

Mrs. White exhibited through the Treasurer, an abbey piece or jetton, found at Canterbury. The obverse presents the sacred monogram I.H.S., and around the legend reads AVE MARIA STELLA DEI MATER. The reverse has a cross ornamented with fleurs-de-lis, dots or pellets, etc., and the legend is repeated around. The manufacture is conjectured to be of Nuremberg, whence they principally came; the piece is thin and the brass has much lapis calaminaris in its composition. It is not earlier than the xv *sæc.* The revenues of establishments requiring much computation, introduced jettons (from jetter to throw), or counters, hence they were employed in monasteries and abbeys, and this piece may have belonged to the abbey of St. Augustine. A similar specimen has been engraved in Snelling's tract on these pieces, plate ii, No. 27.

Mrs. White also exhibited a pretty little patera of Samian ware, found at the Moat, Higham, Kent, ornamented with the ivy leaf; a paalstab from Llangollen, and a leaden figure of the Saviour from a crucifix, found in the sewer at Clerkenwell, near St. John's Gate. It is of the fifteenth century, and of rude execution.

MAY 16.

JOHN LEE, LL.D., F.R.S., F.S.A., V.P., IN THE CHAIR.

Francis Godrich, esq., 12, Sydney Place Brompton,
Henry Algernon West, esq., The Hodge, Mottram in Longendale, Cheshire,
were elected Associates.

Thanks were voted for the following presents :—

To the Society.   Proceedings of the Society of Antiquaries, Nos. 48-52, 1857-59.   8vo.

,,   ,,   List of the Fellows of the Society, May 1859.   8vo.

,,   ,,   Archæologia, vol. 38, Part I.   1860.   4to.

,,   ,,   Proceedings of the Royal Society, No. 38, 1860.   8vo.

To the Publisher.   Gentleman's Magazine for May, 1860.   8vo.

The following communication was received from the Rev. Mr. Kell.

"In a paper in the *Journal* for 1857, p. 207, I stated the existence of some Saxon bone pits at the south-west corner of St. Mary's Road, Southampton, which had been discovered in digging for the foundation of the Deanery Inn, now called the Edinburgh Hotel. These pits, dug out of clay resting on gravel, are a continuation of a large number of similar pits in the adjacent part of St. Mary's parish, which were noticed by the late J. R. Keele, esq., in the *Collectanea Antiqua*, vol. iv, p. 58; and by Mr. Atherley, *Br. Arch. Journal*, vol. v, p. 162. They prove that the ancient site of Southampton in the early Saxon times, was half a mile to the north east of that portion of the present town, as defined by the remains of its fortifications.

"A further corroboration of the existence of these Saxon bone pits, and consequently the extension of the ancient site of Southampton to St. Mary's road, has been afforded by an examination of the site on which the new houses somewhat above the Edinburgh Hotel, in St. Mary's Road, have been lately built. The elevation of the newly formed high-road four or five feet above the natural level of the ground in front of these houses precluded the necessity of making any deep excavations for them, but the excavations that were made for their foundations were sufficiently deep to reveal the site of Saxon pits of the same character as those previously found, viz.:—from six to eight feet long, and from four to six feet broad, and filled with bones of the same description of animals, and with some refuse as before discovered. From the soil dug out from the surface portion of these pits, I obtained from a labourer a Constantine I, bearing on the reverse, victory advancing, and placing her feet on a prostrate enemy, having in one hand a trophy, and in the other a palm branch. In the exergue the letters P.L.V.G. Since then, two other coins have been discovered on the same spot. One of Constantine II, having for its reverse soldiers and standard, with the legend Gloria Exercitus; the other, a penny of Offa, identifying the pits more strikingly with the other Saxon pits. It is in good preservation, and is in the possession of Mr. Henry Rayner, High Street, Southampton, who has kindly sent it for exhibition. On the obverse is the king's head with the letters OFFA. Offa is the first Mercian king to whom coinage can with certainty be assigned. It is restricted to pennies, and the ornamentation of their reverses is so varied, that Mr. Hawkins found them too numerous to be engraved in his work on the *Silver Coins of England*.

He also found them too intricate to describe, but they are of much interest and would appear to give to us in the *obv.* of some of them a portraiture of the monarch. This has been attributed to his having been at Rome, and having probably brought with him Italian artists for the work.

"Ruding represented several, and they will be found on Plates 4, 5, 27, 28, 29, and C, of his work. The example offered for our inspection is that figured in pl. 4, No. 10, but with a slight variation, inasmuch as the dots or pellets behind the monarch's head are only three in number, whilst in Ruding there are five, two being placed laterally, one on each side of the three in his specimen. In all other respects they agree. On the *obv.* there is the profile portrait of the king, and his name, OFFA. On the *rev.* a cross inclosing another cross, also crossed. Between the arms of the cross are the letters EA DH VN, representing the word Eadmund (the moneyer). Other pennies enumerated by Mr. Keele, as found in the adjacent pits and neighbourhood, were those of Coenvulf, Burgred, Ceolwulf, Aethelweard (?) Plegmund, Eadweard, Aethelstan, Eadmund, Eadred, Eadgar, and Aethelred, some silver sceattas, and one of brass.

"Tokens, etc. To these coins may be added a penny of Ceolnoth, Archbishop of Canterbury, from A.D. 830 to 870, lately found, which there is every reason to assign to the same spot, as it was purchased by Mr. Covington, a watchmaker, who lives in St. Mary's Street, from a boy who had found it on "a heap of earth" in the neighbourhood, but was not further questioned. This coin is now in the possession of J. Atkins Barton, esq. It is very thin and the legend on one part is obliterated. On the *obv.* is a full faced bust with the letters Ceolnoth. On the *rev.* a cross with the legend, Here Moneta. This coin is figured in Ruding, pl. 13, No. 7. The characters on the *rev.* are conjectured by Mr. Hawkins to present a monogram signifying, *Dorobernia Civitas.* The coins of Ceolnoth present many varieties. He filled the see from A.D. 830 to 870, and not less than twenty names of his moneyers are known."

Professor Buckman exhibited two fine gold coins of Valentinianus and Valens, lately found at Cirencester.

Few places occupied by the Romans in this country, have been more productive of coins than Cirencester, the site of the ancient Roman town Corinium. Professor Buckman and Mr. Newmarch have given, in their excellent *Illustrations of the Remains of Roman Art in Cirencester,* an extensive catalogue of the various coins hitherto discovered, reaching from Cæsar Augustus, B.C. 29, to Honorius, A.D. 423,—a period of three centuries. Among these, examples of Valentinianus and Valens occur; but no gold coin of the former is included. The present specimen may therefore probably be regarded as the first instance of the discovery of one of this emperor in this locality. Of silver and brass (especially the latter) there have been numerous examples of Valens, the brother of Valentinianus. A gold coin occurs in the list referred to (p. 153); but it differs from the example now laid before the Association, and is thus described : obv., D.N.VALENS.P.F.AVG. ; rev., VICTORIA.AVGG. Victory seated. Of this emperor there are also silver and brass. The examples now forwarded by professor Buckman may be thus described : obv., D.N.VALENTIANVS.P.F.AVG. ; profile of emperor to the right. Rev., the emperor standing holding the labarum by his right hand, and in his left a globe surmounted by a figure of Victory. In the exergue, B.T. Legend, RESTITVTOR REIPVBLICAE. Obv., D.N.VALENS.S.P.F.AVG ; profile of emperor to the right. Rev., same figures with labarum, globe, and Victory. In the exergue, KONS. Legend, RESTITVTOR REIPVBLICÆ. It may be worthy of remark that neither of these coins is enumerated in Akerman's *Catalogue of Rare and Unedited Roman Coins.*

Professor Buckman acquaints us that "these coins were found in the 'Leuses Garden,' near the S.W. corner of the camp of Corinium, a little distance within the walls. With them were also discovered several brass coins, Roman pottery of many kinds, bones, oyster shells, and the usual relics of any digging of consequence in this vicinity. The digging is now being carried on for stones, the *débris* of dwellings long since passed away, being now, as it has been for centuries before, used as a quarry, whence stone is obtained for more modern works. In getting out these stones walls of considerable thickness are frequently arrived at, within which are a confused heap of carved stones, with others, consisting of cornices, bases, and capitals, of such sizes as indicate buildings of great magnitude, and with these are intermixed the lozenge-shaped roofing-tiles, one of which, of the Stonerfield slate rock, had a "clout" form of nail in its perforation. Hand molars, which are interesting, not alone on account of the numbers, forms, and uses, but from the great variety of stones of which they are made, and the distances from which they have been brought, as thus :—1, *Andernach Stone*, a hard volcanic grit presenting a sharp grinding surface ; 2, *Old Red Sandstone*, both grey and red, also sharp silicious stones ; 3, *Old Red Sandstone Conglomerate*, the plum-pudding stone of Nimers, full of silicious pebbles, rounded ; 4, *Mill-stone Grit*, with angular bits of silicious rocks, still much used for mill-stones ; and others. The last three were probably derived from the Forest of Dean, where I fancy I have found the site of their manufacture. The pottery is more remarkable for variety than for completeness, as it is always sadly broken ; at the same time I have recently added some fine and perfect forms to the Corinium Museum. Now, as regards the gold coins, I may mention that they are extremely rare at Corinium, whilst the copper ones are very abundant. These examples are very perfect, though not of so good a style of art as are our earlier coins. The "image" is much alike on both, so also the figure on the reverse, but with different legends." Professor B. intends depositing the coins in the Museum at Cirencester, which owes much to his zealous exertions. This museum, now so rich in Roman remains, leads only to regret, upon reflection, that after all it is only an evidence of the heaps of things which have, in times past, been lost to the district.

Mr. Wills exhibited various fragments of Roman fictilia, glass, and other objects discovered by the Rev. T. A. Wills, in a field at Silchester, Hants. The most important item is a third brass of Carausius. *Obv.*, crowned bust to the right, IMP CARAVSIVS P.F. AVG.; *rev.*, Mars to the right, between the letters s.P. (Spes Publica) VIRTVS AVGGG. Exergue MLXXI.

Mr. C. A. Elliott exhibited a picture in embossed *appliqué*, on white satin, nearly twelve inches high by nearly sixteen inches wide, representing a monarch with an eastern crown, royally robed and seated in a richly carpeted tent, extending his arms, as if welcoming a lady who stands in front; following her is a female attendant, and behind the latter a male figure, bearing in his left hand a charger, or a broad brimmed hat. At the edge of the flowered carpet stands a little dog; in the back-ground is a large tree, and, in the distance, a castle or temple, with butterflies, etc., in the sky. The subject represented in this picture seems to have been a favourite with the artists of the seventeenth century; it is found on the bead basket, dated 1668, described in this *Journal* (i, 311), and there has lately been exposed for sale, in the window of a gold refiner in Old Street, St. Luke's, a large piece of embossed *appliqué* with the same story, but in which the royal tent occupies the centre of the picture, whereas, in the above, it is placed on the sinister side. This example is described by its owner as Nell Gwyn being introduced to Charles II, but Mr. Elliott's specimen is conjectured to be the first meeting of Charles I and Henrietta Maria, or that of Charles II and Catherine of Braganza. The truth would appear to be that all these pieces represent Solomon and the Queen of Sheba in the costume of the seventeenth century, and bear no allusion to English history.

Mrs. White sent for exhibition the following objects in metal, ivory, and wood:

In Metal: Roman key of bronze, the stem divided up its centre, so as to form a four-sided broach, which entered a moveable pipe in the lock, and revolved with the key as it passed the wards. The web or bit is perforated with long and short crosses and circlets, and decorated with punctures. It is looped to an annular bow, one inch and a half in diameter, which hung like a handle in front of the chest when the key was in the lock. In some respects, this specimen may be compared with two keys of much later date, described in this *Journal*, xiii, 335-338. An early key of iron, with flat sided annular bow, broached stem, and the edge of the bit dentated. Brass key, the piped stem sur-mounted by a lozenge-bow, with a boss at each point; the web is de-signed for a five warded lock. Date thirteenth or fourteenth century. These two examples were discovered at Missenden in Buckinghamshire. A leonine animal of bronze, about five inches and five-eighths long, evidently intended for the stand or support of a candle pricket, which fitted into a cylindrical socket perforating the body through the centre of the back. In general design and fabric it bears resemblance to the lavatoria of the thirteenth or fourteenth century.[1] A fragment of a bronze plaque, apparently cast and chased by a cinque-cento artist of consider-able skill. It bears a bearded profile to the right, the only remaining portion of the legend which once surrounded it is the termination of one word and the commencenent of the next, thus: ON HOBO. A German coffret of gilt metal, the sides, top, and bottom engraved with a bird, vases, foliated scrolls, etc. It has a complicated but most insecure lock attached to the cover, and stands upon four balls. Size, two inches and two-tenths high, two inches and five-eighths long, by one inch and three-quarters wide. Date, end of the sixteenth century. Half of a leaden cloth-mark, one inch and seven-twelfths in diameter, displaying the royal arms, crest and supporters; a flat ring projects from the edge, through which the rivet passed. Date, *temp*. Charles II. Found in the Thames. A watch seal of brass, the handle composed of open scroll-work, and the matrix bearing the figure of St. George overcoming the dragon. Date, second half of the seventeenth century. Mr. Cuming has a brass matrix, of smaller size, bearing the same device, recovered from the Thames, in June 1847.

In Ivory : A brace or bracer to guard the left arm of the archer from the friction of the bow-string. It is a semi-cylindrical piece of ivory, about six inches and a quarter long, with two iron studs on one side for the attachment of straps, and two perforations on the other for the ad-mission of the straps which bound the defence to the person. The front is engraved with arabesque borders surrounding the martyrdom of St. Sebastian, the patron of archers.[2] Above is a shield charged with a cross between four mullets, encircled by a wreath dividing the date, 1589. Beneath is the name of its quondam owner, IEHAN HATTE.

The archer's brace is the ectype of the Grecian peribrachionion and Roman brachiale, a defence found upon the left arm of the warriors on Assyrian sculptures, and one which may be traced through various coun-tries and ages down to the present time. Braces of cuir-bouilli were

---

[1] See an example in vol. vii, p. 137.

[2] In the Bernal collection was "a silver-gilt badge in the form of a cross-bow, set with stones, wth a whole length figure of St. Sebastian and three others; inscribed 1551, A.P., and 1554, A.P., and DONAVIT, 1565. This was worn by the captain, of the time being, of the archers' society." (See sale catalogue, p. 279.)

in use in the middle ages, and were sometimes painted with bright colours, hence, Chaucer's yeoman in the prologue to the *Canterbury Tales*, wears " upon his arm a gay bracer." There was formerly preserved at Boulton Hall, Yorkshire, a leathern bracer left by one of the followers of Henry VI, in 1463, which was embossed with a rose and other devices, and bore the words IESVS HELPE on a gilded ground. Bracers of ivory seem to date from the sixteenth century. In the Meyrick collection is a fine example in which the surface is graven with arabesques, a helmeted head in an oval, and a shield charged with a chevron between a sheaf of arrows in base, and a popinjay with the initials M.R. in chief. Strutt in his *Sports and Pastimes*, following Roger Ascham's *Toxophilus* written in 1571, says, " that it was necessary for the archer to have a bracer, or close sleeve, to lace upon the left arm; it was also proper for this bracer to be made with materials sufficiently rigid to prevent any folds which might impede the bow-string when loosed from the hand." In the *Art of Archerie*, printed in 1634, Gervase Markham writes : " These bracers are made for the most part of Spanish leather, the smooth side outward, and they be the best, sometimes of Spanish leather, and the flesh side outward, and they are both good and tolerable, and others are made of hard, stiffe, but smooth bend-leather, and they be the worst and most dangerous." The lower half of an early Hindu sacred box or vessel (shrine ?) shaped like a cup, and wrought of elephant tusk ; three inches and three-quarters high by four inches and half in diameter at top. Four subjects are carved round the outer surface, viz.; 1, Leonine mask, possibly that of Nara-Singh (man-lion), the fourth avatar of Vishnu ; 2, two-headed bird, of the crane family, whose eyes, like those of the mask, are set with black wood ; 3, head of Ganesha, the elephantine son of Parvati ; and, lastly, a unicorn mammal with crested back and long tail.

In Wood : a boat-shaped cup, of beech, four inches and three-quarters long, elaborately sculptured, in the rudest manner, with a quantity of figures, representing on one side, the adoration of the Magi, and on the other, the flight into Egypt." At one end of the cup is a half-length of St. Hubert and the cruciferous stag, and on the oval bottom is carved, A. PETIT, 1663, a name which indicates the vessel to be of French origin.

Mr. Dollman laid before the meeting three drawings relating to the architecture of the Guesten Hall, at Worcester, which formed part of the domestic buildings of the ancient priory, and is among the earliest, and perhaps, the very best examples of an ornamental roof of domestic character, and of decorated date, he has met with. He especially referred to the exceeding richness and elegance of the window tracery, the gracefulness with which the arched " wind braces " are sub-arcuated and cusped, the vigour and freedom of the stone sculpture in the corbels and the label terminations, and the purity of detail in the various mouldings of the roof and windows. The entrance porch has lately been brought to light on the removal of a house which stood at the south-west angle of the hall. It is rumoured that this most valuable and interesting example of mediæval architecture is threatened with destruction; public attention has, however, been directed to this fact, and it may be hoped that so beautiful a building may escape destruction; it calls loudly for restoration, not for removal. The Guesten Hall was built about the year 1320, by Walter de Braunsford.

An account of the examination of an Anglo-Saxon barrow on Bowcombe Down, by Dr. E. Wilkins, rev. Ed. Kell, and Mr. John Locke, was read. (See pp. 253-261 *ante*.)

MAY 30.

T. J. PETTIGREW, F.R.S., F.S.A., V.P., IN THE CHAIR.

The Rev. John Cumming Macdona, of Mossley, near Manchester, was elected an associate.

Thanks were voted for the following presents :

To the Author. Notes on Latin Inscriptions found in Britain. By the Rev. John McCaul, LL.D. Toronto, 1860; 8vo.

    ,,   ,,   Analysis of Ancient Domestic Architecture. By F. T. Dollman and J. R. Jobbins. Part VI. London, 1860; 4to.

To Mrs. Kerr. Melly E., das Westportal des Domes zu Wien. Wien, 1850; 4to.

Mr. G. R. Wright exhibited a fine piece of silver lace of butterfly pattern, three inches and a half wide, which till lately formed a portion of the trimming of a baptismal mantle, or bearing-cloth, of blue satin, which, from the year 1659, was in the possession of the Veseys of Hintlesham priory, Suffolk. The Duke of Glo'ster, in Shakespeare's play of Henry VI (1 p., a. 1., s. 3), tells the bishop of Winchester :

> " Thy scarlet robes, as a child's bearing-cloth
> I'll use, to carry thee out of this place."

And "a bearing-cloth for a squire's child," is spoken of by the old shepherd in the *Winter's Tale* (iii, 3), but, beyond the name, little is now known of this costly item of christening costume, and much is it to be regretted that the Hintlesham mantle no longer exists.

Mr. C. A. Elliott exhibited a posy ring, of gold, of the time of Elizabeth or James I, exhumed in Fulham fields. It weighs seventeen grains. The outside is decorated with a looped pattern, and the interior engraved with—NO FRYND TO FAYTH—a singular declaration for a token of affection, but, perhaps, no worse than one on a ring in Mr. Cuming's cabinet, which sets forth—LOVE YE A JEST.

Mr. E. also exhibited an etui of silver, in form of a fish, five inches and three-quarters long, the body composed of nine imbricated joints, with broad forked tail, and eyes set with garnets. The head takes off and exposes a screw to which a cap was attached. It is of Italian fabric of the seventeenth century. He likewise produced a Chinese girdle appendage, or "chatelain," of silver, analogous to the toilet instruments discovered in Teutonic barrows (see *Journal*, ii, 54), and which may also be compared with a set of the sixteenth century engraved in vol. v, 359. It consists of a flat plate, graven on either side with leaves and flowers, and from which hang by short chains, two tooth-picks, an ear-pick, a glave-shaped nail-pick, a spade-shaped tongue-scraper, engraved with fruit, etc., and a pair of tongs with curved points. In Dunn's Chinese collection was a set of instruments much like the above, described in the catalogue (12 ed., p. 80) as "an apparatus in silver, consisting of a tongue-scraper, tooth-pick, and ear-pick : these are generally appended to the girdle of the dress, attached by a chain of the same metal."

Mr. Edward Roberts exhibited a copper coin picked up near excavations in the moat at Boulogne-sur-Mer in 1856. The reverse presents a shield with two lions rampant ; the obverse has an inscription DVC CEL 1634 (Duchy of Cella in Hanover), surrounded by a wreath.

Mr. Wentworth forwarded some documents, consisting of—An order in council against Papists and Sectaries, dated February 3, 1674-5, signed by Robert Southwell. Two letters from the Duke of Buckingham, from Wallingford House, October 23, 1668, and, London, April 2, 1672; one of these related to the peaceable behaviour and good conduct of a Mr. Hancock, and the other to an order of the lords in council, respecting the impressing of men for His Majesty's fleet. A copy of the order accompanied the latter, signed by Carlisle, Bridgewater, Craven, Holles, etc., etc.

Dr. Palmer exhibited a Newbury token of the rector, 1666-74. On the *obv.*, JOSEPH SAYER RECTOR ; *rev.*, OF NEWBERY + + +. A Bible in the field.

Mr. Winkley, jun., of Harrow, sent a German jetton of the close of the sixteenth century, found at Pinner church. On one side is a circle of crowns and fleurs-de-lys, surrounded by the name of the maker, HANNS KRANWINCKEL IN NV (ernburg); on the other side is the monde and cross, within the conjoined triangle and trefoil, GOTTES GABEN SOL MAN LOB ("God's gifts shall one praise ").

Mr. Syer Cuming made the following observations—

On a Roman Villa at Box, Wiltshire.

A correspondent in the *Gent. Mag.* for June, 1831 (p. 596) was, I believe, the first to draw public attention to the existence of Roman remains at Box, a village near Chippenham, in Wiltshire. Subsequent discoveries have shown these remains to appertain to a Roman villa, of considerable size, whose balineum and apartments were warmed by the hypocaust, whose walls had been decorated with frescoes, and halls and passages floored with tessellæ of stone and terra-cotta, and whose culina and mensa had been well provided with fictilia, the fragments of which are scattered about in endless profusion. The rev. G. Mullins, vicar of Box, gave a brief but interesting notice of these reliquiæ in the *Gent.- Mag.* of April, 1833 (p. 357), from which may be gathered the general character, and somewhat of the dimensions, of the once stately house which must have covered a large portion of land, "the most distant of the pavements being at least fifty yards apart." Some time since a friend took up his abode in a house on the site of the villa, and in a letter to me thus speaks of the remains. He says, "My garden is full of Roman remains—tiles, somewhat ornamented, but broken, bricks, tessellated pavement, fused iron, etc. I send all away to mend the roads; they are a perfect nuisance; we cannot put a spade into the ground without bringing up these impediments to vegetable growth, and a long, very long job will it be to clear the garden. There is a bath, quite perfect, in the centre of the garden; it has been opened, but is covered up, and a beautiful pavement runs all about. The bits I dug up were white and black, very coarse work." It is the consignment of these ancient fragments to the high road that has partly induced me to trouble the Association with these observations; for if no record be made of this act of Vandalism, these transported vestigia will, on re-discovery, at some future period, be accepted as indicia of the site of another Roman villa at Box. I begged my friend to send me up some of the remains from his garden, which he has kindly done, and a selection is now before you, consisting of tessellæ of rather rough hewn dice of white lime-stone, and portions of four square flue-pipes of red terra-cotta, from the hypocaust, which are useful for comparison with examples found in London and elsewhere.[1] The majority of the pipes met with at Box are scored with the common diamond pattern, a few have only bands of parallel lines, whilst one fragment is decorated with a succession of waved or undulated furrows of more novel design. From a careful examination of these air conduits, I am inclined to regard them as the products of different kilns, for they vary both in hardness and colour, and, above all, in the character of the material, which must have been obtained from different localities. The only example of stucco which has reached me is a fragment of the fine variety called albarium, composed of plaster of Paris washed over with white; but much of the walling has been painted in fresco, in imitation of African marbles with elegant coloured borderings. A full account of the discoveries

[1] Examples of ornamented flue-pipes discovered in London and Oxford, are given in the *Journal*, iv, 47, 48 ; vi, 55.

made at Box, is still a desideratum; as yet, we only know sufficient to quicken the desire for more ample details, but, if those details be not collected speedily, we shall have to search and ransack the high-ways and by-ways, for what once constituted the well-appointed dwelling of some opulent Roman family seeking health and recreation in the region of the ancient Belgæ.

. Mr. Thos. Wright forwarded memoranda, by the Rev. Edward Egremont, vicar of Wroxeter, and Dr. Henry Johnson, of Shrewsbury, respecting the more recent discoveries at Uriconium. They consist of ten or twelve hair pins, two more elegantly worked than those hitherto obtained; part of a large and rough fibula; many bones; head of a bird; two good pieces of glass; a large quantity of highly ornamented Samian ware; half of a beautiful bowl; inscriptions and representation of a stag-hunt; a basketful of old crockery fragments; a very fine Samian bowl, six inches in diameter, and three deep. The figures are in high relief and represent a hunting scene—deer chased by a dog, a bushy tree—well executed, and there is also the name of the potter; there have like-wise been found thirty or forty coins, including one of Allectus; spe-cimens of wall-painting, a mark of a dog's foot on a tile, and on another that of a sandal; in the great chamber to the left going in at the gate, has been displayed a chamber, thirty-two feet long, oblong, and of strong masonry, curiously formed stones, as if for folding doors; the wall is sixteen feet long, and at the centre there is a well-formed pillar with a base giving indication of a sort of colonnade. There are also traces of a furnace lined with vitrified clay, and bits of charcoal have been found about it. The top of the column is four feet below the surface of the soil, and is two feet wide. These will be duly recorded in Mr. Wright's papers on Uriconium in this *Journal*.

JUNE 13.

BERIAH BOTFIELD, ESQ., M.P., F.R.S., F.S.A., PRESIDENT, IN THE CHAIR.

The following associates were elected :

> Mrs. Freake, Cromwell House, South Kensington.
> Rev. James Ridgway, M.A., 29, Oakley Square.
> Hilary Davies, esq., Shrewsbury.

Thanks were voted for the following presents:

To the Author. The History and Antiquities of North Allerton. By C. J. D. Ingledew. London, 1858; 8vo.

To the Society. Journal of the Archæological Institute. No. 65. 8vo.

To the Publisher. Gentleman's Magazine for June, 1860; 8vo.

Dr. Kendrick transmitted for exhibition an impression of the seal of Stephen Payn, almoner to king Henry V, which seal has been long employed as the signet of Greatham Hospital, Durham. It is vesica shaped, two inches and five-eighths high, the field occupied by a gothic canopy, beneath which stands an ecclesiastic, supporting in his arms a large nef or ship, filled with money, and provided with low wheels, indicating it to be an offertory vessel, which could be passed about to gather contributions.[1] Above the niche are the arms of Edward the Confessor; somewhat lower on the dexter side is a shield charged with a cross, and on the sinister side are the royal arms of France and England quarterly. The bracket supporting the figure, has on it, STEPHS PAYN, and the verge of the seal is inscribed SIGILLM OFFICI ELEMOS-INARY REGIS HENRICI QVINTI ANGLIE. An engraving of this seal is given in Hutchinson's *Durham* (iii, 103), and Mr. Albert Way makes the following remarks upon it, in a letter addressed to Dr. Kendrick: "This seal is the most curious of its class; at the present time you are no doubt aware that my lord of Oxford, her Majesty's almoner, has a ship in full sail on his official seal, like a high admiral, and I am sure nobody suspects it to be the *navis ad elemosinas*. But the singularity is not yet exhausted; in 1793, the true seal of Greatham was found at Durham, at a brazier's; the design is, of course, totally different, and it is dated 1501, being, probably, a copy of an older seal. As far as I am aware, the seal of the almoner is still used, although no connection can be ascertained between him and bishop Stichel's foundation.[2] It was thought that if superseded by that newly discovered, and, apparently, the true seal, the result might prove inconvenient, as deranging the uniformity of legal documents."

The following notice of the almoner has been furnished by Mr. W. H. Black: "Stephen Payn was one of the king's clerks or chaplains in the beginning of Henry V's reign, and was by that monarch made his almoner, by letters patent, dated 16 Oct., 2 Hen. V, 1414, granting to him all deodands by land or water throughout the kingdom, and enabling him to collect them by himself or his deputies. For the appointment of these deputies an official seal was required, and that now comes to light. He seems to have accompanied king Henry V in his expedition to France. In the royal will his name occurs with other the king's clerks or chaplains, immediately following that of the secretary; to each of them was bequeathed a missal or porteous, of the value of ten pounds. The will was dated at Southampton, 24 July, 1415, before he went abroad. Payn was elected dean of Exeter 28 September, 1415, and confirmed 4 October of the same year. Whilst in France, he was

---

[1] For an account of offertory dishes, see *Journal*, vol. xii, p. 259.
[2] Greatham Hospital was founded by Robert de Stichale, bishop of Durham, in 1272.

appointed one of the commissioners to take musters in the city of Lisieux, etc., under date 11 Jan., 5 Hen. V, 1418.[1] His death took place 17 August, 1419." [2]

Dr. Kendrick sent, for the sake of comparison, an impression of the seal of the present lord high almoner, which is of a circular form, about two inches and seven-eighths in diameter, bearing a ship in full sail, surrounded by the legend, SIGILL : ELEEMOSYN : VICTORIA. D : G : BRITANNIARUM. F : D.

Mr. G. R. Wright, F.S.A., exhibited a leaf which had belonged to a theatrical manager's book, relating to performances at the Cock-pit and other playhouses, in 1638.   Mr. Wright accompanied his exhibition by various historical and biographical notices.[3]   The leaf was found in a MS. volume (also exhibited), lettered "Notitia Dramatica," containing scraps and memoranda collected by the celebrated Isaac Reed, from 1734 to the close of last century.   On the reverse of the leaf, was written, "This old play bill was in the papers late the property of Sir W. Foredice" (Sir W. Fordyce, a well-known physician, who died in 1792). It is not, however, a play bill, as reference to the fac-simile (plate 24) will shew.   Mr. Peter Cunningham, in his extracts from the accounts of the revels at court, published by the Shakespeare Society in 1842, has given a similar list for 1636.

Mr. C. Curle produced a large iron horse-shoe dug up in Hampshire: It measures about two inches and a half from toe to heel, and nearly five inches and three-quarters across the quarters; the margin distinctly fullared, the ends bent up into calkins, and the centre occupied by a bar about two inches wide, probably intended for the protection of the foot, or, as it was suggested, to assist the progression of the animal in very soft lands.

Mr. Curle also exhibited a singular and rather early trumpet of eastern fabric, made of thin metal resembling the mediæval latten, and decorated with red varnish.   The mouth of the instrument represents a tiger's head, with open jaws, showing a broad tongue.   The tube is straight for some distance, and then curves into four circular folds.   On the upper part of the tube is engraved a skull and cross-bones.   It is stated to have been taken from a pirate vessel, and that it has always borne the title of "Paul Jones's trumpet."

Mr. W. H. Forman exhibited a *memento mori* medal of gilt silver, and

---

[1] These notices are gleaned from documents printed in Rymer's *Fœdera* (ix, 113, 292, 334, 543), where also is given an account of materials for clothing issued from the king's wardrobe, for distribution by the almoner at Lambeth.
[2] Le Neve, *Fasti Eccl. Angliæ*, 1716, fol., p. 85.
[3] These will appear in a separate pamphlet, being too extended for our purpose, and not altogether suited for the pages of the *Journal*. To the liberality of Mr. G. R. Wright we are indebted for the fac-simile which accompanies the short notice. (See pp. 275-6 *ante*.)

of oval form, one inch and three-eighths high by one inch and a quarter wide.   On the *obv.* is a profile, to the right, of a queen wearing a spiked or eastern crown, a necklace with pendent jewel, rich zone, and with a scarf thrown loosely about the shoulders, so as to leave the bosom nude. The legend reads, QVÆ SIM POST TERGA VIDEBIS.   The *rev.* displays a human skeleton, its head resting on the right hand, the elbow being placed on the top of a tomb, on which is an hour-glass with the left hand of the figure reclining on it.   Legend, SIC NVNC PVLCHERRIMA QVONDAM (*now thus, once so beautiful*).   On the front of the tomb is inscribed CVM PRIVIL CÆ. C.M. (*by the privilege of the emperor*) the C.M. being the initials of the artist.

This exhibition was accompanied by the following notes by Mr. Syer Cuming :

"The motive of this rare and curious medal may be traced back to a distant æra, when the Egyptians enforced the precept, '*memento mori,*' by introducing at their banquets a small coffin containing the image of a corpse ; which, according to Herodotus (ii, 78), was shewn to each guest with the exclamation,—' Cast your eyes on this figure : after death you yourself will resemble it ; drink then, and be happy."[1]

"Our solemn ancestors, whilst stopping short of the in-coffined corpse, adopted the Egyptian sentiment, and surmounted the festive goblet with the grim emblems of mortality : a curious instance of which custom may be seen in an ivory knop of a hanap of the early part of the sixteenth century, in the South Kensington Museum.   This relic consists of four busts,—one being that of a young man in health and prosperity, with an imp deriding him ; in another he is dying ; the moral admonitions being set forth by a figure of death, and Latin inscriptions referring to the love of the world, etc.

"The warning, '*memento mori,*' floated down the stream of time, and in the middle ages manifested itself in divers fashions, the most conspicuous being the famous '*Dance of Death,*' which seems to have made its *début* in the fourteenth century, and which in the sixteenth century was rendered *immortal* by the pencil of Holbein.[2]

"The very baubles which decorated the persons of grave and gay,

---

[1] Classic representations of skeletons are of the utmost rarity.   One, however, is sculptured on a tomb at Pompeii.   In the sixteenth century, skeletons in shrouds became common on English tombs.   In the South Kensington Museum is a jewelled pendant, of the middle of the sixteenth century, in form of a coffin containing a skeleton, and inscribed, "Through the resurrection of Christe we be all sanctified."

[2] In the Doucean museum is an oval plaque of lead, of the time of Elizabeth, on which is embossed a dance of Death, with the armorial bearings of Death in the centre, viz., a skull and snake ; crest, on a barred helmet, an hour-glass between the bones of two arms supporting a skull.   Skulls and cross-bones figure in family heraldry.   Thus the arms of Boulter are a chevron with three dead men's heads.   Those of Baynes, a shin-bone in pale, crossed by another ; and those of Newton, two shin-bones saltirewise.

bore testimony to the importance of ever keeping the great truth before the mind, that, ' in the midst of life we are in death': hence we find reliquaries, pendants, pomanders, and watches, in form of skulls ; rings bearing Death's heads ; and quaint contrivances redolent of mortality, of which the king James the First's apple, in the Londesborough collection, is a striking example.   It is composed of silver, engraved with a crown between the initials I. R. ; beneath which, in seven lines, is the following : ' A.D. 1623.   'From man came woman, from woman came sin, from sin came death.'   Within the apple is a small skull, the top of which opens like a lid, and discloses representations of the creation and resurrection, with the words, 'Post mortem, vita æternitas.'

" Bifacial busts in ivory, representing the living and the dead, and the single heads,—one half being the person in health, the other a mere skull and habitat of worms,—are sixteenth and seventeenth century developments of the same feeling which prompted the Egyptian custom recorded by Herodotus.   Though several sculptors laboured at the production of these admonitory tokens, none gained so much renown in this line of art as Christof Harrick, who flourished about the time of our Charles I.

" Nor in this summary of memento mori tokens, ought we to omit the watch seals bearing a skull surrounded by the words, ' To this complexion we must come at last.'   Amid these dismal warnings, let us not, however, forget the cheering thought conveyed in the old Latin adage, ' Mors janua vitæ.' "

Mr. Allom exhibited a fine oil painting, executed by himself, of the castles of Europe and Asia on the Bosphorus, from sketches which he had made on the spot.   The historical interest attached to these buildings from their intimate connexion with the overthrow of the Roman power in the East, induced him to submit the picture to the Association.

The nearest castle stands on the European side of the Bosphorus, and is called by the Turks Roumolie Hissar : it was built by Mahomet II in 1452, about one year before his final and successful attack on Constantinople.   The rapidity of its construction must have been for that time extraordinary, which Gibbon accounts for by saying, " Of a master who never forgives the orders are seldom disobeyed."   On the 26th of March the appointed spot of Asomaton was covered with an active swarm of Turkish artificers; and the materials by sea and land were diligently transported from Europe and Asia.   The lime had been burnt in Cataphigia, the timber was cut down in the woods of Heraclea and Nicomedia, and the stones were dug from the Anatolian quarries.   Each of the thousand masons was assisted by two workmen, and a measure of two cubits was marked for their daily task.   The fortress was built in a triangular form, each angle flanked by a strong and massy tower; one on the declivity of the hill; two along the sea shore : a thickness of twenty-two feet was assigned for the walls, thirty for the towers, and the whole building was covered with a solid platform of lead. Mahomet himself pressed and directed the work with indefatigable ardour; his three vizirs claimed the honour of finishing their respective towers; the zeal of the cadhis emulated that of the janizaries; the meanest labour was ennobled by the service of God and the sultan; and the diligence of the multitude was quickened by the eye of a despot, whose smile was the hope of fortune, and whose frown was the messenger of death.

The castle is about six miles from Constantinople, and from this place in the following year, as is well known, Mahomet transported small vessels across the land to the top of the Golden Horn, from which he was enabled to invest the city on the land side. This fortress has long been used as a state prison by the Turks. On the opposite side of the Bosphorus is seen Annadoli Hissar, or the castle of Asia; it was built by the grandfather of Mahomet II, previous to the Turks getting a permanent footing on the European side.

Mr. H. H. Burnell placed before the meeting the remains of a painted window discovered in the chapel on the north side of the chancel of old Chelsea church, built by Thomas Laurence, lord of the manor in the sixteenth century. The glass, which is about twenty inches in width, appears to have been purposely smashed and smeared with mortar before being bricked over; enough, however, exists to shew that it had a border of yellow trefoils and quatrefoils, with tabernacle work in the centre, beneath which stood a figure of St. Osyth or Sitha, with long hair and holding three loaves. The style of execution fixes the date of the painting at about the commencement of the sixteenth century.

A figure of St. Osyth with three loaves is found in the painted glass of the fifteenth century in Mells church, Somersetshire, and her effigy holding keys is also seen in the windows of Winchester cathedral and Norbury church. The churches of Chick, Essex, and Denham, Suffolk, are dedicated to this virgin-consort of Suthred, king of East Anglia; and Stowe, when speaking of Size-lane, London, says: "S. Sithe's lane, so called of S. Sithe's church which standeth against the north end of that lane." St. Osyth suffered martyrdom A.D. 870, and was commemorated October 7.

Mr. Planché read a paper on the Cap of Estate anciently worn by the sovereigns of England, which will be printed and illustrated.

The president adjourned the public meetings over to Wednesday the 28th of November, and intimated that the Seventeenth Annual Congress would be held at Shrewsbury, commencing on the 6th, and terminating on the 11th of August next.

NOVEMBER 28.

T. J. PETTIGREW, F.R.S., F.S.A., V.P., IN THE CHAIR.

The following were elected associates:

William Leman, esq., 7, Porchester-terrace.
Rev. Edward Egremont, M.A., Wroxeter.
William White, jun., esq., Broomhall Park, Sheffield.
Capt. Philip H. Crampton, Shrewsbury.
Henry Hope Edwardes, esq., Netley Hall, Salop.
Rev. C. H. Hartshorne, M.A., Holdenby.
J. T. Mould, esq., 1, Onslow-crescent, Brompton.
Rev. Robt. Wm. Eyton, M.A., F.S.A., Ryton Rectory, Salop.
John Knight, esq., Henley Hall, Ludlow.
William Henry Slaney, esq., Katton Park, Shiffnal.
John Rocke, esq., Clungerford House, Aston-on-Clun.
Edward Levien, esq., M.A., F.S.A., 14, Keppel-street.
Henry T. Wace, esq., College Hill, Shrewsbury.
Capt. Thorneycroft, Tong Castle, Salop.
Edward Smythe Owen, esq., Condover House, Salop.
The earl of Powis, Berkeley-square.
Charles Faulkener, esq., F.S.A., Deddington, Oxon.
Arthur Bass, esq., Burton-on-Trent.
Hon. and rev. George Orlando Bridgeman, M.A., Blymhill.
J. Walter King Eyton, esq., F.S.A., 10, Portsdown-road.
Lord viscount Newport, M.P., Wilton-place.
George Tuck, esq., Victoria-street, Windsor.
Henry Gaze, esq., High-street, Southampton.
James Hughes, esq., Maunamead, near Plymouth.

Thanks were voted for the following presents:

To the Society.   Proceedings of the Royal Society. Nos. 39, 40. 8vo.
  „   „   Proceedings of the Somersetshire Archæological Society, for 1858 and 1859. 2 vols. 8vo.
  „   „   Transactions of the Society of Antiquaries, Edinburgh. Vol. III. Part 1. 4to.
  „   „   Annual Report of the Smithsonian Institution for 1858. 8vo.
  „   „   Journal of the Royal Dublin Society for January and April 1860. 8vo.
  „   „   Antiquarisk Tiddskrift, 1852-57. 8vo.
  „   „   Proceedings of the Royal Society of Northern Antiquaries. Copenhagen. 3 vols., 8vo. 1854-59.
  „   „   The Northmen in Ireland. Ib. 8vo.
  „   „   Journal of the Canadian Institute. Nos. 27, 28, 29. Toronto, 1860. 8vo.

To the Author.   Report of the Superintendent of the U.S. Coast Survey
during 1857.   Washington.   4to.

,,   ,,   Etudes Géologico-Archéologiques en Danemark et en
Suisse, par A. Marlot.   Lausanne, 1860.   8vo.

,,   ,,   George Catlin on Steam Raft.   Manchester, 1860.   8vo.

,,   ,,   Concise Account of Ancient Documents relating to the
Honor Forest and Borough of Clun, in Shropshire; by T. Salt,
esq.   1858.   4to.   Privately printed.

,,   ,,   Observations on Roman Remains in Sedbury, by G. Ormerod, F.R.S.   1860.   8vo.

To the Editor.   The Reliquary.   Nos. 1 and 2.   By Ll. Jewitt.   1860.   8vo.

,,   ,,   Gentleman's Magazine for July to November.   8vo.

Rev. J. L. Petit, M.A.   Eight photographs of Shiffnal church, Salop.
Folio.

Hillary Davies, esq.   Coloured drawing of plan of buildings opened at
Wroxeter, to August 1860.   Folio.

E. Sandford, esq.   Engraving of inscribed stones found at Wroxeter.
Folio.

Rev. James Ridgway, M.A.   Photograph of brass at Lübeck.   Folio.

Mr. Thomas Wright, F.S.A., reported the progress of the excavations
making at Wroxeter, and exhibited various coins of Constantine and
other Roman emperors found in the ruins; also a bronze ornament of a
circular form, and enamelled; together with two portions of mortar, or
cement, bearing the impress of an oak-leaf and nut-galls.   These will
be more particularly described in the succeeding reports on Uriconium.

Mr. T. Wills exhibited the following objects : Screw nut-cracker
of the first half of the seventeenth century; the whole of steel; the
screw being surmounted by an ornate bow; the interior of which is
heart-shaped; the exterior having two circlets at the upper part; the
cracker works within an upright oblong frame, with perforated sides,
having a shell at the back to secure the nut.   On the base is graven
the initials E.C., and the date 16 · ·.   Tobacco stoppers of brass.   The
two oldest are of the early part of the seventeenth century and made
like signet-rings, set on the ends of a slender shaft, one having on its
oval face the figure of a bird, the other a star of eight rays.   The
next in date is of the time of James II, its top being a cast of a
satirical medal issued in Germany on the Reformation, about the
year 1545; on one side are conjoined profiles of the pope and the
devil, ECCLESIA PERVERSA TENET FACIEO DIABOLO; on the other
those of a cardinal and a fool, SAPIENTES STVLTI ALEQVANDO.[1]   Shaft
of a stopper, representing Venus holding the apple of discord in her
right hand above her head; this is of the close of the seventeenth cen-

---

[1] For account of this medal, see *Journal*, viii, 6.

tury; and to about the same period may be assigned an example fashioned like the old tobacconist's sign of "the black boy."

Dr. Kendrick exhibited two objects recently discovered in Bridge-street, Warrington, in excavating for the foundations of some new buildings.   The earliest is a bronze tap, of the sixteenth century, the handle of which is in the form of a cock, and the mouth of the pipe representing the head of a dolphin.   The second, a portion of a two-handled vessel, a "wassail cup," of rather thin earthenware, covered with a deep chocolate-brown glaze, decorated with rudely fashioned bunches of grapes in white slip.   Date, first half of the seventeenth century.

A further contribution from Dr. Kendrick was a fac-simile in gutta-percha, of an Italian cinque-cento medallion in bronze, full three inches and five-eighths in diameter; bearing on one side, Abraham about to sacrifice Isaac, and on the other, Rebecca at the well.

Mr. Edward Roberts presented a drawing of a pig of lead seen by the association upon its visit to Linley Hall, Shropshire, twenty-two inches and a half long, and seven inches wide at the base, and unequally tapering upwards on all sides to twenty inches long by three inches and a half wide.   The upper surface is indented or paneled, and contains an inscription in raised and slightly rounded Roman capitals, IMP. HAD-RIANI AVG.   The weight is about one hundredweight and three-quarters by measurement.   On a close examination, it distinctly shows the marks of the wooden model from which the mould was formed, so much so as to define even the wood itself; it clearly was of oak, and, apparently, tolerably well worn.   There are several marks, distinctly the result of the casting, while others seem to have been made since; of the former, there is one that deserves remark; it appears as a sort of curved branch, and may have been the result of a small piece of foliage imbedded in the sand, which being destroyed by the molten lead, caused a corresponding raised model.   Amongst the latter are several marks of a reticulated hammer, but there are no means of ascertaining their probable date.   The pig was discovered in the neighbourhood of the lead mines at Shelve.

The rev. James Ridgway presented to the association a photograph from a rubbing of a brass at Lübeck, taken by Mr. Christopher, accompanied by the following description by Mr. C. : " This remarkable, but comparatively little known incised monumental brass, is situated in one of the apsidal chapels on the northern side of the choir of the cathedral church at Lübeck, and is to the memory of two bishops who died in 1317 and 1350.   They are represented at full length in rich episcopal robes, with mitres and crosiers of elaborate design; and they repose under foliated canopies, diapered with monsters of the usual North German type.   Each of the canopies is surmounted by two stories of traceried niches, the pattern of the tracery being varied in each case;

these niches contain figures representing the souls of the bishops, each supported by two angels, and attended by others with musical instruments ascending to God the Father, who is seated in the upper stage or story, with the infant Saviour in his arms, in the attitude of blessing, and also attended by angels with censers and candles ; the whole composition is crowned with a series of pinnacles. On the outer sides of, and between the bishops, are five stories of somewhat larger figures, also under richly traceried and crocketed canopies : they represent various apostles and saints, some with and some without their usual symbols, and in most (twelve of these) cases, the second figure is a venerable old man with a scroll; these secondary figures probably represent the twelve minor prophets, who are often placed in juxtaposition with the apostles. The upper group in the centre is the 'Annunciation;' the virgin is an exquisitely drawn figure, as also are many of the other figures. It is interesting to observe that Lübeck, being essentially a brick-built city, the plain surfaces behind the pinnacles, etc., are regularly jointed in what is still technically called 'Flemish bond,' in imitation of brickwork. On what may be termed the plinth or pedestal for the main figures, are two series of smaller figures in groups, representing the chief incidents in the histories of the bishops, their miracles, etc., and some popular legends of the saints, such as the story of St. Dunstan and the devil. The plain panels below this are of great value in the design, as giving a solid base to the whole composition, and have the effect of great breadth and repose, while they enhance the beauty of the elaborate detail with which the rest of the surface is covered. The whole is surrounded by the two inscriptions, with symbols of the evangelists in the angles, and angels with crowns in the centre. The inscriptions are as follow : ' The reverend father lord Burchardt de Serken, bishop of this church, died on the 13th day of March, in the year of our Lord one thousand three hundred and seventeen. May his soul rest in peace. Amen.' 'The reverend father lord John de Mül, bishop of this church of Lübeck, and founder of this chapel, died on the tenth day before the kalends of September (*i.e.*, the 22nd August),in the year of our Lord, one thousand three hundred and fifty, the year of jubilee. Pray for his soul.' I have looked into a history of Lübeck, at the British Museum, but can find no special mention of either of these bishops. The main portion of the brass has apparently been formed of eight sheets or slabs of metal soldered together and the enriched borders afterwards joined on in lengths. This brass contains two figures, fully the size of life, fifty smaller figures of saints, angels, etc., all under canopies adorned with the most varied tracery, and about sixty minor figures in the histories, etc., besides dragons and monsters, displaying a great amount of fancy and originality. It is of great size, twelve feet long and six feet one inch and a half wide, of a good period of art, and, fortunately, in admirable preservation;

and is, I believe, the finest work of the kind in existence. The Schwerin brasses, though somewhat larger, are decidedly inferior in the force and character of their design, and one of the two is of much later date (1471). They are all of Flemish manufacture. In conclusion, I would observe, that in Lübeck, a city abounding in mediæval treasures of architecture and the sister arts, there are especially numerous works in metal, well worthy of study, other 'brasses,' and metal fonts, and statues, and in the Marienkirche (a more important structure than the cathedral) a very remarkable and elaborate 'sacrament haus' in brass of purer and more pleasing design, and almost, if not quite, as rich in ornament as the well-known master-piece of Adam Krafft, in the Lorenzkirche at Nuremberg."

Mr. E. L. Blackburne exhibited a fine series of coloured drawings, illustrated by the following remarks :

"The accompanying figures are from the panels of the chancel and north aisle screens at Southwold, in Suffolk. Those representing the apostles are from the former. The latter has representations of the nine orders of angels, two among the number of which are shown, bearing respectively the emblems of the blessed sacrament and the Holy Trinity. These occupy the end panels, north and south of the aisle screen, and have a very appropriate reference to the dedication of the chapel which the screen encloses, viz., to the Holy Trinity. There is a similar screen at the east end of the south aisle, dedicated in honour of the blessed Virgin. The panels here had originally the greater and lesser prophets painted on them. A very few of these are now discernible to any extent. The figures of Moses and David are the most perfect, though the names of the others are still traceable. The chancel screen has the twelve apostles, of which the drawings give the most perfect, though all the others remain more or less so. The order in which they appear is as follows, St. Peter and St. Paul occupying their accustomed positions right and left of the doorway :

St. Philip.	St. Matthias.	St. James Minor.	St. Thomas.	St. Andrew.	St. Peter.		St. Paul.	St. John.	St. James Major.	St. Bartholomew.	St. Jude.	St. Simon.

"Taking the three screens, there are, altogether thirty-six figures, the whole very richly painted in gold and colour. Those of the centre or chancel screen are particularly so, and the execution is far superior, artistically considered, to the majority of existing examples. The grounds upon which the figures of the apostles are painted, or rather which finish the portions of the panel not occupied by them, are diapered in relief in a kind of mastic and gilt, and in places picked in in colour, to heighten the same. The diaper of the dresses is simply painted in gold and colour. These, and the ornamentation of the nimbi are very interesting.

" The mastic enrichment is continued all over the chancel screen. There is hardly a moulding of it that is not so ornamented. The buttress faces are almost entirely covered with it; the design of the enrichment including in it small figures under canopied niches, some of which have been protected by glass, looking like so many small framed pictures. The tracery of the heads of the six main compartments of which the screen is composed, is remarkably beautiful. It is double tracery of exceeding lightness, composed of a small gilt bead and cuspations placed between a parti-coloured ogee, and a hollow alternately green and red, studded with relieved flowers at intervals, gilt. The screen is altogether one of the richest and best preserved examples to be met with.

" The side screens are less rich in the decorations, but still very beautiful and interesting. Mastic relief is here also adopted in the hollows, and on part of the buttress faces. The tracery of the heads is of the same description as that of the chancel screen. The grounds of the panels are here in colour, powdered with stars and flowers; and the tracery heads of the panels have alternately red and white hollows and gold fillets, the former ornamented with flowers.

" The date of the screens is *circa* 1460.

" In connexion with the chancel screen, or rather with the rood figures which anciently stood above it, there is a very richly painted ceiling representing in its panels angels holding scrolls and the implements of the Passion. It appears to have been a common practice to more highly ornament the bay of the church roof which was immediately over the rood. There are several instances of it in Suffolk."

It is intended to give, on a future occasion, further illustration of these very interesting paintings.

Mr. George Vere Irving, V.P., read the following notes " On the districts of Scotland occupied by the earlier and later branches of the Celtic race."

" Whilst most fully concurring with the statement made by Sir Gardner Wilkinson in his able paper on 'the Rock Basins of Dartmoor,'[1] as to the existence in this island of two distinct branches of the Celtic family, an earlier and a later, whose respective languages consisted of two distinct and easily distinguished dialects, I would venture to submit the following observations on the boundaries assigned by him to these races. On

<hr>

[1] See pp. 101-132 *ante*.

p. 124 he observes : 1. That the descendants of the earlier Celtic tribes still occupy *Scotland ;* and 2. That the greater part of Britain *south of Scotland* had, in the time of Cæsar, been long possessed by those of the later stock.   This general use of the modern term ' Scotland' appears to me to create some ambiguity and confusion, as the various districts which compose that country occupy very different positions as to this matter.   As far as what are now called the Highlands are concerned it is incontestably true, that their inhabitants belonged to the earlier races, but the case appears exactly the reverse as to the Celtic occupants of the Lowlands.   The latter district, as sir Gardner has accurately stated in his note on page 128, is now peopled by an Anglo-Saxon race ; but until the seventh or eighth century it was in the possession of Celtic tribes, of whose language vestiges are still met with in the names of numerous localities, although in many instances the original designations have been superseded by others derived from the dialect used by more modern settlers.   Judging from these remains there can be no doubt that the Lowland, or, as I should rather call them, Intramural Celts, spoke the dialect peculiar to the later immigration of that race.   This is more marked in Lanarkshire and those counties which belonged to the Strathclyde Britons, as they appear to have maintained their possessions till dispossessed by the Anglo-Saxon race.   While we find from Bede and other contemporary writers that in several districts, and especially in the Lothians, a short occupation by portions of the more northern tribes belonging to the earlier Celtic branch was interposed between the two.

" Sir Gardner Wilkinson has furnished us with a very good test of whether the names of a district belong to the earlier or later dialect, in the terms generally used for those of rivers — *Usk* or *Esk* being character- istic of the first, and *Dour* and *Avon* of the last.

" Of *Usk* we have no single instance in Lanarkshire, either in a simple or compound form.   It is certainly met with in Mid Lothian and Dum- friesshire, but in the former case I would assign its origin to the Picts who occupied that district in the seventh century, and were under the care of bishop Trumwine ; and in the latter to the Scotch and Irish who about that time, or shortly after, settled on the shores of the Sol- way.

" Of *Dour*, Lanarkshire furnishes a remarkable example in the Duer, pronounced *Daar*, which gives the second title to the earls of Selkirk, and bears the same relation to the Clyde as the Isis does to the Thames. It is also met with in a compound form, as in Durisdur.   I would with great diffidence suggest for sir Gardner Wilkinson's consideration, whe- ther the name of the Clyde itself is not characteristic of the later dialect, as it is met with in Wales, but does not occur, I believe, either in Ireland or the north of Scotland.

"Of *Avon*, the country possesses no less than two streams of this name; one, a tributary of the Annan, rising at the summit of the Caledonian Railway; the other falling into the Clyde at Hamilton, and giving its name to the barony of Evandale, one of the most important possessions of that ducal house, and also to the prosperous town of Strathaven. It has furnished sir Walter Scott with the name of one of his characters in *Old Mortality*.

"I may state, in conclusion, that Chalmers, in his *Caledonia*, has endeavoured to explain our Lanarkshire Celtic names by reference to the Gaelic. I have recently had occasion to examine most carefully a number of his derivations, and in every case, without exception, I have been forced to the conclusion that they are untenable; while I was at the same time led to the firm conviction, that this is entirely attributable to the learned author having resorted to the Gaelic or earlier, instead of to the Welsh or later dialects of the Celtic.

Mr. H. Syer Cuming, Hon. Sec., exhibited various specimens of bellarmines and other grotesque vessels employed in former times for containing drink.

Bellarmine, grey-beard and *long-beard*, he regarded as synonyms of the same vessel, varying in capacity from half-a-pint to two gallons. The leading characteristics of these are a rotund body, narrow neck, Silenus-like mask in front, and loop handle at back; the material being a greyish coloured stoneware, covered by a mottled brown glaze. Its appellation has been derived from its fancied resemblance to the Jesuit Robert Bellarmine, who died in 1621. *Grey-beard* and *long-beard* are titles given from the grim visage on the neck. Frequent allusion is made to this vessel by the writers of the age of Elizabeth, James, and Charles I.

Mr. Cuming produced a pint bellarmine of the sixteenth century, exhumed in Cannon-street, December 1850. It is of the plainest description, the mask being its only ornament. This mask differs considerably on different vessels. On some it is barely human, whilst on others it is carefully wrought, and even a degree of dignity infused into its lineaments. Beneath the mask is frequently found a round or oval seal, containing some device or armorial bearing, the latter indicating the state or family for whom the vessel was wrought. In this *Journal* (vol. v, p. 35) is engraved a bellarmine, with a shield quartered with the arms of Cleves, Mœurs, Marsh, and Ravensburg; and Mr. Cuming produced portions of three vessels recovered from the Thames in 1847, which display the following heraldic insignia. The first shield is charged as follows: per pale. 1. Three bars; 2. Three chevrons. In chief a lion passant guardant. The second bears: A fess checky between, 1. A lion rampant contourné; 2. Two chevrons; 3. Two bars; 4. A lion rampant. The third shield has on a pale the limb of a tree, with lions rampant for supporters.

The body of the bellarmine is at times stamped with medallion busts, the most common being those of warriors wearing salades of divers fashions. Mr. Cuming exhibited three fragments thus decorated. One in which the salade is a dome-crowned, broad brimmed steel cap, the others being visored salades, having the face-guard thrown back.

Besides busts, arms, and devices, bellarmines occasionally bear dates ranging from 1580 to 1610, some few years after which the mask began to fall into disuse; but vessels of the same general contour long continued to be made in the Low Countries, and have received the sobriquet of *Dutch-men*.[1]

Betty (probably another form of the Anglo-Saxon *bitte*, defined by Bosworth as a bottle or bouget) was, according to Grose, the title of a flask like those for Florence wine.

Boggle (north-country name for a goblin) is a title bestowed on image mugs representing mis-shapen human beings, still manufactured in the Staffordshire potteries, and frequently called *toby pitchers*. The idea of these grotesque figures may be traced back to a classic era, examples having been met with among remains of Egyptian, Greek, and Roman art, and have not escaped the notice of the epigrammatist Martial (*Ep.* xiv, 176, 182. A *boggle* of very superior character and believed to be of the commencement of the fourteenth century, is represented in this *Journal*, iii, 63. A bearded mask forms the lip and neck of the vessel, upon the sides of which appear rudely fashioned arms, the hands resting on the front of the ovate body, which has a low foot, and a loop handle at the back. This rare specimen is of terra-cotta covered with a green glaze. The Mexicans and Peruvians had their boggle drinking cups, which are surpassingly ugly.

George, or *gorge*, is the old title of a pitcher, of which Mr. Cuming conceived there were three varieties, the *brown*, the *white*, and the *stone*. Faulkener, in his *History of Fulham*, says: "In the year 1684, Mr. John Dwight, an Oxfordshire gentleman, who had been secretary to Bryan Walton, Henry Ferne, and George Hall, successively bishops of Chester, invented and established at Fulham a manufactory of earthenware, known by the name of *white gorges*, marbled porcelain vessels, statues and figures, and fine *stone gorges*, and vessels never before made in England; also transparent porcelain, and opaceous red and dark-coloured porcelain, or China and Persian wares, and the Cologne or stonewares. For these manufactures a patent was obtained in the year above mentioned."

[1] For notices of bellarmines, see *Gent. Mag.*, May 1831, p. 386; Marryat's *History of Pottery*, pp. 75, 253; and this *Journal*, xi, 33; xii, 83; xiii, 224.

Jack is mentioned in this place for the sake of correcting an error in vol. xv, p. 343, line 28—instead of *Portugal*-street read *Portsmouth*-street, as the locality where the sign of the *Black Jack* still exists.

Jeroboam is the title of a capacious bowl or goblet, generally wrought of metal, but how it obtained the name of the son of Nebat is by no means obvious. The corporation of Ludlow formerly possessed a great two-handled silver vessel which bore this imposing name, and which was used as a *grace* or *loving cup* at the bailiff's feasts.

Jill, or *gill*, described in vol. xv, 345, is again noticed for the purpose of adding the following definition given in Dyche's *English Dictionary*, London, 1744 : " *Gill*, a measure containing a quarter of a pint, much used by wine-drinkers in a morning."

Kitty, as the name of a drinking-vessel, is derived from the Anglo-Saxon *kitte*, a bottle or leathern bag for holding liquors. Bailey gives the word " *Kithe*, a cup. *Chaucer*." And Hexham, in his *Netherduytch Dictionarie*, Rotterdam, 1648, has " *Kitte*, a great wodden bowle or tancker ;" whatever the exact form of the vessel may have been, it would appear to have been of considerable size.

Rabbits, says Grose, " were a sort of wooden canns to drink out of, now out of use." They are spoken of in the *Praise of Yorkshire Ale*, 1697, p. 1.

Ranter, according to Halliwell, is a large beer-jug ; hence those who indulged in its immoderate use bore the same appellation.

Tall-boy, Grose tells us, is a name given to a bottle or two-quart pot, but more generally applied to the high-stemmed wine-glass of the seventeenth century, in contradistinction to the dwarf drinking cups and tumblers then in use. The Venetian glasses with *ditrina* stems are familiar examples of *tall-boys*, some of them measuring full a foot in height.

Mr. W. H. Forman exhibited a Celtic *Cleddyv*, or sword of bronze, recently recovered from the Thames off Battersea. It is thirty-one inches in length, and well preserved. The tang has a strait slit down its centre, similar to examples in this *Journal* (xiv, p. 327, fig. 1 ; xv, p. 229, fig. 3 and 4). Below the grip, the blade is drilled towards each edge with five rivet holes.

Bronze swords of equal length to the above have been discovered in Denmark, but this is believed to be the longest yet met with in England. The examples from Battersea in Mr. Bateman's collection measure respectively twenty-five and twenty-six inches ; but the latter has lost a portion of its hilt.

Mr. Forman also produced a bronze pin, twenty-six inches long. In its slender shaft and conic head it bears resemblance to an *Acus crinalis*,

---

[1] In this plate, for fig. 1 read 5 ; for fig. 5, read 1.

but its great length forbids its use as such. One idea is that it may have served for some culinary process. It appears to be of Etruscan fabric, but is stated to have been found at Salzburg.

DECEMBER 12.

GEORGE GODWIN, F.R.S., F.S.A., V.P., IN THE CHAIR.

The Rev. S. F. Maynard, B.A., Midsomer Norton, was elected an Associate.

Thanks were voted to the Rev. Dr. M'Caul, of Toronto, for his present of Part VI of *Notes on Latin Inscriptions found in Britain*.

Mr. Wills exhibited a brass spur of the time of Charles I, lately dug up in Trinity Lane, City. The neck curves downward, and is mounted with a rowel of five points.

Mr Wills also exhibited a silver matrix, of an oval form, bearing a view of a castle, said to be that of Windsor, but more likely to be that of some foreign fortress. It has a stout haft of lignum vitæ, the date of which is the end of the seventeenth or early part of the eighteenth century.

Mr. S. Wood produced a beautiful example of Brussels Point (*Point à l'aiguille*), five feet in length, which formed the edging of a muslin tippet of about the middle of the seventeenth century.[1]

Mr. Syer Cuming placed before the meeting two pseudo antiques; one being a matrix of jet or shale, the other a terra-cotta cameo. The matrix is lozenge-formed, about two inches high by one and five-eighths wide. In the centre is a vesica-shaped frame, inclosing a cross patée precisely similar to what appears on the pretended signets of Osbert de Helton, Robert de Avo, and other modern creations. On the verge is the legend SIG. RICARDI DE RYTONE, Ryton being a township in the North Riding of Yorkshire. The cameo is an oval, nearly one inch and three-fourths high by one inch and five-sixteenths wide, and is an impress of a black stone matrix set in a metal verge inscribed CAPVT : SERVI : DEI : SIC : which was pretended to have been found in a grave at Spilsby, Lincolnshire, and of which Mr. Cuming also produced a gutta-percha impression. Both the Spilsby signet and the terra-cotta cameo bear on their reverses the Christian monogram, which the artificer has also engraved on the reverses of the seals of Julia Mamœa and the emperor Maximus, and in the field of the signet of Oswald de Ashton, leaving no doubt of the common parentage of these shameful forgeries. The cameo and matrix were reported to have been exhumed in lowering the churchyard of Horncastle, and purchased by the Rev. H. F. Clinton, rector of

---

[1] For notices of other varieties of lace, see *Journal*, xiii, 229 ; xv, 351.

Bothamsall, who presented them to Mr. J. Clayton, of Southwell, Notts, who has now resigned them to Mr. Syer Cuming.

By permission of Mr. A. W. Franks, Mr. Cuming exhibited a second matrix of jet, which had been purchased in Cambridge. It is vesica-shaped, full two inches long, and bears the figure of a bishop, the legend apparently reading SIIL GOLBIDG + VIFGRBLO. The back of the matrix is convex, sculptured with a mitre, and two pastoral staves in saltire, crossed by a label inscribed with the date 1372. The margin of the back is cut in scallops, in imitation of the silver mountings of cups, etc., of the seventeenth century.

Mr. Pettigrew, V.P., read a paper on the seal of Richard Duke of Gloucester as admiral of England and earl of Dorset and Somerset. It will be printed with illustrations in a future *Journal*.

Mr. Syer Cuming read the following paper :—

On the Use of Vessels and Hollow Bricks in Buildings.

" The present communication is devoted to a brief review of the schemes adopted in various ages and countries, whereby time, weight, and material are economised in the erection of sacred and domestic edifices, by the introduction of vases, tubes, and hollow bricks into the substance of arches, walls, and cupolas—measures apparently suggested by the employment of the chambered-stems of the bamboo for building purposes in the East.

" The mud hut, constantly exposed to the vicissitudes of climate, would, if the walls were not of great thickness, soon yield to the heavy rains and devastating winds of the tropics; but buildings formed of clay inclosing bamboos present a strong and durable defence against the attacks of the elements. Dwellings so constructed are still to be found in Africa; and in Chili and Brazil many of the roofs of the houses consist of canes embedded in mud placed on the rafters and covered with round tiles.[1]

" In localities where canes were sparse or unprocurable, the builders would strive to supply the deficit by the use of earthen pipes and vessels; and thus may we, in all likelihood, trace out the origin of a practice which is believed to have been recognised in ancient Egypt, and is still in vogue in the Thebais—one which was carried to the highest perfection by the Roman architects, and which, with certain modifications, is in full existence among ourselves.

[1] Many of the houses of China have the roof covered with semi-cylindrical tiles resembling the Roman *imbrex*. They are ranged with their concave side uppermost, to serve as channels for the rain. Other tiles are then laid with their concave side downwards, so as to hide the joinings of the tiles. It is believed that this plan was derived from the use of split bamboos, as is customary among the Malays.

" Burckhardt[1] says, ' In Upper Egypt, the walls of the peasants' houses are very frequently constructed in part of jars placed one over the other, and cemented together with mud.   In walls of inclosures, or in such as require only a slight roof, the upper part is very generally formed of the same materials; in the parapets also of the flat-roofed houses a double or triple row of red pots, one over the other, usually runs round the terrace to conceal the females of the family when walking upon it.   *Pots are preferred to bricks because the walls formed of them are lighter, more quickly built*, and have a much neater appearance. They possess likewise another advantage, which is that they cannot be pierced at night by robbers without occasioning noise by the pots falling down, and thus awakening the inmates of the dwelling, while bricks can be removed silently, one by one, as is often done by nightly depredators, who break into the houses in this manner.   If, then, we suppose that pot-walls were in common use by the ancient inhabitants, the large mounds of broken pottery may be satisfactorily accounted for.   As for stone, it seems to have been as little used for the private habitations of the ancient Egyptians as it is at the present day.'   Mrs. Lushington and later tourists describe the houses of Luxor as being built of sun-dried bricks, or lumps of mud, and *baked clay pipes.*   Confirmatory of Burckhardt's theory, that the heaps of broken vessels are the debris of the houses of the early Egyptians, I may state that many of the large terra-cotta jars from Thebes which I have examined have been so covered with indurated mud and lumps of fine white plaster that I have felt convinced they must have been built into walls.

" Although we have the testimony of classic writers that the Greeks used bricks, yet few Grecian structures except those of stone have descended to our time, and it is therefore uncertain whether they ever introduced vessels into their walls as was done in Egypt; but the Roman builders, departing from the straight lines of Grecian architecture, and revelling in the graceful arch and proud cupola, found especial advantage in the employment of bricks ; and, availing themselves of the hint given by the dwellings at Thebes, introduced vessels and tubes into the walls and ceilings of their noblest edifices.

" I exhibit an example of these tubes or hollow cylindrical bricks, of red terra-cotta, discovered among the ruins of the tomb of the Scipios in the Via Appia at Rome.   It weighs ten ounces and a half, measures seven inches in length, and about two inches and a quarter diameter, is surrounded by a spiral channel to afford a firm holding for the mortar, and at the closed end is a conic spike which fitted into the open

---

[1] Travels in Nubia, i, p. 94.   London, 1822.
[2] Bruce says that at Etfa, on the west side of the Nile, all the houses have receptacles for pigeons on their tops, made of earthen pots one above the other, occupying the upper story, and giving the walls of the turrets a light and ornamental aspect.

mouth of the next brick, and when two or three were thus conjoined, they formed a line which might well be likened to the jointed stem of the bamboo, which I believe to have been their archetype.

"Seroux d'Agincourt [1] has recorded several instances of such tubes and various urns and vessels being introduced into domes and walls of Roman buildings.

"I place before you one of the tubes from the dome of the church of St. Vitalis at Ravenna. It is of red terra cotta, slightly curved to give the arc of the cupola, with a broad spiral groove on the exterior, and with the usual short conic stem or spike at the solid end. It is nine inches and three-eighths in length and two inches and three-fourths in diameter. Tubes and vases are found worked into domes and arches of other edifices at Ravenna. They are seen in the ancient baptistry of the cathedral, and at the much more modern church of St. Maria in Porto.

"There are indications that the architects of other continental countries adopted similar modes of economising weight in the domes and walls of edifices as was done in Italy. About the year 1843, were discovered, in one of the walls of the nave of the church of St. Blaise at Arles, a quantity of small fictile 'horns' and pots, which are supposed to have been there placed about the year 1280. Professor Oberlin met with vases in various parts of the vaulted ceilings of the choir of Strasburgh cathedral; and baron Taylor observed that many of the Spanish churches have their vaultings composed of various kinds of pottery. Some have supposed that these several vessels were placed in the buildings for acoustic purposes, the idea being drawn from the *Echea* of the Greek and Roman theatres; but there can be little doubt that the fictilia were really introduced for the sake of lightness, as it was in Italy and elsewhere.

"Did the Romans ever introduce vases, tubes, or any other kind of vessels into the walls, arches, vaults, or domes they erected in Britain? is a question on which our present evidence is too meagre to permit of a decisive reply; further discoveries can alone determine the point, but the subjoined facts may serve to aid us in the inquiry:

"In digging a grave near St. Alban's abbey, in 1826, a number of Roman relics were exhumed, one being the remains of a red terra-cotta tube, channeled spirally on the exterior like those in the cupolas of Italian churches. This curious object fell into the hands of a mischievous person, who wantonly broke it up, saving nothing but the small squared piece which I produce, and which, by careful measurement, is shewn to have been a portion of a tube about nine inches in diameter, the sides being a quarter of an inch in thickness. It would be presumptuous to argue from this isolated atom that the vaults and arches of Veru-

[1] The History of Art by its Monuments, vol. i.

lamium were constructed of tubes like those of Rome and Ravenna, but it is possible that it may have been employed for building purposes in one of those subterranean vaults of the Roman city, which Matthew Paris (l. 1, c. 6, s. 29) says were broken down by Ealred, abbot of St. Alban's, and formed material for the new monastery erected by his successor Eadmer. From this obscure fragment, let us turn to more definite objects, which are, however, of uncertain age. During the removal of London wall, Moorfields, in April 1817, and near the site now occupied by Albion chapel, the workmen in excavating the ground came upon an arch, the arc of which was constructed of hollow bricks of red terra-cotta, similar in paste to the broad flat tegulæ, composing the Roman wall. I place one of these hollow bricks before you, which measures seven inches and a half in height, and weighs three pounds and half an ounce ; it is square at top, and four inches in diameter, the lower end circular, impressed with five concentric rings, and having an orifice in its centre, seven-eighths of an inch in diameter. The cylindrical body of the brick is spirally scored with a sharp-edged instrument, not for the sake of ornament, but as a key for the mortar, some of which still adheres to the surface, and might pass for Roman cement. It has been thought by some that the arch of which this specimen is a portion, was the remains of a music room, the hollow bricks serving for echea,[1] but the late Mr. Montague, the late city surveyor, and under whose supervision this interesting structure was demolished, gave it as his opinion that it was a Roman arch, and that the bricks were made hollow, simply for the sake of lightness, that they were, in short, a modification of the fictile tubes of the ancient Italian architects.

" The sale of the collection of the late Mr. E. B. Price in 1853, brought to my knowledge a more recent discovery of these hollow bricks. Eight of these were described as " found in the London wall," but the exact spot was not given. In the early part of this year, a considerable number were met with in taking down premises belonging to Mr. Norman, situated near to old Norton Folgate. One of these has been forwarded for exhibition by Dr. Kendrick. It bears a resemblance to those which composed the Moorfields arch, but on the square end is the addition of a broad band of curved lines. Mr. Norman states, that ' some were on made ground, others on the clay soil. The walls built on them were erected, I think, by the French refugees, for a large dye-house, but how far this is true I cannot say; some were placed in the walls at different places like ordinary bricks, as though put in to fill

---

[1] The *echea* were bell-shaped sonorous vases of bronze or earth, used to reflect the voices of the actors. They were arranged between the seats of the theatres in niches made for the purpose. According to Vitruvius, such vases were inserted at the theatre at Corinth, whence Lucius Mummius, at the taking of that city in 146 B.C., transported them to Rome.

up ; but the majority were laid as footing to the walls.' Mr. Norman adds that two earthen *water-jars* were found with the hollow bricks, but the workmen smashed them to obtain some hair they contained.

"I am not aware that bricks like those obtained at Moorfields and Norton Folgate, have been met with in Roman erections on the continent, and the Roman arches found in London (such for instance as the one in Old Fish-street Hill), were constructed of flat tegulæ, one projecting over the other from opposite sides, with a single tile for the crown of the arc. But it would be unjust to cite these tegulated arches as positive evidence against the antiquity of the hollow bricks, although they are quite sufficient to make us pause ere we accept them as of Roman fabric. Whatever their actual age may be, it is certain that they are anything but modern, and prove that the invention is of far greater age than generally supposed, and is not due to sir John Soane, who claimed them as his own.

"Hollow, or, as they are sometimes called, ' bottle bricks,' and ' cones,' resembling the various examples described, were extensively employed by the late George Dance, R.A., and Henry Holland, and *afterwards*, in 1792, by sir John Soane, in the dome and arches of the ' stock office,' at the Bank of England. The great ceiling of St. George's hall, Liverpool, completed in 1849, is constructed of about 140,000 hollow bricks, weighing altogether about six hundred tons, each brick being twelve inches long and four inches square.

"The above examples of the use of vases, tubes, and hollow bricks for building purposes, have been selected because they are wide-spread, well-marked, and well-attested. The list might be amplified, but enough has, I trust, been done to elucidate the subject, arrest the attention of the archæologist, and, perchance, explain the intent of some of the cylindrical vessels of terra-cotta discovered in this and other countries."

INDEX.

LIST OF ENGRAVINGS.

WOODCUTS.

ERRATA AND ADDENDA.[1]

Page 48, line 9, for " nails" read " dice."

" 48, " 10, for "crown of thorns" read " a cock," and correct plate iii, fig. 3, by the same.

" 58, last line, add " The two corbels, from which spring incipient groin-arches at the eastern angles of the chancel, are fairly carved heads of a lion and a calf, and in default of any authenticated tradition to the contrary, may be taken probably to indicate that the church was originally dedicated to the Evangelists SS. Mark and Luke."

" 61, line 9, for " sixteenth" read " seventeenth."

" 62, " 26, after " heiress" add " of Adam Head, a branch."

" 87, " 31, for " groins" read " quoins."

" 96, " 42, for " Godfroman" read " Godfroye on."

" 135, " 9, for " Edward" read " Edmund."

" 201, " 21, for " Beckinston" read " Bullington."

" 315, note, for " Isaurianæ" read " Isurianæ."

" 328. The ball of variously coloured clays at Slymbridge is not in the British Museum, but there is a specimen obtained from Lincolnshire. The example of Dr. Mantell proves to be clay, not silicious sandstone, as reported by him.

[1] See also p. 225.

CPSIA information can be obtained
at www.ICGtesting.com
Printed in the USA
BVHW081612220819
556561BV00018B/4064/P

9 781407 636412